★ PRACTICING DEMOCRACY ★

PRACTICING DEMOCRACY

POPULAR POLITICS IN THE ★★ UNITED STATES FROM THE CONSTITUTION TO THE CIVIL WAR ★★

Daniel Peart and Adam I. P. Smith

EDITORS

UNIVERSITY OF VIRGINIA PRESS ★ CHARLOTTESVILLE & LONDON

University of Virginia Press
© 2015 by the Rector and Visitors of the University of Virginia
All rights reserved
Printed in the United States of America on acid-free paper

First published 2015

1 3 5 7 9 8 6 4 2

Library of Congress Cataloging-in-Publication Data
Practicing democracy : popular politics in the United States
from the Constitution to the Civil War / Daniel Peart and
Adam I. P. Smith, editors.

pages   cm

Includes bibliographical references and index.
ISBN 978-0-8139-3770-0 (cloth : alk. paper)
ISBN 978-0-8139-3771-7 (e-book)
1. Political parties — United States — History — 18th century.
2. Political parties — United States — History — 19th century.
3. Political participation — United States — History — 18th century.
4. United States — Politics and government — 1789 – 1815. 5. United
States — Politics and government — 1815 – 1861. I. Peart, Daniel,
1985 – , editor of compilation, author. II. Smith, Adam I. P.,
editor of compilation.
JK2260.P73   2015
320.97309′034 — dc23
2014047343

CONTENTS

Acknowledgments vii

Introduction 1
DANIEL PEART AND ADAM I. P. SMITH

PART ONE

Party Development

"Parties Are Unavoidable":
Path Dependence and the Origins of Party Politics
in the United States 23
DOUGLAS BRADBURN

Rethinking the Origins of
Partisan Democracy in the United States, 1795–1840 46
REEVE HUSTON

Party, Nation, and Cultural Rupture:
The Crisis of the American Civil War 72
JOHN L. BROOKE

PART TWO

Parties and Participation

Jeffersonian Parties, Politics, and Participation:
The Tortuous Trajectory of American Democracy 99
ANDREW W. ROBERTSON

An "Era of No Feelings"?:
Rethinking the Relationship between Political Parties and
Popular Participation in the Early United States 123
DANIEL PEART

Was There a Second Party System?:
Illinois as a Case Study in Antebellum Politics 145
GRAHAM A. PECK

PART THREE

The Place of Parties in American Politics

Legitimacy, Localism, and the First Party System 173
KENNETH OWEN

"Peaceably If We Can, Forcibly If We Must":
Immigrants and Popular Politics in
Pre–Civil War New York 196
TYLER ANBINDER

Small Men, Best Men, and the Big City:
Reconstructing Political Culture in
Antebellum Philadelphia 222
ANDREW HEATH

PART FOUR

A Fresh Perspective

Two Approaches to Democratization:
Engagement versus Capability 247
JOHANN N. NEEM

Afterword 281
DANIEL PEART AND ADAM I. P. SMITH

List of Contributors 287

Index 289

ACKNOWLEDGMENTS

The editors would like to thank all those who contributed to the University College London Commonwealth Fund Conference 2011, "Parties, Politics and the People: Rethinking Popular Political Engagement in the United States, 1789–1860," from which this volume developed. We acknowledge the generous financial support provided by the Commonwealth Fund (UCL) and Institute of the Americas. We are grateful to Iwan Morgan, David Sim, Jonathan Chandler, Britta Schilling, and Olga Jimenez for their assistance in organizing and facilitating the event. And we thank all those who attended and took part in the discussions, especially Erik Mathisen, whose paper from that conference has already been published separately in the *Journal of the Early Republic*.

For the volume itself, we are indebted to Dick Holway and all of the editorial team at the University of Virginia Press. Our two patient readers, Ron Formisano and Mark-Voss Hubbard, provided us with extensive comments, critical and supportive in equal measure, which made our task as editors much easier. And finally, we offer our personal thanks to the contributors, for a very pleasant three days in June 2011 and for all the blood, sweat, and tears we demanded of them thereafter.

★ DANIEL PEART & ADAM I. P. SMITH ★

Introduction

W e have frequently printed the word democracy," wrote Walt Whitman in 1871, "yet I cannot too often repeat that it is a word the gist of which still sleeps."[1] Indeed, the frequency with which "democracy" is invoked in descriptions of the early United States, both by Whitman's contemporaries and by subsequent scholars, is one of the main reasons why its meaning remains so difficult to capture. Delegates to the Philadelphia Convention in 1787 viewed democracy as an antique, and imperfect, form of government, and believed that their task was to check its influence in the nation's new constitution. By the outbreak of the Civil War seventy-four years later, however, democracy had become the ubiquitous shorthand for American politics in totality: a government "of the people, by the people, for the people," in Abraham Lincoln's celebrated phrase. The French Revolution may have done much to revitalize and disseminate the concept of democracy, but by the middle of the nineteenth century, it was across the Atlantic that Europeans looked to see it in action. The writings of Alexis de Tocqueville were instrumental here, but the French aristocrat's choice of title for his most famous publication merely reflected an already common, and common sense, understanding of American institutions, one that was made manifest in Britain, for example, by the frequent use of "Americanization" as a synonym for "democratization."[2] Democracy, in its modern incarnation, came to prominence as an idea that described how Americans practiced their politics—or at least how they were imagined to do so—and it remains so today. Thus while our understanding of how United States politics actually worked between the ratification of the Constitution and the coming of the Civil War remains imprecise, so too must our understanding of democracy.

The purpose of this book is to address this problem. The constitutional roots of American democracy are not difficult to locate. The rhetorical commitment of the Founding Fathers to self-rule was natural enough, given the political categories available to these gentlemen of the Enlightenment. Since sovereignty in the new republic manifestly did not reside in a monarch, it must, by default, reside in the people. But just as constitutional theorists claimed that royal sovereignty in Britain was embodied in Parliament, so there existed an influential discourse in the former colonies which argued—or simply assumed without need for elaborate argument—that popular sovereignty in practice could only be encoded in formally defined institutions. "We the people" was a statement of the constitutionally self-evident in the aftermath of the Declaration of Independence, but its democratic implications for political life in the young nation were far from clear.[3]

Looking back half a century from the heights of Jacksonian triumphalism in the 1830s, the radical editor William Leggett professed bemusement at the concerns of his revolutionary forefathers. Their anxiety to establish checks and balances, to guard against the "turbulence and contention" of a "pure democracy," in James Madison's words, struck him as quaint. "We have no such fears," Leggett wrote, claiming to speak, in some cases certainly inaccurately, on behalf of his fellow citizens.[4] Yet the practices most associated with American democracy, those that have come to define the U.S. political system since the Civil War, were the product of decades of experimentation, a process that was still far from complete when Leggett put pen to paper. Competition between two dominant national political parties, the identification of citizenship with the franchise, a reverence for the Constitution and constitutional procedures, and an exclusive focus on elections as moments of political choice: none of these outcomes were necessarily envisaged by the founding generation, and none were the inevitable consequence of their rhetorical commitment to popular sovereignty.

The oft-repeated narrative of the "rise" of democracy between the American Revolution and the Civil War can obscure as much as it reveals.[5] Historians have found it hard to resist imposing a teleological account of political development onto an era that imagined politics very differently from our own. The familiar story is easily caricatured: a genteel politics dominated by men in silk stockings and powdered wigs was swamped by a rising tide of popular demands for inclusion in the political process, a tide bewigged gentlemen had inadvertently helped to unleash with their frequent paeans to popular sovereignty. Scribblers like William Leggett muscled their way into the political mainstream by deploying the language of democracy to give voice to "the people," while skilled party-builders, typified by Martin Van Buren, crafted the organizations necessary to mobilize a mass electorate. The election of the "People's President," Andrew Jackson, in 1828 heralded the dawning of the "Age of the Common Man." "The first principle of our system," proclaimed the new occupant of the White House, is "that the majority is to govern."[6]

The triumph of this doctrine of majoritarianism, something that one of the Constitution's principal architects, Madison, had plainly warned against, marked a transformation in political practices in the United States.[7] Deferential relationships inherited from the colonial era were swept away, and in a wave of constitution writing and rewriting, the executive and judicial branches of many state governments were firmly subordinated to the legislatures, which claimed sole right to speak with the voice of the people. *Vox populi, vox Dei* was hardly a new slogan, but in the hands of men like the Jacksonian orator and historian George Bancroft, it became the justification for tearing down the elaborate constitutional checks and balances erected by the founders precisely to insulate government from simple majority rule.[8] And as the American people flowed ever westward, they carried their evolving notions of self-government with them, creating roughly egalitarian white men's republics predicated on the idea of universal property ownership.

To commentators like Leggett, this political trajectory appeared both natural and salutary. Jacksonian Democrats considered their party to be the faithful guardian of liberties won in the revolution, and "the instrument by which our institutions have been preserved in the progress of the nation."[9] And if "the Democracy," as the party was known to friends and enemies alike, represented the singular embodiment of the sovereign people, its adversaries must be nothing more than a "false, rotten, insubstantial, effete" minority, often rendered "aristocrats" in shorthand.[10] This Jacksonian self-image has cast a long shadow. The Progressive historians of the early twentieth century adopted as their own its principal tenet: that the transformation of American politics before the Civil War was driven by conflict between a rising popular coalition of western farmers and eastern wage laborers, and a patrician class of landholders, bankers, speculators, and industrialists. This titanic struggle climaxed in the presidential election of 1828, with Jackson, championing the forces of democracy, defeating revolutionary-era throwback John Quincy Adams, the representative of wealth, privilege, and elitism. In this view, expressed most cogently by Arthur Schlesinger Jr. and recently revived by Sean Wilentz, it was Jackson and his loyal lieutenants in the Democratic Party who provided the engine for democratization.[11]

During the 1960s and 1970s, however, a new generation of historians, operating loosely under the label "New Political Historians," began to look afresh
at antebellum politics. Using methodologies borrowed from the social sciences, most notably the statistical analysis of census data and election returns,
scholars including Lee Benson, Michael F. Holt, and Joel Silbey sought to
"grasp the total behavior of all the actors in the political universe, rather than
relying only on the statements, actions, and behavior of prominent leaders and
observers of politics."[12] The concept of "negative reference groups" was employed to explain how party-builders exploited ethnic and religious tensions,
which replaced socioeconomic identities as the primary determinant of political behavior. Voters in this model were committed partisans, marching to the
polls to support their own side, or perhaps more importantly to defeat their
opponents. The Whig Party was no longer a bunch of out-of-touch aristocrats
but a recognizably modern organization willing and able to compete with the
Democrats for popular favor, and it was the establishment of nationwide two-
party competition by 1840, not the election of a single charismatic leader, that
provided the impetus for political change.

As scholars abandoned outdated syntheses organized by presidential administration, political parties offered the foundations for an alternative periodization of U.S. politics. Political scientist Walter Dean Burnham was at
the forefront of this endeavor, proposing that American history be divided
into five "party systems," each defined by a distinctive pattern of partisan
behavior.[13] Following in his footsteps, scholars such as Richard L. McCormick
and Joel Silbey grouped the second and third of these systems, spanning the
decades from the 1830s to the 1890s, together under the label of the "Party
Period," during which "parties dominated political participation" and "voting was more partisan and more widespread than ever before."[14] Parties, they
argued, were a manifestation of "modernization," a welcome replacement for
the personal, hierarchical relationships of an earlier, and less-complex, political era, and a necessary ingredient to make the founders' constitutionalism
function in practice. Party organizations articulated issues in ways that made
sense to ordinary citizens, corralled them to the ballot box in ever-increasing
numbers, and sustained unprecedented levels of popular engagement. They
were also a critical force for integration in what was otherwise a fragmented
national community. Parties were all-encompassing; they "defined the terms
of political confrontation and shaped the behavior of most participants in the
many levels of political activity."[15]

Despite their differences, Progressive historians, practitioners of the New Political History, and subscribers to the Party Period concept were in general agreement on the far-reaching transition from a "traditional, notable-oriented and deferential politics" before the 1820s or 1830s to a "party, electorate-oriented and egalitarian style of politics" thereafter.[16] In recent years, however, this chronology has come under severe scrutiny. Several scholars working on the immediate postrevolutionary period have shown that many citizens did not share the Founding Fathers' concern that American politics was becoming too democratic.[17]

Meanwhile, new studies of the conflict between the first major American parties, the Federalists and Republicans, have uncovered evidence of high election turnouts occurring several decades earlier than previously thought. In his contribution to *Beyond the Founders*, a collection of essays from historians working in this field, Jeffrey Pasley even suggests that "this political culture was successful precisely because it was *not* a standardized national system," a sharp dig at Party Period scholars' admiration for Whig and Democratic organizations that he considers "routinized" and "bloated from too many in-jections of money."[18]

Beyond the Founders also reflects the recent "cultural turn" in the historiography, as scholars have made use of Jürgen Habermas's concept of the public sphere to broaden their definition of the political beyond the corridors of power and the calculus of the polling place, and moved away from statistical analysis to read subjects such as clothing, civic rituals, and even a "Mammoth Cheese" for their political meaning.[19] One consequence of this is that scholars of both the early republic and the antebellum eras have uncovered new evidence for the political engagement of women and African Americans, demonstrating that participation in politics has hardly been limited to legally qualified vot-ers. This is one tale that does not fit neatly into the conventional narrative of democratization, however. As Rosemarie Zagarri has shown, over the decades that followed the ratification of the Constitution, women became less able to play a role in electoral politics, as party development brought more regulation to the world of conventions and committees.[20] Likewise, the access of African Americans to the ballot box measurably worsened during the first half of the nineteenth century, while their participation in public space was made more difficult by virulently racist mobs reacting to the rise of abolitionism.[21]

In spite of the many obstacles conspicuously placed in their paths, these and other disenfranchised groups were far from powerless—even enslaved people could decisively influence the political destiny of the nation, as Stephanie McCurry has recently reminded us.[22] But those who were excluded from formal political channels did not exercise the same kind of power as those who were not. At the very least, African Americans, and to a lesser extent women, exercised what might be called an implied political power in antebellum America since their visibility in the public sphere—particularly, of course, in the abolition movement—was a source of such anxiety to white conservatives. The white political imagination was filled with dystopian images of the anarchy that would result from an ever-greater exercise of power by black people, women, and other marginalized sections of society, such as immigrants.[23] Beyond this implied power, both women and African Americans also participated through the exertion of personal influence on the borders of the public/private divide, and through the establishment and operation of political organizations that existed outside the constitutionally defined realm of electoral politics but nonetheless proved to be remarkably effective at exerting pressure on elected representatives.[24]

The existence of these self-created societies highlights the fact that political parties were just one manifestation of an outburst of associational activity during this period. Revolutionary groups like the Sons of Liberty were among the first to demonstrate that "the people" could adopt a public persona other than that of "the mob," and when the war with Britain was brought to a successful conclusion, citizens of the newly independent United States continued to put this lesson to good use. Some of their organizations, like the fraternal societies and militia companies studied by Albrecht Koschnik, were made to serve manifestly partisan ends.[25] Others, like the Know-Nothings that form the subject of Mark Voss-Hubbard's work, were born out of a persistent strain of anti-partisanship but reached maturity through participation in mainstream politics.[26] Other organizations that we would now think of as pressure groups, championing particular causes such as temperance, Sabbatarianism, tariff reform, or abolition, illustrated the dialectical relationship that existed between parties and nonpartisan movements in terms of ideas, personnel, and organizational techniques.[27] All of these groups, however, played a critical role in expanding the political life of the early United States; "in learning how to volunteer," Neem observes, "ordinary people learned to think and to act as citizens. They ensured that citizenship in a democracy would not be confined to voting and to office holding."[28]

The rich outpouring of literature in the field of early U.S. political history during the last few decades has certainly expanded our knowledge in important ways. Nonetheless, a number of issues remain unresolved, and it is these that this book tackles. The first set of issues concern periodization and party development. The revolutionary generation were profoundly influenced by a republican ideology which taught that politics required the subordination of all private interests to the common pursuit of a unitary public good. Guided by these principles, as Richard Hofstadter has famously detailed, the Founding Fathers "could not see how organized and institutionalized party conflict could be made useful, or could be anything other than divisive, distracting, and dangerous."[29] Subsequent studies have shown that many Americans remained suspicious of political parties long into the nineteenth century.[30] And yet right from the emergence of Federalist and Republican groupings in Congress during the 1790s, Americans certainly spoke and acted as if parties existed. The question then remains, as posed most succinctly by Gerald Leonard, "How did antiparty Americans invent the mass political party?"[31]

It is conventional to divide the period from the revolution to the Civil War into early republic and antebellum eras; we have used this language ourselves in this introduction. Yet as David Waldstreicher has observed, the "continuing power of the traditional narrative, which divides political history—and U.S. history generally—at about 1815 or 1820," is the principal reason that "parallel stories of democratization are being told" about the 1800s and the 1830s.[32] Subscribers to the Party Period model have dismissed evidence of high election turnouts in the preceding decades as insignificant; "popular voting remained volatile," writes Joel Silbey, and "there was little persistent evidence of party loyalty from election to election."[33] In response, Jeffrey Pasley has provocatively countered that "the transition from the loose decentralized parties of Thomas Jefferson and Alexander Hamilton to the mass party organizations of Martin Van Buren and Abraham Lincoln [was] a step back for American democracy."[34] Clearly there were differences between the political practices of the Jeffersonian and Jacksonian eras, but bound by their traditional areas of specialty, recent historians have not attempted to place the two periods in comparative perspective.[35]

Then there is the issue of political realignment. The Party Period concept emphasizes the continuity and stability of the years between the advent of mass parties in the 1830s and the end of the century. Yet in the middle of this era, the nation descended into a bloody civil war, a cataclysm precipitated by the collapse of the Whig-Democrat party system in the 1850s. If parties were so all-powerful, how are we to explain their failure to suppress the rise of sectional tensions and, in the case of the Whigs, to prevent their own demise? Michael F. Holt and William E. Gienapp, among others, have described party leaders' battling against rising public dissatisfaction with the practice of "politics as usual."[36] Hostility to sinister behind-the-scenes "wire-pullers" and a sense that partisanship was corrupting the body politic made sectional compromise and conciliation harder. "The party has failed us," concluded the *New York Times* in 1861. Partisanship had "brought the nation to this state of Armageddon."[37] This crisis of party in the 1850s has major implications for a longitudinal study of democratization and party development.

The first part of the book addresses this theme of political development between the revolution and Civil War. Douglas Bradburn examines the origins of America's first national parties in order to show how their emergence was shaped by forces of "path dependency." Reeve Huston addresses head-on the traditional divide between early republic and antebellum historians to identify what was novel about Jacksonian politics and what was merely a continuation of Jeffersonian practice. And John L. Brooke offers a new dichotomy of "structure" and "liminality" to explain the collapse of the Democrat-Whig party system in the build-up to the Civil War. These three chapters, then, offer a fresh perspective on the origins, evolution, and disintegration of party-driven forms of politics.

A second set of issues, which follow naturally from this groundwork, surrounds the relationship between political parties and popular participation. Parties figure in the conventional narrative as the prime agents of democratization. As Ronald P. Formisano has long since (critically) observed, most historians of this period "believe that a competitive, two-party system opened up political life, brought distant governments closer to more citizens, and made power more responsive to constituent demands," or, in other words, that "party virtually equals democracy."[38] This consensus rests on the voluminous statistical analysis of election returns completed by the New Political Historians, and the assumption, voiced most concisely by William Gienapp, that "the best available indicator of the extent of popular interest in politics in pre–Civil War America, as well as the degree to which the political universe of the nineteenth century was unique, is voter turnout."[39]

A decade ago, however, this conclusion was contested by Glenn C. Altschuler and Stuart M. Blumin, who argued that high turnout can be read as evidence not of "a widespread and deep engagement in politics," but rather of "the extraordinary achievement of American political parties in mobilizing voters, some of whom were ignorant of, uninterested in, sceptical about, or even averse to political affairs." Parties, with all of their "elaborate structures and techniques for nominating candidates, devising platforms, conducting campaigns, and maximizing election-day turnout," represented "the efforts of those who were deeply involved in political affairs to reach and influence those who were not." Instead of genuinely promoting a broad-based participatory democracy, parties became adept at providing a "clearly labeled 'package' of candidates, programs, and images that less thoughtful or less interested voters could 'purchase' without difficulty." In fact, according to Altschuler and Blumin, "the very institutional development that facilitated the more widespread purchase of party packages may have deepened the distance between less engaged citizens and the political process." Precisely because parties were so efficient, "Americans could, if they wished, leave the work [of politics] to the professionals, and go about their other business."[40]

The findings of Altschuler and Blumin have provoked fierce debate. Questions had already been raised about the accuracy of the New Political Historians' data on voter turnout.[41] Now, though, doubts were raised about whether the statistical analysis of election returns, even if properly conducted, could ever provide a reliable indicator of popular engagement with politics. By focusing on the frequently dubious methods employed by party activists to drag voters to the polls, and the priority that party leaders placed on winning elections above all else, some recent studies appear almost to echo Edward Pessen's provocative claim that "the great major parties were in a large sense great hoaxes."[42] In response, others have sprung to the defense of party; Harry L. Watson, for example, writes that "the [political] process depends on leaders who articulate options and attempt to generate interest in them, but public response is not automatic or arbitrary. The people will only 'buy' those options they feel a genuine interest in . . . and endless get-out-the-vote rigmarole will not get them to the polls if they are not inclined to go already."[43] The relationship between parties and popular participation is now more contested than ever before.

The second part of the book approaches this problem from three different perspectives. Andrew W. Robertson reconsiders the role that political parties played in both franchise reform and the fashioning of a deliberative public sphere, and emphasizes the tortuous ways in which American democratic ideology and practices ebbed and flowed in the early republic. Daniel Peart explores the connection between party competition and election turnout during the so-called Era of Good Feelings, and provides new evidence to demonstrate that participation rates at the state level were actually higher where political parties were weak or nonexistent than where two-party competition was more firmly established. Graham A. Peck describes the relationship between voters and politicians in Illinois during the so-called second party system (a phrase that he argues is a misnomer). In his depiction, parties were neither durable nor stable, with voters' support highly "conditional." The central theme that unites all three chapters is the issue of whether parties truly served to expand the democratic possibilities of American politics, or whether their role was less straightforwardly affirmative than the standard narrative would suggest.

The final set of issues concerns the place of parties in American political life. The Party Period paradigm rests on the primacy of parties. Even important critics of particular aspects of the paradigm have not challenged this core assumption; Altschuler and Blumin, for example, conclude that "very little that would happen in American politics, especially in the routine conduct of political affairs, would occur beyond the realm of the party."[44] Yet the plethora of third parties, the variety and vitality of associational activity, and the ultimate collapse of both the Federalist-Republican and Whig-Democrat party systems suggest that parties faced considerable challenges in containing alternative forms of political action and maintaining their own organizational dominance.[45]

Parties were certainly not the only way of organizing politics available to contemporaries, so what made them so distinctive? The term "party" itself needs to be carefully historicized since neither the language of party nor the forms of organization that contemporaries associated with parties were consistent over time.[46] Then there is the issue of how political parties related to, and engaged with, other forms of participation. In his recent survey of populist movements from the revolution to the Civil War, Formisano suggests that by the 1840s, the rise of party meant that "both the public space and contested legitimacy once claimed by populist insurgencies and movements . . . had grown more restricted." While Formisano calls this an "ironic sidebar" on "grand narratives chronicling the 'rise of democracy,'" there is a growing sense that the ironies have now become so imposing as to require that the narrative itself be rewritten.[47]

The third part of the book explores the interaction between political parties and the more broadly defined civil society, which, taken together, provides the sum of American political practices during this era. Kenneth Owen investigates how political leaders exercised power in the years immediately following the ratification of the Constitution, and finds that their success or failure often depended not on their control of the formal institutions of government but on their ability to demonstrate popular support from extra-constitutional representative institutions such as public meetings. Tyler Anbinder compares the experiences of Irish and German immigrants in the antebellum North in a bid to understand whether political parties offered these groups a meaningful share of political power. Finally, Andrew Heath explores the campaign for a new city charter in antebellum Philadelphia, and demonstrates that far from welcoming parties as harbingers of democracy, reformers were motivated by a determination to break the power of the party machines.

Thinking about politics in a more expansive way than was once the case has enormously enriched our understanding of politics in the early United States. Yet there are dangers, too, in the "cultural turn," if a focus on political identity and expression fails to also account for what Formisano has called the "classic considerations of political life . . . who gets what, why, and how?"[48] Stefan Collini's definition of politics as "the important, inescapable, and difficult attempt to determine relations of power in a given space" is useful here since it clearly encompasses much more than formal politics, yet also clarifies the goal to which all political activity must be directed.[49] Politics is about power—and power, by definition, is always relational: one exercises it over those who have less. Power can, of course, be symbolic and cultural, or "soft," but it is fundamentally exercised in the context of which groups and individuals can exert "hard" economic or political power.

That brings us to a theme that runs throughout the book, which is the relationship among citizens, parties, and governance. Different forms of participation must be understood in relation to the objects of that participation. The practice of democracy was not simply an end in itself; it was also a means of influencing political outcomes. One of the apparent strengths of the Party Period paradigm was that it tied parties, elections, and policymaking together. "The same party organizations that mobilized citizens on election day also structured their receipt of government goods," explained Richard L. McCormick, and this "distribution strengthened the parties and helped build bridges between their voters, leaders, and representatives in office."[50] Wary of using government for regulatory or redistributive purposes, politicians instead saw government as a way of apportioning the proceeds of an expanding national domain among their supporters at the polls, through public land sales, tariff protection for domestic industries, and log-rolling development projects. This distributive policymaking, according to McCormick, underpinned parties' centrality to the era just as much as their distribution of public offices in the form of patronage.

While McCormick's "exploratory hypothesis" was swiftly adopted as a central plank of the Party Period concept, it has also provoked its fair share of critics. As Formisano notes, in an article that neatly summarizes the arguments on both sides, the claim "that distributive policies created satisfaction with the two major parties and the political system itself—what might be termed *regime satisfaction*"—is relatively uncontroversial, but a higher burden of proof is required to demonstrate that "parties actually served as vehicles for distributive policies intended to build coalitions or satisfy constituencies." Yet Formisano also rejects the opposite conclusion that "policy and voting were wholly unrelated."[51] Since Formisano's article, some scholars have taken up the challenge of providing the missing evidence for McCormick's hypothesis; Richard Bensel, for example, highlights the crucial role played by local party agents in mediating between elected representatives, seeking to promote their own political agenda on the state or national stage, and voters at the polls, whose support was obtained through negotiations that might have little or nothing to do with considerations of public policy.[52] Others continue to seek alternative explanations for government activity. Robin L. Einhorn on the role of slavery in shaping United States taxation policy, William J. Novak on public regulation to facilitate economic development, and Daniel Peart on the struggle among competing interest groups to determine federal tariff rates are all examples of a growing body of work which again reinforces the point that practicing democracy is about more than just parties and elections.[53]

McCormick's formula may be overly neat, but several contributions to this volume echo one implication of his thesis, which is that parties were strongest and most in control of their fate when issues conducive to distributive policymaking were at the center of political debate. Where parties were vulnerable was in the face of issues that forced governments on the local, state, and national levels to make difficult, often binary, choices — to ban alcohol or not, to restrict slavery in the territories or not, and so on. Single-issue pressure groups, or public opinion leaders like churchmen and newspaper editors, could mobilize voters on these issues without having to worry, as mainstream parties did, about the difficulties of building and maintaining diverse coalitions to win elections. Nineteenth-century American politics revolved around such tensions between party leaders' desires to "routinize" politics and outsiders' desires to impose some sweeping reform (or to stop one).

This notion of politics as a ceaseless struggle over power relationships, expressed in numerous ways but always with a clear goal, underlies the approach taken by the authors of the essays that follow. We do not take parties and elections to be the only meaningful arena for political action, but we do think that it is necessary to clarify what institutions and practices were available to different groups of Americans, and how effectively each could be used to exercise power. We also aim to take on board insights about greater participation in the early period without "flattening" our understanding of change over time. Such methodological issues are the subject of the final essay in this book. Johann N. Neem argues that instead of relying on voter turnout as a proxy for democratization, historians should concentrate on the capability of ordinary citizens to affect political outcomes, an approach that promises to integrate recent work on civil society with more traditional party-oriented perspectives.

Taken as a whole, this book has three main findings:

1. We offer a new way of thinking about American politics across the traditional dividing line of circa 1828. In recent years, historians of the early republic have demolished old assumptions about low rates of political participation and shallow popular partisanship in the age of Jefferson. But this raises the question of how, if at all, Jacksonian politics departed from earlier norms. This book reaffirms the significance of a transition in political practices during the 1820s and 1830s, but casts the transformation in a different light. Whereas the traditional narrative is one of a party-driven democratic awakening, the contributors to this volume offer a more complex reading of changing organizational forms and styles of politics, one that emphasizes both the constricting definition of legitimate "democratic" practices in the decades following the revolution and the proliferation within those bounds of competing public voices in the build-up toward the Civil War.

2. We challenge the conventional wisdom that with the coming of the so-called Party Period, American politics reached its apogee of participation. In

contrast, several contributors to this volume critique the role of political parties in this story, stressing their function to manage the people *as well as* to em-
power them. These two apparently contradictory functions actually coexisted,
though often in continuing tension with one another, as party leaders strove
both to stimulate and to channel voters' energies, spawning unprecedented rates
of sustained electoral participation by the 1840s and 1850s. Equally important,
what this book also suggests is that the major parties' hold on the electorate
was always contested, as the demise of the Whigs very obviously demonstrates.
Political actors from outside the formal party system—Know-Nothings,
abolitionists, temperance campaigners, advocates for the right of labor, pro-
tectionists and free traders, anti-rent protestors, secessionists, and many more
—were frequently able to galvanize the electorate in ways that subverted the
intentions and interests of party leaders. Yet parties remained central to the
electoral process, and it is telling that insurgents, often with single-issue campaigns, usually ended up allying with, or being subsumed by, parties. The
point is that we cannot simply tell the story of American democracy as one of
ever-gradual empowerment of "the people" (however we may define that defi-
antly plural entity). The advent of more formalized and self-conscious parties
in the Jacksonian era was neither the apotheosis nor the nemesis of popular
democracy.

    3. We argue that, while parties were by far the most visible and import-
ant political formations in these decades, they existed in constant interaction
with groups and individuals who could utilize alternative—and sometimes
strikingly effective—non- and anti-partisan means of mobilizing the public.
Seldom were party leaders in complete control of the issues that drove politics
at any particular moment, and their need to construct and maintain a broad-
based, electorally viable coalition made them inherently vulnerable to targeted insurgent campaigns. Furthermore, the traditional American mistrust
for centralized power placed officeholders at a disadvantage against those who
could successfully pose as "outs," representing the people against the "wire-
pullers" of corrupt partisans. Republican electoral advances in 1858–60, for
example, were due to their ability to pose as the antiestablishment insurgents
as well as their antislavery message. Like the Know-Nothing organizations
that swept to dramatic victories in state elections in 1854 and 1855, Republicans claimed their candidates were "fresh from the loins of the people."[54]
This, after all, was a period in which the "rules of the game" were far from
settled, and the practices of politics were themselves frequently the subject of

political conflict, as Americans struggled to reconcile their competing, and often contradictory, interpretations of popular sovereignty.

In sum, then, this book is an effort to crystallize emerging scholarship that resists a teleological reading of progress toward the present-day U.S. political system organized around two competing national parties.[55] The tale that emerges from this volume is not a whiggish one of "democratization," but a more complex, sometimes ironic portrait of the changing ways in which ordinary Americans — "We the People" — could exercise political power in the decades between the ratification of the Constitution and the coming of the Civil War.

Notes

1. Walt Whitman, *Poetry and Prose*, ed. J. Kaplan (New York: Library of America, 1996), 984.

2. Alexis de Tocqueville, *Democracy in America*, 2 vols. (1835–40; New York: Library of America, 2004); John Dunn, *Setting the People Free: The Story of Democracy* (London: Atlantic Books, 2005); Pierre Rosanvallon, *The Demands of Liberty: Civil Liberty in France since the Revolution* (Cambridge, Mass.: Harvard University Press, 2007); Joanna Innes and Mark Philp, eds., *Re-imagining Democracy in the Age of Revolution: America, France, Britain, Ireland, 1750–1850* (Oxford: Oxford University Press, 2013); Axel Körner, Nicola Miller, and Adam I. P. Smith, eds., *America Imagined: Explaining the United States in Nineteenth Century Europe and Latin America* (New York: Palgrave, 2012); Robert Saunders, *Democracy and the Vote in British Politics, 1848–1867: The Making of the Second Reform Act* (Farnham, Eng.: Ashgate, 2011).

3. Ronald P. Formisano, *For the People: American Populist Movements from the Revolution to the 1850s* (Chapel Hill: University of North Carolina Press, 2008); Christian G. Fritz, *American Sovereigns: The People and America's Constitutional Tradition before the Civil War* (Cambridge: Cambridge University Press, 2008); Suzette Hemberger, "A Government Based on Representations," *Studies in American Political Development* 10 (Fall 1996): 289–332; Edmund S. Morgan, *Inventing the People: The Rise of Popular Sovereignty in England and America* (New York: Norton, 1988).

4. James Madison, "The Federalist 10," in *The Federalist Papers*, ed. Lawrence Goldman (Oxford: Oxford University Press, 2008), 52; William Leggett, *A Collection of the Political Writings of William Leggett*, 2 vols. (New York, 1840), 1:262.

5. Daniel Walker Howe, *What Hath God Wrought: The Transformation of America, 1815–1848* (New York: Oxford University Press, 2007); Sean Wilentz, *The Rise of American Democracy: Jefferson to Lincoln* (New York: Norton, 2005); Gordon S. Wood, *Empire of Liberty: A History of the Early Republic, 1789–1815* (New York: Oxford University Press, 2009).

6. *Annual Messages, Veto Messages, Protest Etc. of Andrew Jackson, President of the United States* (Baltimore, 1835), 10.

7. Madison, "Federalist 10," 48–55.

8. George Bancroft, *An Oration Delivered on the Fourth of July, 1826* (Northampton, Mass., 1826), 19–20.

9. "The United States Constitution," *United States Magazine and Democratic Review* 22 (May 1848): 387.

10. *Brooklyn Daily Eagle*, 7 November 1846.

11. Arthur Schlesinger Jr., *The Age of Jackson* (Boston: Little, Brown, 1945); Wilentz, *Rise of American Democracy*.

12. Joel H. Silbey, *The Partisan Imperative: The Dynamics of American Politics before the Civil War* (Oxford: Oxford University Press, 1985), xiv. See also Lee Benson, *The Concept of Jacksonian Democracy: New York as a Test Case* (Princeton, N.J.: Princeton University Press, 1961), and Michael F. Holt, *Forging a Majority: The Formation of the Republican Party in Pittsburgh, 1848–1860* (New Haven, Conn.: Yale University Press, 1969).

13. Walter Dean Burnham, "Party Systems and the Political Process," in *The American Party Systems: Stages of Political Development*, ed. William Nisbet Chambers and Walter Dean Burnham (New York: Oxford University Press, 1967), 277–307. Burnham's work built on V. O. Key Jr., "A Theory of Critical Elections," *Journal of Politics* 17 (February 1955): 3–18.

14. Richard L. McCormick, "The Party Period and Public Policy: An Exploratory Hypothesis," *Journal of American History* 66 (September 1979): 279–98, 281, 283 (quotations). See also Joel H. Silbey, *The American Political Nation, 1838–1893* (Stanford, Cal.: Stanford University Press, 1991).

15. Ibid., 9.

16. Ronald P. Formisano, "Deferential-Participant Politics: The Early Republic's Political Culture, 1789–1840," *American Political Science Review* 68 (June 1974): 473–87. Formisano's notable contribution was to show how this transition took place gradually and unevenly over half a century.

17. Woody Holton, *Unruly Americans and the Origins of the Constitution* (New York: Hill and Wang, 2007); Terry Bouton, *Taming Democracy: "The People," The Founders and the Troubled Ending of the American Revolution* (New York: Oxford University Press, 2009); Michael A. McDonnell, *The Politics of War: Race, Class and Conflict in Revolutionary Virginia* (Chapel Hill: University of North Carolina Press, 2010); Seth Cotlar, *Tom Paine's America: The Rise and Fall of Transatlantic Radicalism* (Charlottesville: University of Virginia Press, 2011).

18. Jeffrey L. Pasley, "The Cheese and the Words: Popular Political Culture and Participatory Democracy in the Early American Republic," in *Beyond the Founders: New Approaches to the Political History of the Early American Republic*, ed. Jeffrey L. Pasley, Andrew W. Robertson, and David Waldstreicher (Chapel Hill: University of North Carolina Press, 2004), 49.

19. These examples are all taken from essays in *Beyond the Founders*.

20. Rosemarie Zagarri, *Revolutionary Backlash: Women and Politics in the Early American Republic* (Philadelphia: University of Pennsylvania Press, 2008), 147–80. See also John L. Brooke, "Spheres, Sites, Subjectivity, History: Reframing Antebellum American Society," *Journal of the Early Republic* 28 (Spring 2008): 75–82. Exceptions to this trend are noted by Susan Graham, "'A Warm Politician and Devotedly Attached to the Democratic Party': Catherine Read Williams, Politics and Literature in Antebellum America," *Journal of the Early Republic* 30 (Summer 2010): 253–78; Elizabeth R. Varon, *We Mean to Be Counted: White Women and Politics in Antebellum Virginia* (Chapel Hill: University of North Carolina Press, 1998); and Ronald J. Zboray and Mary Saracino Zboray, *Voices without Votes: Women and Politics in Antebellum New England* (Durham: University of New Hampshire Press, 2010).

21. Alexander Keyssar, *The Right to Vote: The Contested History of Democracy in the United States* (New York: Basic Books, 2000).

22. Stephanie McCurry, *Confederate Reckoning: Power and Politics in the Civil War South* (Cambridge, Mass.: Harvard University Press, 2012).

23. See, for example, Don E. Fehrenbacher, *Prelude to Greatness: Lincoln in the 1850's* (Stanford, Cal.: Stanford University Press, 1962), and Alexander Saxton, *The Rise and Fall of the White Republic: Class Politics and Mass Culture in Nineteenth Century America* (New York: Verso, 1990).

24. Catherine Allgor, *Parlor Politics: In Which the Ladies of Washington Help Build a City and a Government* (Charlottesville: University Press of Virginia, 2000); Anne M. Boylan, *The Origins of Women's Activism: New York and Boston, 1787–1840* (Chapel Hill: University of North Carolina Press, 2002); Gary Nash, *Forging Freedom: The Formation of Philadelphia's Black Community, 1720–1840* (Cambridge, Mass.: Harvard University Press, 1988); Patrick Rael, *Black Identity and Black Protest in the Antebellum North* (Chapel Hill: University of North Carolina Press, 2002); Richard S. Newman, *The Transformation of American Abolitionism: Fighting Slavery in the Early Republic* (Chapel Hill: University of North Carolina Press, 2002).

25. Albrecht Koschnik, *"Let a Common Interest Bind Us Together": Associations, Partisanship, and Culture in Philadelphia, 1775–1840* (Charlottesville: University of Virginia Press, 2007).

26. Mark Voss-Hubbard, *Beyond Party: Cultures of Antipartisanship in Northern Politics before the Civil War* (Baltimore: Johns Hopkins University Press, 2002).

27. See, for example, Reeve Huston, "Popular Movements and Party Rule: The New York Anti-Rent Wars and the Jacksonian Political Order," in *Beyond the Founders*, and Johann N. Neem, *Creating a Nation of Joiners: Democracy and Civil Society in Early National Massachusetts* (Cambridge, Mass.: Harvard University Press, 2008).

28. Ibid., 82. For an important recent study that combines all of these aspects, see John L. Brooke, *Columbia Rising: Civil Life on the Upper Hudson from the Revolution to the Age of Jackson* (Chapel Hill: University of North Carolina Press, 2010).

29. Richard Hofstadter, *The Idea of a Party System: The Rise of Legitimate Opposition in the United States, 1780–1840* (Berkeley: University of California Press, 1970), ix.

30. Adam I. P. Smith, *No Party Now: Politics in the Civil War North* (New York: Oxford University Press, 2006); Voss-Hubbard, *Beyond Party.*

31. Gerald Leonard, *The Invention of Party Politics: Federalism, Popular Sovereignty, and Constitutional Development in Jacksonian Illinois* (Chapel Hill: University of North Carolina Press, 2002), 3.

32. David Waldstreicher, "The Nationalization and Racialization of American Politics: Before, Beneath, and Between Parties, 1790–1840," in *Contesting Democracy: Substance and Structure in American Political History, 1775–2000*, ed. Byron E. Shafer and Anthony J. Badger (Lawrence: University Press of Kansas, 2001), 37.

33. Silbey, *American Political Nation*, 15.

34. Jeffrey L. Pasley, "Party Politics, Citizenship, and Collective Action in Nineteenth-Century America: A Response to Stuart Blumin and Michael Schudson," *Communication Review* 4 (2000): 48.

35. A comparative perspective was one of the advantages of the "party systems" model favored by many New Political Historians and political scientists, which has since fallen out of favor. For a notable example of this earlier comparative perspective, see Ronald P. Formisano, *The Transformation of Political Culture: Massachusetts Parties, 1790s–1840s* (Oxford: Oxford University Press, 1983).

36. Michael F. Holt, *The Political Crisis of the 1850s* (New York: Norton, 1980); Michael F. Holt, *The Fate of Their Country: Politicians, Slavery Extension, and the Coming of the Civil War* (New York: Hill and Wang, 2004); William E. Gienapp, *The Origins of the Republican Party, 1852–1856* (New York: Oxford University Press, 1987); Mark W. Summers, *The Plundering Generation: Corruption and the Crisis of the Union* (New York: Oxford University Press, 1987); Voss-Hubbard, *Beyond Party;* Smith, *No Party Now;* Michael Thomas Smith, *The Enemy Within: Fears of Corruption in the Civil War North* (Charlottesville: University of Virginia Press, 2011).

37. *The New York Times*, 7 July 1861, quoted in Smith, *No Party Now*, 1.

38. Formisano, "Deferential-Participant Politics," 473.

39. William E. Gienapp, "'Politics Seem to Enter into Everything': Political Culture in the North, 1840–1860," in *Essays on American Antebellum Politics, 1840–1860*, ed. Stephen E. Maizlish and John J. Kushma (College Station: Texas A&M University Press, 1982), 17.

40. Glenn C. Altschuler and Stuart M. Blumin, *Rude Republic: Americans and Their Politics in the Nineteenth Century* (Princeton, N.J.: Princeton University Press, 2000), 79–81.

41. See, for example, Gerald Ginsburg, "Computing Antebellum Turnout: Methods and Models," *Journal of Interdisciplinary History* 16 (Spring 1986): 579–611, and, in response, Walter Dean Burnham, "Those High Nineteenth-Century American Voting Turnouts: Fact or Fiction?" *Journal of Interdisciplinary History* 16 (Spring 1986): 613–44.

42. Edward Pessen, "We Are All Jeffersonians, We Are All Jacksonians; or, A Pox on Stultifying Periodizations," *Journal of the Early Republic* 1 (Spring 1981): 25. See, for example, Philip J. Ethington, *The Public City: The Political Construction of Urban*

Life in San Francisco, 1850–1900 (Berkeley: University of California Press, 2001). Richard Franklin Bensel, *The American Ballot Box in the Mid-Nineteenth Century* (Cambridge: Cambridge University Press, 2004), concurs in the importance that Altschuler and Blumin attach to the role of party agents as mediators between voters and politicians but is more positive about the implications of this relationship for democracy.

43. Harry L. Watson, "Humbug? Bah! Altschuler and Blumin and the Riddle of the Antebellum Electorate," *Journal of American History* 84 (December 1997): 890. See also Mark E. Neely Jr., *The Boundaries of American Political Culture in the Civil War Era* (Chapel Hill: University of North Carolina Press, 2005).

44. It is not surprising that Altschuler and Blumin reach this conclusion given that they explicitly exclude from their analysis such practices as town meetings, local elections, reform groups, and vigilante committees. Altschuler and Blumin, *Rude Republic*, 47. They have been criticized for precisely this reason by Jean Harvey Baker, "Politics, Paradigms, and Public Culture," *Journal of American History* 84 (December 1997): 894–99.

45. These issues have been discussed in a roundtable published in the *Journal of American History*. See Ronald P. Formisano, "The 'Party Period' Revisited"; Mark Voss-Hubbard, "The 'Third Party Tradition' Reconsidered: Third Parties and American Public Life, 1830–1900"; and Michael F. Holt, "The Primacy of Party Reasserted," all in *Journal of American History* 86 (June 1999): 93–120, 121–50, 151–57.

46. Michael Wallace, "Changing Concepts of Party in the United States: New York, 1815–1828," *American Historical Review* 74 (December 1968): 453–91; Marc W. Kruman, "The Second American Party System and the Transformation of Revolutionary Republicanism," *Journal of the Early Republic* 12 (Winter 1992): 509–37.

47. Formisano, *For the People*, 198.

48. Ronald P. Formisano, "The Concept of Political Culture," *Journal of Interdisciplinary History* 31 (Winter 2001): 395.

49. Stefan Collini, "On Variousness; and on Persuasion," *New Left Review* 27 (May–June 2004): 65–97.

50. McCormick, "Party Period," 287. For similar conclusions, see Pasley, "Party Politics"; Silbey, *American Political Nation;* and Stephen Skowronek, *Building a New American State: The Expansion of National Administrative Capacities, 1877–1920* (Cambridge: Cambridge University Press, 1982).

51. Formisano, "'Party Period' Revisited," 93–120, 104, 107 (quotations).

52. Bensel, *American Ballot Box.*

53. Robin L. Einhorn, *American Taxation, American Slavery* (Chicago: Chicago University Press, 2006); William J. Novak, *The People's Welfare: Law and Regulation in Nineteenth-Century America* (Chapel Hill: University of North Carolina Press, 1996); Daniel Peart, "Looking beyond Parties and Elections: The Making of United States Tariff Policy during the Early 1820s," *Journal of the Early Republic* 33 (Spring 2013): 87–108. Richard R. John reviews some of these alternative approaches in "Governmental Institutions as Agents of Change: Rethinking American Political

Development in the Early Republic, 1787–1835," *Studies in American Political Development* 11 (Fall 1997): 347–80, and "Farewell to the 'Party Period': Political Economy in Nineteenth-Century America," *Journal of Policy History* 16 (2004): 117–25.

54. The phrase appeared in numerous newspapers and campaign documents; see, for example, *New York Herald,* 23 August 1856.

55. Further discussion of this emerging scholarship may be found throughout the volume, but see particularly the essays by Reeve Huston and Johann N. Neem.

PART ONE

PARTY
DEVELOPMENT

★ DOUGLAS BRADBURN ★

"Parties Are Unavoidable"

Path Dependence and the Origins of Party Politics in the United States

I n 1804, the U.S. Congress approved a constitutional amendment to fix the rules of presidential selection. The electoral tie in 1800 spooked the people, and the redesigned process was intended to limit the potential for usurpation.[1] The change was necessary. The original mode of selection assumed that the electors would act alone, without collusion—that they would not combine their support for two candidates for the highest office, thus creating an unwanted tie between two candidates who were really intended for different positions. The new amendment, on the other hand, assumed that the electors would operate as a party, to support a "slate" of candidates, for president and vice president. It was the last change to the fundamental character of the Union before the Civil War, the completion of the founding.[2]

Two aspects of the 12th Amendment are remarkable. First, the amendment was a party amendment. The Republicans, in power since the fall of 1800, designed the amendment without meddling from the minority party, the Federalists. Second, people debating the amendment assumed that there would be two national parties. Federalists opposed the amendment, offered substitutes, and asserted the danger of fiddling with the framework of government. But Federalists also admitted the inevitability of national parties. As Delaware's Samuel White argued, the "United States are now divided, and will probably continue so, into two great political parties."[3] James Hillhouse from Connecticut suggested that the "federal and republican parties have had their day—and their designations will not last long." But soon new parties would arise, and "new names and new views will be taken" in the competition for power "as it has been the course in all nations." Hillhouse even suggested that the losing presidential candidate of the opposition party should become vice president, so that the officials would be "checks upon each other."[4]

The belief that the country would "probably" always be divided into two great political parties—acknowledged and institutionalized in the creation of the 12th Amendment—marks the end of the naive hopes of the original framers that national parties would not come to dominate American political life. American democracy, as it evolved over the nineteenth century, would be practiced most obviously through parties. Yet, as this book suggests, parties were not necessary for democracy, so why did parties have so much staying power? Why only two, and not three or more?

As political historians of the last twenty years were moving away from the study of ideology to the study of culture, numerous social scientists were rediscovering the problem of thinking about continuity and change over time. Beginning with work on institutional analysis in economics—especially the work of Douglass North on the role of institutions in shaping and constraining the choices of societies and individuals—political scientists have been giving increasingly sophisticated attention to the historical processes that shape and influence social and economic behavior. As North puts it succinctly in his call for the complete integration of institutions into theories of economic growth and performance, "history matters" not simply as a repository of facts but "because the present and the future are connected to the past by the continuity of a society's institutions." While institutions have always been studied, the recent literature defines institutions broadly, to incorporate not only the formal structures of government or the market but also the "rules of the game," the informal cultures, prejudices, and mores that shape acceptable behavior.[5]

Beyond this, understanding that history and context are essential components of social development means that "time" and "the sequence of events" matter—what happened first effects what happens next, and that in turn effects what might happen years later in social, economic, and political outcomes. Political scientists have latched onto this last problem in their enthusiasm for "path dependence," the belief that "once a country or a region has started down a track, the costs of reversal are very high." Institutions, once "entrenched," obstruct the "easy reversal of the initial choice."[6] As political scientist Paul Pierson has suggested, a proper respect for the problem of path dependence means that "specific timing and sequence matter, a wide range of social outcomes may be possible, large consequences many result from relatively small or contingent events; particular courses of action, once introduced, can be almost impossible to reverse; and consequently, political development is punctuated by crucial moments or junctures that shape the basic contours of social life."[7] While social scientists are still interested in building models that apply throughout time and place, the enthusiasts for institutional analysis are skeptical about the possibility of creating a general theory of politics, and refuse to accept a deterministic approach to the problem of change over time. Institutional analysis promises nothing less than a paradigmatic shift in some branches of the social sciences, as they move out of a Newtonian model of science—in which universal laws govern cause and effect—and move into "complexity science." With such an awareness of contingency and context, as one critic of the concept of path dependence notes, "history becomes the ultimate explanation of all political choices and changes."[8]

Historians might rightly smirk to hear our cousins in the dismal sciences argue, in a provocative manner, that things change, that choices are often determined by what came before, and that human beings often die long before the consequences of their actions can be fully understood and appreciated. But there is much to be gained by embracing this welcome historical turn in the social sciences, and for historians to ignore the trend—which is certainly the case for recent historians of politics in the early republic—is bad for everybody. Historians too often work without attention to the relative usefulness of our work, either for a general public, for a general audience of historians, or for the possible use (or misuse) by social scientists. This chapter considers three problems related to the concept of path dependence in the origin and legacies of the first parties under the Constitution. First, it looks at the "framers" in action to find the relationship among the design of the new institutions of the "more perfect Union," the original polarization in Congress, and the organization of the first parties. Second, it examines "national" parties before the 1790s and the local practices that would shape the character of post–1790s politics. Finally, the essay considers the relationship of ideology to the existence of an American assumption that two parties, not three or four or more, will inevitably shape national political life.

Madisonian Failure and the Birth of Party

One of the key elements of institutional analysis and the interpretation of the path dependence of social, political, and economic outcomes is finding an "original ordering moment" that "triggered particular patterns."[9] Here the originating moment is clear. The Constitution as written, ratified, and amended between 1787 and 1791 marks a clear "original ordering moment" of the new national institutions of government. The original organization of the judiciary, the departments of the executive branch, and the procedures of the U.S. Congress stand out as the beginning of new institutions. But if we understand institutions to also include "the rules of the game," the more informal constraints that limit choice and action, there was still much to be solidified in 1791. In fact, it was differences over the rules of the game that would create the original polarization in Congress—and ultimately drive the formation of the original parties. Fundamental questions about how strictly to interpret the powers granted in the Constitution, the legitimacy of organized opposition to government policies, and the relative usefulness of national party organizations would need to be clarified before the "founding" of the United States under the Constitution was complete. The original polarization in Congress is the place to start.

Too many historians imbibe the prejudices of their subjects in telling the story of the 1790s. Much of the literature on the original leaders of the parties descends from the original polarization. American historians have overwhelmingly been Whig historians and so also have not escaped the impulse toward choosing sides in the ideological and partisan battles of the founding. If history must be moving progressively toward better government or more civil rights—more inclusion, more liberty, more social justice—then anyone who blocks the march of progress must be attacked. There are only two sides; people are either right or wrong. These tendencies have not disappeared in either popular or academic scholarship, nor in contemporary American politics. Balance is rare.

Recent popular biographies of Alexander Hamilton by Richard Brookheiser, Ronald Chernow, and Williard Randall Stern, for example, bring much to the table but rarely a sympathetic treatment of the opponents of their chosen favorite. These studies follow in a tradition that extends back to John Marshall's *Life of George Washington,* which was reinvigorated in Henry Cabot Lodge's important *Alexander Hamilton* of the 1880s, and powerfully renewed in Forrest MacDonald's 1982 biography in which he equates American "decline" with a growing popular enthusiasm for Thomas Jefferson over Hamilton.[10] In these treatments, James Madison emerges as the great betrayer, playing a deep and mysterious game, compelled either by ignorance of the great things

Hamilton was doing or by simple jealousy—positions that mimic Hamilton's opinion at the time. Scholarly studies too often share this view. Stanley Elkins and Eric McKitrick's massive survey of the period, *The Age of Federalism*, puts Hamilton in a position of honor, relegating Madison to the role of a sad confused puppet of Jefferson. Many studies, like *The Age of Federalism*, which intentionally (and incorrectly) conflate the federalists who supported ratification of the Constitution with the "Federalist Party" that Hamilton organized originally as a governing party seem unable to understand Madison as anything other than a turncoat.[11]

Studies of Madison for their part, and of Jefferson as well, too often share a similar myopia. So enamored of their subject's genius, they emphasize the Madison who "wrote" the Constitution and rarely seriously consider Madison in opposition to Hamilton, or if they do, emphasize the least important aspects of Hamilton's design and mimic the rhetoric of Madison's critique. They emphasize Hamilton's arrogance and high tone, his general indifference to the political aspirations of the common man, and his elite style. Added to this literature are the numerous studies of the framing of the Constitution whose organizing assumptions suggest that the drafting and ratification of the Constitution are the completion of "the Revolution" or "the Founding" of the United States in which either democracy is destroyed or genius is enshrined; that the creation of that document anticipated all of the developments of the 1790s, or the 1820s; and thus that the successes and failures of American history can be placed on the mantle of those narrow years. It is time to move beyond these conceptions of these two framers: neither was a villain, neither was confused, each attempted to keep his own vision—which each believed was the best—from being crushed by the designs of the other. Understanding this process remains crucial to understanding the creation of the first parties.

Madison and Hamilton appeal to political scientists, historians of political thought, and rational actor theorists for a simple reason: Madison and Hamilton remind them of themselves. Hamilton built economic and political institutions. He wrote plans and schemes and defenses of the way politics works and economies function. Madison designed institutions with a close attention to historical and contemporary systems of governance. His remarkable series of notes, articles, and polemics on the vices of the political systems of various confederacies, states, and kingdoms presents a thoroughgoing engagement with issues that interest academics today—how to design a government that will work. He believed that all men followed basic impulses, and so human behavior was universal and "natural." Men were, in essence, self-interested and rational.

Thus modern political scientists, historians, and theorists have canonized Madison and Hamilton. They assert that there is something called a "Hamiltonian System," a "Madisonian Republic," a "Madisonian System," a "Hamiltonian economy," "Madisonian Presidential Voting," "a Madisonian Democracy," and so on. A full text search of "Madisonian" in history, economics, political science, and legal journals catalogued by JSTOR lists 1,127 separate articles, while a similar search on "Hamiltonian" brings up over 600.[12] There is even a Hamiltonian Madison and a Madisonian Madison—but not, unfortunately, a Madisonian Hamilton. And there is not, it appears, an "Adamsian" anything.

But the original polarization in Congress emerges from nothing less than a "Madisonian failure." Madison's failures of design were more evident to himself than they are to many historians or theorists, and they were caused, in part, by Alexander Hamilton. Outside of the biases that too many studies of the original polarization bring to their analyses, the biggest error made by political scientists, historians, and jurists who write about the framers of the Constitution is an assumption that Madison and Hamilton were happy with the outcome of the Constitutional Convention. Hamilton's disgust with the tenor of the convention and his impatience with the final Constitution should be the beginning point of any discussion of his behavior as the first secretary of the treasury.

Hamilton believed that the Constitution as drafted contained numerous small problems and some dangerous blunders (like the equal representation of the states in the Senate), which threatened the long-term survival of the national government. A few days before the final signing of the Constitution, Hamilton explicitly revealed his feelings about the plan. He had restrained himself "from entering into the discussions by his dislike of the Scheme of Govt. in General; but as he meant to support the plan to be recommended, as better than nothing, he wished in this place to offer a few remarks."[13] Later, in his final speech to the convention, he reaffirmed that "no man's ideas were more remote from the plan than his [own] were known to be."[14] He was heard in private settings to decry the document as a "shilly shally thing of mere milk and water, which could not last, and was only good as a step to something better."[15] Out of power in 1802, he reemphasized his dislike for the Constitution, calling it a "frail and worthless document."[16]

Nevertheless, Hamilton saw potential for a truly powerful national state in the new executive branch. He recognized that the "administration of government"—understood to be the conduct of foreign affairs, the design and execution of fiscal policy, "the application and disbursement of the public monies in conformity of the general approbation of the legislature," the management of the army and navy, and the direction of "operations of war"—was nicely collected in the executive branch.[17] With the right policies, and the administration of those policies with energy and purpose, the defects of the initial design could be overcome. As Hamilton implied, effective execution of a properly designed policy could serve to "extinguish State Governments gradually."[18]

It is hardly surprising then that Hamilton did not run for any elective office under the Constitution. Indeed, he resisted the efforts of his friends and political allies to support him for senator because he wanted to administer the government from the Department of Treasury.[19] In the Treasury, he could implement his plan for the financial stability and prosperity of the country, the essential purpose of statecraft that he believed, if managed properly, would attach the interest of individuals throughout the country to the national state and help to assure the growth of national loyalties, patriotism, and solidarity. "Imagining a nation" was never enough—the interests of the people needed to be bound together with the power of the state. Although George Washington, James Madison, and Thomas Jefferson believed that the Department of State would be the most important executive department—concerned as it was with both foreign and internal affairs—Hamilton knew better. Money was the life-blood of government, and as Hamilton succinctly noted, "most of the important measures of every Government are connected with the Treasury."[20] Washington asked Hamilton to take over the Treasury a few days before his inauguration as president, and as soon as Congress organized the department, Hamilton began implementing his vision.

The creation of the first two national parties began with a competing mobilization in Congress. Hamilton had the upper hand for two reasons. First, he drove the legislative agenda. As secretary of the treasury, he was tasked by Congress to present them with plans concerning the debt and public credit of the country, and he possessed a strategic vision for the future strength and development of the country, and the national state. Congress offered Hamilton the ball, and Hamilton ran with it.

Hamilton's political behavior reflected powerful assumptions about how the eighteenth-century British political system functioned. Governments, he believed, could not depend on the virtue of the people. People's interests needed to be connected to the positive goods that governments provided. "Men love power," he argued, and citizens loved the power that provided the essential blessings of government, power that protected their interests: security of property, protection of persons, the distribution of justice, and the maintenance of law and order.[21] With patronage power, with policies intended to separate creditors from local fiscal policies, and with his ability to persuade and manage votes in Congress, he ran the government like the lord treasurer of Great Britain. As such, Hamilton sought to create a governing coalition — "a party in government" — to assure the success of his plans.

Along with his plans, which have received the bulk of attention by historians, came his centralization of political power and national authority in the Treasury Department. He was building a governing party. By the end of 1792, Hamilton controlled the direct and indirect appointment of nearly one thousand positions, across every state and territory of the Union. These positions, which included the comptroller, auditor, numerous clerks, all the customs officials, surveyors and inspectors of the revenue, port inspectors, commissioners of loans, officers of the revenue cutters, and even the numerous employees of the post office, commanded a total compensation from the national state amounting to nearly $300,000 in 1792.[22] Within a year, Hamilton had gained control of the patronage of the excise department, which he carefully designed and with which he intended to extend his influence into the backcountry.[23] The leading proponents of Hamilton's funding system and supporters of the National Bank found themselves rewarded and connected to the sinews of the Hamiltonian state.[24] Compared to the other executive departments, Hamilton's patronage machine was overwhelming. Thomas Jefferson, secretary of the Department of State, possessed direct control over the appointment of only seven clerks, with annual salaries worth a paltry $4,100 in 1792. Outside of his immediate office, Jefferson also controlled the mint, which had four employees in 1792, with salaries worth $5,012.[25]

To fight for his agenda, Hamilton cultivated and mobilized a group of supporters in Congress. Notable among the initial directors of the bank were staunch political supporters of Hamilton including South Carolinian William

Loughton Smith, who championed Hamiltonianism in the House of Representatives; New Yorker Rufus King, who led Hamilton's program in the Senate; and the scions of New England Federalism, Congressman Fisher Ames
and Senator George Cabot.[26] Unlike the other executive department heads,
Hamilton was required to appear in Congress to receive instructions and respond to oversight. Hamilton used these occasions to great advantage, and
turned what was intended as a position of control into a position of influence.
He was often in Congress, presenting his own reports, meeting with members, and participating in the writing of legislation. During the debates over
funding and assumption, Hamilton was seen spending "most of his time in
running from place to place among the members."[27]

In addition, Hamilton often drafted important legislation respecting the
structure of the Treasury and the design of his financial plan, or participated
in the drafting of other bills by meeting and corresponding both formally and
informally with the congressional committees working on the bills.[28] During
the debates over the excise bill, for instance, Hamilton personally participated
in the committee to draft the final bill in the Senate. Using his influence,
Hamilton insisted on the creation of excise districts that did not correspond
to any existing state or local jurisdictions, a plan that the excitable William
Maclay considered part of Hamilton's drive for "the annihilation of State government."[29] In some extraordinary instances, Hamilton even wrote speeches
for his leading advocates to deliver in the legislature.[30] Hamilton freely min-
gled in all the policies of the executive branch. Legitimately concerned as he
was with problems of money, supply, and contracting in the War Department,
as well as international trade, loans, and credit in the State Department, he
nevertheless took advantage of numerous opportunities to insinuate his own
leadership in issues outside of his immediate purview—as when he marched
with the army to put down the Whiskey Rebellion or when he met with British
diplomats to contradict a hard line taken by Thomas Jefferson.[31] By 1792 Hamilton was behaving as a prime minister. He considered the emerging opposition
to the government as an assault upon "my administration." When defending
his system, he spoke of himself in the third person as "The Minister."[32]

For James Madison's part, although he was pleased with the ratification
of the Constitution and believed it needed to be maintained inviolate, he also
quickly came to see the fabric as flawed. He used politics to try to make it work
properly. Throughout the 1790s, he operated as if certain clarifying principles
and new political organizations were necessary to shore up the Constitution.

He thought it did not need a Declaration of Rights but then proceeded to draft numerous restrictive amendments and guided their passage through Congress. He hoped the design of the Constitution would frustrate the emergence of a national party but then proceeded to organize and lead a national party. He hoped the reinvigorated Union could frustrate the myopia of the states only to provide extensive theoretical justifications for state power by the end of the 1790s. But he was no hypocrite as many, beginning with Hamilton, have suggested. How can we understand Madison's political moves?

First, Madison believed that the whole system would fail without a neutral arbiter. While scholars treat Madison's Federalist 10 as a powerful analysis of the problem of factions and how to deal with them, the short essay was never intended to be a complete theory. "Extending the sphere" of the republic to assure that a majority interest could not be organized—and therefore not use the state to destroy the minority—was only one half of Madison's solution. As he wrote to Thomas Jefferson (after reviewing arguments that would later appear in *Federalist* 10), without a neutral arbiter, "a defensive concert" would prove too difficult to establish in an extensive republic. Only a general government with an ability to veto state legislation could hold an effective balance between the parties of particular states, and be at the same time "sufficiently restrained by its dependence on the community, from betraying its general interests." Without such a power, he noted, there would be inevitable encroachments, instability, and ultimately "injustice."[33]

Why would Madison present Federalist 10 without incorporating his belief in the need for a neutral arbiter? Because the *Federalist Papers* were not intended to be a systematic explication of Madison's political thought. Instead, they were polemical arguments in a partisan contest. If he pointed out what was wrong with the Constitution as proposed, he would play into his opponents' hands. Many scholars continue to read the Federalist essays as an objective analysis of the Constitution. But they are not. They are party papers.

Second, it is clear that Madison underestimated the immediate threat of *minority* tyranny. Obsessed as he was with the failures of the states to control simple majoritarianism, a concern that shaped his hopes for the "extended sphere" of the American federal republic, he assumed that the checks and mixing of the powers of the branches of government would assure that no one branch could usurp authority. He did admit the possibility of the general government's encroaching on the states, or one branch encroaching on the other, but he believed these concerns to be much less likely than states behaving badly. But he appears to have been dumbfounded that Hamilton could so quickly achieve success for his plans—plans that Madison believed were at first poor policy and later as unconstitutional and against the "real interest" of the country.

The policies were not entirely new. Assumption and funding had been debated in the 1780s, the possibility of a national bank had been around for a decade or more, and Madison must have had some familiarity with Hamilton's vision, given their close collaboration. What seemed to upset Madison most was not that Hamilton was pursuing these policies, but that people were actually listening to Hamilton, and that Hamilton was winning by using the very institutions that Madison believed would check and control usurpation of authority and power. Madison helped to design not only the Constitution but the executive departments and the judiciary. When he considered his "Vices of the Political system" in the 1780s, nowhere did he suggest that an individual could so corrupt the system so quickly. The dangers and vices were all in the behavior of the states. There were "majority interests" galore in the states, skewing the policy toward their own factions and violating the laws of nations, the interest of the Union, and the rights of individuals—but there were very few actual people in any of Madison's analyses, very few designing men at the root of these problematic factions. Who were the faces of these policies in the states? He allowed for the possibility that factions would be based on a charismatic leader, but throughout his debates and letters on the problems of the political system, he failed to name names. His analysis was academic, and although obviously based on experience as well as deep reading, it was abstract.[34]

But Hamilton's successes in Congress were tangible—and from Madison's point of view, simple to understand. Madison believed that Hamilton was using corrupt means to win votes on crucial pieces of legislation that would otherwise fail. Madison saw the moneyed interest and "stockjobbers" as "the pretorian band of the government—at once its tools and its tyrants; bribed by its largesse, and overawing it by clamors and combinations."[35] In his battles against the treasury department in the legislature, Madison began to believe that "he could at all times discover a sympathy between the speeches and the pockets of all those members of Congress who held certificates."[36] This corrupt group was not playing by the rules, so the checks and balances of his design were worthless. As he noted, complaining about Hamilton's flexible interpretation of the powers of Constitution, "the federal government has been hitherto limited to the specific powers, by the greatest champions for latitude in expanding those powers. If not only the means, but the objects are unlimited, the parchment had better be thrown into the fire at once."[37] The Constitution as designed was not working; it was not enough.

But what could Madison do? His choices were already path dependent. It would be too costly and risky to have another Constitutional Convention, and he could not amend the Constitution because he could not defeat Hamilton in the legislature. As Madison wanted a neutral arbiter at the top of his system, it seemed at first that George Washington might be able to play that role. But Madison failed to convince Washington of the deeply pernicious and danger-ous tendencies of Hamilton's plans. Madison and Jefferson moved to establish an opposition newspaper immediately after they failed to convince Washing-ton to veto the bank bill. Ultimately, Madison would need to marshal a stable winning majority of votes in Congress to stop Hamilton. He could not depend on ad hoc coalitions of different regional groups. The stakes had simply gotten too high. No more dinner table bargains could be made with Hamilton.

So Madison moved to mobilize a majority faction — a political party — to combat and check what he considered to be a minority party using *corruption* to win votes in Congress. As he would write in early 1792, "In every political society, parties are unavoidable." The large extent of the sphere of a republican government had failed to dissipate the danger of factions. To assure that one interest did not come to control the government, something had to be done. To "combat the evil," Madison argued, it was necessary for "one party [to be] a check on the other, so far as the existence of parties cannot be prevented, nor their views accommodated." He continued, "If this is not the language of reason, it is that of republicanism."[38] Abstract reason had failed; party politics was now essential. So he would build an organization to improve the original design of the Constitution, another check against imbalance. By the beginning of the third Congress, with the arrival of the first group of legislators created by a clear party effort to elect Madison's winning majority, the polarization of partisan behavior had begun — and American politics forever after has been defined by the waxing and waning of national parties.[39]

Other Paths to American Party Politics

There are countless studies of the original polarization in Congress, which focus on the creation of the first parties from the perspectives of Madison and Hamilton. But Madison did not consider his the *first* moment of parties in the United States. Writing on the eve of elections in the fall of 1792, he argued that the country was experiencing a *third* period of national party competition. As it was the job of every "contemplative statesman to trace the history of parties in a free country," and the "duty of the citizen at all times to understand the actual state of them," he paused to consider the past examples of American party politics. For Madison, the first national parties were between "those who espoused the cause of independence and those who adhered to the British claims." This first period of parties ended with the Treaty of Paris. It was not the end of parties, per se, for from "1783 to 1787 there were parties in abundance," but they were "local" rather than "general," and so not within "the present review." The second period of national party politics, he noted, was the fight over the ratification of the federal Constitution: "Every one remembers it, because every one was involved in it." He argued that this second period ended after "the regular and effectual establishment of the federal government in 1788." The third "division" grew out of disputes over "the administration" of the new government, "which being natural to most political societies, is likely to be of some duration in ours."[40]

Two aspects of Madison's analysis deserve consideration. First, he understood the conflict between patriots and loyalists from 1774–83 as a period of party politics. Second, he understood that parties existed in numerous states in the 1780s. Both of these realities would have a powerful relationship to the birth of party politics in the 1790s, and both drew on continuities from the colonial period that have rarely entered serious analysis of the "first" (or, as Madison would have it, "third") period of American party politics.

A continuing weakness of the history of U.S. politics is the lack of analytical connections between the colonial and early national periods. Of course, in the colonial period, there was no *national* politics — until the mobilizations against Parliament. Or was there? Much of the new imperial history has extended the courtesy of a *sense* of British nationhood to the provincial North American polities. In fact, some recent analyses have interpreted the coming of independence as a reaction against the mother country's haughty denial of the "Englishness" of the colonial elite.[41] But these somewhat loose analyses fail to describe a clear relationship of English party politics to the development of American politics.

One hundred years before Madison wrote his newspaper essay on American parties, numerous colonies were polarized around Court and Country factions that engaged closely with party politics in London, if not throughout North America. Both Whigs and Tories in Parliament and the court strove to use colonial allies and issues to weaken their opponents, to craft winning governing coalitions, and to shape policy—including much of the original institutions of the eighteenth-century British Empire. In 1715, the possibility that some colonial parties would become drawn into imperial party politics in a semi-permanent way remained a very real possibility.[42] But that did not happen.

There was a breakdown in the engagement with imperial parties after the rise of Robert Walpole in the 1720s and the fracturing of the Tory opposition. The trend was not irreversible. Party alliances could have emerged from significant political fights in the 1720s and 1730s. The contest over a new excise policy at the beginning of the decade, the passage of the Molasses Act, and efforts to stop the growth of an American lead industry were all issues that could have drawn some colonial interests into a broader trans-Atlantic party movement. But as it happened, no shared interests could be clearly articulated or discovered between Walpole's desire to crush colonial manufacturing on the one hand and the opposition's interest in mobilizing the lesser London merchants on the other. The great colonial interests involved in these English party disputes—the South Sea Company, the West Indian sugar lobby, and the East India Company—had only incidental connections to the party fights in North America. When Lewis Morris, "the American Craftsman," appeared in London to try to find political support for his ongoing fights in New York and New Jersey, he was a stranger in a strange land and found no takers. He was completely ignored by the original Craftsmen—Henry St. John, Viscount Bolingbroke, and William Pulteney—who were in the midst of building an alliance with London merchants and artisans whose interests were mercantilist and protectionist. There continued to be an imperial politics, of course, but it was not a party politics, and even *national* party politics within England began to break down by the 1750s and 1760s.

Nevertheless, the rhetoric of English party politics—developed from the Exclusion Crisis in 1678–81, through the Glorious Revolution, and culminating in the South Sea Bubble and subsequent domination of Walpole—proved essential to American party politics. The Court and Country coalitions that formed in many colonies drew freely on English authors, embellished their visions, and created an expectation of party conflict.[43] Although there was no reason to organize an "American" party before the 1760s, the quickness by which an intercolonial opposition party was fashioned is remarkable. Using shared rhetoric and basic organizational practices—including the widespread employment of crowd mobilization, popular petitioning, circular letters, and the expansion of the press—the opponents of the Stamp Act were clearly able to build on a mature foundation of party activity to mobilize a broad movement against the hated legislation. The Stamp Act opposition astonished imperial observers who were always more prone to emphasize the differences among the North American colonies and their political establishments than their similarities.[44] After the crisis, parties in the colonies would continue to mobilize around elections with an eye to both local and imperial issues, and continuing efforts to *nationalize* colonial resistance aided in the creation of the first period of general party conflict remembered by Madison.

While imperial *party* politics seems to have largely disappeared by the 1760s, there were other institutions of imperial rule through which political agents operated.[45] There were many people in the colonies who were supposed to represent the interest of the crown, and who were themselves products of an active politics in England. Royal governors, councilors, military officials, judges, customs officials, Indian agents, and others were an important component of the political world that shaped the development of colonial politics. These men would form the core of the "Tory" or "Loyalist" party after 1774. The revolutionary experience between 1774 and 1783—thought of at the time as a party dynamic between the "friends of order" and the "friends of liberty"—shaped many attitudes about party in the 1790s, when the same monikers would again dominate the way people talked about the ideological commitments of the Federalists and Republicans.[46]

But as Madison pointed out in the 1790s, while any semblance of a national party dynamic ended with American independence, between "1783 to 1787 there were parties in abundance" within the states. These parties, local as they might be, were themselves not entirely new and would have a formative influence on the operations of the national party period of the 1790s. Madison's desire to organize a majority faction in opposition to Hamilton would require close attention to existing party coalitions in the states—and the path dependence which shaped that movement is still only vaguely sketched out. So while the Republican and Federalist coalitions were new, the parties that would often serve as the foundations of their local power were not. Recent efforts have made great strides in exploring some of the nationalizing cultural tendencies of the early republic, and the place of the newspapers as organizers and popularizes of political polarization, but a synthetic narrative of the process by which the polarization in Congress was achieved on the ground, of the links by which these local parties were shaped into a national political conversation, remains to be written.[47]

Such a work would need to have a sophisticated sense of the various political systems and cultures of the different states at the time Madison began to attempt to create a stable majority against Hamilton, as well as the halting, nonlinear pace of his successes and failures. In Virginia, Pennsylvania, and New York, the coalitions that were for and against the ratification of the Constitution were reshuffled, but not entirely redefined, by the emerging polarization of the Federalists and Republicans. Specific regions still tended to be in opposition to other regions, and socioeconomic issues remained important measures of political behavior. But in some areas, rising populations, increasing urbanization, and internal migrations were creating wholly new polities, which were incorporated into existing state coalitions at the same moment that they found their voices on the national stage. By the end of the 1790s, as Kenneth Owen's essay in this volume partly illustrates, the "national" party coalitions of Federalists and Republicans were a heterogeneous mash-up of local political practices and personalities, some of which reflected "modern" political organization, others depending on long tendencies of local political behavior, and some defying easy categorization.[48]

And yet, a well-articulated party politics in a given state did not always immediately translate into an easy link with emerging national party politics. Rhode Island is an excellent case in point, and perhaps a unique case. As Edward M. Cook Jr. has shown, Rhode Island possessed a fully articulated competitive party politics as early as the 1730s, complete with presession caucusing of party members, high mobilization of rural voters, centralized regulation of freeman membership, and, "by the 1740s," printed ballots. In the 1760s, as much as 80 percent of the eligible voters participated regularly. Popular, if not democratic, this party politics was a "modern" system in many senses of the term. But even so, this local machine politics did not easily match up to the national polarization of the 1790s—Rhode Island remained insular, with the two parties sending Federalists to the Senate throughout the 1790s and supporting John Adams in 1800. Only after 1800, when the Country Party "warily proclaimed themselves Republicans," did alliances within the state begin to coordinate and mimic the competitive fashion of national politics.[49]

The continuities and discontinuities that shape the emergence of the first national parties in the 1790s, therefore, would be deeply shaped by the structures, cultures, and assumptions of politics already in place in the states—by the path dependence of earlier eras. We might thus conceptualize the rise of "American party politics" in the 1790s and beyond in a much more capacious way—as the reconstruction of an imperial system of politics and an integration of local politics into a national polarization, which served the cultural assumptions, material needs, and ideological imperatives of the new citizenry in a better way than the failed politics of the British Empire, in which no imperial parties existed to channel discontent into electoral contests rather than a contest of arms.

The Past and the Future:
The Original Dialectic of American Politics

Finally, when considering why American politics has been associated with *two* national parties, we need to distinguish the problem of why Americans have two national parties today—at a time when Democratic and Republican parties have rigged election rules, congressional rules, and campaign finance laws to block the emergence of a third party—from the original polarization of the 1790s. As previously noted, most political science treatments of the problem tend to be transhistorical and begin with the 1790s, never the 1780s or the revolution, and analyze the problem up to the present. There are certainly some structural reasons why two parties emerge more readily than three or four in the American system—particularly the "winner take all" elections—but some of these reasons make more sense after the popular election of senators in the twentieth century and the rise of the presidency to tremendous power and influence, and few seem to be definitive—given the lack of competitiveness of numerous elections in many regions of the country for much of its history. As I have suggested, Madison needed to win stable majorities in Congress not to govern but to stop Hamiltonian legislation, so he had no interest in the creation of numerous regional parties building informal coalitions.

But there are powerful cultural and historical influences that shaped the expectations of Americans and pushed them to believe that there always had been and always would be two great sides to any conflict of significance. While the United States is one of the very few modern political systems with only two dominant parties, Americans of the 1790s assumed *all* political systems would be contests between two sides. James Hillhouse thought the rise of two parties in the United States was inevitable, as quoted earlier, because "it has been the course in all nations." The men who built the first party politics in the United States, like many of their biographers, were ideological Whigs whose histories of England were filled with sharp dialectical fights between advocates for prerogative power and martyrs for liberty. Whether in the case of Prince John versus the barons, the Roundheads against the Cavaliers, or the Whigs against the Tories, the popular narrative of English history and law were centered on conflicts between two parties. Such a dynamic fit well with the Christian-based assumption of eschatological struggle — with a notion that history was leading to a great fight between the saved and the forces of Satan — and distinguished American political analysis from ancient authors, like Aristotle or Polybius, who stressed cyclical chance and change. American authors on politics did not limit their own perspective to English history but extended their interpretation into the ancient past as well. Such a worldview deeply informed American attitudes toward contemporary politics in the 1790s — particularly after the French Revolution reified the transhistorical significance of their own moment.

The polarization of American political rhetoric in the 1790s reflected this widely held assumption about the nature of political history. As Jefferson wrote later in life, at the beginning of his reconciliation with John Adams, "The same political parties which now agitate the U.S. have existed thro' all time." One party sought to exult "the power of the people," the other strived for the prerogatives of the "αριστοι," the "aristocrats."[50] Since Jefferson became the leader of the opposition against the Federalist government, and as he obviously saw himself as one of those serving the interests of the people, the Federalists could easily be fused into proponents of aristocracy and monarchy, enemies to the "principles of '76." Jefferson, like all good revolutionaries, had little time for splitting hairs. In the 1790s, Adams apparently was on the wrong side of the question, and there were only two sides. Even Hamilton, who seems like such a practical man, building his governing party with patronage and planning, and who originally understood Madison's opposition as personal pique, would come to see his fight in clear Manichean terms. As he wrote in 1801, "The contest between us is indeed a war of principles," not between "monarchy and republicanism" but "between tyranny and liberty." At least on this point, he and Madison could agree.[51] The United States possesses two great political parties in part because the original organization of party politics happened at a time when many Americans saw the world, and the history of their country, in a dialectical fashion.

When Martin Van Buren—a son of a tavern-keeper, a most practical American politician of the type that organized, managed, and ran the machinery of American politics—set about to write his history of American parties, be began by noting that the "true character and principles of the parties" could be discovered in the dichotomy between "Cavaliers or Roundheads," between "Jacobites or Puritans and Presbyterians," and between "Whigs or Tories." Names had changed, but the parties were the same. He may be right. History matters.[52]

Many Americans concerned with politics today still see the world in these terms, as a casual perusal of the world of blogs, the rhetoric of campaigns, and recent foreign policy announcements makes all too evident. Even when we can see that formal institutions assist in blocking the emergence of competing third parties, the cultural bias toward a politics of two sides remains an important part of American life. It is a powerful legacy of having created advanced representative institutions in an Age of Revolutions, a legacy of path dependence that colors the character of life in the United States and shapes the way too many American historians still write the history of their country.

Notes

1. The problem of close elections continued, as can be seen from controversies over the elections of 1824, 1876, and 2000.

2. For my understanding of 1804 as the political settlement of the American Revolution, see Douglas Bradburn, *The Citizenship Revolution: Politics and the Creation of the American Union, 1774–1804* (Charlottesville: University of Virginia Press, 2009).

3. William Duane, *Report of a Debate, in the Senate of the United States, on a Resolution for Recommending to the Legislatures of the Several States, an Amendment to the Third Paragraph of the First Section of the Second Article of the Constitution of the United States, Relative to the Mode of Electing a President and Vice President of the Said States* (Philadelphia, 1804), 18–19.

4. Ibid., 90.

5. Douglass North, *Institutions, Institutional Change and Economic Performance* (Cambridge: Cambridge University Press, 1990), vii, 3–5.

6. Margaret Levi, "A Model, a Method, and a Map: Rational Choice in Comparative and Historical Analysis," in *Comparative Politics: Rationality, Culture, Structure,*

ed. Mark I. Lichbach and Alan S. Zuckerman (Cambridge: Cambridge University Press, 1997), 28.

7. Paul Pierson, "Increasing Returns, Path Dependence and the Study of Politics," *American Political Science Review* 94 (June 2000): 251–66, 251 (quotation); Paul Pierson, *Politics in Time: History, Institutions, and Social Analysis* (Princeton, N.J.: Princeton University Press, 2004).

8. Shu-Yun Ma, "Political Science at the Edge of Chaos? The Paradigmatic Implications of Historical Institutionalism," *International Political Science Review* 28 (January 2007): 57–78, 64 (quotation).

9. Pierson, "Increasing Returns," 263.

10. Richard Brookheiser, *Alexander Hamilton, American* (New York: Free Press, 1999); Ronald Chernow, *Alexander Hamilton* (New York: Penguin Press, 2004); Williard Randall Stern, *Alexander Hamilton: A Life* (New York: HarperCollins, 2003); John Marshall, *The Life of George Washington: Commander in Chief of the American Forces, during the War Which Established the Independence of His Country, and First President of the United States*, 5 vols. (Philadelphia, 1804–7); Henry Cabot Lodge, *Alexander Hamilton* (Boston, 1889); Forrest MacDonald, *Alexander Hamilton: A Biography* (New York: Norton, 1982), 363.

11. Stanley Elkins and Eric McKitrick, *The Age of Federalism* (New York: Oxford University Press, 1993).

12. No more than 650. Exactitude in the number of "Hamiltonian" references that apply to Alexander Hamilton is difficult; apparently the mathematician Richard Hamilton gets some due.

13. "Constitutional Convention. Remarks on the Election of the President," 6 September 1787, *Papers of Alexander Hamilton*, ed. Harold C. Syrett et al., 26 vols. (New York: Columbia University Press, 1961–79), 4:243, hereafter *PAH*.

14. Max Farrand, ed., *The Records of the Federal Convention of 1787*, 4 vols. (New Haven, Conn.: Yale University Press, 1966) 2:645–46.

15. Thomas Jefferson in Conversation with Washington, 1 October 1792, *Papers of Thomas Jefferson*, ed. Julian P. Boyd et al., 40 vols. to date (Princeton, N.J.: Princeton University Press, 1950-), 24:435.

16. Alexander Hamilton to Gouverneur Morris, 27 February 1802, quoted in Gerald Stourzh, *Alexander Hamilton and the Idea of Republican Government* (Stanford, Cal.: Stanford University Press, 1970), 39.

17. James Madison, "The Federalist 72," in *The Federalist Papers*, ed. Lawrence Goldman (Oxford: Oxford University Press, 2008).

18. Farrand, ed., *Records of the Federal Convention*, 4:83.

19. James Roger Sharp, *American Politics in the Early Republic: The New Nation in Crisis* (New Haven, Conn.: Yale University Press, 1993), 32–33.

20. Alexander Hamilton to Edward Carrington, 26 May 1792, *PAH*, 11:442.

21. Farrand, ed., *Records of the Federal Convention*, 1:285.

22. Civil List, year ending 1 October 1792, *American State Papers: Documents*

Legislative and Executive, of the Congress of the United States, 38 vols. (Washington, D.C., 1832–36), 1:57–68.

23. See Alexander Hamilton to Charles Cotesworth Pinckney, 3 August 1791, *PAH*, 10:280.

24. See, for example, George C. Rogers Jr., *Evolution of a Federalist: William Loughton Smith of Charleston, 1758–1812* (Columbia: University of South Carolina Press, 1962), 191–92, 227–30.

25. *American State Papers*, 1:57.

26. Rogers, *Evolution of a Federalist*, 230; David Hackett Fischer, *The Revolution of American Conservatism: The Federalist Party in the Era of Jeffersonian Democracy* (New York: Harper and Row, 1965), 2–6.

27. William Maclay, *The Journal of William Maclay, United States Senator from Pennsylvania, 1789–1791* (New York: A. and C. Boni, 1927), 185.

28. See, for instance, his "Draft of an Act to Incorporate the Bank of the United States," *PAH*, 7:399.

29. Maclay, *Journal*, 378.

30. See, for instance, the speech of William Loughton Smith in March 1794, quoted in Dumas Malone, *Jefferson and the Ordeal of Liberty* (Boston: Little, Brown, 1962), 182–83.

31. See George Hammond to William Lord Grenville, 8 June 1792, *PAH*, 11:454–55. On Hamilton's behavior, see John C. Miller, *Alexander Hamilton: Portrait in Paradox* (New York: Harper and Brothers, 1959), 366–68, and "Conversation with George Hammond, December 15–16, 1791," *PAH*, 10:374. See also Hamilton's Conversation with George Beckwith, 19–20 January 1791, *PAH*, 7:440–42. For a different view, see MacDonald, *Hamilton*.

32. "Defense of the Funding System, July 1795," *PAH*, 19:4. See also MacDonald, *Hamilton*, 392n18, 285–307.

33. James Madison to Thomas Jefferson, 24 October 1787, *The Papers of James Madison, Congressional Series*, ed. William T. Hutchinson et al., 17 vols. (Chicago: University of Chicago Press, 1962–77, and Charlottesville: University Press of Virginia, 1977–91), 10:205–28, hereafter *PJM*.

34. James Madison, "Vices of the Political System of the U. States," *PJM*, 9:345–58.

35. James Madison to Thomas Jefferson, 8 August 1791, *PJM*, 14:69–70.

36. Conversation with Benjamin Rush, *PJM*, 14:272n1.

37. James Madison to Henry Lee, 1 January 1792, *PJM*, 14:179–81.

38. "For the *National Gazette*," 23 January 1792, *PJM*, *14:197–98*.

39. For an excellent quantitative analysis of the polarization and partisanship of voting behavior in the first, second, and third Congresses, see John F. Hoadley, "The Emergence of Political Parties in Congress, 1789–1803," *American Political Science Review* 74 (September 1980): 772–91.

40. "For the *National Gazette*," 22 September 1792, *PJM*, 14:370–72.

41. Linda Colley, *Britons: Forging the Nation, 1707–1837* (New Haven, Conn.: Yale

University Press, 1992); John Brewer, "The Eighteenth Century British State: Contexts and Issues," in *An Imperial State at War: Britain from 1689–1815,* ed. Lawrence Stone (London: Taylor and Francis, 1994), 52–71; Kathleen Wilson, *The Sense of the People: Politics, Culture, and Imperialism in England 1715–1785* (Cambridge: Cambridge University Press, 1995); Jack P. Greene, "Search for Identity: An Interpretation of the Meaning of Selected Patterns of Social Response in Eighteenth Century America," in *Imperatives, Behaviors and Identities: Essays in Early American Cultural History* (Charlottesville: University Press of Virginia, 1992), 43–173.

42. For a classic statement on the party period after the Glorious Revolution, see John P. Kenyon, *Revolution Principles: The Politics of Party, 1689–1720* (Cambridge: Cambridge University Press, 1977); Alison G. Olsen, *Anglo-American Politics, 1660–1775: The Relationship between Parties in England and Colonial America* (Oxford: Clarendon Press, 1973); and Douglas Bradburn, "The Visible Fist: The Chesapeake Tobacco Trade in War and the Purpose of Empire, 1690–1715," *William and Mary Quarterly,* 3rd series, 68 (July 2011): 361–86. On colonial factions and parties in New York, see Charles W. Spencer, *Phases of Royal Government in Colonial New York, 1691–1719* (Columbus, Ohio: Fred J. Heer, 1905).

43. Still essential is Bernard Bailyn's *The Origins of American Politics* (New York: Vintage Books, 1967).

44. P. D. G. Thomas, *British Politics and the Stamp Act Crisis: The First Phase of the American Revolution, 1763–1767* (Oxford: Oxford University Press, 1975).

45. Alison G. Olsen, *Making the Empire Work: London and American Interest Groups in the Seventeenth and Eighteenth Centuries* (Cambridge, Mass.: Harvard University Press, 1992).

46. In South Carolina, Pennsylvania, and New York, former loyalists and "Tories" during the 1770s would play prominent roles in the Federalist coalitions in those states, in politics, law, and business.

47. The best histories of the party coalitions in the states in the 1790s, now a generation or more old, include Ronald P. Formisano, *The Transformation of Political Culture: Massachusetts Parties, 1790s–1840s* (New York: Oxford University Press, 1983); Paul Goodman, *The Democratic-Republicans of Massachusetts* (Cambridge, Mass.: Harvard University Press, 1964); Carl E. Prince, *New Jersey's Jeffersonian Republicans: The Genesis of an Early Party Machine, 1789–1817* (Chapel Hill: University of North Carolina Press, 1967); Norman K. Risjord, *Chesapeake Politics, 1781–1800* (New York: Columbia University Press, 1978); and Alfred F. Young, *The Democratic Republicans of New York: The Origins, 1763–1797* (Chapel Hill: University of North Carolina Press, 1967). All these histories recognize that the histories of these parties begin before the revolution. American political scientists seem to have little awareness of this.

48. For my analysis of the diversity of political "types" that characterized the different regions and states in the late 1790s, see Douglas Bradburn, "A Clamor in the Public Mind: Opposition to the Alien and Sedition Acts," *William and Mary*

Quarterly, 3rd series, 65 (July 2008): 565–94, and Bradburn, *Citizenship Revolution,* 139–205.

49. Edward M. Cook Jr., "Enjoying and Defending Charter Privileges: Corporate Status and Political Culture in Eighteenth Century New England," in *Cultures and Identities in Colonial British America,* ed. Robert Olwell and Alan Tully (Baltimore: Johns Hopkins University Press, 2005), 244–45.

50. Thomas Jefferson to John Adams, 27 June 1813, *The Adams-Jefferson Letters: The Complete Correspondence between Thomas Jefferson and Abigail and John Adams,* ed. Lester J. Cappon, 2 vols. (Chapel Hill: University of North Carolina Press, 1959), 1:335.

51. Alexander Hamilton, "An Address to the Electors of the State of New York," 21 March 1801, *PAH,* 25:370.

52. Martin Van Buren, *Inquiry into the Origin and Course of Political Parties in the United States* (New York, 1867), 8. On Martin Van Buren as the quintessential American organizing politician and campaign manager, see Joel H. Silbey, *Martin Van Buren and the Emergence of American Popular Politics* (New York: Rowman and Littlefield, 2002), xii.

★ REEVE HUSTON ★

Rethinking the Origins of Partisan Democracy in the United States, 1795–1840

Since the publication of Ronald P. Formisano's *The Transformation of Political Culture* in 1983, two interpretations have dominated writing about the origins of partisan democracy. One school, dating back to Arthur M. Schlesinger Jr.'s *Age of Jackson*, holds that partisan democracy first began during the late 1820s and 1830s.[1] Formisano, on the other hand, argues that partisan politics began during the 1790s. Before the 1830s and 1840s, he argues, partisanship was a half-hearted affair: partisan organizations were unstable "proto-parties"; voter loyalty was ephemeral; voters and political leaders were ambivalent partisans, practicing party warfare while denouncing parties. In this earlier period, the United States had parties but only in 1840 did it have a "party system."[2] According to both schools of thought, full-fledged partisan democracy (defined as a political system organized around partisanship, dominated by "modern" political parties, with a wide suffrage and high levels of popular mobilization) did not appear until the years between 1828 and 1840.

This belief has been challenged from at least two directions in recent years. Since the mid-1990s, historians of American politics have been steadily uncovering evidence of widespread partisan activity and popular electoral mobilization in the 1790s, 1800s, and early 1810s. There is now a rich and growing body of scholarship on party and popular politics during the 1790s and the Republican ascendancy. The new scholarship does not yet match in volume the work on Jacksonian politics, but it is sufficiently robust to offer a fundamental challenge to both earlier schools of thought. While several contributors to the new scholarship suggest that their work challenges dominant understandings of Jacksonian politics, none, to my knowledge, has attempted to think broadly about *how* it does so.[3]

More recently, Sean Wilentz, John L. Brooke, and Donald J. Ratcliffe have, in markedly different ways, presented democratization and party development as a cumulative process that spanned the "Jeffersonian" and "Jacksonian" eras (or, in another widely used formulation, the first and second party system). In Wilentz's synthesis, Jacksonian democracy built on the accomplishments of the Jeffersonians. Although he depicts Jacksonian democracy (and more emphatically Lincoln's Republican Party) as a fuller expression of democracy, Wilentz presents each era as a germinal moment in a longer process. Both Brooke and Ratcliffe argue that the basic methods and institutions of partisan mobilization changed very little between the first decade of the nineteenth century and 1840; both see partisan appeal, partisan loyalty, and popular mobilization widespread and effective in the earlier period. Brooke's and Ratcliffe's books focus on a single county or state, while Wilentz's work examines the making and breaking of party coalitions and political movements and on those coalitions' and movements' ideas and policies, rather than on political practice.[4]

This chapter takes these two bodies of work as a starting point for rethinking the origins of partisan democracy in the United States. Focusing exclusively on political practices and on people's ideas about how politics ought to be practiced, it offers a preliminary synthesis of this scholarship, the "New Political History," and some of my own research on the Era of Good Feelings. Along the way, it offers some suggestions for revising the conceptual apparatus with which we think about democratization. The argument that partisan democracy began between 1828 and 1840 is simply no longer tenable, and Formisano's model of an unstable, weak partisan politics before 1840, while still useful in some respects, needs revision. On the other hand, it does not make sense simply to move our periodization back by thirty years and declare that partisan democracy began in the 1790s or the first decade of the nineteenth century. There were significant differences between the democratic mobilizations of the two periods, and these need to be reexplored in the light of new scholarship.

The heyday of the New Political History, between the 1960s and 1980s, brought with it a broad consensus about how political practices and institutions changed during the Jacksonian era. Between the late 1810s and the late 1830s, something close to universal white male suffrage was achieved in all but a handful of states. Partisan organizations, capable of mobilizing these new voters, were created, albeit at different times in different states. These parties became highly organized and stable. Party activists created a hierarchy of committees and conventions and a network of communication that reached from state party leaders to local activists and the rank and file in nearly every school district in the republic. Parties were held together by partisan discipline. Leaders permitted freewheeling debate within the party over candidates and policies, but required every member to wholeheartedly endorse candidates and policies once the proper caucus or convention had adopted them. Each party was thus held together by a single set of candidates, a specific set of policies, and (after 1837) a clear ideology.[5]

Jacksonian parties moved heaven and earth to educate and mobilize the rank and file. By 1840, most county seats had both Whig and Democratic newspapers. These organs trumpeted each party's messages and policies (not to mention vilifying its opponents) year round. State parties organized electoral committees in each county, town, and school district. These committees filled the month before each election, as well as civic holidays, with meetings, parades, picnics, dinners, and other partisan events. These rituals drew voters (and often their wives and children) into the cause. Along with newspapers and other printed materials, the speeches, songs, visual images, and slogans taught participants to identify themselves as Democrats and Whigs and to think in partisan ways. At their best, electoral committees canvassed each ward or school district; classified each voter as Democrat, Whig, or doubtful; sought to persuade the doubtful; and stampeded the faithful to the polls.

By the 1840s, most historians of the period agree, these innovations had transformed American political culture and practice from top to bottom. As William Gienapp insisted, "Politics seem[ed] to enter into everything." Unprecedented numbers of citizens became active in partisan committees and joined party rituals. Voter turnout reached levels never seen before or since. Voters learned to identify themselves as Democrats or Whigs and to think about public issues in Whig and Democratic ways: party activists succeeded in creating "a party in the electorate." Joel Silbey writes that by the mid-1840s, "Parties had become communities — the sense of loyalty to them, as to a family, a tribe, a religion, or a nation, overwhelmed all else." With the exception of the realignment of the 1850s, most sons inherited their partisan loyalties from their fathers and voted for the same party in every election. With these innovations, the Jacksonian parties ushered in a flood of democratic participation that lasted into the 1890s, one that some historians see as a golden age of American democracy.[6]

The key question is: was this party democracy new? Recent work on the Jeffersonian era poses important challenges to arguments that it was unprecedented or had hitherto appeared in an enfeebled form. One such challenge lies in new findings about how political leadership changed before the War of 1812. As Alan Taylor, Joanne Freeman, and others have shown, gentlemen dominated national politics and maintained a decisive influence over public life in the states at least until 1800 and often later. The class was open to newcomers, but entry was limited to those who had money, connections with powerful families, and the ability to demonstrate their gentility through their dress, speech, consumption patterns, and bearing. Gentry politics was above all a contest for honor and preeminence: among other things, it was a confirmation of a gentleman's *social* status. Gentlemen achieved and maintained political power through patron–client relationships. They sought the favor of their social superiors by providing them with political services; they also solicited the services of their inferiors, who conducted campaigns for them. These "friends" of a great man, in turn, solicited the help of their subordinates, including ordinary voters, whose votes they courted through a combination of treating, wheedling, and subtly applied pressure. This mode of doing politics turned social dependency into political capital. It also hinged on honor. Political rivalries were contests for public honor, and political combat frequently involved attacking an opponent's reputation and defending one's own.[7]

Two historians have found that a new class of political leaders emerged during the late 1790s and early decades of the nineteenth century to challenge the gentry's political primacy and their mode of conducting politics. Alan Taylor has shown how, on the Maine and New York frontiers, prosperous, self-made men with no pretensions to gentility challenged genteel Federalists for office. These men gravitated toward the Republicans, and they adopted a new political style. Where Federalist gentlemen presented themselves as benevolent "fathers" of their constituents, Republican upstarts assumed the mantle of the people's "friends." They embraced popular egalitarianism, attacking their opponents' claims to social superiority.[8]

Jeffrey L. Pasley tracks the rise of a related but different cadre of leaders: plebeian party activists. These men, who also favored the Republicans, appointed themselves as organizers and publicists in the cause. Mostly middling-born printers, they identified proudly as mechanics. Operating outside of gentlemen's networks of clientage, they championed a radical break from genteel rules of politics. They embraced partisanship as salutary to the political order. They attacked political deference as a form of slavery, and they appealed to a broad public in stridently egalitarian terms. They embraced what Max Weber called a "charismatic" approach to politics: they saw the Republican Party as a noble cause and devoted their lives to it. But they also treated politics as a way to make a living. They published partisan newspapers as a way both to serve the Republican cause and to earn money. Unfortunately, party papers were rarely profitable enterprises, and printers (as well as other self-appointed activists) pressed Republican governors and cabinet members for patronage jobs, which they saw as their rightful reward for faithful labor in the cause. In this they failed. The Republican gentlemen who controlled the presidency and governorships reserved appointments for men from good families; upwardly mobile activists failed to establish standards of reward for political service or to create a career track in politics.[9]

Pasley's work upends a consensus shared by historians since Richard Hofstadter's *The Idea of a Party System:* that all citizens of the early republic believed parties to be dangerous and destructive, even when they engaged in party conflict.[10] While most genteel political leaders indeed disdained partisanship and popular mobilization, activists of humbler origins embraced them. Far from being universally accepted, anti-partisanship was a matter of fierce conflict conducted largely along class lines.

Scholars of politics before the War of 1812 also challenge the belief that widespread popular mobilization of ordinary voters was unknown before 1828. David Waldstreicher, Simon Newman, Andrew W. Robertson, and others have analyzed the rich calendar of political rituals during the early republic, one that drew thousands of people into active partisan combat. Adapting prerevolutionary and revolutionary traditions of civic festivals, deferential election rituals, and other practices to partisan ends, both Republican and Federalist activists organized parades, public dinners, and similar celebrations. They also mobilized preexisting institutions like militia musters to the cause. In addition, as Albrecht Koschnik has shown, both Federalists and Republicans formed an array of clubs. These organizations and rituals pulled ordinary (as well as not-so-ordinary) people into the party cause, encouraging them to embody their partisan commitments in public by marching with their fellow Republicans or Federalists, wearing their political commitments on their sleeves (usually in the form of black Federalist cockades or Republican tricolor ones), singing partisan songs, and skewering party enemies in toasts, celebrations, and mock funerals. Such events also taught participants to think in partisan ways. Federalist rituals and songs celebrated national leaders and emphasized participants' loyalty and deference toward the constituted authorities, teaching participants to submit to national authority. Republican rituals, on the other hand, instructed the rank and file in a more universalist Enlightenment nationalism, one centered on universal liberty and committed to the French Revolution. These activities and associations trained their participants in partisan identities and ways of living, teaching them to adopt, for example, a distinctly Federalist or Republican masculinity.[11]

Popular mobilization also included less celebratory elements. As Donald Ratcliffe, Andrew Robertson, and John Brooke have shown, partisan electoral mobilization was rampant in places as widely dispersed as Virginia, Pennsylvania, New York, and Ohio as early as 1799–1801. Robertson's essay in this volume shows that mobilization peaked in most states between 1808 and 1815, as Thomas Jefferson's embargo and war with England revived the Federalist Party and sent Republicans scampering to maintain their political dominance. The tools of mobilization were those that have long been assumed to have been pioneered in the 1820s: nominating conventions with delegates elected by earlier, local conventions; electoral committees; partisan clubs; mass meetings; partisan newspapers, broadsides, and handbills; official party tickets; and pre-prepared party ballots. In Columbia County, New York, more than 10 percent of voters joined party electoral committees in the years after 1801. In all four states, candidates were widely identified by party. In Ohio (and possibly elsewhere), voters tended to vote straight partisan tickets, with their loyalties remaining constant election after election. Donald Ratcliffe argues that by 1804 in Ohio, "Politics in the new state had come . . . to be dominated by a deep-rooted sense of political polarization, which divided politicians and voters into two camps." Partisan mobilization and identification did not take place everywhere. Political institutions and practices varied a great deal from location to location.[12]

The new partisan politics was carried out in a different register than gentry politics. As Robertson argues, where deferential politics depended on "personal relationships set within a localized, physical community," partisanship rested on "abstract relationships—ideology, interest, and common affiliation—among individuals" who were tied together into a virtual community through print. Partisanship itself was just such an abstract relationship, tying individuals to strangers on the basis of a shared, voluntary identity. While gentry politics brought people together in the name of a single, public good, partisan appeals tended to be pluralistic, at least in the cities, where Republicans reached out to specific religious and ethnic communities (not to mention mechanics and farmers) on the basis of their particular class, religion, or ethnicity.[13] Politics of this sort did not always destroy the gentry's political power, but it weakened its old basis by undercutting personal relationships as a nexus of political control and by fragmenting community allegiances.

Scholars disagree about the level of party organization before 1815. Pasley insists that "the early political parties were organizationally almost nonexistent," consisting of scattered activists and newspapers without any "central direction or funding." Ratcliffe, on the other hand, insists that parties became a long-term, institutionalized presence in Ohio after 1802, with a consistent presence of partisan conventions, committees, newspapers, and activist cadre in many (though not all) counties. Brooke's recent work suggests a similar pattern of intensive, permanent organizational presence in New York, varying significantly by county.[14]

These studies confirm Ron Formisano's depiction of the early republic as marked by a hybrid political culture. They extend his insight considerably, showing how that culture was stratified by class and varied by region and locality. At the national level, and often among state and local leaders, politics was a gentlemen's game, conducted by alliances and rivalries among great men and by mobilizing clientage networks on their behalf. Gentlemen disdained to campaign actively among the electorate; their subordinates did so by marshalling dependencies and through rituals of treating and deference. Alongside gentry politics there emerged a newer politics of popular appeal and mobilization. As Kenneth Owen's essay in this volume demonstrates, this mobilization took place in both parties—though each conceived of the public and its place in politics in a distinct way. Republican activists celebrated ordinary citizens' capacities for self-government, skewered genteel pretensions to power, and celebrated partisanship as devotion to the people's cause. Federalists, on the other hand, played a delicate game of rallying ordinary citizens to play the role of loyal, deferential citizens. Activists in both parties mobilized and educated people, creating a genuinely popular politics and, in some places, a party in the electorate. Appeals to partisan principles and loyalties sometimes replaced and sometimes complemented the mobilization of dependencies and personalist politics. Clientage seems to have gone into steep decline in central New York after 1800, but the two styles of political appeal coexisted and even merged in Pennsylvania, Massachusetts, and North Carolina.[15]

Whatever the precise modes of mobilizing voters, they were extremely effective. Figures on the numbers of participants in partisan rituals are notoriously unreliable, but newspapers and diarists in large cities generally estimated that they included between one and eight hundred participants; partisan commemoration of very important events like the death of George Washington gathered people in the thousands. Electoral committees provide a more reliable index of participation. John Brooke has found that a hefty 3 to 13 percent of the electorate participated in electoral committees in the mid–Hudson Valley Region between 1791 and 1820, though the percentage varied dramatically between counties. The most reliable indicator of popular participation in electoral politics (though not of popular political belief) is voting returns. Andrew Robertson's chapter in this book demonstrates conclusively that, in all but a handful of states, peak voter turnout during the Jefferson and Madison administrations was greater than in 1828. In many states, these earlier peak turnouts were greater than peak national turnout rates during the 1840s.[16]

The new work on politics in the early republic requires a fundamental rethinking of the origins and timing of partisan democracy in the United States. It is no longer tenable to suggest that mass political mobilization, democratic rhetoric, unapologetic partisanship, or stable partisan divisions in the electorate first emerged in the 1820s or 1830s. Nor will it suffice to acknowledge precedents in the earlier period but minimize their importance because they failed to measure up to ideal types or later models of democracy. One virtue of the new scholarship on politics in the early republic is that it takes political practices, ideas, and institutions on their own terms; we need to emulate it in this respect. On the other hand, it will not do simply to move our periodization back by thirty years. Formisano's basic approach, purged of anachronistic measures of political development, is worth imitating. Partisan democracy emerged over a long period between 1790 and 1840; our job is to figure out what changed when, and how political practices, ideas, and institutions changed within that period.

This reperiodization ought to be part of a broader rethinking of democracy as an always unfinished, ever-contested project. The democracy that emerged in the fifty years after the adoption of the federal Constitution excluded a lot of people, many of whom launched movements to challenge their exclusion.

While the vast majority of white men got the vote, it took another 80 years before white women could participate in elections and another 120 before the suffrage rights of African Americans, American Indians, and other nonwhites were established on a permanent basis. Nor are conflicts over access to the ballot over, as today's clashes over felon disfranchisement, same-day registration, and voter identification laws make clear. The basic rules of politics established before 1840 (party discipline, major party duopoly of nominations, constitutionalism, limiting political action to electoral and legislative means, etc.) were repeatedly challenged by democratic dissidents, from the Workingmen's Party to the Progressives and the New Left. In bringing Jefferson's generation into the story of democratization, we need also to acknowledge that this was simply an early stage of a much, much longer story, not a golden age.[17]

If we take this approach to the history of democratization, we must abandon all hope of finding a clean, clear beginning or end to the process. We may profitably apply to the process of democratization a concept coined by Leon Trotsky and appropriated by social and economic historians to describe industrialization: combined and uneven development. As scholars have begun to recognize over the last decade, American politics has always involved a *combination* of disparate, even contradictory practices. In different places and times, politically active people have alternately clashed over these practices, practiced them peacefully alongside other methods, and combined different routines to create hybrid politics. From the 1790s through at least the early 1820s, a genteel politics based on personal alliances and rivalries, patron-client relationships, and voter deference coexisted with a newer politics of newspaper wars and popular mobilization. Sometimes activists combined these styles into a single campaign; at others they clashed over them. During the same period but especially after 1830, various kinds of political practices centered on voluntary associations established several quite different ways of conducting public life. Often these associations served partisan purposes; frequently they provided a nonparty means of affecting policy and public life; sometimes they explicitly challenged partisan practices and sought to supplant them.

The Arab Spring and various "occupy" and *"indignante"* movements in Europe, Latin America, and North America have demonstrated anew that in moments of political crisis and opportunity, people experiment with new ways of conducting politics, hoping to overcome the limitations and corruptions of existing political repertoires. Democracy has never resided in a single way of doing politics. Indeed, it has usually developed through clashes *among* competing ways of conducting politics. To pick just two American examples, the collision between the Democratic-Republican Societies and the Federalists in 1793–95 and between the Mississippi Freedom Democratic Party and the leadership of the national Democratic Party in 1964 both played midwife to a dramatic expansion in popular participation in politics. When we think about American democratic development, we need to look for it in multiple, competing, or complementary sets of practices—in voluntary associations as well as partisan electoral struggle, in community organizing and mass protest as well as two-party competition.[18]

Democratization has also been *uneven*. Partisan organization and participation in Columbia County, New York, reached levels in 1801–2 not seen in most areas until 1840—and not seen in South Carolina until Reconstruction. The ability of gentlemen to exert significant control over the votes of their social inferiors seems to have fallen into steep decline in Oneida County, New York, in 1800, but it continued until the 1820s just a few counties away, in parts of Columbia, Albany, and Rensselaer counties, as well as in parts of Massachusetts and North Carolina. The politics of personal influence continued in Mississippi and South Carolina into the 1850s and probably beyond. Expansion of the suffrage to include propertyless white men took place in fits and starts between 1786, when Vermont enfranchised almost all white men, and Radical Reconstruction, when South Carolina dropped the property requirements for voting for the upper chamber of the state legislature (not to mention enfranchising African American men). Partisan nominating conventions were common in New York from the 1790s on, if not earlier; Illinois did not adopt them until the 1830s. Southern states had a far lower density of partisan newspapers than their northern counterparts during the early nineteenth century. The disparity in the number and power of voluntary associations and reform movements was, if anything, greater—a fact that led George Fitzhugh to depict reform movements as a symptom of the social disorder created by capitalist wage labor in the North.[19]

Tracing the trajectory of democratization, I want to suggest, requires that we recognize the geographic and temporal unevenness of the process, that we pay attention to multiple forms of democratic practice, and that we search for multiple lines of political development. The temptation in taking this approach is to avoid all generalizations about what was happening at any one moment. This would be a mistake, because repertoires of political mobilization were put to use and affected outcomes only in particular moments of political conflict (including, but not limited to, elections). If we want to understand why William Henry Harrison won the presidency in 1840, we need to know what the broad pattern of political institutions, ideas, and practices were during that election. Still, we should look not for *one* pattern but for several: Whig practices in New York were not the same as those of the Mississippi Whigs, or of the New York Liberty Party, or the New York Garrisonians. Furthermore, things *did* change over time on a national level, even if they did not do so in a uniform or synchronized way. We still need to assess how, on a national level, the congeries of political practices changed between one era and the next.

For the remainder of this essay, I make some generalizations about the continuities and differences between Jeffersonian and Jacksonian democracy. Once we acknowledge that democratic development was robust before 1828, and that many of the trademark elements of Jacksonian politics were inheritances from an earlier era, the question becomes, how were the two eras different?

The most well-known differences between Jeffersonian and Jacksonian democracy were constitutional, though reform of organic law actually bridged the two periods. Constitutional conventions were called in most states between the 1790s and 1850s, though most assembled between the late 1810s and 1830s. With a few exceptions, the constitutions adopted by these conventions ended property requirements for the suffrage, significantly enlarging the electorate. We do not know the extent of the increase in most states, but New York's 1821 constitution tripled the number of electors for the state senate and increased those who could vote for the state assembly by 50 percent. In North Carolina, those qualified to vote for state senators increased by half. In addition, most conventions made many previously appointed offices subject to popular election. They also provided that representation in the state legislatures be allocated according to population, ending the historic underrepresentation of western and nonslaveholding regions. Voting rights became more racialized and gendered, as most states for the first time adopted requirements that voters be white or that subjected black men to special restrictions. Most states excluded aliens and paupers as well. New Jersey, the sole state to give propertied women the vote, disfranchised them in 1807. Power at the ballot box was extended to propertyless and middling white men on equal terms with the wealthy, and that power could now be exercised over a far greater number of officials. These changes took place in both the Jeffersonian and Jacksonian eras, but their cumulative effect was far greater in the later period.[20]

These constitutional changes were part of a broader shift in the boundaries of the political community. At no point in American history was participation in political life limited to legally qualified voters. Before 1829, the disfranchised wives of prominent politicians played a central part in Washington's political world, acting as brokers and mediators between powerful men. Andrew Jackson and his allies dealt a death blow to this "parlor politics" during the Eaton affair in 1829. After being increasingly marginalized in festive partisan culture during the Republican ascendancy, women were largely excluded from street politics during the 1820s and 1830s (though Whigs brought them back in during the 1840s). White crowds began to drive African Americans violently from election-day rituals and other civic celebrations, and to segregate public spaces in the North during the 1810s. But by the late 1820s, African American men and women of both races had begun to create a vibrant place for themselves in public life through voluntary associations and evangelical reform. African American men used these associations to press for full citizenship; women would do so by the 1840s. As electoral and legislative politics became limited to adult white men, women and African Americans helped to create a new and more inclusive kind of politics in a different public arena.[21]

An equally important change occurred in the character of political leadership. After 1815, second and third generations of middling-born, self-appointed, upwardly mobile political activists came to enter politics. Like their Jeffersonian forbears, these activists specialized in grassroots mobilization and popular appeal, embraced partisanship as a positive good, and sought to make nominations and appointments the reward for party service. Unlike their forbears, the political bourgeoisie of the postwar period overcame gentry control of politics and came to lead state and national political parties. The leadership of the Bucktails in New York, the Reform–New Court Party in Kentucky, and the Concord faction of the New Hampshire Republicans were composed of new men. During the 1810s and 1820s, these factions gained control both of their state Republican parties and of their state governments. Such men also came to prominence in other states, but they usually shared power with gentry politicians. Where they gained control over the party and state government, these politicians made the political practices, identities, and rhetoric of the first generation of humble-born activists the new rules of the game. Full-throated partisanship, once practiced only by a decidedly ungenteel minority of activists, became the norm. Party leaders embraced a charismatic approach to politics, at least in their rhetoric: "the party" was celebrated as a noble cause, not disdained as a necessary evil. The new leaders explicitly rejected gentlemen's views of politics as a contest for honor between great men. Politics became a clash of *organizations;* individuals were expected to subordinate their preferences and personal ambitions to the good of the party. Nominations and appointments were openly distributed as a reward for service in the party cause. Because of rotation in office, most individuals held positions for only a few years, but in each state, a handful of talented and energetic activists were able to make a career out of politics.[22]

Another important change was in the geographic spread and intensity of partisan electoral practices. The middle-class political leaders of the postwar period revived the methods of Jeffersonian activists—newspaper polemic, speeches on the hustings, appeals to the dignity of laboring men, nominating conventions, electoral committees, party rituals, and partisan clubs. And they applied those methods far more *systematically* than their predecessors had. In the earlier period, certain states and localities—most notably New York and Pennsylvania—were hotspots of partisan activity. During the late 1810s and 1820s, when most political leaders were retreating from partisanship and popular mobilization, activists in some of these hotspots (all of them middling-born new men) continued to use and refine these practices. Other new men came to power by leading both grassroots and faux grassroots political rebellions; they began using similar methods to mobilize their rank and file. Most of these men became Jacksonians by 1828. Their methods were transformed from a series of rump phenomena to a national model when Martin Van Buren took command of Andrew Jackson's presidential campaign in that year. The success of Van Buren's methods ensured their continued adoption in new places; in 1838–40, even the Whigs adopted them. Here was an instance of the path dependent development described by Douglas Bradburn elsewhere in this volume. But in this case, the established path taken was consciously chosen by a particular cadre of activists, deeply shaped by those activists' class, and fiercely contested by other groups in the political arena.[23]

In the process, the plebeian Jeffersonians' techniques of mass persuasion and mobilization became both more widespread geographically and more intensively used in most areas. In much of the Old Northwest and South outside of Virginia and North Carolina, partisan, democratic practices made little headway before 1828, and were fiercely resisted after Jackson's elevation to the presidency. By 1840, however, New York methods were adopted throughout the old Southwest and Old Northwest, and in much of the Southeast. The contagion of party took place within states as well. Donald Ratcliffe notes that partisan ritual, organization, and voting "existed in many, but not all counties" of Ohio before 1816, but became operational in every county during the 1820s. No historian of the period before 1815 has unearthed anything that approached the sheer magnitude of popular mobilization that occurred in 1840. As Ratcliffe concludes, parties fundamentally shaped political behavior during the earlier period, but they did not do so with the same "effectiveness" that the Jacksonian parties enjoyed.[24]

The period after 1828 did not usher in new political practices or an unprecedented commitment to popular mobilization, but it did witness an organizational revolution in electoral politics. At the core of Van Buren's political methods was an insistence on party discipline. Debate was encouraged within the party (at least in theory), but once the appropriate party institution (usually a caucus or convention) chose a candidate or a policy position, all party members were expected to fight for the candidate or position, regardless of personal preference or dictates of conscience. Those who broke ranks were excoriated in the party press, shunned by their compatriots, and excluded from consideration for nominations and patronage posts. In addition, the Democrats (and by the 1840s, the Whigs) standardized party institutions and routinized party decision-making. Elaborating on and regularizing plebeian Jeffersonians' practices in New York and Pennsylvania, both parties adopted a hierarchy of conventions at the school district, town, county, state, and national levels, with the delegates from each convention selecting the delegates for the level above them. A similar structure of ward, town, county, state, and national electoral committees became the norm as well. Newspapers adopted a looser chain of command, but in state and presidential contests, the party's semiofficial mouthpiece (the Jacksonian *United States Telegraph* in 1828; the Whig *Albany Evening Journal* in 1840) established a clear campaign message, which editors in the provinces replicated — or, just as often, simply reprinted.

This organizational revolution was intimately tied to the growing political power and electoral importance of the presidency during the early nineteenth century. The first political campaign coordinated from a national headquarters (actually two, in Nashville and Washington, D.C.) was that of Andrew Jackson in 1828. Most people who adulated Old Hickory did not seem to be strong supporters of partisan methods. Still, Martin Van Buren used their enthusiasm to build a national party committed to those methods. Once in office,

Jackson dramatically elevated the importance of the presidency by insisting that the chief executive was the sole legitimate mouthpiece for the entire nation and by making himself the lightning rod for both the adulation of his supporters and the fears of his opponents. After 1840, presidential campaigns routinely became national elections, with turnout for the first time exceeding that for gubernatorial races.[25]

The new importance of the presidency encouraged voters and political advocates to focus on national rather than state politics. It allowed for national coordination of campaigns, which in turn facilitated a more intensive and widespread use of old methods of popular mobilization. It is no accident that the presidential campaign managers who played midwives to the revival of partisan democracy were both middling-born New Yorkers: Martin Van Buren in 1828 and Thurlow Weed in 1840. These men sought to make the New York model of partisan mobilization the norm for their respective parties. They did not triumph everywhere, but they won in the Northeast, Old Northwest, and Upper South. By 1840, openly partisan appeals, newspaper wars, electoral committees, mass meetings, nominating conventions, and partisan rituals—all centrally coordinated at the state and (during presidential elections) national level—became standard procedure in most of the United States.[26]

It is important not to exaggerate the uniformity of electoral practices after 1828. National political parties were still alliances of state parties. Each state organization continued to be shaped by local conditions, existing local hierarchies, and local alliances and arrangements that often predated the second party system. The long-lasting influence of nullifiers in the deep South and the growing conflict over slavery everywhere were the most obvious—but hardly the only—examples of the importance of local and regional factors in shaping the political landscape. In the Northeast, Old Northwest, and Upper South, these conditions and alliances did not prevent the adoption of the New York model, though it often met with resistance. Indeed, the great number of emigrants from New York and Pennsylvania (where partisan mobilization also had a long history) to those regions may have facilitated that process; in Illinois, it was Yankees from New York who championed their adoption.

Still, the receptions and effects of partisan democracy differed enormously from place to place. Party conflict became common throughout New England, but highly unequal party strength and the proliferation of nonparty and antiparty movements kept turnout low. Political development was even more uneven in Virginia and the Deep South. Fearful that residents of the state's intervale and mountain regions were hostile to slavery, Virginia's slaveholders fought all efforts to widen the suffrage and equalize the apportionment of the legislature until 1851. Still, partisan, democratic rhetoric, party organization, and popular mobilization took firm hold during the 1830s. Louisiana, too, lived with the paradox of relatively restrictive property and taxpaying requirements for suffrage and robust popular mobilization. South Carolina slaveholders erected the strongest barriers to democratization. Poor men could vote for representatives to Congress and the lower house of the state legislature, but high property requirements blocked them from voting for the state senate and governor. Most offices remained appointive, and officeholders were subjected to high property requirements. As a result, the planter elite retained firm control of politics, and the state's political leaders openly denounced democracy and formulated constitutional doctrines designed to protect slave property from majority rule. Alone of all the states, South Carolina avoided having its electorate divided into Jacksonians and Whigs. Planters in other slave states embraced a wide suffrage, partisanship, and popular mobilization but managed to keep democracy within bounds. As Erik Mathisen has argued, the high bonds required of southern officeholders kept them dependent on wealthy men.[27]

Even where they embraced partisan democracy, southerners proved selective in their appropriation of the New York model. Most slave-state partisans enthusiastically adopted partisan appeals, democratic rhetoric, and the techniques of popular mobilization. Outside of South Carolina and Louisiana, voters turned out in larger proportions than in New England. But southern politicians tended to be skeptical of partisan organizations and party discipline. Leaders cherished the doctrine of legislative independence, maintaining their autonomy in matters of policy from both party counsels and constituents. Newspapers, another cornerstone of party organization, were far less thick on the ground than in the North and West. As John Brooke has found, newspapers were directed at an audience of gentlemen, who mediated and passed on their messages to a plebeian audience through oratory and face-to-face interaction. Despite very high voter turnout, Mississippians remained averse to partisanship. Local and county party organizations languished, party identification mattered little in races below the state level, and voters frequently switched parties. Politics centered not on issues or abstract partisan identities but on direct community relationships, local hierarchies, and the imperatives of masculinity and honor. All in all, the adoption of the New York model was uneven across space, especially but not exclusively in the South.[28]

Another major difference between Jeffersonian and Jacksonian democracy was that they took place in starkly dissimilar international contexts. Republicans and Federalists clashed in the shadow of the French Revolution and monarchical reaction. To both, democracy was not bounded by national borders; it was the central aim of a worldwide revolutionary movement. Republicans and their progenitors celebrated French military victories and sang paeans to the guillotine; Federalists saw in every opposition meeting and Republican electoral victory the imminent arrival on American shores of France's atheism, bloodshed, and social upheaval. The democratic movements behind Andrew Jackson and his successors and opponents, on the other hand, took place in a world of monarchical reaction and failed revolution. Scholarly work is sorely lacking on the international context of American democracy after 1828, but a few tentative observations are in order. Where both its champions and its enemies saw democracy as an import and part of a worldwide movement during the 1790s, after 1828 both Whigs and Democrats depicted it as a key marker of American exceptionalism. For them, as well as for the democratic movements that emerged in England and Europe after 1835, the United States was the *source* of democratic inspiration and ideas, not the recipient. The political ideas and styles that Americans borrowed from abroad after 1815 tended to be nondemocratic—especially those of Napoleon and Edmund Burke.[29]

Perhaps the most important manner in which Jacksonian democracy differed from its earlier versions lay in the fact that partisan mobilization was just one version of democracy (albeit the most widely practiced one) competing for dominance in the public sphere. As Terry Bouton, Woody Holton, Kenneth Owen, Alan Taylor, and others have shown, democratic aspirations and practices were widespread outside of the major parties under the Articles of Confederation and into the 1790s. Regulator movements, agrarian rebellions, popular meetings and conventions, and collective efforts to obstruct the enforcement of unpopular laws all gave form to popular efforts to expand the power of nonelites in public life. But the Federalists were committed to crushing these democratic efforts in all their forms, while Republican leaders defended them halfheartedly at best. More often, Republicans pressured movement activists to abandon their extralegal tactics while appealing to their grievances. Federalist officials crushed regulator movements like the Whiskey Rebellion and Fries's Rebellion, and hounded Democratic-Republican societies out of existence; Republican leaders, for the most part, accepted the repression while appealing to the regulators' hatred of high taxes and Democratic-Republicans' devotion to the French Revolution. Where Republicans fought back was in defending the right of town meetings to debate and criticize the actions of federal officials during the discussion over the Jay Treaty. They succeeded. But the timing of their success was crucial: it took place at the very moment that the popular opposition to the Federalists was merging with the elite Republican opposition. Opponents carved out some space for democratic opposition at the same time that their movements became incorporated into the Republican Party.[30]

By the time of Jefferson's elevation to the presidency in 1801, no significant democratic movement existed outside of the Republican Party. After Fries's Rebellion, backcountry regulator movements disappeared, except for a few rump riots in places like Maine. Voluntary associations multiplied, but they tended to be either partisan, or respectable to the genteel in their membership, or both. Nonparty associations were mostly undemocratic in their aspirations, aiming at literary or scientific advancement, preserving the moral and social order, or advocating gradual, nondisruptive reform. Between 1789 and 1800, extra-partisan democratic movements were vibrant, widespread, and quickly crushed. Between 1800 and 1815, the only organization or movement committed to increasing ordinary citizens' power in public life was the radical wing of the Republican Party.[31]

This was not the case after 1815. Membership in nonpartisan associations skyrocketed after the War of 1812. Their character changed as well. Where in the earlier period most voluntary associations enjoyed an almost uniformly respectable, and often a largely genteel, membership, by the 1830s and 1840s, such organizations drew in large numbers of skilled wage earners, small farmers, and young, marginal members of the middle class. Mechanics' institutes gave way to trade unions; membership in agricultural societies changed from gentlemen to prosperous farmers; temperance societies drew in people from all classes. The number of female and African American activists grew exponentially. At the same time, the stance of many voluntary associations toward the social and religious order changed. Organizations aimed at gradual, nondisruptive reform or at preserving social order, like the American Tract Society and the American Colonization Society, grew during the later period. But so did societies that sought fundamental, often disruptive social or religious change: trade unions, utopian communities, and Garrisonian abolitionism, to name a few. Third parties, unknown in the earlier period, briefly proliferated during the late 1820s and early 1830s, just as the Jacksonians were spreading the New York system of electioneering across the United States, and reappeared again in the 1840s and 1850s.[32]

These newer, less respectable, more radical associations and movements often posed fundamental challenges to the major parties' way of doing business. The 1820s marked a momentous break from the first party system: A multitude of movements and organizations dedicated themselves to expanding ordinary citizens' participation and power in public life. Workingmen's parties and the Anti-Masons used mass mobilization techniques to galvanize members and voters in an effort to make government an extension of the will of a sovereign people. Evangelical reform, movements for political autonomy among American Indians, and a newly assertive African American politics in the North brought into public life women, African Americans, and Indians who had been excluded from electoral politics. Many, though not all, of these movements explicitly condemned major party politics as a sham democracy and sought to change the rules of the political game in what they saw as a more democratic direction. The Workingmen's Parties condemned the "interested, self-appointed individuals" and the "office holders" who controlled the major parties, and they sought institutional changes that would make parties and government more responsive to the will of the rank and file. Evangelicals condemned the unchristian competition, false witness, and ruthless pursuit of power that they saw as rampant in party politics. They sought to create a different kind of politics, based on mass mobilization and persuasion, which changed the world by transforming individual hearts rather than gaining state power. The more radical among them looked to open that politics to all individuals regardless of race or sex. In short, where before the War of 1812 partisan mobilization was the only democratic movement with staying power, the Jacksonian era gave rise to multiple democracies, each championing a different set of political practices and ideals.[33]

For a long time, many historians have considered the 1820s and 1830s as ushering a single, more or less unitary democracy centered on partisan mobilization. In reality, that democracy was not new but represented the intensification and refinement of trends begun in the late 1790s. Nor is it easy to conclude, as many historians do, that the era gave rise to unprecedented popular power in politics. The organizational revolution that overtook party politics in the 1820s and 1830s had a paradoxical effect on power and participation at the grassroots. On the one hand, the proliferation of conventions and electoral committees, along with the meetings, dinners, and parades that those committees organized, facilitated a spectacular increase in popular participation in electoral politics, as measured in both local activism and voter turnout. In the process, the parties dramatically enhanced the civic capabilities of tens of thousands of middling and poor citizens—a process that Johann N. Neem describes brilliantly in this volume. On the other hand, increased party discipline, the standardization of the institutions and routines of intraparty governance, and the establishment of genuinely national party ideologies and policies all helped to establish a degree of centralized control over the parties that had never been seen before. After 1828, American political parties developed the ability not only to nominate candidates and adopt policies but to *enforce* them at the local level. The autonomy exercised by local parties during the 1790s and 1800s became increasingly attenuated—at least until the sectional crisis began to split the parties along sectional lines. Similarly, party organizations developed sophisticated means to silence dissent within their ranks.

This combination of intensifying popular mobilization (and the rank-and-file efficacy that went with it) and centralized control of the party methods and message contributed mightily to the most distinctive characteristic of Jacksonian politics: the proliferation of competing blueprints for democracy. This *was* genuinely new; the first party system had no sustained counterpart to the Anti-Masons, the abolitionists, or the labor movement. Far from giving rise to a new partisan democracy, the Jacksonian era gave birth to a political arena that encompassed much more than electoral politics. For the first time in U.S. and world history, politics came to be defined by powerful, regimented partisan organizations, challenged on all sides by movements that rejected their policies, their ideas, and, crucially, their ways of conducting politics. This was the signature contribution of the Jacksonian era to the American democratic tradition. We live with it still.

Notes

1. Arthur M. Schlesinger, *The Age of Jackson* (Boston: Little, Brown, 1945); Charles Sellers, *The Market Revolution: Jacksonian America, 1815–1846* (New York: Oxford University Press, 1994); Harry L. Watson, *Liberty and Power: The Politics of Jacksonian America* (New York: Farrar, Straus, and Giroux, 1990); Watson, *Jacksonian Politics and Community Conflict: The Emergence of the Second Party System in Cumberland County, North America* (Baton Rouge: Louisiana State University Press,

1981); Gerald Leonard, *The Invention of Party Politics: Federalism, Popular Sovereignty, and Constitutional Development in Jacksonian Illinois* (Chapel Hill: University of North Carolina Press, 2002).

2. Ronald P. Formisano, *The Transformation of Political Culture: Massachusetts Parties, 1790s–1840s* (New York: Oxford University Press, 1983). See also Joel H. Silbey, *The American Political Nation, 1838–1893* (Stanford, Cal.: Stanford University Press, 1991.

3. See, for example, the introduction and the essays by Pasley and Robertson in Jeffrey L. Pasley, Andrew W. Robertson, and David Waldstreicher, eds., *Beyond the Founders: New Approaches to the Political History of the Early American Republic* (Chapel Hill: University of North Carolina Press, 2004). For a fuller inventory of this body of work, see notes 11–15 in this essay.

4. Donald J. Ratcliffe, *Party Spirit in a Frontier Republic: Democratic Politics in Ohio, 1793–1821* (Columbus: Ohio State University Press, 1998); Ratcliffe, *The Politics of Long Division: The Birth of the Second Party System in Ohio, 1818–1828* (Columbus: Ohio State University Press, 2000); Sean Wilentz, *The Rise of American Democracy: Jefferson to Lincoln* (New York: Norton, 2005); John L. Brooke, *Columbia Rising: Civil Life on the Upper Hudson from the Revolution to the Age of Jackson* (Chapel Hill: University of North Carolina Press, 2010). Rosemarie Zagarri, Albrecht Koschnik, and Johann Neem also frame their recent histories of women's politics and voluntary associations, respectively, to encompass both periods. Zagarri, *Revolutionary Backlash: Women and Politics in the Early American Republic* (Philadelphia: University of Pennsylvania Press, 2007); Koschnik, *"Let a Common Interest Bind Us Together": Associations, Partisanship, and Culture in Philadelphia, 1789–1840* (Charlottesville: University of Virginia Press, 2007); Neem, *Creating a Nation of Joiners: Democracy and Civil Society in Early National Massachusetts* (Cambridge, Mass.: Harvard University Press, 2008).

5. Silbey, *American Political Nation;* Formisano, *Transformation of Political Culture;* Watson, *Liberty and Power;* Watson, *Jacksonian Politics;* Amy Bridges, *A City in the Republic: Antebellum New York and the Origins of Machine Politics* (New York: Cambridge University Press, 1984). This and the following two paragraphs draw on these works.

6. William E. Gienapp, "'Politics Seem to Enter into Everything': Political Culture in the North, 1840–1860," in *Essays on American Antebellum Politics, 1840–1860*, ed. Stephen E. Maizlish and John J. Kushma (College Station: Texas A&M University Press, 1982); Silbey, *American Political Nation,* 126. For the Jacksonian era as a golden age, see Robert H. Wiebe, *The Opening of American Society: From the Adoption of the Constitution to the Eve of Disunion* (New York: Knopf, 1984), and, in a more qualified way, Michael A. McGerr, *The Decline of Popular Politics: The American North, 1865–1928* (New York: Oxford University Press, 1986).

7. Alan Taylor, "The Art of Hook and Snivey: Political Culture in Upstate New York during the 1790s," *Journal of American History* 74 (March 1993): 1371–96;

Taylor, *William Cooper's Town: Power and Persuasion on the Frontier of the Early American Republic* (New York: Knopf, 1995), 141–69; Alfred F. Young, *The Democratic Republicans of New York: The Origins, 1763–1797* (Chapel Hill: University of North Carolina Press, 1967); Joanne Freeman, *Affairs of Honor: National Politics in the New Republic* (New Haven, Conn.: Yale University Press, 2001).

8. Alan Taylor, "From Fathers to Friends of the People: Political Personas in the Early Republic," *Journal of the Early Republic* 11 (Winter 1991): 465–91; Taylor, *William Cooper's Town*, 227–91. See also Wilentz, *Rise of American Democracy*, 125, 138, 177.

9. Jeffrey L. Pasley, *"The Tyranny of Printers": Newspaper Politics in the Early American Republic* (Charlottesville: University Press of Virginia, 2001); Pasley, "A Journeyman, Either in Law or Politics: John Beckley and the Social Origins of Political Campaigning," *Journal of the Early Republic* 16 (Winter 1996): 531–69; David Waldstreicher and Stephen R. Grossbart, "Abraham Bishop's Vocation; or, The Mediation of Jeffersonian Politics," *Journal of the Early Republic* 18 (Winter 1998): 617–57; Max Weber, "Politics as a Vocation," in Weber, *The Vocation Lectures*, ed. David Owen and Tracy B. Strong, trans. Rodney Livingstone (Indianapolis: Hackett, 2004).

10. Richard Hofstadter, *The Idea of a Party System: The Rise of Legitimate Opposition in the United States, 1780–1840* (Berkeley: University of California Press, 1968). Hofstadter's interpretation, which took the sentiments of gentry politicians to be universal, was endorsed by almost all historians writing after him. See Formisano, *Transformation of Political Culture;* James Roger Sharp, *American Politics in the Early Republic: The New Nation in Crisis* (New Haven, Conn.: Yale University Press, 1993); and Stanley Elkins and Eric McKitrick, *The Age of Federalism* (New York: Oxford University Press, 1993).

11. David Waldstreicher, *In the Midst of Perpetual Fetes: The Making of American Nationalism, 1776–1820* (Chapel Hill: University of North Carolina Press, 1997), 108–245; Simon Newman, *Parades and the Politics of the Street: Festive Culture in the Early American Republic* (Philadelphia: University of Pennsylvania Press, 1997); Andrew W. Robertson, "Voting Rites and Voting Acts: Electioneering Ritual, 1790–1820," in Pasley et al., eds., *Beyond the Founders*, 66–75; Koschnik, *Let a Common Interest*.

12. Ratcliffe, *Party Spirit*, 98; Brooke, *Columbia Rising*, 288–303; Robertson, "Voting Rites"; Jeffrey L. Pasley, "The Cheese and the Words: Popular Political Culture and Participatory Democracy in the Early American Republic," in Pasley et al., eds., *Beyond the Founders*, 39.

13. Robertson, "Voting Rites," 67–69.

14. Pasley, *"Tyranny of Printers";* Ratcliffe, *Party Spirit;* Brooke, *Columbia Rising*, 288–303, 437–52.

15. Taylor, *William Cooper's Town;* Formisano, *Transformation of Political Culture;* Watson, *Jacksonian Politics*.

16. Pasley, "Cheese and the Words," 47–48; Brooke, *Columbia Rising,* 289–94; Watson, *Jacksonian Politics,* 63. For national turnout rates during the 1830s and 1840s, see Silbey, *American Political Nation,* 145.

17. Alexander Keyssar, *The Right to Vote: The Contested History of Democracy in the United States* (New York: Basic Books, 2000); Reeve Huston, *Land and Freedom: Rural Society, Popular Protest, and Party Politics in Antebellum New York* (New York: Oxford University Press, 2000); Ronald P. Formisano, *For the People: American Populist Movements from the Revolution to the 1850s* (Chapel Hill: University of North Carolina Press, 2008); Mark Voss-Hubbard, *Beyond Party: Cultures of Antipartisanship in Northern Politics before the Civil War* (Baltimore: Johns Hopkins University Press, 2002); Elizabeth S. Clemens, *The People's Lobby: Organizational Innovation and the Rise of Interest Group Politics in the United States, 1890–1925* (Chicago: University of Chicago Press, 1997); William H. Chafe, *Civilities and Civil Rights: Greensboro, North Carolina, and the Black Struggle for Freedom* (New York: Oxford University Press, 1980); Charles M. Payne, *I've Got the Light of Freedom: The Organizing Tradition and the Mississippi Freedom Struggle* (Berkeley: University of California Press, 1995); Barbara Ransby, *Ella Baker and the Black Freedom Movement: A Radical Democratic Vision* (Chapel Hill: University of North Carolina Press, 2003).

18. See, for example, Kimberly K. Smith, *The Dominion of Voice: Riot, Reason, and Romance in Antebellum Politics* (Lawrence: University Press of Kansas, 1999); Wilentz, *Rise of American Democracy;* Huston, *Land and Freedom;* Huston, "Popular Movements and Party Rule: The New York Anti-Rent Wars and the Jacksonian Political Order," in Pasley et al., eds., *Beyond the Founders,* 355–86; Pasley, *Tyranny of Printers;* Pasley, "Cheese and the Words"; Robertson, "Voting Rites"; Brooke, *Columbia Rising;* Koschnik, *Let a Common Interest;* Neem, *Creating a Nation of Joiners;* Voss-Hubbard, *Beyond Party;* Clemens, *People's Lobby;* Chafe, *Civilities and Civil Rights;* Payne, *I've Got the Light of Freedom;* Ransby, *Ella Baker.*

19. Taylor, *William Cooper's Town,* 256–87, 346–63; Huston, *Land and Freedom,* 30–33, 59; Brooke, *Columbia Rising,* 284–341, 437–52; Formisano, *Transformation of Political Culture,* 128–40; Watson, *Jacksonian Politics,* 82–108; Christopher J. Olsen, *Political Culture and Secession in Mississippi: Masculinity, Honor, and the Antiparty Tradition, 1830–1860* (New York: Oxford University Press), 71–147; Keyssar, *Right to Vote,* 92–93, appendix, tables A.1 and A.2; Leonard, *Invention of Party Politics;* William G. Shade, *Democratizing the Old Dominion: Virginia and the Second Party System, 1824–1861* (Charlottesville: University Press of Virginia, 1996); John L. Brooke, "To Be 'Read by the Whole People': Press, Party, and Public Sphere in the United States, 1790–1840," *Proceedings of the American Antiquarian Society* 110 (2000): 41–118; Koschnik, *Let a Common Interest;* Neem, *Creating a Nation of Joiners;* George Fitzhugh, *Cannibals All! or, Slaves without Masters* (1852; reprint edn., Cambridge, Mass.: Harvard University Press, 1960). Several scholars emphasize the unevenness of democratization; see Richard P. McCormick, *The Second American Party System: Party Formation in the Jacksonian Era* (Chapel Hill: University of North Carolina Press, 1966); Wilentz, *Rise of American Democracy;* Brooke, "To Be Read."

20. Keyssar, *Right to Vote*, 26–67; Wilentz, *Rise of American Democracy*, 183–200.

21. Catherine Allgor, *Parlor Politics: In Which the Ladies of Washington Help Build a City and a Government* (Charlottesville: University Press of Virginia, 2000); Zagarri, *Revolutionary Backlash*, 140–80; Shane White, "It Was a Proud Day: African Americans, Festivals, and Parades in the North, 1741–1834," *Journal of American History* 81 (June 1994): 13–50; Gary Nash, *Forging Freedom: The Formation of Philadelphia's Black Community, 1720–1840* (Cambridge, Mass.: Harvard University Press, 1988); Anne M. Boylan, *The Origins of Women's Activism: New York and Boston, 1787–1840* (Chapel Hill: University of North Carolina Press, 2002); Carole Smith-Rosenberg, *Disorderly Conduct: Visions of Gender in Victorian America* (New York: Knopf, 1985); Patrick Rael, *Black Identity and Black Protest in the Antebellum North* (Chapel Hill: University of North Carolina Press, 2002); Richard S. Newman, *The Transformation of American Abolitionism: Fighting Slavery in the Early Republic* (Chapel Hill: University of North Carolina Press, 2002); Julie Roy Jeffrey, *The Great Silent Army of Abolitionism: Ordinary Women in the Abolitionist Movement* (Chapel Hill: University of North Carolina Press, 1998).

22. Michael Wallace, "Changing Concepts of Party in the United States: New York, 1815–1828," *American Historical Review* 74 (December 1968): 453–91; Donald B. Cole, *Martin Van Buren and the American Political System* (Princeton, N.J.: Princeton University Press, 1984); Cole, *A Jackson Man: Amos Kendall and the Rise of American Democracy* (Baton Rouge: Louisiana State University Press, 2004); Cole, *Jacksonian Democracy in New Hampshire, 1800–1851* (Cambridge, Mass.: Harvard University Press, 1970).

23. Brooke, *Columbia Rising*, 288–341, 437–52; Wallace, "Changing Concepts"; Cole, *Martin Van Buren*, 14–232; Cole, *Jackson Man*, 55–143; Cole, *Jacksonian Democracy;* Wilentz, *Rise of American Democracy*, 301–11; Lynn Hudson Parsons, *The Birth of Modern Politics: Andrew Jackson, John Quincy Adams, and the Election of 1828* (New York: Oxford University Press, 2009), 133–58; Silbey, *American Political Nation*, 18–45.

24. McCormick, *Second American Party System*, 175–320; Leonard, *Invention of Party Politics;* Ratcliffe, *Politics of Long Division*, 17; Silbey, *American Political Nation*, 47–108, 125–58; Brooke, "To Be Read"; Olsen, *Political Culture;* Manisha Sinha, *The Counterrevolution of Slavery: Politics and Ideology in Antebellum South Carolina* (Chapel Hill: University of North Carolina Press, 2000).

25. Robert V. Remini, *Andrew Jackson and the Course of American Empire, 1767–1821* (New York: Harper and Row, 1977); Remini, *The Election of Andrew Jackson* (Philadelphia: J. B. Lippincott, 1963); Cole, *Martin Van Buren*, 101–215; Silbey, *American Political Nation*. My deep thanks to Kenneth Owen for suggesting this line of analysis to me.

26. Pasley, "Cheese and the Words," 39; Silbey, *American Political Nation*, 46–124; Formisano, *Transformation of Political Culture*, 72–79, 84–96; Wilentz, *Rise of American Democracy*, 305, 515; Waldstreicher, *In the Midst*, 201–16; Wallace, "Changing Concepts"; Cole, *Martin Van Buren*, 101–215; Glyndon G. Van Deusen, *Thurlow Weed, Wizard of the Lobby* (Boston: Little, Brown, 1947).

27. McCormick, *Second American Party System;* Shade, *Democratizing the Old Dominion;* Sinha, *Counterrevolution of Slavery;* 2–3, 33–61; Erik Mathisen, "'Know All Men by These Presents': Bonds, Localism, and Politics in Early Republican Mississippi," *Journal of the Early Republic* 33 (Winter 2013): 727–50; John M. Sacher, *A Perfect War of Politics: Parties, Politicians, and Democracy in Louisiana, 1824–1861* (Baton Rouge: Louisiana State University Press, 2003), 12. My thanks to Daniel Peart for pointing out Louisiana's restrictive suffrage requirements and boisterous democratic mobilization.

28. McCormick, *Second American Party System;* Olsen, *Political Culture,* 13–15, 17–37; Kenneth S. Greenberg, *Masters and Statesmen: The Political Culture of American Slavery* (Baltimore: Johns Hopkins University Press, 1985); Brooke, "To Be Read."

29. Matthew Rainbow Hale, "I Am a Democrat: The French Revolution and the Emergence of Jeffersonian Democracy" (paper, "Jeffersonian Democracy, Theory and Practice" conference, Princeton University, Princeton, N.J., 17–19 May 2012); Hale, *The French Revolution and the Forging of American Democracy* (Charlottesville: University of Virginia Press, forthcoming); Hale, "For the Love of Glory: Napoleonic Imperatives in the Early American Republic" (unpublished paper in author's possession); Seth Cotlar, *Tom Paine's America: The Rise and Fall of Transatlantic Radicalism in the Early Republic* (Charlottesville: University of Virginia Press, 2011); Milena Bianco, *L'Associazionismo Politico Inglese e la Democrazia Europea* (Florence: Centro Editoriale Toscano, 2012); Daniel Dewey Barnard, *Man and the State, Social and Political* (New Haven, Conn., 1846); Jean H. Baker, *Affairs of Party: The Political Culture of Northern Democrats in the Mid–Nineteenth Century* (Ithaca, N.Y.: Cornell University Press, 1983), 53–54, 187–90.

30. Terry Bouton, *Taming Democracy: "The People," the Founders, and the Troubled Ending of the American Revolution* (New York: Oxford University Press, 2007); Woody Holton, *Unruly Americans and the Origins of the Constitution* (New York: Hill and Wang, 2007); Kenneth Owen, "Political Community in Revolutionary Pennsylvania, 1774–1800" (Ph.D. diss., University of Oxford, 2011); Thomas Slaughter, *The Whiskey Rebellion: Frontier Epilogue to the American Revolution* (New York: Oxford University Press, 1986); Eugene P. Link, *The Democratic-Republican Societies, 1790–1800* (New York: Columbia University Press, 1942); Paul Douglas Newman, *Fries's Rebellion: The Enduring Struggle for the American Revolution* (Philadelphia: University of Pennsylvania Press, 2004); Alan Taylor, *Liberty Men and Great Proprietors: The Revolutionary Settlement on the Maine Frontier* (Chapel Hill: University of North Carolina Press, 1990), 209–32; Sharp, *American Politics.*

31. Bouton, *Taming Democracy;* Neem, *Creating a Nation of Joiners;* Newman, *Transformation of American Abolitionism;* Brooke, *Columbia Rising,* 117–70, 228–79; Robert Abzug, *Cosmos Crumbling: American Reform and the Religious Imagination* (New York: Oxford University Press, 1994). I am indebted to John Brooke for his insight about the disappearance of regulator movements coinciding with the Republican victory of 1800.

32. Brooke, *Columbia Rising*, 458–74; Koschnik, *Let a Common Interest;* Sean Wilentz, *Chants Democratic: New York City and the Rise of the American Working Class, 1789–1850* (New York: Oxford University Press, 1984); Newman, *Transformation of American Abolitionism;* Smith-Rosenberg, *Disorderly Conduct;* Rael, *Black Identity;* Jeffrey, *Great Silent Army;* Paul Goodman, *Towards a Christian Republic: Antimasonry and the Great Transition in New England, 1826–1836* (New York: Oxford University Press, 1988); Formisano, *For the People;* Huston, *Land and Freedom.*

33. *Mechanics' Free Press* (Philadelphia), 31 May, 23 August 1828; Reeve Huston, "What We Talk about When We Talk about Democracy: Re-engaging the American Democratic Tradition," *Common-Place: The Interactive Journal of Early American Life* 9, no. 1 (October 2008), common-place.org/vol-09/no-01/huston/; Formisano, *For the People;* Goodman, *Towards a Christian Republic;* Wilentz, *Chants Democratic;* Newman, *Transformation of American Abolitionism;* Aileen Kraditor, *Means and Ends in American Abolitionism: Garrison and His Critics on Strategy and Tactics, 1834–1850* (New York: Vintage Books, 1969); Huston, *The Origins of Jacksonian Democracies* (unpublished book manuscript, in progress); Smith, *Dominion of Voice.* The political practices of voluntary associations also showed a lot of continuity between the two periods.

★ JOHN L. BROOKE ★

Party, Nation, and Cultural Rupture

The Crisis of the American Civil War

T he causes of the Civil War stand as a central question in American history, and the debate has generated an enormous and contentious literature. Very broadly, the battle is drawn between fundamentalists and revisionists. Fundamentalists see slavery as the obvious and long-term cause, with the war grounded in deep-running structural tensions between a free North and a slave South. Revisionists focus on the play of contingent events in national party politics and the explosion of ethno-religious conflict in the early 1850s, arguing that internal rifts both North and South marginalized sectional extremists, who might have been suppressed and war avoided. Both of these interpretations have their problems, and Edward Ayers has recently called for an effort to bridge the gap between fundamentalists and revisionists through a reconsideration of the "catalysts that emerged in the two to three decades before the war began."[1] This chapter argues that a more fluid conversation between political and cultural histories can help to identify these catalysts and resolve this interpretive struggle.

The revisionists are quite right in arguing that Civil War causation was deeply entangled with the role and structure of political parties in the early republic. National leaders and party politicians from the revolution forward worked assiduously to keep the question of slavery off the national agenda. But explaining why the South waited until 1860–61 to secede from the Union is not that much of a puzzle. As a distinguished body of fundamentalist literature has made clear, the South's membership in the Union from the 1787 Constitutional Convention forward was contingent on a primal compromise: no union without slavery.[2] The course of the southern majority was relatively plain: despite challenges in 1790, 1821, 1832, and even 1850, most southerners saw their interests protected within the Union by the national political parties.

Whatever their differences, the two major parties stood behind the 1787 compromise as the pillar of national unity; the dominance of the Democratic Party in particular seemed to ensure that slavery would expand into new territories, as demanded by the interests of the cotton economy. Thus, understanding the trajectory into the Civil War has to rest on one essential point: when did a *decisive strategic bloc* in northern opinion coalesce around a party that would challenge this founding compromise, agreeing with the argument that slavery was antithetical to the ideals and future of the American republic? The war, as the South argued many times, was caused not simply by southern secession but by a successful northern "agitation" over slavery.

Despite the unstinting efforts of early antislavery activists, however, the critical mobilization did not arrive until the rise of the Republican Party between 1854 and 1856. But what caused this decisive mobilization? Political historians have focused considerable attention on the events surrounding the passage of the Kansas-Nebraska Act in the early months of 1854. Focusing on a rising tide of anti-immigrant and anti-Catholic opinion in the North, these historians argue that the northern public was apathetic about slavery in the years immediately following the Compromise of 1850. They are virtually unanimous in pointing to the galvanizing impact of an "Appeal of the Independent Democrats in Congress," published by six antislavery senators in January 1854, which attacked the Kansas-Nebraska bill "as a gross violation of a sacred pledge, as a criminal betrayal of precious rights; as part and parcel of atrocious plot" to convert the West "into a dreary region of despotism, inhabited by masters and slaves." Assessments from both sides of the modern interpretive divide concur on its galvanizing significance. In Eric Foner's estimation, the "Appeal" was "one of the most effective pieces of political propaganda in our history"; Michael F. Holt describes it as "a desperate effort by a few Free-Soilers to "perpetuate their party and their own political careers."[3]

Why was the "Appeal" so effective, essentially launching the rise of the Republican Party, if the northern electorate in the years immediately preceding was so "unconcerned about slavery"?[4] The political historians of the period uniformly describe the "Appeal" in total isolation from its rhetorical context. That context, unfolding from the summer of 1850, had prepared the northern public for this moment in a series of events and experiences that fall outside the purview of routine politics and traditional political historical writing. Indeed these events and experiences forged a northern nationalism that steeled strategic communities to endure four years of grueling war to defend the Union and end slavery, a nationalism that would then define the national center for the next half-century.[5] The early 1850s must be seen as a liminal, revolutionary rupture, melting away the structural glue that for decades the parties had worked to maintain, and building a new structure in its place.

This account stretches our common understanding of causal forces in the domain of "the political." The northern experience of the early 1850s was a multifaceted crisis of structure and legitimacy. At a moment of profound social and economic transformation, the Fugitive Slave Law broke the grip of the Compromise of 1787 on broad constituencies across the northern United States. As this crisis unfolded, cultural actors stepped into the breach, re-shaping the arena of formal politics.[6] The collective culture was inflected into a new consensus through the metaphoric, performative action of text, song, and theater. Expressive interventions led by Harriet Beecher Stowe's *Uncle Tom's Cabin*, Stephen Foster's song-writing, and their fusion in theater literally changed the public soundtrack across the North, shaping the climate of opinion that drove the ferocious response to the Kansas-Nebraska Act. Thus the seeming calm of the years immediately following the Compromise of 1850 masked a powerful shift in the northern center of gravity that—when mobilized by the Nebraska debates—manifested itself in a new political party and, more broadly, a new social imaginary, a new definition of American nationality. In this opening of James McPherson's "Second American Revolution," a broad coalition of northern men and women arrived at a fundamentally new understanding of the proper constitutional order of the republic, the roots of what Bruce Ackerman has called the "Second American Republic."[7]

Before I turn to the particulars of the 1850s, however, we need to explore briefly a set of problems neglected by many modern historians: the analysis of the "event," its place in what we now call the "public sphere," and its relationship with what anthropologists once called "structures." If this interpretation has anything useful to contribute regarding the coming of the Civil War, it does so in dialogue with this simple but useful theoretical framework.

OVER THE LAST SEVERAL decades, a number of historians have been exploring the utility of Jürgen Habermas's theory of the "public sphere," first introduced in 1960.[8] Very broadly this work has argued that the public sphere as a zone of discourse and association provides a literally material space mediating among the social, the political, and the cultural. But if the concept of the public sphere provides an analytical space at the intersection of society, culture, and politics, its deployment is still oddly rigid and abstract. The current literature on it does not encompass the contingent agency of human actors on the day-to-day or month-to-month chronology of events that frame lived experience, or of how events might have a transformative impact. Of course, historians abandoned "the event" long ago; certainly by the time that Bernard Bailyn described a general turn from manifest history to latent history, from a study of consciously experienced events to unconsciously lived processes and structures.[9] Since then, the "linguistic turn" has moved us from social to cultural structures, but an enduring queasiness with politics has left the event out in the cold. Perhaps we need to bring the event back in, to think carefully about how public occurrences are sequenced, experienced, and then synthesized into enduring collective culture.

One approach to a theory of events focuses on the role of the media in reinforcing cultural structures, deploying "narrative frames," and presenting "media events" to serve the needs of established interests.[10] This literature certainly describes how events are managed to serve the needs of the status quo, in a mode of analysis originated by Émile Durkheim, but it does little to explain how events might transform structures of opinion and even power.[11] William H. Sewell Jr., however, has proposed an analysis of transformative events, grounded in the anthropology of the "routinization of charisma" and the "rite of passage" running back to Victor Turner, Marshall Sahlins, Arnold van Gennep, and ultimately Max Weber. Very simply, this framework posits a three-step process: an established structure falters and, in the open-ended liminal space created by this collapse of authority, creative actors emerge to shape the mythic terms of a new political structure. Bridging historical practice and anthropological theory, Sewell usefully argues that historical time is lumpy and punctuated, rather than smooth and continuous: transformative event-clusters rupture entrenched structures and shape foundational myths for new structures.[12]

This model, as Sewell is well aware, is an obvious truism among historians, though somehow forgotten. It opens up some useful avenues of interpretation. Crisis events alter both political and cultural structures, and that alteration is driven by "liminality," an indeterminate, open-ended condition closely linked to domains of metaphor, myth, emotion, and even ecstatic experience. Established rules break down and new alignments of meaning and power emerge.

Quite literally, all events partake in the liminal to varying degrees. In the right circumstances, event sequences can spiral into liminal rupture, a rupture operating along multiple dimensions and pathways.

In most circumstances, however, the liminal quality of events is hedged in and contained by the effective management of various social and political routines. Among these routines, the political party emerged and developed as an institution designed to manage events in a postrevolutionary society. It was designed to direct the course of governance at a pace and trajectory suiting the interests of leaderships and their key constituencies, and to defend a revolutionary settlement against another breakdown, another rupture in the body politic and body social. "Political party" and "liminal rupture" are thus diametrically opposed terms. For most of modern history, major political parties and their leaderships have been deeply invested in utterly nonliminal, routine politics, protecting the status quo with processes of event management first described for religion by Émile Durkheim. Parties incorporate huge swaths of the public behind limited platforms of governmental action, constrained by Constitution and statute to particular channels of policy and political action. The potential for liminal breakout is hedged in by the rules governing lawmaking, and ultimately limited to the tense anxieties of an election season.

Antebellum partisanship rested on the legitimacy of the constitutional settlement of 1787: union with slavery. The dyadic party system comprised a "structure" in exactly the sense that Turner and Sewell intended. It defined and constrained the boundaries of the politically possible. Both of the great antebellum political parties inherited the preservationist nationalism of the early republic—the compelling mission to protect the Constitution and the Union against all challenges. In the wake of the Missouri Crisis of 1819–21, Martin Van Buren worked assiduously to reinforce that structure, to turn public attention away from slavery by "draw[ing] anew the old Party lines." Conflict over slavery threatened the Union; party could suppress the slavery debate. "Party attachment in former times furnished a complete antidote for sectional prejudices by producing *counteracting feelings*," he wrote in his famous letter to Thomas Ritchie, editor of the *Richmond Enquirer*, in January 1827. Party would protect the nation from disaster.[13]

The "counteracting feelings" of party identity that Van Buren invoked against both the decline of party and the rise of antislavery would soon coalesce into the great struggle over the "Money Power" of the Second Bank of the United States, the central trope of the debate between Whigs and

Democrats over the power of the state in the general economy. Men of both parties strove to maintain this focus on the economy and divert attention from slavery. By the late 1840s, this would become increasingly difficult, as state constitutional reforms seemed to solve the issue of public corruption, and then the lure of incorporated profit during the economic boom undermined any real distinctions between the two parties.[14] But if by the early 1850s the ideological structures dividing the two parties were crumbling, their behavioral structures were firmly in place.

Parties as institutions develop trajectories of their own—linking the personal interests of party notables to both policy advancement and group preservation. The entire fabric of party patronage—a widely ramifying range of administrative and judicial positions—comprised literal "structure." Established politicians simply could not afford to risk their household incomes—the "bread of office"—that flowed from loyal attachment to party discipline. Political parties were and are powerful engines of self-perpetuation, practically inventing their own physical laws of friction and inertia. Joel H. Silbey has captured the essential features of the antebellum parties in describing them as "wide-ranging management institutions," and arguing that "policy advancement, partisan organization, popular mobilization, and the art of management all went hand in hand."[15] If voter identity was not always quite as tribal as Silbey would have it, party management was closely calculated, since the loss of an election would ruin many a loyal soldier in the ranks of federal, state, and county leadership. And with this control of party rank and file, party managers could be reasonably confident that they could control the flow of events, or at least restrict them to a narrow channel.

FOR MANY YEARS, Silbey and others have argued for the primacy of this managed, stable party contest running in a "party period" down to 1896. But this happy story is maintained only by forgetting the constitutional crisis of the Civil War, when political violence left at least 750,000 dead.[16] Quite simply, during the early 1850s, the party managers lost their power to control events. In William Sewell's language, the structure failed, and a rupture with liminal qualities broke through. When a new structure emerged, its critical mythology had been forged in this era of crisis.

This essay opened with the suggestion that the central problem of Civil War causation requires defining and explaining a strategic shift of northern public opinion. While antislavery mobilization in the public sphere was from the mid-1830s more advanced and pervasive than proslavery mobilization in the South, it failed for many decades to achieve a synthesis that would recruit a northern majority to the antislavery cause. Most importantly, the antislavery coalition lacked two key and mutually dependent elements: effective leaders and voting majorities. Without votes, political leaders would not break from their patronage systems; without convincing leadership, voters would not vote. The Liberty Party received only a tiny fraction of the northern vote in 1840 and 1844. In 1848, even after the drama of the southern-driven Mexican War and the rise of the first widely resonant assault on the "Slave Power," Free Soil attracted less than 15 percent of the free-state vote. Six and eight years later, the story was quite different. With the passage of the Nebraska bill in May 1854, northern newspapers were filled with attacks on the "slave power." The November election for the Thirty-fourth Congress brought victory to a mixture of "anti-Nebraska" candidates, Republican and nativist, across the North, consigning the Democrats to the minority among northern congressmen for decades to come. In the 1856 presidential election, the new antislavery Republican Party nearly quadrupled the 1848 Free Soil strength to 1.3 million votes (an increase of 360%). This was the great break in nineteenth-century American politics: the Republican victory in 1860, with 1.8 million votes (a 37% increase) only built on the sea-change of 1854–56.

What had altered between 1848 and 1854? The revisionists stress that growing nativist hostility toward Catholicism, immigrants, their drinking habits, and their threat to wages drove the sudden rise of the Know-Nothings and the breakup of the Whig Party.[17] There is much to be said for this argument, because both nativism and the anxieties behind it were very real, as the recovery from the depression of 1837–43 was powered by a technologically driven shift toward a new economy.[18] Under these pressures, and given the salience of ethnic hostility in later nineteenth-century politics, it is not all that surprising that many in a deeply Protestant culture lashed out against Catholic immigrants. What is surprising is how quickly and easily the nativist impulse was sidelined by the antislavery imperative. Most historians of the northern Know-Nothings and Republicans agree that these groups held elements of both nativist and antislavery sentiment to varying degrees.[19] In the end, antislavery, not nativism, framed the agenda of the northern public.

The rise of antislavery in the 1850s was complicated by the organizational politics of both the 1854 and 1856 elections. A Republican Party would have to be constructed from top to bottom, while the Know-Nothings exploited the flexibility and popularity of the fraternal lodge, then in a renaissance across the North.[20] Thus, particularly in New England, where the Whigs refused to abandon their local party structures, Know-Nothing voting was the only available vehicle for opposition to the Kansas-Nebraska Act. Rhode Island Know-Nothings announced that "the people of the North had got heartily sick of the old organizations, and chiefly because they had truckled with the South in every matter of great interest." In Massachusetts, George Frisbie Hoar was of the opinion that great numbers voted nativist for an election or two "simply in order that they might get rid of the old parties, and prepare the state as with a subsoil plow."[21] Such conditions also explain at least some of the nativist voting in the Mid-Atlantic, while in the Midwest, the weakness of Whig organizations allowed the election of antislavery candidates to Congress in 1854. But if they were successful in some northern states in 1854 and 1855, the nativists were doomed as a national party by the impossibility of their uniting enough support in both the North and South: Native American conventions in July 1855 and February 1856 collapsed when schisms erupted over slavery planks, schisms orchestrated by antislavery delegates.[22]

The nativist Know-Nothings thus failed fundamentally to define the politics of the 1850s. Their support in the North was interwoven with powerful opposition to the Kansas-Nebraska Act and the threat of slavery in the West, precluding any possibility of a national nativist coalition. If critical events in Kansas and Washington in May 1856 — the sack of the city of Lawrence and the caning of Senator Charles Sumner — would widen support for antislavery, the fact remains that voters with these sentiments appeared in decisive numbers in the fall of 1854. How did this come to pass?

In the revisionist position, antislavery opinion was of minimal significance until early 1854, when it was kindled by "irresponsible" politicians in two steps. First, Stephen Douglas launched a bid for the presidency with the Kansas-Nebraska Act, which would overturn the Missouri Compromise of 1821 and open the Louisiana Purchase to slavery by local vote, so-called popular sovereignty. Second, six antislavery politicians immediately launched their "Appeal of the Independent Democrats," attacking the Nebraska bill in what revisionists universally term "propaganda."

How did the "Appeal of the Independent Democrats" have such an impact, if the northern electorate was so "unconcerned about slavery"?[23] The answer is that the northern public had been *prepared* for this moment by a series of events and experiences that fall outside the purview of routine politics. The political history of the early 1850s has tended to dismiss the massive new literature on the Fugitive Slave Act and the impact of cultural performances unfolding in its wake. The 1854–56 northern shift in voting and party was not "the event" itself but rather the result of a prior "event," cultural action in a liminal rupture acting on a large bloc of the northern public between 1850 and 1854.

LET US CONSIDER the Turner-Sahlins-Sewell model of structural crisis, liminal rupture, and rebuilding structure in relation to the politics of the early 1850s. A structural crisis is certainly evident in the sequence of events between 1846 and 1850: rising northern demands that slavery be kept out of any territories conquered from Mexico were met by demands for a solution that would "end all agitation" against slavery. This was a desperate effort to shore up received structures. In January 1850, President Zachary Taylor sent a message to Congress hoping that the legislature would "remove all occasion for the unnecessary agitation of the public mind," and Henry Clay introduced his omnibus resolutions "as a great national scheme of compromise and harmony." In March, Daniel Webster invoked the "trusts that now devolve upon us for the preservation of this Constitution . . . guarded by legislation, by law, by judicature, and defended by the whole affections of the people."[24] When rising Democratic star Stephen Douglas finally pushed a patchwork of bills through Congress late that summer, conservative business interests and religious authorities across the North called for the full enforcement of the compromise: the support of "law and order," of "government and civil society" was paramount; the Union was "the Palladium of our National Happiness"; the people of the North had a "religious duty of obedience to law."[25] Such was the language deployed in 1850 to reinforce an essential political structure: the 1787 compromise on Union with slavery.

There were two tracks in northern political culture in these years, partisan and extra-partisan. Historians have almost completely ignored the massive petitioning against the compromise during the winter and spring of 1850.[26] All told, about a thousand of these petitions protested the extension of slavery into the territories, while slavery in the District of Columbia and the Fugitive Slave Law each were the subject of about 480 petitions. The passage of the compromise that September spawned protest meetings across the North, which led to a second wave of petitioning; 364 petitions were submitted to the U.S. House between December 1850 and March 1851, all directed at the Fugitive

Slave Act. In sum, there were 840 fugitive slave petitions to the Thirty-first Congress, just a few hundred less than the petitions regarding the territories, potentially involving as many as eighty thousand signers.[27] The Fugitive Slave Law petitions were then reinforced by a massive wave of attention to the new law in the press and a host of public meetings across the North in the fall and spring of 1850 to 1851.

It is clear, therefore, that there was powerful popular opposition to the Fugitive Slave Law from the late winter of 1850, driving petitions and meetings well into the spring of 1851. Most of the petitions framed their appeal in a demand that all accused fugitives be given the rights of habeas corpus and a trial by jury.[28] Beyond this central issue of legal rights lay a series of constitutional questions. While President Taylor might argue that slavery was "left exclusively to the respective states," and thus "not expected to become topics of national agitation," the Fugitive Slave Law effectively nationalized slavery.[29] In requiring northern cooperation with fugitive rendition, the law violated the terms of the federalism that Taylor himself upheld as the pillar of the Union. Where southerners had long upheld the internal regulation of slavery as a right under a doctrine of state sovereignty, now the tables were turned and northerners saw their state autonomy threatened. If the Constitution stood as a national structure, northerners saw it shifting and changing shape before their eyes.

Under the Fugitive Slave Law, slavery became a direct and palpable experience for northern whites, driving a shift toward the public play of emotion and passion. Just as the massive petition drive unfolded outside the domain of formal politics, the experience of the Fugitive Slave Law lay outside the political routine, in local and personal dramas of both rendition and rescue — experienced sometimes directly but more often in print. This was a profoundly dissonant experience. Essentially respectful of law, white northerners were witness to a law-sanctioned violence that violated constitutional norms of due process and state sovereignty, as well as common decency and sensibility. All of these events put a host of disturbing images into the public arena, images that were the essence of liminality: dangerous movement between extremes of civil condition.[30] At the center lay the physical image of the fugitive slave, bag slung on a stick, on the move outside the law, venturing through the dark wilderness to civilization, threatened with death while moving toward life. Fugitives moved from slavery to freedom, across state and national lines, while captives returned to slavery. Black families took flight for British

Canada, calling into question the certainties and securities of life in the American North.

By the end of 1851, however, a seeming quiet had developed among the northern public. Pressed by both Democrats and pro-compromise Webster Whigs, antislavery Whigs were defeated in scattered elections across the North. Fugitive renditions—and rescues—dropped off considerably in 1852, and as the North settled into a reluctant enforcement of the law, press attention to the issue began to fade toward a trough of interest in 1853. It would appear that the petitioning and rescue activism—dramatic as it was—involved mostly committed communities of abolitionism and Liberty Party sentiment. Ronald P. Formisano describes late 1851 as the last moment of a "dying sectional storm."[31] But if partisan political attention to the Fugitive Slave Law faded, cultural attention began to intensify and ramify in widening circles in American society. In an explosion of commercialized celebrity, and a formative moment in American popular culture, two figures stepped into this opening to drive the emotional forces set in motion by the Fugitive Slave Act. Their explosive work in novel and song imperfectly but effectively fused in theater, Harriet Beecher Stowe and Stephen Foster provided the narrative and soundtrack of the liminal image of the fugitive slave that worked to shift the hard structural realities of American slavery politics.

HARRIET BEECHER STOWE began to conceptualize *Uncle Tom's Cabin* in December 1850, and published chapters serially in the abolitionist *National Era* from May 1851 through April 1852, when the novel was published as a book. Selling 310,000 copies within a year, *Uncle Tom's Cabin* became the first bestseller in the modern American book market.

There was a carefully calibrated strategy to Stowe's interpretive choices. Framing a gradualist message in the familiar tropes of sentimental domesticity, the book was centrally written to influence opinion among a carefully chosen audience. Stowe's goal was to gently push conservative evangelical white women and children out of their comfort zones; to that end, she crafted a tale that would have as many comfortable connections as discomforting traumas. First building an initial audience in the conservative wing of the antislavery community and then reaching a national and international audience with the published book, Stowe set in motion a tide of personal, private, intuitive epiphanies that dramatically extended the liminal impact of petition, protest, and resistance against the Fugitive Slave Law.[32] Diaries hint at its impact.

Ellen Wheaton in Syracuse, New York, wrote in April 1852 that her husband "Charles bro't home *Uncle Tom's Cabin* the other night, & the children are devouring it." The young James Garfield in October 1850 had thought that Congressman Joshua Giddings was "laboring" for a "carnal" cause when Giddings spoke for three hours on the Fugitive Slave Act. Garfield first began reading *Uncle Tom's Cabin* a year and a half later; in March 1853, he may have had something of a conversion crisis: "I commenced reading *Uncle Tom's Cabin*. Read after went to bed. Rested uneasy in night." The previous December, John Jay, the New York abolitionist, had written to Senator Charles Sumner that "'Uncle Tom' has created a new feeling in regard to slavery, which I am confident will shew itself the moment an opportunity is afforded for its embodiment."[33]

Stowe reignited a controversy that had seemed to be fading away but did so in a manner that transcended the typically "political," and thus achieved the purchase in northern imagination that had eluded the abolitionists since the 1830s. The impact of *Uncle Tom's Cabin* lay in the dynamic between the deeply entrenched sentimental mode and the volatile state of opinion in the North in the months following the passage of the Compromise of 1850 and the Fugitive Slave Act. Returning to our theoretical frame, the experience of sentimental reading shaped transformational epiphanies of personal identification, moments of sympathetic breakthrough, that are prime examples of the metaphoric action, the linkage of previously unlinked categories, which Victor Turner saw at the heart of the liminal experience.[34] The public reception of Stowe's *Uncle Tom's Cabin* was a dramatic manifestation of this metaphoric action, as these intuitive epiphanies began to break through the barriers that northern majority opinion had erected against the antislavery movement.

The full effect of this breakthrough did not rest on this text alone. *Uncle Tom's Cabin* was part of the first truly national wave of commercially driven popular culture, and this commercialization carried its message forward in increasingly attenuated and simplified forms. Commercial tie-ins — engravings, decorative plates and figurines, toys, games, and even clothing — were all spun off in vast quantities.[35] American publishers issued at least eighteen other extended treatments of slavery between 1852 and 1856, including Solomon Northrup's *Twelve Years a Slave*, Frederick Douglass's *The Heroic Slave*, Stowe's *Key to Uncle Tom's Cabin*, and her second novel, *Dred: A Tale of the Great Dismal Swamp*. And a powerfully multivocal and liminal vector for Stowe's message developed in song and theater. The nineteenth-century songsheet industry was a major enterprise, and seems to have reached into virtually every household in the country, filtering out into the streets and taverns. By July 1852, the first of several waves of sentimental renditions of *Uncle Tom's Cabin* were on the market, but the most important musical accompaniment to Harriet Beecher Stowe would come from Stephen Foster.[36]

A long scholarship has demonstrated that a powerful ambiguity regarding race and slavery ran through Stephen Foster's song-writing and the Jim Crow minstrel tradition in which he wrote.[37] The dominant interpretation labels the blackface minstrel show as an entirely racist attack on black America, and the longer arc of performance reaching down to vaudeville, the early movies, and even television is solid evidence. But recent historians of blackface present a counter interpretation, focusing on the earlier decades down to the mid-1850s, that argues for a more complex, ambiguous picture. Rather than simply being fundamentally racist, the early Jim Crow and minstrel players, this interpretation argues, interwove a vicious parody of the African American with his trickster persona, a fumbling buffoon who rendered biting critiques — disguised and explicit — of the cruelties of slavery and the oppression of a master class both southern and northern. Taking off in exactly the years of the emergence of the American abolitionist movement, British emancipation, and anti-abolitionist riots, the early blackface shows were a means through which working-class white audiences wrestled with the emerging possibility of black emancipation. For the restless young white men of the growing industrial cities, minstrelsy was also a means of self-assertion, a rejection of the smooth sentimentalism of the parlor for the harsh, raw jangle of the tavern. The early blackface tradition was thus exceptionally multivocal, enforcing the racial boundary while it critiqued class and slavery. It comprised an extended white commentary on the American condition as a multiracial society, grounded — as one recent historian has put it — in "a deep recognition of African American charisma."[38]

In the early 1840s, as the country emerged from deep economic depression, the blackface tradition shifted from a more volatile working-class venue toward a new commercialized performance, increasingly shaped by a careful calculus of the tastes and demands of middling audiences.[39] Foster had his start in blackface in the early informal period and came of age with the commercializing trajectory. He sang his first songs at the age of nine in a neighborhood blackface group, and as a teenager he wrote songs for Thomas D. Rice, who had pioneered the genre in 1832 with his wildly popular "Jump Jim

Crow" dance. Immersed in African American work songs while clerking on the Cincinnati docks in the late 1840s, Foster sold the rights to his most important songs to one of the new commercial groups, E. P. Christy's Minstrels, in the early 1850s.[40]

The contradictory messages of blackface meant that it could serve as a bridge between popular culture and the antislavery movement. The first important and obvious such bridge was forged by the Hutchinson Family Singers in 1845, when they set their powerful abolitionist song "Get off the Track (for Emancipation)" to the tune of "Old Dan Tucker," recently popularized by the commercial Virginia Minstrels.[41] This bridging between blackface and antislavery was also manifested in Stephen Foster's popular hit "Oh Susannah" in the late 1840s: a sentimental song lamenting the division of a slave couple by sale became the theme song of the Gold Rush that immediately followed the Mexican War, the Wilmot Proviso debates, and the rise of the Free Soilers. Nostalgia, domesticity, slavery, and the frontier were all fused in the experience of this song.[42]

These ambiguities—and a coming cultural explosion—seem to have been expressed in Frederick Douglass's changing opinion of the minstrel shows. In 1848, writing in the *North Star* to defend the Hutchinson Singers from proslavery Democrats, he condemned the Virginia Minstrels and Christy's Minstrels, among others, as "the filthy scum of white society, who have stolen from us a complexion denied to them by nature, in which to make money, and pander to the corrupt taste of their white fellow-citizens."[43] In 1855, addressing the antislavery women of Rochester, New York, Douglass had changed his opinion:

It would seem almost absurd to say it, considering the use that has been made of them, that we have allies in the Ethiopian songs; those songs that constitute our national music, and without which we would have no national music. They are heart songs, and finest feelings of human nature are expressed in them. "Lucy Neal," "Old Kentucky Home," and "Uncle Ned," can make the heart sad as well as merry, and can call forth a tear as well as a smile. They waken the sympathies for the slave, in which antislavery principles take root, grow and flourish.[44]

Douglass's change of opinion may have been shaped by the slippery fusion of Foster's songs with Stowe's novel sweeping northern theaters since 1852. The publication of Foster's "Old Folks at Home," "Massa's in the Cold

Ground," and "My Old Kentucky Home" between June 1851 and January 1853 tracked the arc of the fugitive slave drama and then the rising popularity of *Uncle Tom's Cabin*. There was mutual borrowing: Stowe's novel was itself shaped by the blackface tradition, presenting the first rendition of African American dialect in sentimental prose; Foster's original model for his "Kentucky Home" was Stowe's Uncle Tom's cabin in Kentucky. Perhaps not coincidentally, both Stowe and Foster had spent formative years on the Ohio River in Cincinnati, literally a battleground of slavery and freedom. Both also shared a common sentimental, increasingly nostalgic culture, ironically driven by the same commerce that was overturning an idealized past. And both Stowe and Foster were immediately brought together in theaters across the North. Starting in the late summer of 1852, multiple theater companies were staging versions of *Uncle Tom's Cabin* in towns and cities throughout New England, New York, and the Midwest, and in Washington, Baltimore, and St. Louis. By early 1854, when it was regularly showing in towns across the Midwest, there were two shows running simultaneously in both Philadelphia and Boston, and five in New York City.[45]

Foster's songs immediately became a central feature of all of the *Uncle Tom's Cabin* productions. But these shows did not all share Stowe's message. Among the various texts, the George Aiken version, which in July 1853 started a long run in New York's National Theater, advanced Stowe's abolitionism, while the Henry Conway version, moving from Boston to P. T. Barnum's American Museum, was the model for a host of proslavery "Old Tom" shows that ran for decades following. Just as historians of American religion see the Civil War prefigured in the sectional schisms among Presbyterians, Methodists, and Baptists, historians of the stage see the Civil War prefigured in a theater war over *Uncle Tom's Cabin* running from the summer of 1852 to the spring of 1854—and an ensuing resolution of the implicit contradictions in the minstrel tradition. For the rest of the decade, the blackface minstrels—including Foster— wrote and sang the proslavery song of happy slaves, while antislavery forces— including both the Hutchinsons and the Republican Party—borrowed Foster's texts and tunes to convey the contrary message of the inhumanity of slavery.[46]

Thus there were complex interactions between the culture of race and the politics of slavery in the aftermath of the Compromise of 1850. Stowe's novel, Foster's songs, and the theatrical Uncle Tom concentrated attention on race and slavery. Some antislavery, some proslavery, some ambiguous: they all worked together to draw attention to linkages among slavery, domesticity, sentiment, and nostalgia in bourgeois culture; they were all involved in an explosion of cultural discourse on race and slavery that was unprecedented in scale and scope. Ironically, Stephen Douglas, the architect of the Kansas-Nebraska Act, missed this sea-change in northern culture, departing for a five-month grand tour of Europe in April 1853.[47] The white North was by no means suddenly converted to radical abolition. But the constant presence and power of the narrative, sound, and imagery created by Stowe, Foster, and the theater companies drove metaphoric action in a liminal moment, raising the political stakes of the slavery debate to new heights.

THESE STAKES CAME into play with a vengeance in the opening months of 1854 when Congress took up the Kansas-Nebraska bill, which by 23 January had morphed into explicit repeal of the Missouri Compromise and the virtual promise of a slaveholding future for the new Kansas Territory. Well before the Nebraska bill was enacted in late May, political antislavery sentiment had surged throughout the North, most formatively in the launching of local Republican parties in the upper Midwest.[48] Its first manifestation was another onslaught of petitions to Congress — typically couched as a constitutional protest "against the repeal of the Missouri Compromise." By the end of May, roughly 1,650 petitions were received by the U.S. House alone.[49]

   The congressional debate over and the protest against the Nebraska bill was played out in a public sphere resounding with the narrative, sounds, and images forged by Stowe, Foster, and the theater. In December 1853, when a thirteen-part series of antislavery lectures began at New York's Broadway Tabernacle, three different versions of Uncle Tom's Cabin were open in New York City, including P. T. Barnum's production at his American Museum. On 9 January, five days after the Nebraska bill was introduced in the Senate, the National Theater added a pivotal scene from the novel to the Aiken production, in which the Ohio senator apologized for supporting the Fugitive Slave Act in 1850, and his wife specifically condemned it.[50] On 16 January, the day before Stowe's brother Henry Ward Beecher spoke in the Tabernacle series, another version of the play opened at the Bowery Theater, with Thomas D. Rice playing the lead as Uncle Tom. A report in the New York Daily Tribune was thunderous, if perhaps overstated: the Bowery performance before "a sweaty steaming audience" of three thousand seemed to reflect "a gross, robust, unreasoning, sentiment of hatred of slavery in the very ground tier of society, that may be the germ of a tremendous social explosion. Do slaveholders count on the steady support of the masses . . . ? Let them as well reckon upon the quiet of the rumbling volcano."[51] In late February, *Uncle Tom's Cabin* was playing to packed houses in Harrisburg, Pennsylvania, the scene of many fugitive renditions. During that same week, a local pro-Nebraska meeting was taken over by antislavery men who voted overwhelmingly to condemn Douglas's effort to put Kansas "within reach of slavery." In the middle of March, a traveling production arrived in Milwaukee — two days after fugitive slave Joshua Glover had been rescued from federal authorities.[52] Stowe herself entered the political arena, leading a petition from 1,100 Massachusetts women, publishing her own "Appeal to the Women of the Free States." She also funded the circulation of a petition signed by 3,050 New England clergymen: their condemnation of the Nebraska bill as a "great moral wrong" and "subversive of all confidence in national engagements" reversed the strident defense of the Compromise of 1787.[53]

THE FULL IMPACT of the election of November 1854 was delayed for over a year, since the Thirty-fourth Congress would not convene until December 1855. Over these thirteen months, antislavery's hold on the northern public would coalesce from sentiment to structure. In that election, Democrats were reduced from a 63 percent majority among northerners in the Thirty-third Congress to a bare 18 percent in the Thirty-fourth, but their opponents were divided between declared anti-Nebraska Republicans (28%) and nativists (54%), more than half of whom had stated some sort of antislavery position. Over the course of 1855, while the nativists did well in the politics of a few states, the tide turned against them at the national level. The schism over slavery in their convention in the summer of 1855 undermined hopes for a united nativist front, while by autumn, armed conflict had broken out between proslavery and free-soil governments in Kansas. When the Thirty-fourth Congress convened in December 1855, its first order of business was the election of a speaker of the house, a struggle that lasted for three months and ended with the election of the Republican choice: antislavery nativist Nathaniel P. Banks. The result was a disaster for the nativists, since the speaker controlled committees in the House. But antislavery forces were jubilant:

"Banks's election" was, Theodore Parker wrote to Charles Sumner, "the first northern victory . . . since 1787."[54]

The election of 1854 was thus a fundamental realignment in the political order of the American North. But this transformation was not simply a result of the impact of the Kansas-Nebraska debate on the northern electorate. Rather, it was the result of a sequence of events unfolding between 1850 and 1854, one that is best understood in terms of a dynamic model of liminality and structure. The Fugitive Slave Act of 1850 put northern loyalties to "structure"—the Compromise of 1787 that linked Union and slavery—under extreme stress. Challenges to this cultural "structure" and its glue of national party advanced from massive petition drives to violence in the streets; if most northerners did not participate, they had to consider the implications of their cause, the liminal figure of the fugitive slave. Compounding these stresses was a background that I have touched on only very lightly—the destabilizing dynamic of economic recovery, sharp technological transition, and rapid urbanization. In this volatile and liminal environment, cultural interventions in text, music, and theater—some driven by antislavery conviction, some by ambiguity, some by commercial profit—were rapidly reshaping the public imagination in exactly the months when Senator Douglas was advancing the Nebraska bill.

The closing crisis in this prolonged drama thus came in the spring of 1854, and its resolution, the restructuring out of an anti-structural liminal "moment," came with the elections of 1854 and 1856. This was the critical break in antebellum politics, the forging of a strategic bloc of northerners who were now mobilized to oppose the interests of slavery and willing to rethink the Compromise of 1787. Decades later, Henry Wilson, the nativist-turned-Republican senator from Massachusetts, wrote that *Uncle Tom's Cabin* "was both a revelation and a summons." The book, Wilson argued, had been a "needful preparation for the arguments and appeals of Republican presses and speakers that were soon to follow." In the 1856 election, "many votes cast for Fremont were but the rich fruitage of seed broadcast by Harriet Beecher Stowe." And the sympathetic break that Stowe and Foster had forged would work upon many Union soldiers as they marched into the South during the Civil War.[55]

Notes

1. Edward Ayers, *What Caused the Civil War? Reflections on the South and Southern History* (New York: Norton, 2005), 132–42, 138 (quotation). See also the discussion in Elizabeth Varon, *Disunion: The Coming of the American Civil War, 1789–1859* (Chapel Hill: University of North Carolina Press, 2008), 3–4.

2. Staughton Lynd, "The Compromise of 1787," *Political Science Quarterly* 81 (June 1966): 225–50; Paul Finkelman, *An Imperfect Union: Slavery, Federalism, and Comity* (Chapel Hill: University of North Carolina Press, 1981); David Waldstreicher, *Slavery's Constitution: From Revolution to Ratification* (New York: Hill and Wang, 2009); George Van Cleve, *A Slaveholders' Union: Slavery, Politics, and the Constitution in the Early Republic* (Chicago: University of Chicago, 2010), 107–83.

3. Eric Foner, *Free Soil, Free Labor, Free Men: The Ideology of the Republican Party before the Civil War* (New York: Oxford University Press, 1970), 94–95; Michael F. Holt, *The Fate of Their Country: Politicians, Slavery Extension, and the Coming of the Civil War* (New York: Hill and Wang, 2004), 107. See also David Potter, *The Impending Crisis, 1848–1861* (New York: Harper and Row, 1976), 163–65; William Gienapp, *The Origins of the Republican Party, 1852–1856* (New York: Oxford University Press, 1987), 72; and Varon, *Disunion,* 107. Quotation from "Appeal" in *Congressional Globe,* Senate, 33rd Cong., 1st sess., 281–82. For a dissenting voice arguing that the impact of the "Appeal" has been entirely overblown, see Mark F. Neely Jr., "The Kansas-Nebraska Act in American Political Culture: The Road to Bladensburg and the *Appeal to the Independent Democrats,*" in *The Nebraska-Kansas Act of 1854,* ed. John R. Wunder and Joann M. Moss (Lincoln: University of Nebraska Press, 2008), 13–46.

4. Holt, *The Fate of Their Country,* 107.

5. Graham Alexander Peck, "Abraham Lincoln and the Triumph of an Antislavery Nationalism," *Journal of the Abraham Lincoln Association* 28 (Summer 2007): 1–27; Melinda Lawson, *Patriot Fires: Forging a New American Nationalism in the Civil War North* (Lawrence: University Press of Kansas, 2002); Susan-Mary Grant, *North over South: Northern Nationalism and the American Identity in the Antebellum Era* (Lawrence: University Press of Kansas, 2000).

6. Here I concur with and extend David Reynolds's *The Pen Is Mightier Than the Sword: Uncle Tom's Cabin and the Battle for America* (New York: Norton, 2011).

7. James M. McPherson, *Abraham Lincoln and the Second American Revolution* (New York: Oxford University Press, 1992); Bruce Ackerman, *We the People,* vol. 1, *Foundations* (Cambridge, Mass.: Harvard University Press, 1991).

8. Jürgen Habermas, *The Structural Transformation of the Public Sphere: An Inquiry into a Category of Bourgeois Society,* trans. Thomas Burger (Cambridge, Mass.: Harvard University Press, 1989); Habermas, *Between Facts and Norms: Contributions toward a Discourse Theory of Law and Democracy,* trans. William Rehng (Cambridge, Mass.: Harvard University Press, 1996).

9. Bernard Bailyn, "The Challenge of Modern Historiography," *American Historical Review* 87 (February 1982): 1–24.

10. Daniel Dayan and Elihu Katz, *Media Events: The Live Broadcasting of History* (Cambridge, Mass.: Harvard University Press, 1992); William Gamson, *Talking Politics* (New York: Cambridge University Press, 1992); Todd Gitlin, *Media Unlimited: How the Torrent of Images and Sounds Overwhelms Our Lives* (New York: Metropolitan Books, 2002).

11. Émile Durkheim, *The Elementary Forms of the Religious Life*, trans. Joseph Ward Swain (New York: George Allen and Unwin, 1915), esp. 463–74.

12. William H. Sewell Jr., *Logics of History: Social Theory and Social Transformation* (Chicago: University of Chicago Press, 2005), 225–70; Victor Turner, *Dramas, Fields, and Metaphors: Symbolic Action in Human Society* (Ithaca, N.Y.: Cornell University Press, 1974), 37–42, 275–94; Max Weber, *The Theory of Social and Economic Organization*, trans. A. M. Henderson and Talcott Parsons (New York: Oxford University Press, 1947), 358–78, 386–92; Sabini Mihelj, "National Media Events: From Displays of Unity to Enactments of Division," *European Journal of Cultural Studies* 11 (November 2008): 471–88. See also the essays in the "Special Section: Logics of History," *Social Science History* 32 (Winter 2008): 535–95.

13. Martin Van Buren to Thomas Ritchie, 13 January 1827, Martin Van Buren Papers, Library of Congress. For a key analysis of the parties comprising structures, see Donald J. Ratcliffe, "The Decline of Antislavery Politics, 1815–1840," in *Contesting Slavery: The Politics of Bondage and Freedom in the New American Nation*, ed. John Craig Hammond and Matthew Mason (Charlottesville: University of Virginia Press, 2011), 267–90.

14. Michael F. Holt, *The Political Crisis of the 1850s* (New York: Norton, 1978), 101–20; John Joseph Wallis, "Constitutions, Corporations, and Corruption: American States and Constitutional Change, 1842–1852," *Journal of Economic History* 65 (March 2005): 211–56; Wallis, "Founding Errors: Making Democracy Safe for America" (unpublished paper, December 2008).

15. Joel H. Silbey, "'To One or Another of These Parties Every Man Belongs': The American Political Experience from Andrew Jackson to the Civil War," in *Contesting Democracy: Substance & Structure in American Political History, 1775–2000*, ed. Byron E. Shafer and Anthony J. Badger (Lawrence: University Press of Kansas, 2001), 68.

16. Joel H. Silbey, *The Partisan Imperative: The Dynamics of American Politics before the Civil War* (New York: Oxford University Press, 1985); Silbey, *The American Political Nation, 1838–1893* (Stanford, Cal.: Stanford University Press, 1991); Richard L. McCormick, *The Party Period and Public Policy: American Politics from the Age of Jackson to the Progressive Era* (New York: Oxford University Press, 1988); J. David Hacker, "A Census-Based Count of the Civil War Dead," *Civil War History* 57 (December 2011): 306–47.

17. Holt, *Political Crisis of the 1850s;* Gienapp, *Origins of the Republican Party.*

18. Robert W. Fogel, *Without Consent or Contract: The Rise and Fall of American Slavery* (New York: Norton, 1989), 354–69; Michael F. Holt, "The Politics of Impatience: The Origins of Know Nothingism," *Journal of American History* 60

(September 1973): 309–31; Mark Voss-Hubbard, *Beyond Party: Cultures of Antiparti-sanship in Northern Politics before the Civil War* (Baltimore: Johns Hopkins University Press, 2002), 17–37.

19. For different approaches to nativist-antislavery "fusion," see Tyler Anbinder, *Nativism and Slavery: The Northern Know Nothings and the Politics of the 1850s* (New York: Oxford University Press, 1992), 44–45, 52–102; Bruce Laurie, *Beyond Garrison: Antislavery and Social Reform* (New York: Cambridge University Press, 2005), 279–82; Voss-Hubbard, *Beyond Party*, 127–28, 171–75; and Ronald P. Formisano, *The Birth of Mass Political Parties: Michigan, 1827–1861* (Princeton, N.J.: Princeton University Press, 1971), 242–43.

20. Mark C. Carnes, *Secret Ritual and Manhood in Victorian America* (New Haven, Conn.: Yale University Press, 1989).

21. *Tribune* (Providence), quoted in *Harrisburg Herald*, 24 December 1854, quoted in Anbinder, *Nativism and Slavery*, 99; George F. Hoar, *Autobiography of Seventy Years* (New York: Scribner's and Sons, 1903), 189.

22. Anbinder, *Nativism and Slavery*, 164–74, 206–10; Gienapp, *Origins of the Republican Party*, 179–85, 259–64; Potter, *Impending Crisis*, 254–55.

23. Holt, *The Fate of Their Country*, 107.

24. Holman Hamilton, *Prologue to Conflict: The Crisis and Compromise of 1850* (Lexington: University of Kentucky Press, 1964), 168–72, 43–44; Varon, *Disunion*, 210–31; *Congressional Globe*, House, 31st Cong., 1st sess., 21:195 (Taylor, 21 January); 21:244 (Clay, 29 January); Appendix:276 (Webster, 7 March).

25. *American* (New York), excerpted in *North Star* (Rochester), 24 October 1850, 3; Richard J. Carwardine, *Evangelicals and Politics in Antebellum America* (Knoxville: University of Tennessee Press, 1997), 180–86, 181, 184 (quotations). See also Laura L. Mitchell, "'Matters of Justice between Man and Man': Northern Divines, the Bible, and the Fugitive Slave Act of 1850," in *Religion and the Antebellum Debate over Slavery*, ed. John R. McKivigan and Mitchell Snay (Athens: University of Georgia Press, 1998), 134–65, and Stanley W. Campbell, *Slavecatchers: Enforcement of the Fugitive Slave Law, 1850–1860* (Chapel Hill: University of North Carolina Press, 1968), 63–79.

26. For example, see Edward Magdol, *The Anti-Slavery Rank and File: A Social Profile of the Abolitionists' Constituency* (Westport, Conn.: Greenwood Press, 1986), 130–31; Campbell, *Slavecatchers*, 25.

27. I have not attempted to count the petitions for the entire period, but a keyword search in the *Journal* of the House (in "A Century of Lawmaking for a New Nation," http://memory.loc.gov/ammem/amlaw/) for "slavery" and "petition" or "memorial" between 1815 and 1861, generating the number of days when these terms appear, shows high points in 1835–39 and 1847–51. Detailed petition counts for the 25th and 31st–33rd Congresses indicates that the 1837–39 Gag Rule and Texas petitioning campaigns clearly generated the highest volume, followed by 1850–51 and then 1854–55.

28. *Congressional Globe,* Senate, 31st Cong., 1st sess., 21:236 (Seward, 28 January).

29. Zachary Taylor, "Special Message, to the Senate of the United States," 23 January 1850, in Gerhard Peters and John T. Woolley, The American Presidency Project, www.presidency.ucsb.edu/ws/?pid=68071.

30. William L. Andrews, *To Tell a Free Story: The First Century of Afro-American Autobiography, 1760–1865* (Urbana: University of Illinois Press, 1986), 167–204; Nancy Kang, "'As If I Had Entered a Paradise': Fugitive Slave Narratives and Cross-Border Literary History," *African American Review* 39 (Fall 2005): 431–57.

31. Michael F. Holt, *The Rise and Fall of the American Whig Party: Jacksonian Politics and the Onset of the Civil War* (New York: Oxford University Press, 1999), 635–72; Formisano, *Birth of Mass Political Parties,* 210 (quotation).

32. Michael D. Pierson, *Free Hearts, Free Homes: Gender and American Antislavery Politics* (Chapel Hill: University of North Carolina Press, 2003), 71–96, 150–63; Dawn Coleman, "The Unsentimental Woman Preacher of Uncle Tom's Cabin," *American Literature* 80 (June 2008): 265–92.

33. *The Diary of Ellen Birdseye Wheaton,* ed. Donald Gordon (Boston: N.p., 1923), 131; *The Diary of James A. Garfield,* vol. 1, *1848–1871,* ed. Harry James Brown and Frederick D. Williams (East Lansing: Michigan State University Press, 1967), 145–46, 181; John Jay to Charles Sumner, 20 December 1852, Charles Sumner Papers, Harvard University. See also Barbara Hochman, *Uncle Tom's Cabin and the Reading Revolution* (Amherst: University of Massachusetts Press, 2008), 14–19, and Ronald J. Zboray and Mary Saracino Zboray, *Everyday Ideas: Socioliterary Experience among Antebellum New Englanders* (Knoxville: University of Tennessee Press, 2006), 94, 123, 132, 185, 249–50, 263–64.

34. Turner, *Dramas, Fields, and Metaphors,* 25–32; Hochman, *Uncle Tom's Cabin,* 26–50.

35. Jo-Ann Morgan, *Uncle Tom's Cabin as Visual Culture* (Columbia: University of Missouri Press, 2007), 3, 10n28, 31, 74–82, 189; Stephen A. Hirsch, "Uncle Tomitudes: The Popular Reaction to *Uncle Tom's Cabin,*" *Studies in the American Renaissance* (1978): 317–19, 322; Reynolds, *Mightier Than the Sword,* 132–36; *Bangor Daily Whig and Courier,* 25 December 1852, 2.

36. Hirsch, "Uncle Tomitudes," 311–15.

37. Robert C. Toll, *Black Up: The Minstrel Show in Nineteenth-Century America* (New York: Oxford University Press, 1974); Eric Lott, *Love and Theft: Blackface Minstrelsy and the American Working Class* (New York: Oxford University Press, 1993); Dale Cockrell, *Demons of Disorder: Early Blackface Minstrels and Their World* (New York: Cambridge University Press, 1997); Ken Emerson, *Doo-Dah! Stephen Foster and the Rise of American Popular Culture* (New York: Simon and Schuster, 1997); W. T. Lhamon, *Jump Jim Crow: Lost Plays, Lyrics, and Street Prose in the First Atlantic Popular Culture* (Cambridge, Mass.: Harvard University Press, 2003). See also Heather S. Nathans, *Slavery and Sentiment on the American Stage, 1787–1861: Lifting the Veil of Black* (New York: Cambridge University Press, 2009); Melinda

Lawson, "Imagining Slavery: Representations of the Peculiar Institution on the Northern Stage, 1776–1860," *Journal of the Civil War Era* 1 (March 2011): 25–55. For the more established understanding, see Jean Baker, *Affairs of Party: The Political Culture of the Northern Democrats* (Ithaca, N.Y.: Cornell University Press, 1983), 213–247, and Alexander Saxton, *The Rise and Fall of the White Republic: Class Politics and Mass Culture in Nineteenth-Century America* (New York: Verso, 1990), 165–83.

    38. Toll, *Black Up,* 33–34, 73–76; Lott, *Love and Theft,* 111–35; Lhamon, *Jump Jim Crow,* 91 (quotation).

    39. Toll, *Black Up,* 30–33; Lott, *Love and Theft,* 136–68; Cockrell, *Demons of Disorder,* 32–54, 149–62.

    40. Emerson, *Doo-Dah!* 50–71; Toll, *Black Up,* 36.

    41. Scott Gac, *Singing for Freedom: The Hutchinson Family Singers and the Nineteenth-Century Culture of Reform* (New Haven, Conn.: Yale University Press, 2007), 177–82.

    42. Lott, *Love and Theft,* 190–210.

    43. "The Hutchinson Family—Hunkerism," *North Star* (Rochester), 27 October 1848, 2.

    44. Frederick Douglass, *The Anti-Slavery Movement: A Lecture by Frederick Douglass, before the Rochester Ladies Anti-Slavery Society* (Rochester, 1855), 40, published in *Frederick Douglass' Paper* (Rochester), 23 March 1855, 2–3. See also Gac, *Singing for Freedom,* 203–205.

    45. Harry Birdoff, *The World's Greatest Hit: Uncle Tom's Cabin* (New York: S. F. Vanni, 1947), 101–26; Hirsch, "Uncle Tomitudes," 320–25; Thomas F. Gossett, *Uncle Tom's Cabin and American Culture* (Dallas: Southern Methodist University Press, 1985), 260–83; Reynolds, *Mightier Than the Sword,* 136–46.

    46. Birdoff, *The World's Greatest Hit,* 87–99, 107–26; Toll, *Black Up,* 91–97; Lott, *Love and Theft,* 223–33; Emerson, *Doo-Dah!* 191–200, 237–38; Sarah Meer, *Uncle Tom Mania: Slavery, Minstrelsy, and Transatlantic Culture in the 1850s* (Athens: University of Georgia Press, 2005), 19–130; Mark E. Neely Jr., *The Boundaries of American Political Culture in the Civil War Era* (Chapel Hill: University of North Carolina Press, 2005), 97–128.

    47. Robert W. Johannsen, *Stephen A. Douglas* (New York: Oxford University Press, 1973), 382–86.

    48. Richard H. Sewell, *Ballots for Freedom: Antislavery Politics in the United States, 1837–1860* (New York: Oxford University Press, 1976), 239–51, 264.

    49. Petition count from House *Journal,* 33rd Cong.

    50. Birdoff, *The World's Greatest Hit,* 101; Lynck C. Johnson, "'Liberty Is Never Cheap': Emerson, 'The Fugitive Slave Law,' and the Antislavery Lecture Series at the Broadway Tabernacle," *New England Quarterly* 76 (December 2003): 259–324.

    51. *New York Daily Tribune,* 17 January 1854, 7. See also Lhamon, *Jump Jim Crow,* 90–91.

    52. Gerald G. Eggert, "The Impact of the Fugitive Slave Law on Harrisburg: A Case Study," *Pennsylvania Magazine of History and Biography* 109 (October 1985):

568–69; H. Robert Baker, *The Rescue of Joshua Glover: A Fugitive Slave, the Constitution, and the Coming of the Civil War* (Athens: Ohio University Press, 2006), 59–60.

53. Harriet Beecher Stowe, "An Appeal to the Women of the Free States," *Independent* (New York), 23 February 1854, 57; *Congressional Globe*, Senate, 33rd Cong., 1st sess., 617–23 (14 March 1854); *Right of Petition. New England Clergymen. Remarks of Messrs. Everett . . . on the Memorial of Some 3050 Clergymen . . . Remonstrating against the Passage of the Nebraska Bill* (Washington, 1854).

54. Theodore Parker to Charles Sumner, 16 February 1856, Charles Sumner Papers, Harvard University; Anbinder, *Nativism and Slavery*, 164–74, 197–202; Gienapp, *Origins of the Republican Party*, 179–85, 240–48; Nicole Etcheson, *Bleeding Kansas: Contested Liberty in the Civil War Era* (Lawrence: University Press of Kansas, 2004), 28–88; Fred H. Harrington, "The First Northern Victory," *Journal of Southern History* 5 (May 1939): 186–205.

55. Henry Wilson, *History of the Rise and Fall of the Slave Power in America*, 3 vols. (Boston, 1872–1877), 2:519. See also David Grant, "Uncle Tom's Cabin and the Triumph of Republican Rhetoric," *New England Quarterly* 71 (1999): 429–48, 430 (quotation). On Union soldiers, see Chandra Manning, *What This Cruel War Was Over: Soldiers, Slavery, and the Civil War* (New York: Knopf, 2007), esp. 120, 269n35, and James Oakes, *Freedom National: The Destruction of Slavery in the United States, 1861–1865* (New York: Norton, 2013), 48–83, 163–71, 302–8, 533–34n13.

PART TWO

PARTIES
AND
PARTICIPATION

★ ANDREW W. ROBERTSON ★

Jeffersonian Parties, Politics, and Participation

The Tortuous Trajectory of American Democracy

Since Alexis de Tocqueville published his famous work, the idea of American democracy has often seemed inextricably bound up with the notion of American exceptionalism. The scholarship of the past twenty years, however, especially among colonial historians, has called this exceptionalism into question. Atlantic historians, global historians, and early modern European historians working in a comparative context have all contributed to a far more complicated understanding of the ideological, institutional, and cultural *origins* of American democracy. Historians of the eighteenth-century United States now generally accept the idea that the ideology, discourses, and practices of a larger world intruded on and heavily influenced Americans' ideas of self-rule.[1]

The same cannot be said for scholarship on the expansion of American democracy in the nineteenth century, however. Historians of American democracy in this era have been almost universally exceptionalist, and many still apply a whiggish historical gloss to the period after 1800 — particularly to the years when America is said to have achieved "universal" manhood suffrage and ushered in the Age of the Common Man. The whiggish historians, who have generally celebrated the extension of liberty over the course of history, have seen steady progress toward democratization from the American Revolution onward. They have also assumed a causal link between the extension of suffrage laws to unpropertied adult white males and the surge in voter turnout at the polls. For these whiggish historians and their latter-day followers, the election of Andrew Jackson marks a watershed event in the democratization of American political culture.[2]

This uncomplicated trajectory ignores the tortuous ways in which American democratic ideology and practices ebbed and flowed — in fact, were redefined and sometimes reduced—in the years preceding the Civil War. First of all, turnout waxed and waned from the 1790s to the 1850s. For the most part, sharp rises in turnout did not immediately follow changes in suffrage laws. Second, issues more than anything else drove elections in the period from 1800 to 1816. Third, the first party system was in actuality twenty-four state party systems; party competition and identity were based on longstanding local political rivalries and, equally importantly, on durable Atlantic affinities with either Britain or France. Fourth, at the same time some northern Jeffersonian Republicans were working to secure voting rights for unpropertied white males, they also began exploiting gender and race prejudice to disqualify women and free men of color from voting.

Suffrage Laws and Participation: Challenging Myths of Democratization

One of the most persistent myths about the democratization of American political culture is the idea that the election of Andrew Jackson was a watershed event. In fact, empirical evidence gathered in the 1960s by J. R. Pole and Richard P. McCormick shows that turnout in many states was significantly higher in the age of Jefferson than it was in 1828 (see table 1).[3] Yet Pole's and McCormick's evidence still has not been accepted by such recent political historians as Sean Wilentz, Alexander Keyssar, or Daniel Walker Howe. In *Rise of American Democracy,* Wilentz maintains that politics somehow did not engage the public at large until 1828.[4] Keyssar's *Right to Vote* and even Howe's magisterial *What Hath God Wrought* also emphasize that political practice became more democratic after 1828.[5]

Yet the ascendancy of the unpropertied white male voter was hardly a new phenomenon in 1828. As table 1 indicates, between 1800 and 1820, upward of 60 percent of adult men were voting in states like New Hampshire, Massachusetts, and Pennsylvania, and similar turnout levels were evident among white males in states like North Carolina and Tennessee.[6]

A central reason that many historians see the Jacksonian era as pivotal is because they assume that suffrage laws changed prior to the 1828 election to include propertyless adult white males. Even the most widely respected college textbooks still assert that turnout rose as a direct and immediate result of those changes in suffrage laws. In other words, Jackson's election ushered in "The Age of the Common Man," and voters trooped to the polls.

Table 1. Pre-1828 peak turnout and 1828 turnout

State	Pre-1828 peak turnout (% and year)	1828 turnout (%)
Maine[a]	62.0 (1812)	42.7
New Hampshire	80.8 (1814)	76.5
Vermont	79.9 (1812)	55.8
Massachusetts[a]	67.4 (1812)	25.7
Rhode Island	49.4 (1812)	18.0
Connecticut	54.4 (1819)	27.1
New York	41.5 (1810)	70.4
New Jersey	71.8 (1808)	70.9
Pennsylvania	71.5 (1808)	56.6
Delaware	81.9 (1804)	—[b]
Maryland	69.0 (1820)	76.2
Virginia	25.9 (1800)	27.6
North Carolina	70.0 (1823)	56.8
South Carolina	—[c]	—[b]
Georgia	62.3 (1812)	35.9
Kentucky	74.4 (1820)	70.7
Tennessee	80.0 (1817)	49.8
Alabama	97.6 (1819)	36.3
Mississippi	79.8 (1823)	53.6
Louisiana	34.2 (1812)	36.3
Ohio	46.5 (1822)	75.8
Indiana	52.4 (1822)	68.3
Illinois	55.8 (1822)	51.9
Missouri	71.9 (1820)	54.3

Note: Pre-1828 peak turnout was most typically derived from gubernatorial elections because the power and patronage rewards in the first party system were concentrated in the states.

[a] Figures for the District of Maine before 1820 are treated separately from Massachusetts, and the figures for Massachusetts do not include Maine.
[b] Delaware and South Carolina did not have popular votes for president in 1828. The presidential electors were selected by the legislatures.
[c] South Carolina voting data is incomplete.

Table 2 Pre-1828 peak turnout and suffrage reform

State	Pre-1828 peak turnout (% and year)	Year of suffrage reform
New Hampshire	80.8 (1814)	1792
Vermont	79.9 (1812)	1791
Massachusetts	67.4 (1812)	1821[a]
Rhode Island	49.4 (1812)	1842
Connecticut	54.4 (1819)	1818
New York	41.5 (1810)	1826[b]
New Jersey	71.8 (1808)	1807[c]
Pennsylvania	71.5 (1808)	1790
Delaware	81.9 (1804)	1792
Maryland	69.0 (1820)	1801
Virginia	25.9 (1800)	1850
North Carolina	70.0 (1823)	1842[d]
South Carolina	—[e]	1865
Georgia	62.3 (1812)	1789
Kentucky	74.4 (1820)	1792
Tennessee	80.0 (1817)	1796
Alabama	97.6 (1819)	1819
Mississippi	79.8 (1823)	1817
Louisiana	34.2 (1812)	1845
Ohio	46.5 (1822)	1803
Indiana	52.4 (1822)	1816
Illinois	55.8 (1822)	1818
Missouri	71.9 (1820)	1820

Note: "Year of suffrage reform" is the year in which all property and taxpayer requirements for adult (white) males to vote were eliminated.

[a] Massachusetts figures exclude Maine for 1812. The property requirement for voting in Massachusetts was sufficiently low and sufficiently leniently enforced as to permit most adult male inhabitants to vote. See Keyssar, *Right to Vote*, 331, and Williamson, *American Suffrage*, 190–94.

[b] The New York constitution of 1821 abolished the two-tier suffrage and all property requirements for adult white male inhabitants. It continued, however, a property requirement for free men of color. In 1826, New York abolished the taxpaying requirement for suffrage.

[c] The New Jersey constitution of 1776 provided that "all inhabitants" could vote, without specifying race or gender, if they were heads of household worth £50 New Jersey currency. After 1807, the legislature extended the suffrage to those

This was in fact true in one important but exceptional case. New York abolished its property requirements for adult male suffrage in 1821 and its tax requirements in 1826.[7] In 1828, with the suffrage extended to all adult male New Yorkers, the state's voter turnout spiked.[8] Moreover, because New York had the largest population of any state, that election marked a national tipping point: for the first time, a majority of adult white male Americans could vote.

The larger story, however, is much more complicated than this suggests because political culture varied dramatically from state to state. First of all, New York State lagged behind all other northern states except Rhode Island in expanding its suffrage; in fact, by the time New York eliminated property and taxpayer requirements for voting, seventeen other states, North and South, had already done so. Second, in twelve of those states, changes in suffrage laws did not lead immediately to a surge in turnout. Third, in a few exceptional cases such as New Jersey, voters who were not formally qualified to vote had turned out anyway, and the suffrage laws were subsequently adjusted to reflect the new reality.

Table 2 indicates when each state eliminated property and taxpaying requirements for suffrage. A few states in addition to New York did experience a spike in turnout immediately following the extension of the suffrage. Both Connecticut and New Jersey witnessed a sharp increase in turnout after property restrictions were dropped, although New Jersey is again a special case. Alabama and Missouri both experienced their highest turnouts in the first election following their admissions as states. In New Hampshire, Vermont, Pennsylvania, Delaware, Maryland, Georgia, Ohio, Kentucky, and Tennessee, voter turnout did not peak until significantly after the suffrage was extended. In Massachusetts, adult male participation was already very wide in 1812, although formal property requirements were not actually eliminated until 1821. North Carolina's turnout peaked in 1823 at 70 percent, although that state did not completely repeal its property requirements until 1842.[9]

---

propertyless white males who paid any taxes but also eliminated woman suffrage and the vote by free people of color.

[d] North Carolina abolished its two-tier suffrage entirely in 1835 with a new state constitution. The property requirement for the lower tier of suffrage had been sufficiently lenient that 70 percent of free adult male inhabitants could vote in 1823. The constitution of 1835 also eliminated the right of free men of color to vote.

[e] South Carolina voting data is incomplete.

Turnout in the 1790s:
Rising Competition and Mobilization

Party competition in the 1790s tended to focus on the governor because the state executive exercised the most power in the voters' lives. State policy was far more important than federal policy in the early years of the republic. The governor held the levers of patronage, which were much more important than the few federal positions available through the federal executive or legislative branches. Presidential elections registered consistently lower turnout than gubernatorial elections in the 1790s because many states changed their laws regarding the selection of presidential electors. Massachusetts, New York, Pennsylvania, and Virginia changed from popular to legislative elections in the years from 1788 to 1800.[10] In almost all of the states, turnout remained at a level between 30 and 50 percent of adult white males before 1800; this was true even in those states where turnout before the American Revolution has been estimated at higher than 50 percent.

Why were elections such relatively low-turnout events in New England in the 1790s? Part of the reason seems to be that the political parties did not really develop a mass base until 1796. Before that, elections were not contested under party labels, and newspapers did not assume that part of their function was to rally readers to vote consistently for one political party over another. Party organizations were only embryonic affairs in the 1790s, and perhaps most importantly, the mass base of New England voters were not mobilized, polarized, or actively engaged in mass participatory politics at election time.

In the Middle States, the situation was similar. Pennsylvania had the broadest suffrage of any state in the 1790s, and New Jersey allowed property holders of £50 freehold, not restricted by race or gender, to vote. New Jersey's suffrage was wider than it might seem, since the law stipulated that the freehold be valued in the vastly depreciated Revolutionary War currency.

Despite relatively few restrictions on voting, participation levels in all of the Middle States hovered around 30 percent until the very end of the 1790s. Why this was so is an interesting question. Again, the reason was not restrictions on voting but the lack of sufficient incentive for voters to go to the polls. The issues that engaged political elites and the middling sort in the first half of the 1790s—Hamiltonian funding and assumption, the Bank of the United States, and the Jay Treaty—did not provoke a surge in turnout. Voters, as opposed to officeholders, had not yet found an efficacious means of expressing themselves at the polls. In order to vote, the mass base needed to be engaged in the issues in a deliberative fashion, deciding what needed to be done, a point that Daniel Peart demonstrates applied just as forcefully during the waning years of the first party system as it did at the outset. The parties had to feel a credible need to compete for voters. They needed to have a communications network through the press that allowed them to communicate with their mass base. The parties needed to feel this competition so clearly that they would court the voters by embracing policy alternatives and engaging or exploiting local rivalries and interests to woo potential voters to the polls.

Beginning in 1798, three factors came together that helped propel a surge in turnout, particularly in the South and Middle States. The Quasi-War with France provoked a longstanding rivalry between the Federalists and the Republicans, and the Federalists vehemently raised the cry of a French invasion after the XYZ Affair. Nascent Atlantic rivalries between the pro-British Federalists and the pro-French Republicans helped to stir durable allegiance to the rival parties. In addition, the real fears connected to a French invasion and later the very real antagonism by the Republicans to the passage of the Alien and Sedition Acts, and the selective enforcement of the Sedition Act against Republican editors, made the Republicans all the more energized to go to the polls.

At the very end of the 1790s, turnout figures show a rise in the vote for governor. At this point, for the first time, the parties began competing for voters by presenting the issues as stark alternatives. This engaged electors. By 1799, the parties in Pennsylvania had begun to successfully exploit longstanding local and ethnic rivalries that extended back to the beginning of the eighteenth century. The Federalist Party was able to mobilize the prosperous eastern counties surrounding Philadelphia including Chester, Montgomery, and Lancaster. The Federalists were also successful in fielding candidates and attracting the interests of voters in the rapidly growing area around Pittsburgh. The Republicans, on the other hand, mobilized the urban middling and lower orders to vote along with the Scots-Irish in the central portion of the state, and in the mountainous regions of northeastern and western Pennsylvania.

In Maryland, turnout figures for congressional elections fluctuated greatly by county in the years before parties became well-established as mass-based organizations. Over the course of the 1790s, counties on the western shore of the Chesapeake Bay generally had consistently higher turnouts than the counties of southern Maryland or the lower eastern shore. Landholding, local organization, and local interest determined whether voters turned out in a particular county during the 1790s. By 1800, however, with a very competitive presidential election, an antithetical presentation of issues, the proliferation of party newspapers, and the extension of party organization, the turnout levels in Maryland were generally above 50 percent throughout the state.

In Virginia, as in Maryland, voter turnout rose in the 1790s and spiked in the years 1798 to 1800. These last years of the eighteenth century marked the highest turnout recorded in Virginia, and in some counties, these turnout rates were not surpassed until the elimination of all property requirements in 1850. Only congressional and presidential electors were elected by popular vote, and surviving county-level records of 1790s congressional elections are uneven. From the congressional records that have survived, however, there is a clear trend toward higher turnout in the later 1790s. In the extant records, the last two congressional election years, 1797 and 1799, show a clustering around 40 percent of the total adult white male population. This is all the more remarkable given Virginia's history of low-turnout elections, which extended through most of the Jacksonian era, continued after Reconstruction, and extended well into the late twentieth century. These last few elections of the eighteenth century in Virginia may have constituted a brief moment of uncharacteristically democratic activity, when both parties were competitive and mobilized around critical issues.

Republican Mobilization after the Revolution of 1800: Issues Drive Elections

Historians who see mass political mobilization as occurring for the first time during the Age of Jackson often describe pre-Jacksonian political mobilization as centering on personality and deference.[11] Although personality politics and the politics of deference played a role, the Jeffersonian era also saw a very different dynamic. For the most part, serious policy considerations—issues involving international trade and foreign affairs, federal taxation and banking policies, the relationship of church and state, and others—drove elections during this period.

In the period between 1808 and 1816, Jeffersonian participation in many states reached its peak, and this high point of Jeffersonian participation was driven in large part by the issues (see discussion below). The period from 1790 to 1824 saw the rise of ad hoc political organizations, some closely connected to the parties and some arising from popular ferment. These included democratic societies, literary societies, coffee house tontines, militias, and formal party organizations, all of which were enlisted and exploited by the Republican and Federalist parties.[12] In many ways, these highly political social organizations served as direct conduits for focusing public opinion. Such issues were publicized by a burgeoning network of partisan newspapers, which tended to frame issues in symmetrical, binary fashion.[13]

The year 1800 marked the first successful national mobilization effort by both Republicans and Federalists. In those states that held popular elections for the presidential electors, the contest between the electors pledged to John Adams and Charles Cotesworth Pinckney and those pledged to Thomas Jefferson and Aaron Burr was quite keen.

International issues frequently intruded on American politics. For instance, foreign policy questions obsessed elites and the broader public from the Genet Affair through the Treaty of Ghent in 1814. Other critical issues also drove public debate and mass participation: the relationship of church and state was one visible issue. Popular historians like to cite the quote from the *Gazette of the United States:* "At the present solemn moment the only question to be asked by every American, laying his hand on his heart, is 'Shall I continue in allegiance TO GOD — AND A RELIGIOUS PRESIDENT; or impiously declare for JEFFERSON — AND NO GOD!'"[14] This invocation demonstrates that the cultural conflict in the election of 1800 was as vituperative as the culture war politics of our own era. Yet that characteristically blunt statement from the flagship Federalist newspaper actually makes reference to a much larger and more serious issue that engaged the parties. The New England Federalists referred to Jefferson's alleged "atheism" to secure their base among observant Congregationalists and Episcopalians. But among Baptists and other dissenting sects, Jefferson was hailed as the apostle of religious liberty. Federalists hoped that the "atheism" issue would prompt observant Christians from these denominations to abandon the Republican Party and join the Federalists, an attempt that was mostly unsuccessful. The relationship of church and state was one of the more fraught issues facing partisans between 1790 and 1800. Although personality and scandal certainly intruded into popular politics, particularly in the 1790s, serious issues including trade, taxation, and state's rights frequently emerged in debates for mass consumption in the Jeffersonian era.

In the years after 1800, a new generation of politicians began to contest elections. The younger generation of Federalists and Republicans were getting more adept at campaigning than their elders, as Kenneth Owen's essay in this volume illustrates; they were growing accustomed to the idea of popular deliberation, and the voters responded with the beginnings of a consistent party identification.

The years after 1800 were a time of increasing turnout, as table 3 indicates. These elections from 1800 to 1807 occurred at a time when the property restrictions for voting had already disappeared from many states. In the North, Massachusetts and New Jersey retained only minimal property requirements. In the southern states, limited property restrictions in Tennessee and North Carolina applied to both free white men and free men of color. In all of these states except New Jersey, a majority of free men began voting. In states where the governor was elected by popular vote, the turnout fluctuated between 31 and 58 percent in Massachusetts, 39 and 68 percent of adult males in New Hampshire, and 47 and 55 percent of adult males in Pennsylvania.

Energized by issues that favored them, such as repealing the Alien and Sedition Acts, greater separation of church and state, and the Louisiana Purchase, northern Republicans began to mobilize in the years after 1800. They recruited new voters to the polls in New England and the Middle States, and began winning decisive majorities in congressional elections throughout the North and trans-Allegheny West. By 1804, the Republicans had captured the governorships of New Hampshire, Vermont, Massachusetts, Rhode Island, New York, Pennsylvania, Maryland, and Delaware. It was this Republican mobilization in the North in the first decade of the nineteenth century that led to the unprecedented turnout figures between 1800 and 1807.

The Federalists, by contrast, were demoralized by the election of 1800, and their vote between 1801 to 1807 was depressed. (In the presidential election of 1804, for instance, the Federalists won only the electoral votes of two states, Delaware and Connecticut.) The outlook for the Federalist Party after 1804 seemed decidedly bleak. Their older leadership was depleted by death and retirement. The death of Alexander Hamilton was particularly demoralizing. Jefferson's success in gaining ratification of the Louisiana Purchase meant the long-term endangerment of the party, since it had no foothold whatsoever in the further reaches of the West.

The story in the South was mixed. The southeastern states—Virginia, North Carolina, South Carolina, and Georgia, as well as Maryland—did not have popular elections for governor, and even presidential electors were often selected by the legislatures. Thus, party competition tended to embody

Table 3 Gubernatorial turnout in selected northern states, 1800–1807

Year	Massachusetts (%)	New Hampshire (%)	Pennsylvania (%)
1800	31	44	—[a]
1801	37	40	—
1802	39	48	47
1803	33	53	—
1804	41	60	—
1805	47	68	55
1806	55	49	—
1807	58	39	—

[a] Pennsylvania elected its governor triennially.

local interests and lacked statewide competition. Where local interests had a rough parity statewide, as they did in Maryland and North Carolina, voters of both parties went to the polls. Where the Republican Party dominated, party competition did not serve as a mobilizing force to get new voters to the polls. This was the case in Virginia, Georgia, and South Carolina, all of which kept property restrictions on voting. As a result, the turnout for congressional and presidential elections mostly hovered around 25 percent of adult white male inhabitants.

Although the Federalist Party never seriously established itself in any southwestern state except Louisiana, this area, especially Tennessee, had high levels of turnout.[15] High turnout in Tennessee may have been the result of competitive factional politics. The southwestern states of Mississippi and Alabama permitted white manhood suffrage from the time they were admitted to the Union. Tennessee and Kentucky, moreover, allowed free manhood suffrage— albeit briefly in Kentucky from 1792 to 1799—but free men of color were allowed to vote in Tennessee from 1796 to 1834.[16]

The High Point of Jeffersonian Participation, 1808–1816

In the last year of the Jefferson administration, the political dynamics between the parties changed dramatically north of the Potomac. The president sought to prevent the United States from becoming embroiled in the constant violation of its neutrality rights by the British and French in the Napoleonic Wars. His solution, the Embargo Act, was passed by Congress in 1808 and prohibited U.S. merchant vessels from engaging in trans-Atlantic trade. Jefferson imagined that the withdrawal of U.S. exports—especially foodstuffs and staples—would force the belligerents to respect American neutrality. In the short term, it did not force either the British or the French to make overtures to the Americans about respecting their neutrality. It did, however, wreak economic havoc on the entire Northeast, which was critically dependent on the Atlantic trade for its prosperity.

Although the Embargo Act provided loopholes through which many a merchantman sailed for Europe with impunity, most of the nation's merchant fleet was grounded, and the economies of the New England and Middle States ground to a halt. Without the trade in foodstuffs, merchants, sailors, dockworkers, and commercial farmers faced a devastating economic blow. For the first time in U.S. history, a policy inaugurated by the federal government was seen as causing overwhelming economic hardship. The opposition Federalists wasted little time in proclaiming their opposition to the foolish and destructive trade policies of the Republicans.

The Southeast, although dependent on the export of staple crops, was not yet entirely in the thrall of cotton production. The frontier areas in an arc from Maine (still part of Massachusetts) through northern New York and southward through western Pennsylvania, Virginia, North Carolina, South Carolina, and Georgia had everything to gain from the embargo and little to lose. The frontier areas abutting British Canada and Spanish Florida could only benefit from British or Spanish recognition of American rights. Moreover, these subsistence farming regions were not affected by the interruption of the Atlantic export trade.

For the next eight years, Federalists and Republicans in the northern states were joined in a fiercely partisan battle over foreign policy, trade policy, and the politics of war. That debate was sufficient to jump-start a full-fledged participatory democracy in the American republic. In the years after 1808, both parties contested every popular election, competing for what they believed were the highest stakes imaginable. Table 4 indicates that turnout levels peaked at 68 percent in Massachusetts, 81 percent in New Hampshire, and 70 percent in Pennsylvania of adult male inhabitants, and the presidential election of 1812 was by far the closest such election between 1800 and 1824. In

Table 4 Gubernatorial turnout in selected northern states, 1808–1817

Year	Massachusetts (%)	New Hampshire (%)	Pennsylvania (%)
1808	56	36	70
1809	64	70	—[a]
1810	61	71	—
1811	55	70	33
1812	68	69	—
1813	64	75	—
1814	64	81	43
1815	59	74	—
1816	59	77	—
1817	50	70	61

[a] Pennsylvania elected its governor triennially.

the years after 1808, the turnout in gubernatorial elections in states north of the Mason-Dixon Line set records, some of which would not be broken until the so-called Log Cabin Campaign of 1840.

Explaining the Rise in Turnout, 1808–1817

In the years after 1808, three factors came together: (1) party competition; (2) the critical salience of economic issues; and (3) persistent rivalries, now extended to the local level, of complementary national press networks. In the years after 1808, a real debate ensued over the issues, both parties vigorously joined the debate, and they competed energetically to get their bases to the elections. Participation rose dramatically thanks to party competition. This competition over critical issues, tied to longstanding local rivalries and international trans-Atlantic preferences, gave the Federalist and Republican parties a coherence they had hitherto lacked.[17] For New Englanders, the fears of France extended back more than a century, reached a fever pitch in the French Revolution, and never abated in the Napoleonic era. For southerners and many in the Mid-Atlantic and West, the bitter memories of the British depredations in the American Revolution were nurtured by the Republicans. For the first time in American history, or in the history of republican government, ordinary Americans found identities in the Federalist and Republican political parties, and those identities became as durable components of political culture as patriotism, civil religion, or local identity.

We can see how issues drove elections in this period in Massachusetts in 1808 and Maryland in 1812. In Massachusetts, Republican supporters and Federalist opponents of the embargo oriented their appeals explicitly around Jeffersonian policy. Before the state elections in 1808, a letter addressed "To the People of the County of Essex" appeared in the Federalist *Columbian Centinel*, for example. The letter declared that "the Embargo must be raised, or the ruin of our country is inevitable." The letter went on to enumerate and discuss the Essex Federalists' position on "1. The restrictions of the colonial trade by Great Britain. 2. The impressment of her seamen from our merchant vessels. 3. The attack on the Chesapeake. 4 The Orders of Council."[18] In the same year, a letter in Boston's Republican *Independent Chronicle* appeared "To the Selectmen of the Town of Boston" after Bostonians petitioned Jefferson to amend or repeal the embargo. The letter declared, "We consider it to be unworthy the character of a true American to meet with so little fortitude the privations occasioned by the Embargo."[19]

In the year 1812, the declaration of war with Great Britain and the conduct of the war became the most salient rallying points for Federalists and Republicans. Nowhere were the issues and passions of the war more inflamed than in Baltimore. The office of the Baltimore *Federal Republican* was attacked by a Republican mob angry at the newspaper's antiwar orientation. In Baltimore, the party newspapers and committees sometimes used hortatory language to rally their adherents, but the *Federal Republican* also addressed the issue of war in a sober, deliberative fashion, reporting on one meeting in Anne Arundel County of those who took a moderate antiwar position. It "is premature and impolitic at the present crisis to declare war against G. Britain, because the country is not in a sufficient state of preparation to afford reasonable calculations of success."[20] The *Baltimore Patriot*, a Republican newspaper, also appealed in 1812 for honest deliberation, saying, "In the collision of sentiment, truth is oft times elicited; and honest discussion is the only road to correct decision."[21]

Lockean versus Athenian Definitions of Democracy

As we have seen, Jeffersonian political culture was marked by a high degree of issue-centered voting. In this sense, it seems far away from the Log Cabin Campaign of 1840. Yet even though the Republicans and Federalists often stuck to the issues in their fiercely competitive politics, they sometimes also took the low road. We see this in examining the interesting case of New Jersey politics from 1802 to 1808.

After the critical election of 1800, the debate in the United States between Federalists and Republicans turned from defining the role the people should play in representative government to defining the makeup of the people who would participate in government. In the first decades of the nineteenth century, Americans fiercely debated the boundaries of a democratic universe. Intense competition between the Federalists and Republicans resulted in two different definitions of political inclusion. One, embraced more enthusiastically by the Federalists, relied on property qualifications, which following John Dunn, we might call the Lockean version of democracy. The other, promoted increasingly by Republicans, hinged on demographic identity and, again following Dunn, we might call the Athenian version of democracy.[22]

In the late eighteenth century, the nearly universal operative requirement for suffrage in the Anglo-American world was property. In William Blackstone's words, this would "exclude such persons as are in so mean a situation as to be esteemed to have no will of their own."[23] Ironically, this very insistence on property as the defining characteristic of popular participation permitted some Americans to think of radically extending the franchise in demographic terms. In northern states, free men of color who met the property requirement were accorded the right to vote. In fact, in 1790, only three states—Virginia, South Carolina, and Georgia—explicitly confined the vote to whites. The New Jersey constitution of 1776 also permitted women to vote if they were heads of household and possessed a minimal freehold. This definition of inclusion by property-holding allowed for a remarkable practice in New Jersey.

In the prerevolutionary era, colonial legislatures rarely troubled to specifically exclude women from voting, but there is depressingly scant evidence of women acting to take advantage of the law's failure to exclude them. Women in New Jersey did vote after 1776, however. The legislature took no action until the Republicans seized on the issue of women and blacks voting in New

Jersey to mobilize unpropertied white males and get them to the polls.[24] New Jersey Jeffersonians proclaimed themselves in favor of a different definition of inclusion, one centered on boundaries of race and gender. Two definitions of inclusion collided — one defined by property and the other by race and gender identity. Republicans argued that women and free blacks, whatever their property holdings, by virtue of their identity lacked "independence." In 1808, New Jersey Republicans achieved their goal, simultaneously eliminating property-holding as the defining characteristic for voter suffrage and restricting the vote exclusively to whites and males.

The High Road and the Low Road: New Jersey, 1802–1808

The New Jersey elections of 1802 and 1806 were too close for the Republicans' comfort, and subsequently, party leaders blamed women and black voters for "corruption" (i.e., fraudulent voting). Republican leaders targeted both groups for exclusion from the suffrage. In doing so, they were not *simply* scapegoating.

It turns out that in the early nineteenth century, there was a gender gap at the polls. The women of New Jersey showed a Federalist preference in the early 1800s: contemporary reports drawn from newspapers on both sides tell us that women *property* holders preferred the Federalists to the Republicans, perhaps for both religious and economic reasons. Free blacks also tended to vote Federalist because of the overall connection in black voters' minds of the Republican Party with slaveholders' interests. Thus, it became the Republicans' mission in New Jersey to deny women and blacks the vote.

Rosemarie Zagarri in *Revolutionary Backlash* describes the politics behind the New Jersey Republicans' efforts to deny women the vote.[25] A referendum was held in 1806 in Essex County to determine whether the county seat should be moved from Elizabeth (which was strongly Federalist) to Newark (which was strongly Republican). Thanks in part to the property restrictions on the vote, Federalist Elizabeth retained its courthouse and Republican Newark, which had a larger population but fewer qualified voters, had its wishes thwarted.[26] In the following year, the number of votes cast in Essex County went up another 60 percent. This time the vote was augmented by unpropertied white men who were not legally entitled to vote. In the aftermath of that election fraud, women and blacks in New Jersey were completely disbarred, the £50 property qualification was eliminated, and all adult white men were legally allowed to vote.

The low road politics of Republicans in New Jersey—race and gender scapegoating and subsequent election fraud—extended beyond Essex County into Hunterdon County, on the Delaware River surrounding Trenton. It turns out that the Republicans' charges of vote corruption did not originate in Essex County in 1806. In Hunterdon County in 1802, we see a similar pattern of voting, and similar charges were made. In the legislative election of 1802, the Hunterdon Republican machine succeeded in winning the only election for a seat in the legislative upper house, the Governor's Council. It also succeeded in winning one seat in the lower house of the legislature, the assembly, and lost another assembly seat by a single vote: voters cast 1,825 votes for Republican Joseph Hankinson and 1,826 votes for Federalist Benjamin Van Cleve. In this close election, charges of "corruption" were raised by the Republicans. When an election was close, partisans had learned that charging election fraud could be a useful tactic.

The importance of this close vote went beyond courthouse politics. New Jersey's governor and U.S. senators were not popularly elected at this time; they were elected by the state legislature. In order to elect either a governor or a senator, the legislature met in joint session. The result of the 1802 election was a Governor's Council and an assembly tied between the two parties at twenty-six votes each when they met jointly. The legislature was consequently deadlocked, and New Jersey was unable to elect either a governor or federal senator in that year.

As we saw in the 2000 election dispute in Florida, which some have blamed on the butterfly ballots in Palm Beach County, a seemingly trivial polling event can have enormous consequences. In 1802, New Jersey Republicans had benefited from a national landslide in congressional elections. But for the lack of a single vote in Hunterdon County, they were unable to deliver on their mandate and elect either a Republican governor or U.S. senator. That may very well have been the moment when Republican Party leaders decided to augment their support at the polls—by playing the gender and race cards.

Immediately after the October 1802 election, Republican partisans in Hunterdon County formed "an Association for the Preservation of our Electoral Rights." The following month, a state legislative committee held hearings to determine the extent of voter fraud in Hunterdon Country, and the

Republicans gave evidence that "women voted, citizens of Philadelphia, ne-groes and slaves, and those possessing less than £50 freeholds" (presumably this last category were unqualified Federalists). The legislative committee eventually dismissed all the allegations of partisan unfairness, concluding that the Republicans received as many fraudulent votes as the Federalists did. Re-publicans then charged the Federalist-dominated committee with conducting the investigation unfairly.[27]

Following their defeat in the legislative committee, the Republican Party in Hunterdon decided on a two-pronged strategy, one deliberative and the other demagogic. Party leaders James Linn and James J. Wilson launched a series of open meetings to "disseminate correct information on public officers among [their] fellow citizens."[28] This approach testifies to one of the remark-able features of Jeffersonian politics: party leaders encouraged and assimilated an extended audience into critical policy deliberations. The strategy of en-couraging the dissemination of "correct information" among voters was one of the hallmarks of Jeffersonian democracy.

But Jeffersonian politics was not without its low appeals to race and gen-der prejudice. Republican Party organizers also fostered and nurtured blatant race prejudice among poorer whites, who were disfranchised themselves and resented any blacks being given the right to vote. The demagogic attack on women voters was more subtle and couched in the tone of gentle reproofs to women for seeking to vote. The following letter in the Trenton *True Ameri-can*, a strongly Republican newspaper, gives a vivid illustration of the strategy and represents an early illustration of the ways in which the "cult of domes-ticity" would later be used to restrain women from exercising a public role. The newspaper at the outset struck a chivalric tone. "Among the numerous striking scenes which our election presents to the disinterested observer," it said, "none is more amusing than the fight of whole wagon-loads of those 'privileged fair,' who from the lucky circumstance of being possessed of fifty pounds, and of being disengaged at the age of twenty-one are entitled to a vote." Then the newspaper took a reproving position:

> From the moment when party spirit began to rear its hideous head, the female votes became its passive tools and the ill consequences of their admiration have increased yearly. This year their number arose to an alarming height; in some townships I am told they made up almost one fourth of the total number of votes, and we cannot blame the apprehen-

sions of an old farmer who feared "that the next election would be left entirely to the ladies." This defect in our constitution certainly deserves the notice of our government, and if not attended to may in a few years cause the most fatal confusion; for until it is amended, each party will of course muster all its female champions, from an apprehension that its antagonists will do the same.

Let not our fair conclude that I wish to see them deprived of their rights. Let them rather consider that female reserve and delicacy are incompatible with the duties of a free elector . . . that a female politician is often the subject of ridicule . . . and they will recognize in the writer of this a sincere

FRIEND TO THE LADIES[29]

In the 1803 election, the vote in Hunterdon County jumped by nearly 50 percent, from 3,689 to 5,271. Whether or not women voted in great numbers, as "Friend to the Ladies" had warned, the total vote for the Republicans swamped the Federalists and was probably fraudulent. Only two-thirds of the men in the county would likely have met the £50 pound requirement, and the county's total vote was 25 percent higher than the total adult male population. Moreover, the surge in the vote came from Republicans, who were much more likely to be have-nots.

In 1806, the Republicans were still charging vote "corruption." The editor of the Republican Trenton *True American* indignantly addressed the Federalists, playing up race resentments against African Americans, gender resentments against "misses," and class resentments directed downward against paupers and upward against Princeton students: "Why admit Princeton students? Why shove in votes of those who declared they were *not worth a cent?* — and of vast numbers of blacks who were *known* to be worth nothing? — Why bring in misses yet in their teens, and pass them off by oath or assertion as of full age[?]"[30]

The following election shows exactly the outcome that J. R. Pole described in his early studies of election turnout. One might call this the "boots on the ground" effect: unpropertied or unqualified voters turned out at the polls and forced a retroactive extension of the suffrage. Men were prompted to the polls in part by antipathy — nurtured and sustained by Republican Party organizers — to the political power allegedly enjoyed by propertied women and prosperous free African Americans.

The Republicans in Hunterdon County achieved their aims after the election of 1807. In that year, turnout surged again by about 25 percent. Once again, the total vote was higher than the total adult male population of the county. After this election, the newly elected Republican state legislators eliminated property qualifications for white male voters, and all women and African Americans were explicitly denied the vote.

In one sense, Republicans were the agents of democratization. They eliminated the property requirements in New Jersey for all adult males nearly two decades before neighboring New York followed suit. Furthermore, by promoting meetings providing "correct information on public officers among [their] fellow citizens," Republicans encouraged a politics of widespread deliberation.

At the same time, however, Republicans in New Jersey were also the agents of democratic restriction. New Jersey was the first northern state to restrict the definition of political eligibility to adult white males only. Remarkably, at the beginning of the early republic in 1790, only three states (Virginia, South Carolina, and Georgia) explicitly confined the vote to whites; by 1855, only five states, all in New England, allowed blacks to vote on the same basis as whites.

This is a collision between two conceptions of democracy that emerged in the years between the American Revolution and the Jacksonian era. In some states, the property requirement was minimal, and no further stipulations were required. Only in New Jersey, where women had borne an exceptionally heavy burden during the revolution, was the suffrage consciously and explicitly extended to women, but in ten of the thirteen states, propertied men of color could vote without any more restrictions on them than on their white neighbors.[31]

The election of 1807 in New Jersey marks the beginning of a turning point from the Lockean definition of citizenship to an Athenian concept of American democracy defined by race, national origin, and religion. Here is a successful attempt to seize political power for unpropertied white men and to wrest the imagined political power away from those "privileged" propertied women and African Americans. Poor white men, themselves the victims of class prejudice and economic oppression, were motivated not just to gain a voice for themselves but to deny that voice to others. That pattern repeated itself in American politics many times with great success, most extensively in the Age of Jackson. It occurred in the antebellum North in states like New York, which eliminated all property restrictions on white males, only to impose new property and residence restrictions on African American voters. Pennsylvania, Tennessee, and North Carolina went even further. In the 1830s, when these states eliminated all remaining obstacles to white male suffrage, they also excluded free black male suffrage entirely.[32]

In New Jersey in 1807, at least party leaders had hoped to extend the audience for serious political deliberation. Repeated appeals to race and gender prejudice, however, "dumbed down the discourse" over the course of years, and party leaders who appealed to these prejudices saw less and less need to reach a wide audience for serious policy debates.

The high turnout of American politics in the years from 1800 to 1816 seems to have been caused by a combination of high- and low-road tactics by Republicans and Federalists. New Jersey's action was only the first in a depressing series of decisions by leaders of all parties to take the "low road" in American politics. Amid the several important differences between Jeffersonian and Jacksonian democracy identified by Reeve Huston elsewhere in this volume, one feature that certainly distinguishes this earlier period is the leaders' frequent assumption (call it naive or high-minded) that appeals to the high road in politics was necessary

Although the case of New Jersey was unusual in the Jeffersonian era, its action in 1808 put it in the vanguard. Even as the definition of democracy expanded along one axis in the first decades of the nineteenth century, it narrowed significantly along others. Between 1824 and 1860, all new states admitted to the Union adopted racial exclusions for voting. Pennsylvania eliminated African American suffrage entirely. Connecticut followed New Jersey's lead, entirely depriving its African Americans of the right to vote. Free people of color in Maryland and North Carolina also lost their voting rights. The party competition between the Federalists and Jeffersonian Republicans in the 1790s and early 1800s witnessed the flowering of a direct and forceful style of popular discourse, one that presented the American public with clear and potent — if exaggerated — comparisons of party alternatives in economic and foreign policy. In the later Jacksonian era, that style of discourse began its long decline in favor of blatant appeals to race, ethnic, and religious prejudice. Even the now-hallowed Lincoln-Douglas debates were accompanied in the Republican newspaper of Springfield, Illinois, with the slogan "No Nigger Equality!"

The Peculiarity of American Democracy

Rather than describing American democracy as "exceptional," with all the normative baggage that word entails, I might apply a term that allows for idiosyncrasy but dispenses with teleology. A word that better describes these twists and turns in the history of American democracy is "peculiar." It captures the unusual and puzzling features of popular government in America then and now. The peculiarity of American democracy is precisely what warmed Tocqueville to this subject, and the word occurs frequently in his two volumes. I would argue that American democracy is America's other "peculiar institution," and this connotative link to slavery points to the increasing salience of race in defining the limits of inclusion.

Notes

1. See, among many others, Bernard Bailyn, *Atlantic History: Concept and Contours* (Cambridge, Mass.: Harvard University Press, 2005); David Waldstreicher, *In the Midst of Perpetual Fetes: The Masking of American Nationalism, 1776–1820* (Chapel Hill: University of North Carolina Press, 1997); Michael Durey, *Transatlantic Radicals and the Early American Republic* (Lawrence: University Press of Kansas, 1997); and Seth Cotlar, *Tom Paine's America: The Rise and Fall of Trans-Atlantic Radicalism in the Early Republic* (Charlottesville: University of Virginia Press, 2011).

2. The nineteenth-century historian George Bancroft celebrated the presidency of Andrew Jackson as the culmination of the ideals of the American Revolution. See his eulogy on the death of Jackson delivered at Washington, 21 June 1845, in *Life and Public Services of Gen. Andrew Jackson*, ed. John S. Jenkins (Buffalo, 1850); see also Arthur Schlesinger Jr., *The Age of Jackson* (Boston: Little, Brown, 1945), written by Bancroft's descendant Arthur Schlesinger Jr. Schlesinger depicts the Jacksonian era as ushering in an American democratic revolution. Sean Wilentz, following in the tradition of Schlesinger, hails the election of Jackson in *The Rise of American Democracy: Jefferson to Lincoln* (New York: Norton, 2005), 312–29.

3. See especially Richard P. McCormick, "New Perspectives on Jacksonian Politics," *American Historical Review* 65 (January 1960): 288–301, and the collated turnout figures that are assembled from Pole's many articles on the subject in J. R. Pole, *Political Representation in England and the Origin of the American Republic* (London: St. Martin's Press, 1966), 543–64.

4. Wilentz, *Rise of American Democracy*, esp. 72–99, 138–40.

5. Alexander Keyssar, *The Right to Vote: The Contested History of Democracy in the United States* (New York: Basic Books, 2000), esp. 26–52; Daniel Walker Howe, *What Hath God Wrought: The Transformation of America, 1815–1848* (New York: Oxford University Press, 2007), esp. 282–84.

6. The data in all the tables is derived from the Philip J. Lampi Collection of Early National Voting Data at the American Antiquarian Society, Worcester, Massachusetts. This data is made available via A New Nation Votes: American Election Returns 1787–1825, http://elections.lib.tufts.edu/. I have computed the turnout figures by the following method. For those states that permitted all adult white male inhabitants to vote, I have taken the total vote cast for an office (e.g., governor) and divided it by the total number of adult male inhabitants. In states where only free adult men could vote, I divided the vote by the free adult male population. In those states that restricted the

vote to white males, I used the appropriate figures, and for New Jersey, I used all adult free inhabitants through the election of 1808. To determine the adult male population, I added the cohorts of adult males (dividing by 2 the 16–26 age cohort). To estimate the population between decennial census years, I used linear interpolation.

7. New York had a two-tiered suffrage until 1821, with a larger body of voters permitted to vote for Congress and the New York State assembly and a more restricted group of voters permitted to vote for the New York state senate. See Chilton P. Williamson, *American Suffrage from Property to Democracy, 1760–1860* (Princeton, N.J.: Princeton University Press, 1960), 195–207.

8. In New York, voter turnout was determined as the number of votes cast for an office divided by the adult male population. In those states that prohibited all people of color from voting, I have used the adult white male population.

9. North Carolina, like New York, had a two-tiered suffrage. The constitution of 1835 abolished the property requirement for the lower tier of suffrage. It also completely eliminated the right of free men of color to vote. See Williamson, *American Suffrage*, 234–36.

10. For consistency and comparability, turnout is calculated as the vote cast for an office divided by the free adult male population. In those states that completely prohibited African Americans from voting, the vote is divided by the adult white male population.

11. For the best summary of this original and skeptical view of the first party system and what the author perceives as "deferential-participant" political culture, see Ronald P. Formisano, "Deferential-Participant Politics: The Early Republic's Political Culture, 1789–1840," *American Political Science Review* 68 (June 1974): 473–87.

12. See the introduction to this volume, notes 25–28.

13. There are many examples of this. For some of the most striking instances, see *Gazette* (Boston), 2 September 1802; *Independent Chronicle* (Boston), 1 April 1805; and *Aurora* (Philadelphia), 13 October 1812. See also Jeffrey L. Pasley, *"The Tyranny of Printers": Newspaper Politics in the Early American Republic* (Charlottesville: University Press of Virginia, 2000).

14. *Gazette of the United States* (Philadelphia), 14 October 1800.

15. James Broussard, *Southern Federalists, 1800–1816* (Baton Rouge: Louisiana State University Press, 1978).

16. Keyssar, *Right to Vote*, 328–45.

17. For a trenchant analysis of the many examples in the first party system in which high turnout could not have been fostered by party competition, see Daniel Peart, *Era of Experimentation: American Political Practices in the Early Republic* (Charlottesville: University of Virginia Press, 2014).

18. Boston *Columbian Centinel*, 12 October 1808. See also *Salem Gazette*, 14 October 1808.

19. Boston *Independent Chronicle*, 13 October 1808.

20. Baltimore *Federal Republican and Commercial Gazette*, 10 June 1812.

21. *Baltimore Patriot*, 28 December 1812.

22. John Dunn, *Democracy: A History* (New York: Atlantic Books, 2005), 24–44, 71–118.

23. William Blackstone, *Commentaries on the Laws of England: A Facsimile of the First Edition of 1765–1769* (Chicago: University of Chicago Press), 1:165–66.

24. For an excellent work that probes the efficacy of the African American vote in the first party system, and analyzes the connection between free black voting and party competition, see Christopher Malone, *Between Freedom and Bondage: Race, Party and Voting Rights in the Antebellum North* (New York: Routledge, 2008), esp. the discussion of New York, 23–56, which in important ways parallels New Jersey.

25. Rosemarie Zagarri, *Revolutionary Backlash: Women and Politics in the Early American Republic* (Philadelphia: University of Pennsylvania Press, 2007).

26. See "A New Nation Votes: The Case of Female Suffrage in New Jersey, 1776–1807" (paper, Society of Historians of the Early American Republic Conference, Worcester, Mass., 22 July 2007).

27. Carl E. Prince, *New Jersey's Jeffersonian Republicans: The Genesis of an Anti-Party Machine, 1789–1817* (Chapel Hill: University of North Carolina Press, 1964), 84n25.

28. Ibid., 84–85; *True American* (Trenton), 3, 17 January, 4 April, 25 July 1803; *To the Republicans of the County of Hunterdon* (Philadelphia, 1812), New Jersey Pamphlets Collection, Sinclair New Jersey Collection, Rutgers University Library, New Brunswick, N.J.

29. *True American* (Trenton), 25 October 1802.

30. *True American* (Trenton), 27 October 1806.

31. Undoubtedly women bore a significant burden during the war in every state. But every state did not share the horrors of war equally. Historians of the American Revolution point out that New Jersey was a target of British and Hessian terror. See, for example, David Hackett Fischer, *Washington's Crossing* (New York: Oxford University Press, 2004), 31–65, 346–62.

32. Keyssar, *Right to Vote*, 328–45; Malone, *Between Freedom and Bondage*, 57–100.

★ DANIEL PEART ★

An "Era of No Feelings"?

Rethinking the Relationship between Political
Parties and Popular Participation
in the Early United States

Democracy is *unworkable* save in terms of parties."[1] This bold statement, by political scientist John H. Aldrich, echoes an assumption that has shaped much of what has been written on the politics of the early United States. Recent syntheses by Sean Wilentz and Daniel Walker Howe speak of "the rise of American Democracy" and "the democratization of American life" during the first half of the nineteenth century, and both place political parties at the forefront of this tale.[2] These works reflect a broad consensus that the gradual establishment of nationwide two-party competition between the revolution and Civil War opened up public life to mass participation and made government more responsive to the people. As Andrew W. Robertson's essay in this volume shows, this process was sometimes "tortuous," as "democratic ideology and practices ebbed and flowed" across the period. And yet still, the standard narrative suggests, the overarching trajectory was always toward an identifiably "democratic" future: the present-day political system organized around two competing national parties.

This teleological trend in the literature is problematic, for few contemporaries would have equated democracy so completely with political parties. This caveat is particularly true for the decade following the War of 1812, which witnessed the demise of party competition across much of the Union. This chapter presents new data on voter turnout which challenges the conventional view that most citizens simply lost interest in politics during this period, and suggests how these findings can help us to rethink the relationship between political parties and popular participation in the early United States.

The phrase "Era of Good Feelings" was coined by Boston newspaper editor Benjamin Russell in reference to the cordial welcome that greeted President James Monroe on his tour of New England in 1817. Russell, like many New Englanders, was a Federalist, yet he candidly voiced his hope that the visit of this new Republican chief magistrate would signal an end to hostilities between those two political parties. This sentiment was widely shared. The incompetence of James Madison's administration during the War of 1812, and the ill-fated proceedings of the Hartford Convention at the climax of that conflict, had sullied the reputations of both parties. The republican creed to which most Americans subscribed had always held partisanship in disrepute, and now political leaders scrambled to put these principles into practice. Federalists united with Republicans in praising Monroe for his pursuit of political harmony, and in 1820, the president was reelected to a second term effectively without opposition. Surely, contemporaries agreed, Russell had been right; the United States was enjoying an Era of Good Feelings the likes of which had not been seen since George Washington first occupied the White House.[3]

The "Era of Good Feelings" label remains in common use among scholars today, usually referring to the ten years or so that stretched from the close of the War of 1812 to the inauguration of John Quincy Adams in 1825. We have long known, of course, that good feelings were actually in short supply during this period, as politicians squabbled over the presidential succession and the Missouri crisis brought open talk of disunion onto the floor of Congress. Yet the phrase still persists, a convenient shorthand to describe a decade that most historians now contend was defined by widespread apathy toward politics among the general populace. Indeed, this interpretation has become so entrenched that one recent survey concludes, "the Era of Good Feelings, the label commonly attached to the post–1815 decade, might more accurately be called the Era of No Feelings."[4]

"No Feelings" is certainly an apt characterization of popular opinion with regard to Monroe's reelection in 1820. In Richmond, capital of the president's native Virginia, a mere seventeen tickets were taken at the polls.[5] Throughout the nation as a whole, as few as one in ten of those who were eligible took the trouble to vote for the unchallenged incumbent. Four years later, this figure was little improved. In 1824, five serious contenders competed for the White House, and newspapers trumpeted that the contest was "the all-absorbing topic of every circle."[6] But a full seven-tenths of the electorate failed to cast their ballots. "The election of a president is a great political curiosity," mused venerable Virginia Senator John Taylor. "Partisans are zealous, and a great majority of the people indifferent."[7]

The particular apathy of Americans toward presidential elections during this period becomes even more conspicuous when placed in a broader context. Turnout surged above 50 percent for the first time in 1828 when "the People's President," Andrew Jackson, was hoisted into the White House, and again to a new high of 80 percent in 1840 following the famous "Log Cabin and Hard Cider" campaign. Thereafter, as Walter Dean Burnham originally demonstrated, the participation rate was sustained roughly between 70 and 80 percent throughout the nineteenth century, before dropping away significantly thereafter; even the recent peaks, relatively speaking, of 2008 and 2012 only hovered around the 60 percent mark. And this trend was mirrored in midterm elections too, where Burnham calculated that turnout averaged approximately 64 percent during the second half of the nineteenth century, several points below that in presidential contests but still much higher than to what we have since become accustomed.[8] Indeed, Burnham's figures were so striking that they subsequently became the basis for an entirely new periodization of U.S. politics, endorsed most notably by Joel H. Silbey and Richard L. McCormick, with the decades from the 1830s to the 1890s labelled as a "Party Period" in which "Americans repeatedly turned out to vote in record numbers at all levels of electoral activity."[9]

The uniqueness of these Party Period levels of electoral activity has been challenged, however, by recent work on the Federalist-Republican competition that preceded the Era of Good Feelings. Historians such as Andrew Robertson, Rosemarie Zagarri, and Jeffrey Pasley have suggested that, in the words of the last, "this early partisan political culture . . . was one of the most participatory and transformative that the United States has ever experienced, despite its utter lack of many elements that came to define party politics later."[10] In support of this claim, Pasley produces evidence that while turnout in national elections remained relatively low, participation rates for state elections "approached 70 percent of adult white males" in many parts of the nation between 1800 and 1816.[11]

For all their differences, these conflicting interpretations share two crucial points in common. First, they both identify parties as responsible for raising turnout, whether they date this process to the 1800s or to the 1830s. Indeed, the notion that "national parties were central to the initial stimulation and continued maintenance of a mass, *voting* electorate" has now become almost axiomatic among political historians.[12] For those who concur with Silbey's claim that "parties and partisanship did not significantly affect the political nation before 1838," it consequently follows that sustained popular participation was also impossible prior to this point in time.[13] Critics of this perspective, meanwhile, are happy to concede that a "participant political culture emerged from strenuous party competition." They simply locate both developments several decades earlier.[14]

Consensus on the relationship between parties and participation leads to the second conclusion on which both schools agree: the absence of popular engagement with politics during the Era of Good Feelings. For subscribers to the Party Period concept, these years represent merely a continuation of the "deference to social elites and mass indifference that characterized the nation's politics" prior to the advent of recognizably modern political parties.[15] Their detractors, conversely, declare that the "summit of participatory democracy" was scaled as early as the Jeffersonian era, but with the disintegration of the Federalist Party following the War of 1812, "popular participation in the midst of political vacuousness withered into apathy lasting another decade."[16] Without partisan competition to sustain their attention, it is generally agreed, most citizens simply would not have been interested in politics.

This image of indifference and apathy is shattered, however, by data recently made available by the A New Nation Votes project, an online archive of election returns from 1787 to 1825, many of which were previously assumed to be lost. When used in conjunction with census reports to calculate participation rates in congressional and gubernatorial elections occurring between 1820 and 1825, the results are remarkable. Of the twenty-four states admitted to the Union by this point, twelve breached Pasley's 70 percent barrier *at least once* during this short period, and eight maintained an *average* turnout equal to or in excess of Burnham's 64 percent for comparable contests during the Party Period (see tables 1, 2). In sum, this was most certainly not an "Era of No Feelings."[17]

But the significance of these findings extends far beyond merely correcting a longstanding misapprehension about election turnout during this period. They also challenge our conventional understanding of the relationship between political parties and popular participation. In the national capital, the Republican Party reigned supreme; no candidate would contest a presidential election under the banner of Federalism after 1816, and by the beginning

Table 1 States with at least one turnout of 70 percent or higher in congressional and gubernatorial elections, 1820–1825

State	Single highest turnout (%)
Alabama	95
Rhode Island	89
Georgia	85
Illinois	83
Mississippi	82
Tennessee	80
Indiana	76
Missouri	76
Kentucky	74
New York	72
Maryland	72
Delaware	71

Table 2 States with an average turnout of 64 percent or higher in congressional and gubernatorial elections, 1820–1825

State	Average turnout (%)
Alabama	80
Tennessee	78
Missouri	74
Kentucky	72
Illinois	69
Indiana	66
Mississippi	65
Delaware	64

of Monroe's second presidential term, Federalist numbers in Congress had dwindled to less than forty.[18] As one contemporary observed, the Federalist Party "received its death blow during the war of 1812. . . . They have lingered ever since, in the councils of the nation, without strength and without hopes, as a political party."[19] Two-party competition on a national scale, then, cannot have provided the catalyst for mass participation in politics during the early 1820s.

Descending the rungs of the federal system, the situation becomes more complex, for political practices differed greatly from region to region. To illustrate this point, let us look in more detail at two states: Massachusetts and Illinois.

While Federalist leaders in the Bay State joined Benjamin Russell in pledging their "good feelings" toward Monroe's geographically distant administration, party conflict raged unabated in their own backyard. Indeed, the Federalists' continued electoral success into the third decade of the nineteenth century led Richard P. McCormick to conclude in his comprehensive survey of party formation that "the stability, durability, and balance of the parties in Massachusetts was, by contrast with other states, most extraordinary."[20] Yet still, some scholars have questioned whether the term "party" should even be applied to these political groupings. According to Joel Silbey, the most vocal champion of this perspective, "persistent partisan political alignments and behavior" simply did not exist prior to the Party Period. "Consistency in political procedures and behavior was lacking," he argues, "as were organizational structure and, most of all, commitment." In sum, "there was always an intermittent, ad hoc quality, a casual attitude," toward what Silbey calls "partisan forms."[21]

This portrait of a political world without parties would have been unrecognizable to an inhabitant of Boston, the state's Federalist headquarters, in the early 1820s. Here, the party's organization was fully institutionalized, comprising a pyramidal structure of multiple local committees reporting to a single central body, all of which were ostensibly subject to election by party members. The method used to nominate candidates for office, which involved party leaders meeting with delegates chosen from each municipal ward to make their choices on the principle of majority rule, likewise bears a remarkable resemblance to modern practices.[22] The town's Republican cohort organized in a similar manner, and both sides could count on the support of several friendly newspapers to advocate their cause.[23] Between elections, the competing forces employed volunteer militia companies, fraternal societies, and rival 4th of July celebrations to recruit new partisans and publicize their rival persuasions.[24] And when polling day arrived, they appointed agents to patrol the streets, distributing pre-prepared ballot papers and exhorting every supporter to vote the straight party ticket.[25] Viewed in the context of Boston's crowded electoral calendar, with various state and local offices to be filled each year in March, April, and May, followed by biennial contests for its single seat in the U.S. Congress in the fall, these arrangements appear as anything but intermittent, ad hoc, or casual.

Even more significant than the practical details of partisan machinery, however, is the perception held by contemporaries that their political lives were ruled by party. "This system has been pursued in Boston twenty years, more or less, and for the whole of that period there never has been a single free and uncontrolled election," complained Joseph T. Buckingham, proprietor of the *New-England Galaxy*, on the eve of Monroe's reelection to the White House.[26] Buckingham was an ardent Federalist, but his disillusionment with the party's grandees led him to demand a greater voice for the rank and file in decision-making. "The Republican Institution and the [Federalist] Central Committee . . . have taken from the good citizens of the town all the labor of investigation into the characters and claims of candidates for officers," the editor declared. "He who would not give his vote as one or other of these self-created bodies of aristocrats and demagogues should dictate, might as well stay at home."[27] If change was not forthcoming, Buckingham warned, the citizens of Boston would abandon their traditional allegiances and form a new party.

Two years later, Buckingham's prediction was fulfilled, as popular discontent finally erupted in the form of a protest movement calling itself the Middling Interest. These insurgents nominated their own candidates for office, complaining of the established parties that "the moderator of a caucus has *convenient ears;* he never hears the name of an independent man; but he can hear *whispers* from the well known, tried and faithful servants of the aristocracy, or he can, upon an emergency, take *nods* and *winks* for a nomination."[28] The group also condemned the practice of partisan editors' only publicizing their own tickets at election-time: "We hope we shall never feel impelled to adopt that narrow-minded, exclusive sort of policy," wrote Buckingham, "which would seal up the press of this free and enlightened country, against the expression of the will and sentiments of a majority of citizens, and open it only at the will and pleasure of a cabal."[29] These criticisms transcended the partisan divide. "The Federalists have their aristocracy, and the Republicans have theirs," a rebel handbill reminded its readers, "but they are both equally united on some occasions against the Middling Interest. . . . Their object is power to be used for themselves, as they have done, and not always for the benefit of the people."[30]

The state's political elite were unmoved by this manifestation of the people's dissatisfaction with their leadership, however. "Three parties can no more continue in a country, than three men can continue to fight in single combat," declared Harrison Gray Otis, the Federalist gubernatorial candidate in 1823 and 1824. "It will happen of necessity, that two must beat the other, before they can fight themselves, and perhaps in that very act, they become such friends, as to bury the hatchet."[31] Historians have often assumed that those heading up the first American parties, and particularly those of the Federalist creed, never really accepted the legitimacy of partisan competition.[32] Yet here Otis dismissed the Middling Interest insurgency precisely because it did not fit into a political order structured around two entrenched parties. His words would prove prophetic. The Republicans struggled to wrest the state government from Federalist control in a series of bitter contests through the early 1820s, but in 1825, with both facing grassroots pressure to reform, the old rivals united in nominating a single candidate for governor. The long-delayed Era of Good Feelings, it seems, had finally arrived in Massachusetts.[33]

One thousand miles away in Illinois, the political landscape looked very different. The Federalist-Republican division had never penetrated deeply into the Prairie State, where all politicians of note claimed allegiance to the Jeffersonian persuasion. Those factional alignments that did develop out of personal rivalries among the state's political leaders were loosely defined and lacked dedicated popular followings. Parties of the kind that existed in Massachusetts, with their nominating caucuses and Central Committees, were completely alien. Instead, as one commentator noted, "every candidate nominat[es] himself, and travers[es] his district with gingerbread in one end of his saddle-bags and whiskey in the other, soliciting every man whom he [meets] to support him at the next election."[34] If anywhere in the nation truly approached the "prepartisan political culture" described by Silbey then it was certainly this frontier state.[35] By Russell's measure, since its admission to the Union in 1818 Illinois had known nothing but "Good Feelings."

The state's politics were thrown into turmoil in February 1823, however, when advocates of a scheme to legalize slavery succeeded in forcing a referendum on the subject, to be determined at the next elections in August 1824. In the absence of existing mechanisms for mobilizing popular support, opponents of the peculiar institution moved swiftly to establish a network of voluntary associations tasked with disseminating antislavery publications; as one participant later recalled, "the Anti-Convention party had the whole State under their control, and the question virtually decided, before their opponents

Table 3 Turnout in Massachusetts and Illinois congressional and
gubernatorial elections, 1820–1825

Year	Massachusetts (%)		Illinois (%)	
	Congressional	Gubernatorial	Congressional	Gubernatorial
1820	22	45	67	—
1821	—	40	—	—
1822	20	40	66	67
1823	—	52	—	—
1824	28	57	83	—
1825	—	28	—	—

got up a public organization."[36] Not content with blocking any constitutional change, the friends of freedom also arranged nominating meetings to concentrate their strength, with the aim of driving the proslavery faction from office. When election day finally arrived, one observer recorded, "the aged and crippled were carried to the polls, and men voted on this occasion that had not seen the ballot box before in twenty years."[37] The result signaled a clear, if closely contested, rejection of the legislature's proposal, which ensured that the future home of Abraham Lincoln would remain barred to human bondage.[38]

Taking this context into consideration, a brief comparison of turnout in Massachusetts and Illinois demonstrates the necessity of rethinking the relationship between parties and participation. Throughout the early 1820s, as few as one in five citizens of Massachusetts cast their ballots in the choice of representatives for Congress. Even the highly charged, ultra-partisan gubernatorial races from 1820 to 1824 frequently failed to bring a majority of eligible voters to the polls. In Illinois, meanwhile, participation rates in both types of election consistently exceeded the 64 percent average cited by Burnham for the Party Period, and peaked at an extraordinary 83 percent in the referendum of 1824 (table 3).

If we return to those state-by-state figures for turnout in congressional and gubernatorial elections between 1820 and 1825, we find this pattern replicated across the United States. Of the eight states with an average turnout of 64 percent or higher, the first seven were, according to Richard P. McCormick, places with "little or no experience of conducting politics on a party basis," in

Table 4 Average turnout in congressional and gubernatorial elections in
selected states, 1820–1825

Ranking	State	Average turnout (%)
1	Alabama	80
2	Tennessee	78
3	Missouri	74
4	Kentucky	72
5	Illinois	69
6	Indiana	66
7	Mississippi	65
8	Delaware	64
12	New York	59
14	Pennsylvania	55
19	Massachusetts	34

which "candidates for elective office and those who voted for them did not be-
have as partisans," and there was "little use of formal devices of political management, such as caucuses, conventions, or committees." Delaware, where
"the old parties still retained their original identity and undiminished vigor,"
came in eighth on the list, but Massachusetts, the only other state where this
was also true, languished in nineteenth.[39] As for New York, recently described
by one scholar as "an advanced laboratory of political sophistication, where the
foundations were being laid for the emergence of the mass political parties of
the nineteenth century," it ranked only twelfth.[40] And Pennsylvania, another
state often identified as being at the forefront of new forms of party politics,
fell shorter still in fourteenth (table 4). Taken as a whole, these results suggest
that voter participation during this period was most vibrant where parties
were weakest.

Admittedly, this division between "party" and "no party" states is somewhat arbitrary. In Kentucky, for example, the Panic of 1819 generated new
political issues that provided the foundation for a clearly defined "Relief"–
"Anti-Relief" axis to dominate the state for several years.[41] These alignments
may not meet the strict criteria for party formation set down by Party Period
scholars, but they certainly acted as parties in selecting candidates for office
and seeking to mobilize electoral support behind them, and contemporaries
evidently considered them in these terms. James Roger Sharp suggests that

such groupings might best be described as "proto-parties," but such language seems unhelpfully anachronistic; no one has ever set out to create a "proto-party," or been censured for their "proto-partisanship."[42] Instead, the case of Kentucky illustrates the importance of not forcing the diversity of American political life during this period into abstract categories invented by modern scholars. By acknowledging that "party" meant different things to different people in different contexts, we can address the surely more significant question: why did one form of competition in Kentucky drive participation rates above the 70 percent mark, while a very different model in Massachusetts, more sophisticated by modern standards, struggle to bring half that proportion of the electorate to the polls?

Further examples tend toward the same conclusion. The Illinois slavery referendum of 1824 involved a well-defined and controversial issue, with the opposing sides evenly matched and making great efforts to secure a popular mandate, and resulted in an 83 percent turnout. Evidently "binary pluralism," intense competition, and sustained organization, all things associated with two-party politics (although, in this case, appearing in the absence of such a system), can play an important role in raising participation rates.[43] Two years earlier, in stark contrast, the state had been host to a four-way gubernatorial race where candidates flaunted their lack of organizational backing and failed to take any clear stance on a confusing melee of public concerns. Yet writing during that campaign, Horatio Newhall, a recent emigrant from New England, confidently predicted that "when party politics were at the highest pitch in Massachusetts, there was, probably, never an election more warmly contested than our next election will be for *all* our state and national officers."[44] Newhall's boast is borne out by the numbers. In 1822, 67 percent of the Illinois electorate cast their ballots, not as many as in 1824, certainly, but a figure that compares favorably not just to Massachusetts that same year but also to equivalent contests in New York and Delaware, all states where party conflict was the norm. Again, this poses the question: in what circumstances do "binary pluralism," competition, and organization promote participation, and in which circumstances might they have the opposite effect?

This question may help to resolve the clear discrepancy between participation rates in congressional and gubernatorial elections on the one hand, and presidential elections on the other. The occasion of Monroe's re-coronation in 1820 was singularly uncompetitive of course, and the same could also be said for some regions in 1824; across New England, for example, John Quincy

Adams took four of every five ballots cast. Elsewhere that year, however, the race was far closer. Andrew Jackson outpolled Adams by less than one hundred votes in Maryland, Henry Clay triumphed by a single percentage point in Ohio, and in the three electoral districts of Illinois, no winning candidate managed to muster more than a plurality.[45] But nowhere did turnout really reflect these results. Maryland's respectable 54 percent was the highest across the whole nation, but in Ohio, only slightly more than one-third of those eligible bothered to register their preference. And in Illinois, just three months after fourth-fifths of the electorate thronged to the polls to keep their state free from slavery, barely one-third returned to determine the next occupant of the White House. In only two states across the Union did the vote in 1824 equal or exceed average turnout in congressional and gubernatorial elections across the period, and in the case of Connecticut at least, that outcome says more about how low participation rates were generally than it does about popular enthusiasm for the presidential contest (table 5).

For the most part, historians have interpreted this discrepancy as merely "reflecting what many Americans believed to be the greater importance of politics below the national level."[46] Yet average turnout in congressional elections across the Union hovered around the 50 percent mark from 1820 to 1825, nearly double that for the selection of Monroe's successor in 1824, and significantly greater than we expect to see today.[47] Likewise, as Noble E. Cunningham Jr. has long since observed, the sheer volume of letters and petitions directed to congressmen by their constituents "contradicts the arguments that legislators in Washington were isolated from the people they governed and that the people themselves were indifferent to what the national government did."[48] More work is needed then to explain John Taylor's "great political curiosity": What was it about the presidency specifically during this period that made most Americans indifferent come election day? And given that we have rightly moved beyond old fairytales about Andrew Jackson playing the Pied Piper, why did this situation change so dramatically over the following two decades?[49]

What these findings most clearly do is problematize the standard narrative that celebrates the rise of parties for replacing the deferential politics of the prerevolutionary period with a robust and rambunctious democracy.[50] In colonial America, it is said, the rule of the few was sustained by a somewhat vague formula involving wealth, reputation, and virtue, a combination that, according to contemporary understanding, made them alone capable of governing.[51]

Table 5 Comparison of presidential and congressional/gubernatorial turnout in selected states

Ranking (by presidential election turnout)[a]	State	Turnout in 1824 presidential election (%)	Index of competition for 1824 election[b] (%)	Average turnout across gubernatorial and congressional elections, 1820–1825 (%)
1	Maryland	54	0	60
2	Alabama[c]	50	52	80
3	Mississippi[c]	46	31	65
6	Ohio	38	1	51
7	Illinois	33	6	69
8	New Jersey	31	10	19
18	Connecticut	15	59	15

[a] Presidential electors were chosen by popular vote in eighteen states and by the legislature in the remaining six. Connecticut's was therefore the lowest turnout of the eighteen states that used the popular method.

[b] Percentage of vote for winning candidate minus percentage of vote for nearest competitor. The larger the number, the less competitive the election.

[c] Alabama and Mississippi are included here to show that their relatively high turn-outs in 1824 were achieved in the absence of any real competition, since Jackson won both states easily, or sustained efforts to mobilize the electorate. Once again, the conventional "party equals participation" model cannot account for these results.

That these qualities carried less authority by the first decades of the nine-teenth century cannot be doubted, and their decline in preeminence may well be attributed, at least in part, to processes attendant on party formation. But this did not automatically make politics more democratic. Instead, the advent of parties introduced the people to a new set of masters, exchanging party rank for social status as the most important determinant of political power.

This was certainly the opinion of Joseph Buckingham in Massachusetts. "The majority of the people in the state," he wrote in the *New-England Galaxy*:

seldom trouble their heads about public matters, unless private, and per-sonal interest is to be in some shape or another affected. They mind their own domestic concerns, and leave the affairs of state to be settled by

juntoes, caucuses, central committees, and a few demagogues, who, having by management, seated themselves in office, are determined to keep
their places and establish themselves as perpetual dictators. Whatever is
said by General ——, or Major ——, or the Hon. Mr. ——, or . . . Esq.
is received as right and expedient; and if there should happen to be a
slight difference of opinion, as to the measure proposed, it is wrong to
suggest it, because opposition duly weakens and divides the party, and
hurts the feelings of these honorable and patriotic gentlemen.[52]

Buckingham's complaint suggests that not only could deference and parties
coexist, but in fact parties actually relied on forms of deference in order to
function. Party leaders, by definition, took the lead and expected the party
faithful to follow. Politics was managed by means of "juntoes, caucuses, [and]
central committees," and power was concentrated in the hands of those who
commanded this machinery. The role of the partisan press was to regulate access to information, which, as Richard D. Brown has shown, was an effective
way to ensure a compliant electorate.[53] And the concept of party discipline
further served to legitimate the continuing deference of the many to the few;
decisions from on high had to be obeyed, because "opposition duly weakens
and divides the party." The effect of all this was to channel, control, even
curb popular expression. Or as "Brutus," another *Galaxy* correspondent, succinctly put it: under the prevailing arrangements, "'We the people' have no
political existence."[54]

Partisan management is not necessarily a barrier to mass participation at
the polls, of course; both Pasley's and Burnham's figures stand as testament
to that. But in the decade that followed the War of 1812, the Federalist and
Republican parties also faced the problem of having outgrown the original
points of conflict that had previously energized them. "We cannot make our
children know, and feel, and understand, all the reasons which induced our
fathers to differ in the time of Jay's treaty," noted Buckingham in an editorial
that accurately predicted the demise of old party labels, "nor bequeath to
them the animosities which were roused, and perhaps justly roused, by the
embargo and non-intercourse laws, and the measures which led to the late
war."[55] With increasingly little to differentiate between the two parties in re-
gards to policy, at both federal and state level, party leaders became ever more
reliant on an appeal to traditional loyalties to mobilize their supporters, just
as these loyalties were themselves losing their meaning.

Here then is an explanation for the disparities in turnout witnessed across the United States during the early 1820s. In some states with little experience of party conflict, such as Illinois and Kentucky, the injection of new issues, new alignments, and new (sometimes nonpartisan) modes of organization served to inflate participation rates. Meanwhile, in Massachusetts, and probably elsewhere too, well-established and comparatively elaborate party forms proved unable to sustain enthusiasm for an entrenched system in which many citizens no longer felt they had any stake. As for presidential elections, the 1824 campaign introduced an element of competition that was noticeably lacking four years earlier, but still the race for the White House impacted little on the lives of most Americans; a contest "between those in office—and them who want their places" was how one commentator characterized it.[56] This was a subject about which, as Taylor discovered, "partisans are zealous, and a great majority of the people indifferent," and so it would remain until party-builders succeeded in connecting the battle for the presidency with real issues of popular concern.[57]

The grievances of men like Buckingham and "Brutus" did not pass unnoticed in those parts of the nation that remained free from party management. "Whoever has seen, as we have, how regularly drilled and organized, is the system of elective nomination, in the eastern states, . . . would see how specious, how plausible [sic], and yet how pernicious, is this course," declared "Zero" in the *Illinois Intelligencer* in 1820. "Instead of the direct individual influence of the candidate, on the community at large, arising from the open declarations of his pen; his public demonstrations of the interests of his country at *the Hustings* . . . instead of all this, he is enshrined as the Juggernaut of his party." In a passage that could have come straight from the columns of the *New-England Galaxy*, the writer deplored the "little private caucuses" that "cut and dried" the choice of candidate long before the actual nominating meeting took place. "Experience has shewn," he concluded, that "caucuses, nominations [and] delegations . . . are political machines in the hands of the designing, the wealthy, and the vicious, by which they essay to influence, guide, and govern popular opinion."[58]

Statements such as this shed light not only on political practices during this period but also on popular attitudes toward parties. In seeking to explain the pervasiveness of antiparty sentiment in the half-century following the revolution, historians have often cited the continued power of increasingly outdated republican principles or the influence of an idealistic strain of evangelical

Protestantism.[59] Critics like "Zero" and Buckingham, however, and many others who joined them in resisting the spread of parties, derived their convictions not from theoretical treatises or utopian sermons but from a certain knowledge of the consequences of partisan hegemony. Far from welcoming the rise of party as a harbinger of democracy, these political prophets deplored it as a new tool by which a handful of men could maintain their grip on government, a tool made necessary, in some areas at least, by a preceding upsurge in participation that rendered traditional modes of politics built on personal connections obsolete. Or, to quote another lifelong opponent of party, John C. Calhoun, a youthful first-time contender for the presidency in 1824 when he wrote these words, "If the [spirit of aristocracy] favored the few against the many, the few wealthy and well born against the body of the people, so does [the spirit of combination and political management] favor the cause of the few, not indeed the same class, but the few intriguers and managers against the people."[60]

Finally, turnout data underlines the sheer diversity of political life in the early United States. No longer can we afford to dismiss the decade that followed the War of 1812 as an "Era of No Feelings." But what label might we put in its place? The new periodization scheme must be flexible enough to encompass the remnants of the Federalist-Republican system in Massachusetts and Delaware, the first stirrings of the Democrat-Whig system in parts of the Mid-Atlantic, and a host of other state-level alignments that bore little or no relationship to national politics. It must cover both 85 percent and higher participation rates in Alabama, Georgia, and Rhode Island, and single-figure turnouts in Connecticut and New Jersey. And it must find room for men like Harrison Gray Otis, who considered two-party competition to be the natural order of things, and for men like "Zero," who sought to conduct their politics without recourse to party. This was a period of vitality and innovation, with fluidity in forms and uncertainty in outcomes, where a political system organized around two competing national parties was only one of many possible futures. In sum, this was an Era of Experimentation during which a generation of Americans grappled with the democratic potential inherent in the principle of popular sovereignty that lay at the heart of the young republic.

Notes

1. John H. Aldrich, *Why Parties? The Origin and Transformation of Political Parties in America* (Chicago: University of Chicago Press, 1995), 3.

2. Sean Wilentz, *The Rise of American Democracy: Jefferson to Lincoln* (New York: Norton, 2005); Daniel Walker Howe, *What Hath God Wrought: The Transformation of America, 1815–1848* (Oxford: Oxford University Press, 2007), 489 (quotation).

3. "Era of Good Feelings," *Columbian Centinel* (Boston), 12 July 1817.

4. Morton Keller, *America's Three Regimes* (Oxford: Oxford University Press, 2007), 72. For similar assessments, see Glenn C. Altschuler and Stuart M. Blumin, *Rude Republic: Americans and Their Politics in the Nineteenth Century* (Princeton, N.J.: Princeton University Press, 2000), 14, and Michael Schudson, *The Good Citizen: A History of American Civic Life* (New York: Free Press, 1998), 112.

5. "Presidential Election," *Richmond Enquirer*, 7 November 1820.

6. *Western Carolinian* (Salisbury, North Carolina), 8 June 1824, cited in Albert Ray Newsome, *The Presidential Election of 1824 in North Carolina* (Chapel Hill: University of North Carolina Press, 1939), 140.

7. John Taylor to John H. Bernard, 8 April 1824, John Taylor Papers, Library of Virginia, Richmond.

8. Walter Dean Burnham, "The Changing Shape of the American Political Universe," *American Political Science Review* 59 (March 1965): 7–28. See also Burnham, "Table I: Summary: Presidential Elections, USA, 1788–2004," *Journal of the Historical Society* 7 (December 2007): 521–80.

9. Joel H. Silbey, *The American Political Nation, 1838–1893* (Stanford, Cal.: Stanford University Press, 1991), 144 (quotation); Richard L. McCormick, "The Party Period and Public Policy: An Exploratory Hypothesis," *Journal of American History* 66 (September 1979): 279–98.

10. Jeffrey L. Pasley, "The Cheese and the Words: Popular Political Culture and Participatory Democracy in the Early American Republic," in *Beyond the Founders: New Approaches to the Political History of the Early American Republic*, ed. Jeffrey L. Pasley, Andrew W. Robertson, and David Waldstreicher (Chapel Hill: University of North Carolina Press, 2004), 45. The scholars named here are all contributors to the *Beyond the Founders* volume, which places this interpretation at its core. See also Donald J. Ratcliffe, *Party Spirit in a Frontier Republic: Democratic Politics in Ohio 1793–1821* (Columbus: Ohio State University Press, 1998).

11. Pasley, "Cheese and the Words," 46. Limited work has been done on state-level voter turnout prior to the 1830s, but two important exceptions are J. R. Pole, *Political Representation in England and the Origins of the American Republic* (Berkeley: University of California Press, 1971), which includes data on several states from previous articles by the same author; and Donald J. Ratcliffe, "Voter Turnout in Early Ohio," *Journal of the Early Republic* 7 (Autumn 1987): 223–51. Burnham's figures for this period are based on limited data and only break down the results by region. Walter

Dean Burnham, "Critical Realignment: Dead or Alive?" in *The End of Realignment? Interpreting American Electoral Eras,* ed. Byron Shafer (Madison: University of Wisconsin Press, 1991), 123.

12. William Nisbet Chambers and Philip C. Davis, "Party, Competition, and Mass Participation: The Case of the Democratizing Party System, 1824–1852," in *The History of American Electoral Behavior,* ed. Joel H. Silbey, Allan G. Bogue, and William H. Flanigan (Princeton, N.J.: Princeton University Press, 1978), 196.

13. Silbey, *American Political Nation,* 9–10.

14. Andrew W. Robertson, "Voting Rites and Voting Acts: Electioneering Ritual, 1790–1820," in Pasley et al., eds., *Beyond the Founders,* 67. For an older, but perceptive, caution against the tendency of scholars "to exaggerate the causal impact of party organization in raising turnout and creating interest in politics generally," see Ronald P. Formisano, "Deferential-Participant Politics: The Early Republic's Political Culture, 1789–1840," *American Political Science Review* 68 (June 1974): 483, and Frank J. Sorauf, "Political Parties and Political Analysis," in *The American Party Systems: Stages of Political Development,* ed. William Nisbet Chambers and Walter Dean Burnham (Oxford: Oxford University Press, 1967), 33–55.

15. William E. Gienapp, "'Politics Seem to Enter into Everything': Political Culture in the North, 1840–1860," in *Essays on American Antebellum Politics, 1840–1860,* ed. Stephen E. Maizlish and John J. Kushma (College Station: Texas A&M University Press, 1982), 15.

16. Pasley, "Cheese and the Words," 49; Andrew W. Robertson, "'Look on This Picture . . . And on This!': Nationalism, Localism, and Partisan Images of Otherness in the United States, 1787–1820," *American Historical Review* 106 (October 2001): 1280.

17. The data in the following tables was calculated by dividing the number of votes cast in an election by the estimated size of the electorate. To calculate the size of the electorate, I used federal and state census data, adjusted according to the restrictions on the franchise in each state, and interpolated for intervening years. The figures for votes cast were taken from A New Nation Votes: American Election Returns 1787–1825, http://elections.lib.tufts.edu/, supplemented by other sources where necessary.

My methodology is modeled on that employed by both Burnham and Pasley in order to facilitate comparison. I recognize that certain criticisms have been leveled at this methodology, such as that it does not account for the tendency of nineteenth-century censuses to undercount eligible voters. I make no claim, therefore, that my figures are accurate right down to the last voter, but they do provide a frame of reference for comparing both between states and across time periods. Or, to put it another way, I acknowledge that any flaws in the model pioneered by Burnham apply equally to my calculations, but I consider this to be a strength as well as a weakness of this approach.

Burnham's 64 percent figure applies only to off-year elections between 1850 and 1898, whereas my figures in table 2 also include the presidential years of 1820 and

1824. During the early 1820s, however, presidential elections were held on different dates to other elections in every state except Massachusetts and New Jersey, and in any case, turnout in the presidential elections of 1820 and 1824 was so low that it could hardly have exerted a coattails effect on turnout in other elections even where these were held concurrently.

For a sample of recent work that makes use of the A New Nation Votes database, see the special issue of the *Journal of the Early Republic* 33 (Summer 2013).

18. Any measure of partisan affiliation during this period of political flux is somewhat inexact. This analysis is based on data from *Biographical Directory of the United States Congress 1774–Present*, http://bioguide.congress.gov/biosearch/biosearch.asp.

19. "Virginius," *Richmond Enquirer*, 7 November 1820.

20. Richard P. McCormick, *The Second American Party System: Party Formation in the Jacksonian Era* (Chapel Hill: University of North Carolina Press, 1966), 40.

21. Silbey, *American Political Nation*, 14–15. The debate over whether the Federalists and Republicans should qualify as parties is summarized in Ratcliffe, *Party Spirit*, 2–5.

22. Detailed contemporary descriptions of the Federalist organization and nominating procedure may be found in "Federal Caucus, for the Nomination of City Officers," *Boston Commercial Gazette*, 8 April 1822, and "Federal Caucuses," *Boston Daily Advertiser*, 18 May 1822.

23. On the functions of the partisan press, see John L. Brooke, "To Be 'Read by the Whole People': Press, Party, and Public Sphere in the United States, 1789–1840," *Proceedings of the American Antiquarian Society* 110 (2000): 41–118, and Jeffrey L. Pasley, *"The Tyranny of Printers": Newspaper Politics in the Early American Republic* (Charlottesville: University Press of Virginia, 2001).

24. The activities of partisan auxiliaries between elections are explored by Albrecht Koschnik, *"Let a Common Interest Bind Us Together": Associations, Partisanship, and Culture in Philadelphia, 1775–1840* (Charlottesville: University of Virginia Press, 2007), and David Waldstreicher, *In the Midst of Perpetual Fetes: The Making of American Nationalism, 1776–1820* (Chapel Hill: University of North Carolina Press, 1997).

25. See, for example, "More Central Committee Dictation," *Boston Patriot & Daily Mercantile Advertiser*, 25 March 1820; and "Federal Vote Distributors" and "Vigilance," both in *Boston Commercial Gazette*, 1 April 1822.

26. "Our Representative to Congress," *New-England Galaxy* (Boston), 3 November 1820.

27. "Municipal Elections," *New-England Galaxy* (Boston), 9 March 1821. The Republican Institution and the Federalist Central Committee were the bodies at the heads of the respective party hierarchies.

28. "Federal Caucus," *New-England Galaxy* (Boston), 12 April 1822.

29. "Impartiality of Editors," *New-England Galaxy* (Boston), 12 April 1822.

30. *The Middling Interest* (Boston, [March] 1822), American Broadsides and Ephemera Database.

31. [Harrison Gray Otis], "Speech before a Federalist Caucus, Spring of 1822,"

[12 May 1822], reel 8, Harrison Gray Otis Papers, Massachusetts Historical Society, Boston.

32. The classic text on this theme is Richard Hofstadter, *The Idea of a Party System: The Rise of Legitimate Opposition in the United States, 1780–1840* (Berkeley: University of California Press, 1970).

33. More detail on Massachusetts politics during this period may be found in Ronald P. Formisano, *The Transformation of Political Culture: Massachusetts Parties, 1790s–1840s* (Oxford: Oxford University Press, 1983), and Daniel Peart, *Era of Experimentation: American Political Practices in the Early Republic* (Charlottesville: University of Virginia Press, 2014), ch. 1. It is worth noting that while 1825 effectively marked the demise of the Federalist-Republican system in Massachusetts, two-party competition under those labels persisted longer there than the Democratic-Whig system would in most states. The stability, or otherwise, of the latter is the subject of Graham A. Peck's essay in this volume.

34 "Aristides," *Edwardsville Spectator* (Illinois), 5 February 1822.

35. Silbey, *American Political Nation*, 16.

36. John Mason Peck to Hooper Warren, 27 March 1855, in *Governor Edward Coles,* ed. Clarence Walworth Alvord (Springfield: Illinois State Historical Library, 1920), 334. The opponents of slavery were labeled anti-conventionists because they opposed the calling of a constitutional convention.

37. John Reynolds, *My Own Times: Embracing Also, the History of My Life* (Chicago, 1879), 155.

38. Of ballots cast, 57 percent were against a change to the constitution, and 43 percent in favor. For differing interpretations of this episode see Peart, *Era of Experimentation,* ch. 2, and James Simeone, *Democracy and Slavery in Frontier Illinois: The Bottomland Republic* (DeKalb: Northern Illinois University Press, 2000).

39. McCormick, *Second American Party System,* 177, 320, 151.

40. Ronald P. Formisano, *For the People: American Populist Movements from the Revolution to the 1850s* (Chapel Hill: University of North Carolina Press, 2008), 101.

41. McCormick, *Second American Party System,* 212–15.

42. James Roger Sharp, *American Politics in the Early Republic: The New Nation in Crisis* (New Haven, Conn.: Yale University Press, 1993), 8.

43. On the importance of these factors see, for example, Robertson, "Look on This Picture."

44. Horatio Newhall to J. & J. Newhall, 11 May 1822, folder 1, Horatio Newhall Letters and Journal, Abraham Lincoln Presidential Library, Springfield, Illinois.

45. All of these figures are either from A New Nation Votes or direct from Phil Lampi, who first collected much of the data now made available via that site.

46. Silbey, *American Political Nation*, 13. For similar conclusions, see John L. Brooke, "Cultures of Nationalism, Movements of Reform, and the Composite-Federal Polity: From Revolutionary Settlement to Antebellum Crisis," *Journal of the Early Republic* 29 (Spring 2009): 6, and Ronald P. Formisano, "State Development in the Early Republic: Substance and Structure, 1780–1840," in *Contesting Democracy:*

Substance and Structure in American Political History, 1775–2000, ed. Byron E. Shafer and Anthony J. Badger (Lawrence: Kansas University Press, 2001), 19. These works follow in the footsteps of James Sterling Young, *The Washington Community, 1800–1828* (New York: Columbia University Press, 1966). For a recent revisionist interpretation, see Brian Balogh, *A Government out of Sight: The Mystery of National Authority in Nineteenth-Century America* (Cambridge: Cambridge University Press, 2009).

47. Congressional turnout was 46 percent in 1820–21, 47 percent in 1822–23, and 51 percent in 1824–25. Gubernatorial turnout across the whole period, by comparison, was 58 percent.

48. Noble E. Cunningham Jr., *The Process of Government under Jefferson* (Princeton, N.J.: Princeton University Press, 1978), 300.

49. John Taylor to John H. Bernard, 8 April 1824, John Taylor Papers, Library of Virginia, Richmond.

50. Richard R. Beeman helpfully defines, without endorsing, the concept of deference as "a means of describing a society that . . . [seems] consensual in its social and political relations but hierarchical in its distribution of power and authority." Beeman, "Deference, Republicanism, and the Emergence of Popular Politics in Eighteenth-Century America," *William and Mary Quarterly*, 3rd series, 49 (July 1992): 403.

51. The usefulness of deference as a concept for explaining colonial politics continues to be the subject of much debate. See, for example, Roundtable on "Deference in Early America: The Life and/or Death of an Historiographical Concept," *Early American Studies* 3 (Fall 2005): 227–401. In his contribution, John Smolenski writes that "historians have afforded deference an important place in a larger metanarrative about the rise of American democracy. Rather than studying deference itself, they have used it as the centrepiece of a 'before' picture that will be swept away by the political and social changes the American Revolution wrought; the existence of deference in a pre-Revolutionary America lends relief to the 'after' picture." In this respect, the challenge posed by Smolenski and his collaborators to the conventional story of democratization as it is commonly told about the colonial period parallels my own concerns with regard to the early United States. Smolenski, "From Men of Property to Just Men: Deference, Masculinity, and the Evolution of Political Discourse in Early America," *Early American Studies* 3 (Fall 2005): 253–85, 257 (quotation).

52. "The Constitution," *New-England Galaxy* (Boston), 6 October 1820.

53. Richard D. Brown, *Knowledge Is Power: The Diffusion of Information in Early America, 1700–1865* (Oxford: Oxford University Press, 1989).

54. "Brutus," *New-England Galaxy* (Boston), 29 September 1820. The analysis of Buckingham and "Brutus" anticipates, by 180 years, the conclusion reached by Glenn Altschuler and Stuart Blumin: precisely because parties became so effective at what they did, "Americans could, if they wished, leave the work [of politics] to the professionals, and go about their other business." Altschuler and Blumin, *Rude Republic*, 81. The point that new parties often assimilated, rather than dissolved, older forms of deference is also stressed by Formisano, "Deferential-Participant Politics," 473–87.

To those who would argue that the situation in Massachusetts was unique because the unusual persistence of Federalism there delayed the democratizing reforms promoted by Republicans elsewhere in the nation, I would reply that in Thomas Jefferson's own Virginia, property qualifications on the franchise, which barred somewhere close to half of the adult white male population from voting, were maintained into the 1850s, as the legislature consistently blocked popular efforts to obtain a more equitable reapportionment of political power. By this measure at least, there appears little reason for crediting the Republican planter aristocracy of the Old Dominion over the Federalist merchant princes of Massachusetts, where property qualifications were eliminated in 1821.

55. *New-England Galaxy* (Boston), 9 April 1824.

56. Edward Patchell to James Hall, 4 September 1823, box 1, folder 2, Henry Eddy Papers, Illinois History and Lincoln Collections, University of Illinois at Urbana-Champaign.

57. John Taylor to John H. Bernard, 8 April 1824, John Taylor Papers, Library of Virginia, Richmond.

58. "Zero," *Illinois Intelligencer* (Vandalia), 9 June 1819, cited in Gerald Leonard, *The Invention of Party Politics: Federalism, Popular Sovereignty, and Constitutional Development in Jacksonian Illinois* (Chapel Hill: University of North Carolina Press, 2002), 59–60.

59. For a summary of these arguments, and further references to their sources, see Michael F. Holt, *The Rise and Fall of the American Whig Party: Jacksonian Politics and the Onset of the Civil War* (Oxford: Oxford University Press, 1999), 30–31.

60. John C. Calhoun to Lewis Cass, Washington, 14 October 1823, *The Papers of John C. Calhoun*, ed. Robert L. Meriwether et al., 28 vols. (Columbia: University of South Carolina Press, 1959–2003), 8:312.

★ GRAHAM A. PECK ★

Was There a Second Party System?

Illinois as a Case Study in Antebellum Politics

Over the past fifty years, the concept of the second party system has come to exercise a powerful influence on antebellum historiography. That a party system existed is rarely questioned, and the Second Party System is a familiar, proper noun in monographs and textbooks. The concept even shapes the defining debate in antebellum politics—explaining the origins of the Civil War—because the triumph of the antislavery Republican Party and the consequent secession of southern states required the prior or concurrent collapse of the party system. Historians, therefore, began debating why the party system failed nearly fifty years ago, only shortly after the introduction of the concept itself. The debate has not yet achieved resolution, but its vigor underscores the importance of historians' widespread presumption that a re-alignment of the party system in the 1850s requires special explanation.[1]

This essay challenges that presumption. It argues that voters' allegiances could not be taken for granted, that party loyalties were less entrenched than is often acknowledged, that the stability of the party system has been corre-spondingly overstated, and that historians should consequently rethink how they use the concept of a party system, if they use the terminology at all. In this telling of antebellum history, viewed through the prism of Illinois's vot-ers, antebellum party politics was at root unstable, changing dynamically to reflect voters' interests and judgments. While the party systems concept pre-supposes that voters' partisan affiliations largely determined how they voted, this chapter argues that voters cared primarily about issues. In the 1820s and 1830s, voters' intense interest in the fate of democracy and economic develop-ment spurred their participation in the political system, led to the rise of the Democratic and Whig parties, and influenced which issues politicians tackled. But in the 1840s and 1850s, voters' growing interest in slavery's influence on economic opportunity and the meaning of freedom led them to experiment with various alternatives to the established parties. Democratic and Whig politicians tried to deflect or coopt this experimentation, but despite their efforts to recruit additional party members and maintain the allegiance of existing ones, most voters by the 1850s fashioned new party allegiances.

We must begin with the concept of a party system, which political scientists developed during the 1950s and 1960s in order to explain American political history. It had its origin with V. O. Key Jr.'s 1955 article on critical elections, or elections that marked a sharp discontinuity with previous elections and thus realigned the electorate.[2] Using this concept, other political scientists, most notably Walter Dean Burnham, developed the idea of party systems. Party systems characterized the stable periods in American political history, with one party system giving way to another after a critical election. In 1967, Burnham described this realignment process as "long-term continuity abruptly displaced by an explosive but short period of change." The realignments changed who voted, shuffled existing voters into different parties, and produced major, polarizing changes in national policy. Burnham identified five party systems in American history, the first three being the *"experimental system"* between Federalists and Jeffersonians, the *"democratizing system"* between Democrats and Whigs, and the Civil War system between Democrats and Republicans. The first dealt with political challenges faced by Americans after the adoption of the Constitution, the second addressed democratization in American society, and the third confronted the related problems of slavery and national economic development.[3] Burnham's bold ideas created a blueprint for his discipline, and in the ensuing decades the party system concept took deep root among political scientists, who valued its explanatory power and admired its elegant theory, which seemed all the more persuasive given their presumption that long-term party affiliation was the most critical factor in explaining voter behavior. This presumption did not paint an especially flattering portrait of the electorate, but post–World War II political scientists did not consider the average American voter sufficiently knowledgeable, rational, or sophisticated to participate in politics on any other basis.[4] If such voters indeed predominated, political scientists could logically infer stable party systems periodically disrupted by critical elections.

But the party system concept was never adopted wholesale, and certainly not by historians. Burnham himself acknowledged that the first party system remained competitive for only about a decade, and that the second party system's "dramatic collapse" after 1854 "disclosed its essential fragility."[5] He was not alone in finding exceptions to his generalizations, and over the next decade political scientists criticized the ideas of critical elections and realignment theory on a number of other fronts.[6] Historians, with their characteristic focus on comprehending the particularistic aspects of an alien past, understandably tended toward a less overarching view from the start. In 1966, Richard P. McCormick contended in *The Second American Party System* that each of the "party systems that has existed in the United States since the 1790's must be viewed as a distinctive entity, differing so fundamentally from one another as to constitute separate models." McCormick considered the regional character of antebellum politics to be especially distinctive, and attributed the "relatively brief duration" of the second party system to its "artificial" need to avoid "explicitly sectional issues."[7] Even Michael F. Holt, who has applied party systems theory to Jacksonian politics in the most sophisticated and comprehensive way, concedes that vibrant party competition existed only during the eleven years between 1837 and 1848, notably less than the thirty-year period postulated by Burnham's realignment theory.[8]

Nevertheless, most political historians since the 1960s have incorporated the party system concept into their work. The result is an historical literature deeply tinctured by Burnham's ideas. Historians have produced many studies of various aspects of Jacksonian party conflict over the past half-century, and the second party system has won wide acceptance as a concept necessary to understanding antebellum politics. In a 1998 historiographical essay, Holt articulated the core conviction behind this literature, writing that the "concomitant realignment/party system synthesis argued that American political history from the 1790s to at least the 1960s could best be understood in terms of five successive two-party systems that were distinguished from one another less by the content of the issues and policies over which their constituent parties fought than by the durability of voter allegiance to the rival parties."[9]

Yet historians have struggled to incorporate the model's assumption of political stability. For instance, in *Rude Republic: Americans and Their Politics in the Nineteenth Century*, Glenn C. Altschuler and Stuart M. Blumin declare that "if the constituent elements of the partisan system were not so very stable —the Whigs would disappear within two decades, and Free Soil, American, and other parties would come and go—the system was stability itself."[10] But to boil down the party systems concept to the persistence of two-party competition is to boil it away altogether. Burnham did not seek to explain the persistence of two-party competition. Rather, he sought to identify a critical aspect of it: realignments that explained major shifts in the distribution and use of partisan power.

Ironically, even Michael Holt has had difficulty presuming political stability. As he points out, people "who lived during the nineteenth century never knew they were experiencing the realigning or stable phase of a party system." Rather, they experienced the "political flux and uncertainty" of day-to-day politics.[11] To Holt's credit, his own histories brim with uncertainty, emphasizing possibilities that could have radically altered American history. Yet his emphasis on contingency, a characteristically historical preference, undermines the party system concept. After all, if contingency is so central to historical explanation, historians cannot easily accept an interpretive model that privileges a small number of critical elections over so many other ones. The dilemma inherent in historians' use of the party systems model is reflected in Holt's magnum opus, *The Rise and Fall of the American Whig Party*, which seeks to explain the Whig Party's collapse in the 1850s. Holt focuses on this problem precisely because the presumption of political stability in the second party system makes the Whig Party's death a central event in nineteenth-century politics. Without it, no third party system could arise, and probably no Civil War.[12] Yet the extraordinary complexity of the story Holt tells about the history of the Whig Party makes it hard to credit the presumption of political stability in the 1840s. Holt's remarkable work is perhaps the best evidence of the model's limitations.[13]

Historians' continued attachment to party systems is especially ironic given that contemporary political scientists have adopted historical concepts to critique the party systems model and its underlying propositions. Dissatisfied with the idea that party affiliation primarily determined voter behavior, Morris P. Fiorina developed a retrospective voting model in 1981 that incorporated multiple factors he believed influenced voters: their prior party affiliation, their issue preferences and future expectations, and their retrospective assessment of the results produced by past party decisions. After testing his model against polling and election data from twentieth-century American political history, Fiorina concluded that voters made rational decisions based on issue preferences and retrospective judgments, and that their votes held politicians and parties accountable for past conduct.[14] Voters' vigilance compelled politicians such as Franklin Delano Roosevelt to take responsibility for governance. Rather than assuming a quiescent electorate in a stable party system, Roosevelt and other politicians exercised leadership in order to solve problems and win voters' support. Although Fiorina's equation-laden model appears quite distinct from historical methodologies, his portrayal of the relationship between politicians and voters reflected what political historians prior to the emergence of party systems theory had always assumed: that politicians sought to influence voters who ranged in political knowledge, sophistication, and engagement, but who voted self-interestedly by calibrating future desires against past experiences.[15] These were not the dullards presumed by mid-twentieth-century political scientists. Instead of following politicians like sheep, they influenced political outcomes in contingent and unpredictable ways, and by postulating such voters, Fiorina's work undercut an important presumption of realignment theory.

More recently, David R. Mayhew took more direct aim at the theory and advocated "abandoning the terminology entirely." Unable to identify critical elections in American political history after reviewing studies of election returns, he judged that it would be quixotic to search for periods of electoral stability between them.[16] He instead concluded that American politics has been unpredictable due to contingency, short-term party strategies designed to recruit voters before elections, and voters' practice of judging parties as much on "perceived government management" as on policy issues. Despite political scientists' desire to create predictive models, he argued that the historical record is proof against "the system-building ambition of the realignments genre."[17] Central to Mayhew's argument is an insight he shares with Fiorina: that in "the real world," voters must make judgments "all the time." They do not slumber for thirty years before awakening to issue new directives to the country's political elite.[18] Voter attitudes matter to electoral outcomes in each and every election.

Fiorina's and Mayhew's insights encourage examination of antebellum voters' concerns. Although Fiorina's model requires polling data not available to historians of the nineteenth century, his contention that twentieth-century voters' attitudes shaped policy decisions and electoral outcomes underscores the importance of comprehending the perspective of nineteenth-century voters.[19] Historians have never ignored this task, but they generally have focused far more attention on politicians than voters, an understandable emphasis given the greater availability of politicians' records, not to mention politicians' greater influence in shaping policy and politicizing events.[20] Nevertheless, politicians can only illuminate so much about antebellum politics. Constrained by broader social discourse, they cannot and do not say whatever they wish, and in fact are typically circumspect in when and how they appeal to voters. Hence much can be learned about antebellum politics by thinking about how voters perceived it. Prospects for economic opportunity, which drove generations of settlers west and brought waves of immigrants to eastern shores, probably loomed largest in their thinking. The country's political experiment was also of great significance: Who would get to vote? How would they get to vote? What would they get to vote on? Powerful cultural attitudes, such as evangelicalism, nativism, and nationalism also deeply shaped Americans' participation in politics, as was evident in debates over Indian removal, expansion, immigration, and a host of other matters.

Such broad-ranging economic, political, and cultural issues interwove in complex and unpredictable ways during the antebellum years, and the fate of the Democratic and Whig parties hinged substantially on the particular constellations they formed. As John L. Brooke has argued elsewhere in this volume, the parties shaped and managed American politics but did not control political outcomes. They were in a dialogue with voters about contemporary issues, and knew that voters could replace them. Voters certainly had frequent opportunity to do so. Between 1830 and 1880, the average service tenure of representatives at the beginning of each Congress was about two years, or one term, the lowest average tenure in American history. Correspondingly, only about 60 percent of representatives sought reelection during those years, one of the lowest rates in American history.[21] Inadequate compensation and extended separation from families spurred many congressmen to leave Congress during those years, but, whatever the reasons, the rapid turnover gave voters the opportunity to select new representatives on a regular basis.[22] As this essay seeks to demonstrate, voters selecting those representatives cared deeply about issues.

Illinois's history helps us to gauge the issue orientation of antebellum voters. At the state's inception in 1818, Illinoisans were a mix of migrants from other states, with poor southern whites predominating. Almost all settlers sought to acquire land, and their ability to survive largely on its proceeds gave them a proud and prickly independence that infused politics with a democratic character from the start. The arrival of migrant streams from northeastern and Mid-Atlantic states altered Illinois in the 1830s, spurring the growth of markets and economic exchange, and contributing to partisan feuding between the Democratic and Whig parties over banking and internal improvements.

The continuing flow of migrants from other states in the 1840s began to put price pressures on the land and influenced partisan debates over expansion, while the arrival of Irish and German immigrants, who poured into Chicago and other urban areas in the 1840s and 1850s, fueled social divisions and political unrest over temperance, Catholicism, poverty, and crime. Meanwhile, the significance of slavery ebbed and flowed. Intense antislavery sentiment surfaced in the 1820s as a response to proslavery politicians who sought to legalize human bondage, but antislavery politics quelled quickly thereafter and remained a subordinate issue despite the rise of abolitionism in the later 1830s. Political debate over slavery, however, reemerged forcefully in the 1840s, when the prospect of slavery's expansion into national territories convulsed the country, and by the 1850s abolitionist ideas animated Republican Party assaults on slavery. Illinois's history from statehood until the Civil War thus reflects the major developments of mid-nineteenth-century American history fairly well. While the state's residents were not perfectly representative of the country as a whole, they participated in politics as Americans did elsewhere, and debated the key issues that shaped antebellum politics.

Notably, the state's history suggests that we cannot presume coherent and persisting blocs of Whig and Democratic voters. To be sure, between 1828 and 1848, many voters developed firm party ties, and certain locales became partisan strongholds. Nevertheless, those party connections took time to develop and were never written in stone. Political issues related to slavery, for instance, predated the party system yet were not resolved by it, and hence lurked as potentially disorganizing influences. More generally, some issues corresponded to a partisan framework, such as banking and internal improvements, but others did not, such as slavery and nativism. In those latter cases, voters often carved new paths, working in tandem with either emergent politicians or seasoned politicians who were themselves breaking from party loyalties. A dialogue between voters and politicians about issues and parties thus characterized antebellum politics, shaping Illinoisans' responses to the major political issue of each decade: the slavery convention battle in the early 1820s, national and state banking in the 1830s, national expansion in the 1840s, and slavery's extension in the 1850s. Each issue mattered deeply to the citizens of Illinois and stimulated voter participation before subsiding in significance and being replaced by a more pertinent issue. Illinois history highlights the dynamism and fluidity of antebellum politics, not the straitjackets of party loyalty.

Well before Jacksonian party politics, Illinois's slavery convention battle demonstrated that voter mobilization depended on the salience of issues. During the territorial period, from 1809 to 1818, voters played a limited political role, and what little politicking occurred typically addressed local issues such as transportation improvements.[23] Illinois's voters came to life after statehood, however, in response to politicians who sought to legalize slavery. A thin documentary record makes it impossible to follow the tracks of proslavery politicians precisely, but they were evidently emboldened by the three-year congressional battle over Missouri's admission as a slave state, from which Missouri's slaveholders emerged triumphant in 1821. Hopeful of a similar outcome, Illinois's proslavery advocates sought in 1823 to convene a convention to revise the state's constitution.[24] Their stratagem produced a bitter eighteen-month contest that dominated state politics. As one Illinoisan reported to his Massachusetts relatives in 1824, partisan feeling largely eradicated "all social intercourse between persons of different parties." Future governor Thomas Ford later recalled that the "rank and file of the people were no less excited than their political leaders," while John Reynolds remembered "aged and crippled" men being "carried to the polls," and apolitical men bestirring themselves to vote. This passionate engagement, as Daniel Peart shows elsewhere in this volume, led Illinoisans to organize extensively and vote in droves, producing a turnout of about 80 percent of the eligible voters in the 1824 election.[25]

This extraordinary turnout occurred only because ordinary people believed that the state's future hinged on slavery's status. The convention party's central argument was a potent lure: that slavery would invigorate the state's faltering economy. As land agent David Robson wrote to his employers in 1823, land would "sell much better" should Illinois legalize slavery. Meanwhile, John Reynolds, who ultimately voted for the convention, hesitated only "on account of the General Government: every other object would be answered by [slavery's] introduction."[26] But most Illinoisans were not convinced by this logic; they concluded instead that slavery would diminish the extent of economic opportunity and fundamentally alter the meaning and practice of freedom in Illinois. Slaveholders engorged "large tracts" of land, charged "Aristides," and had "little interest" in improving the country through "roads, bridges, canals, and literary institutions." Likewise, land agent Alfred Cowles judged that slavery's introduction would preclude "advances in improvement which the free states exhibit."[27] Illinoisans opposed to slavery also worried that it would necessarily undermine liberty. Advocacy of slavery requires "a change in our political institutions" that merits the "execrations" of posterity, wrote one newspaper contributor, while "A Friend to Freedom" remonstrated against introducing inhabitants who "would be ready, at the first opportunity, to cut our throats, poison our families, and burn our dwellings." Sympathetic to this concern, state senate candidate John Warnock wrote that nothing was more dangerous "to the peace and safety of the community" than to create an oppressed and vengeful caste."[28]

In the end, Illinoisans' desire to preserve liberty prevailed. A decisive 57 percent of the state's voters opposed the convention, whose defeat quickly pushed slavery to the margins of Illinois politics.[29] As one participant observed, the "question being decided in August, the anti-convention party disbanded, the county societies died, and in a very few months there was not a single prominent man (save in St. Clair county,) who would own he was in favor of introducing slavery within the State."[30] With freedom assured, more pressing issues took center stage.

The banking issue helped to spark the formation of the Democratic Party in Illinois. Banking mattered to Illinoisans, just as it did to Americans generally, because bank notes played a critical economic role, while bankers played an influential political one. This was evident in Illinois as early as 1821, when the Illinois state legislature sought to forestall widespread bankruptcies by creating the State Bank of Illinois. The legislature directed the bank to issue $300,000 worth of bank notes, intending them to be distributed to debtors, and attempted to force creditors to accept the notes at face value. But because the legislature did not back the notes with specie, or make them redeemable on demand, the state's first foray into banking deranged the credit market and repressed economic activity in the state, all courtesy of bank notes that taxpayers eventually had to redeem at great loss.[31] This lesson was not lost on Illinoisans in 1832, when President Andrew Jackson vetoed a bill rechartering the Second Bank of the United States, charging in his veto message that the bank benefited the wealthy at the expense of the poor and the powerful at the expense of the powerless, and thus violated the government's mandate to treat all citizens equally.[32] Jackson's message received mixed reviews in Illinois, but its undeniable economic implications made banking the first core issue for party organizers like Stephen A. Douglas, who challenged anti-partisan attitudes by establishing a Democratic Party organization, believing it to be the only mechanism for ascertaining and implementing the majority's will.[33] By 1835, the newly established state Democratic Party marched in tandem with Jackson by denouncing the national bank as an "instrument" of the aristocracy that had threatened the "liberties of the people."[34] Illinois Democrats by no means necessarily opposed state banks, or even a national bank, but they did demand, as Democratic Congressman Zadoc Casey put it, that any national bank be "debarred" from "participating in the general politics of the nation."[35] To achieve this end, and any other the people desired, the state party introduced conventions in order to "embody and give effect to the popular will."[36]

The intertwined issues of banking and partisan formation subsequently precipitated the formation of Illinois's Whig Party. Many Americans throughout the country considered the Democrats' partisan organizing a threat to America's republican political tradition of independent office-holding. Yet because partisan organizing seemed to be the only way to prevent the Democrats from controlling American politics, anti-Jacksonians morphed into partisan Whigs during the late 1830s. The banking issue helped to push them further down this road. After all, supporters of the national bank had good reason to consider Jackson's bank veto foolhardy. Credit flows were critical to the American economy, not least in frontier states like Illinois. The market in land, Illinois's economic engine, rested entirely on credit, as did the trade market that provided the revenue streams farmers and land speculators required to meet their debt obligations.[37]

Jackson's assault on a national bank that issued stable bank notes and controlled the issue of other banks' currency seemed preposterous to the many Illinoisans and other Americans who feared the possible repercussions. They did not need to look far to understand how important currency was. As New Salem farmer Charles Clarke wrote to his mother, farmers cared less for "fine buildings" than they did for "adding land to land."[38] But purchasing land required credit, and often the assistance of loan sharks. Fully aware of these circumstances when first running for elected office in 1832, twenty-three-year-old Abraham Lincoln declared against "the practice of loaning money at exorbitant rates of interest." He considered this "baneful and corroding system" so "prejudicial to the general interest of the community" that he advocated for a law limiting "the rates of usury." Unsurprisingly, given his desire to promote trade and economic opportunity, he later became a strong advocate of state banking as a leading Whig politician. For Lincoln and many others, access to credit was an eminently practical yet profoundly important concern.[39]

Economic issues, however, did not spur Illinoisans to forge attachments to the Democratic or Whig parties immediately. In the mid-1830s, voters thirsted for increased trade, increased immigration, and rising land values, and thus they urged politicians, regardless of party affiliation, to promote economic opportunity. Expanding credit was the first step to that end. To accomplish that object, the state legislature extended an existing bank's charter and established a new state bank in 1835, with Democrats providing the majority of pro-bank votes in each house.[40] Properly managed, these institutions would have benefited the state's residents. Bank notes redeemable on demand and bills of exchange that facilitated interregional trade reduced uncertainties in the exchange process and spurred economic growth.[41] Creating outlets for trade was the second step in the process, and public outcry spurred Illinois's state legislators to enact a mammoth system of internal improvements in 1837. Public celebrations followed passage of the measure, and politicians from both parties eagerly claimed credit for it. But the plan vastly outstripped the state's resources. Largely for this reason, the legislature tried to fund the improvements by investing $3 million in the state's banks, mostly by purchasing bank stock with state bonds. Legislators hoped that the banks' profits would enable the state to avoid taxing its hardscrabble and tightfisted farmers. Yet by swamping the banks with capital, this decision precipitated a disastrous expansion of note circulation and speculative investment.[42] When the Panic of 1837 hit months later and an economic depression followed over the next five years, the improvements projects stalled, the banks contracted their note issues, and deflation produced a flood of bankruptcies. By 1840, lawyer David Davis estimated that bankruptcy proceedings constituted eighty percent of the circuit court cases.[43]

These conditions precipitated sharper partisan conflicts. By 1839, most Illinois Democrats denounced banking and sought to shutter the state's banks, claiming that illegal bank speculation and corruption checked "the true channels of commerce," allocated capital unfairly and inefficiently, and created a form of "political slavery" for the people.[44] Whigs, however, fought stubbornly to preserve the banks, and the subject of banking roiled state politics until a legislative compromise put the banks into liquidation in 1842.[45] Subsequently, with the Democratic Party ascendant in the state, the banks in liquidation, and no money available for internal improvements, the political agitation over paper money and improvement projects unsurprisingly died down. The party loyalties forged by Illinoisans' forays into state-sponsored banking and internal improvements would be tested by new issues.

The lure of cheap western land, and the national expansion necessary to acquire it, would absorb voters' interests by the mid-1840s. This political issue, like most others, came to the forefront courtesy of politicians, but its resonance with voters stemmed from its centrality to their lives. Since the arrival of the English on American shores in the seventeenth century, population pressure on the land had generated westward migration. This dynamic continued unabated despite the growth of colonial seaports in the eighteenth century and manufacturing centers in the nineteenth. Farm families created a voracious American appetite for land. Demography was thus the first and most critical factor producing westward expansion. The second was the absence of a population capable of resisting American settlers. While overpopulation led to poverty among the landless in Europe, in America it led to a steady encroachment on Indian land, punctuated repeatedly by wars that led to Indian land cessions. The third factor was the immense value of the land Americans thus acquired. While poor settlers hewed down the trees and brought forests and prairies into cultivation, rich investors bought the property and profited from the rise in land values. Many other Americans profited as well. Indeed, in the early nineteenth century, the country's creed of economic opportunity was more deeply rooted in the availability of land than it was in the words of Thomas Jefferson and Benjamin Franklin. By the 1840s, many of the migrants who settled on the land; many of the speculators who financed its settlement; many of the merchants, teamsters, and sailors who traded and moved its fruits; and many of the villagers and townsmen who lived on its abundance perceived the benefits of continued national expansion. By midcentury, expansionism was a powerful elixir of national pride, progressive social theory, and naked self-interest, and the Democratic Party was its devoted peddler. In frontier states like Illinois, Whigs also endorsed it.[46] This enthusiasm was understandable. The land's production was the nation's prime source of wealth.[47]

Illinois's Democratic Party embraced expansionism because it was popular with voters. As Democratic Party politician James Shields wrote to Illinois's Democratic senator Sidney Breese in April 1844, "the Oregon question is becoming more and more exciting in this State," with the public "feeling" mounting for Oregon's acquisition. Shields added that the "passion" for Texas in southern Illinois was even "more exciting and more absorbing than the Oregon question," and he promised Breese that a "strike for Texas" will "do you credit which will astound you."[48] Support for the acquisition of both Oregon and Texas ran deep in Illinois. In 1842, Illinois Senator Samuel McRoberts urged Congress to facilitate settlement in Oregon by donating land to emigrant farmers, and in subsequent years, Illinois's other congress-men prodded Congress to extend American law over Oregon. They felt pro-tective of the stream of Illinoisans immigrating to Oregon, and they coveted Oregon's soil, fisheries, and ports for Asian trade. Texas offered similar in-ducements. As Governor Thomas Ford observed in 1844 at a meeting of "The Friends of the Immediate Re-Annexation of Texas," Texas's cotton planters "will need a vast amount of provisions from the valley of the Mississippi."[49] Sentiments such as these led Illinois's Democratic Party delegates to support the nomination of Tennessee expansionist James K. Polk at the 1844 Demo-cratic national convention. With him as the party standard bearer, Illinois's Democrats rolled to victory in the November election, winning seventy-one of the state's ninety-nine counties in the presidential campaign, and six of the seven congressional districts.[50]

Yet national expansion brought slavery back into politics. Once elected, Polk precipitated a war with Mexico. The train of military triumphs that followed eventuated in the Treaty of Guadalupe Hidalgo, which transferred a mas-sive tract of Mexican land to the United States. The country's new territory compelled Americans to determine slavery's national status, and that was no simple matter. Abolitionists had inveighed against slavery since the 1830s, and in 1840 antislavery voters organized the Liberty Party to free the nation from slavery. They had little success initially, but the war with Mexico gave trac-tion to their arguments. Abolitionist minister Owen Lovejoy was not the only Illinoisan alarmed by slavery's possible extension when he contended in 1848 that it was "a matter of solemn obligation upon Congress utterly and forever to prohibit the existence of slavery" in all of the nation's territories. Although subversive of the Union, this radical doctrine followed necessarily from Love-joy's nationalism: as he put it, the government was founded on the proposition of human equality and was established to protect "inalienable rights," and hence was "a means and not an end." Lovejoy was a true evangelist, tireless and persuasive, and these ideas would come to hold great weight in the decade to follow, not least with fellow Illinoisan Abraham Lincoln, who would chart his political course under the conviction that the Union and the Constitution were made to "*adorn*, and *preserve*" the Declaration of Independence.[51]

The idea of a national antislavery policy appealed to many Illinois Whigs and Democrats. In 1845, central Illinois's Whig congressman John J. Hardin denounced the southern argument that the government had an obligation to extend and perpetuate slavery. He called slavery the nation's "greatest curse,"

and declared that while the "immense majority" of northerners had no intention or desire to interfere with slavery, they did desire "that the government
keep free from any connection with slavery further than the constitution now
recognises it."[52] Hardin's position dovetailed with central Illinois's premiere
Whig newspaper, the *Alton Telegraph*, whose editor repeatedly admonished
against the "extension and perpetuation of the curse of slavery," which gave
"the slave holding interest the preponderance in the nation."[53] Northern Illinoisans expressed even stronger antislavery sentiments, led by the *Chicago
Journal*, a Whig paper that criticized slave power throughout the war, and the
abolitionist *Western Citizen*. Reading the tea leaves, Chicago's leading Democratic politician, Congressman John Wentworth, also endorsed a national antislavery policy. Speaking in the House of Representatives in 1847, he warned
southerners that opening Mexican territory to slavery would anger "millions
of wronged freemen," whose antislavery sentiment would grow "until every
portion of the Union gets its deserved share of the protection and privileges
of this government."[54] Once again relevant, the slavery issue quickly roused
strong passions among the people of the state.

Illinoisans' antislavery sentiments created powerful cross-pressures within
the state's Democratic Party in the late 1840s. Democrats were not of one
mind. Central and southern Illinois Democrats generally supported the
policy of the national Democratic Party, which would come to be known as
popular sovereignty. It permitted a territory's settlers to choose whether to
incorporate slavery into their state constitution. But many northern Illinois
Democrats wanted Congress to exclude slavery in the territories, and in the
1848 presidential election thousands of them defected to the newfound Free
Soil Party, an amalgam of abolitionists, free-soil Democrats, and antislavery
Whigs. Although the Free Soilers only had a few months to organize their new
party prior to the November election, their pledge to stop slavery's expansion
attracted 15,702 voters in Illinois, or 12.6 percent of the overall state tally, with
a large majority coming from northern counties.[55]

Illinois's Whigs did not experience such strong divisions until 1850. They
did not have nearly as many antislavery defectors as the Democrats in 1848
because most Illinois Whigs already considered their party to be antislavery. But the dangerous congressional impasse over slavery that imperiled the
Union in 1850 soon dampened the antislavery ardor of Whig politicians and
voters. After passage of the compromise measures that year, the state's more

conservative Whigs joined with Democrats to repeal instructions against slavery's extension that the General Assembly had sent to Illinois's U.S. senators in 1849. Whig legislators had unanimously approved the instructions in 1849. In 1851, however, southern and central Illinois Whigs voted twenty-two to four in favor of repeal. In this reversal, they reflected the shifting will of their constituents, whose unionist sympathies had supplanted antislavery convictions. But the protracted debate over slavery made one thing clear to Democrats and Whigs alike: party loyalties alone could not bind voters to the Union.[56]

Indeed, by the early 1850s, the two parties' convergence on issues had weakened Illinoisans' political allegiances. Both parties supported a homestead grant for settlers, land grants for railroad construction, and freer incorporation laws within the state. Both also supported river and harbor improvements, although the strict constructionist doctrine that led President Polk to veto several rivers-and-harbors bills in the 1840s encouraged Illinois's Democratic senator Stephen A. Douglas to propose locally instituted tonnage duties for river and harbor improvements.[57] Even banking had become a regional rather than partisan issue, with northern Illinois Democrats voting with Whigs to establish a new banking system in 1851.[58] Meanwhile, the parties responded with similar unionist appeals in the wake of the crisis over slavery, each condemning further "agitation of the slavery question," and each promising to abide by the 1850 compromise measures.[59]

Illinois's demographics also undermined partisan loyalties. The turnover of the electorate was astonishing. Despite the continual outmigration of Illinoisans to the West, Illinois's population tripled in the 1830s, doubled in the 1840s, and doubled again in the 1850s.[60] Meanwhile, migratory urban and farm laborers routinely moved within and across state borders to pursue economic opportunities.[61] These demographic flows altered the state's voter rolls. Most notably, southern-born settlers became a smaller portion of the population, replaced primarily by Irish and German immigrants, whose numbers grew rapidly during the late 1840s and early 1850s.[62] The immigrants typically clustered together in city wards or farming districts, and frequently altered the composition and concerns of the local electorate. Indeed, their presence provoked a surge in nativism throughout the North and intensified the significance of issues like temperance reform, which cut across existing party loyalties and threatened to reorganize the electorate.[63] All of these factors produced a state of political flux. Politicians could no longer assume either the engage-ment or loyalty of party voters.[64] As southern Illinois farmer Gershom Flagg reported to his son after the 1850 elections, "Whigs and Democrats voted together with no regard to the usual party lines."[65]

Stephen A. Douglas's attempt to reinvigorate party loyalties in 1854 reveals the limited ability of antebellum politicians and parties to shape voter behav-ior. He had judged in an 1853 letter to a political confidant that the "party is in a distracted condition & it requires all our wisdom, freedom & energy to consolidate its power and perpetuate its principles."[66] He had a bold plan, however, that seemingly offered an ideal solution. Organizing western terri-tories under the principle of popular sovereignty would enable frontier set-tlement, open a route for a transcontinental railroad, spur economic growth, and rededicate the Democratic Party to territorial expansion. If successful in these objects, the plan would likely revitalize the enthusiasm of Democratic voters and create preconditions for expansion into the tropics.[67] Thus hopeful that popular sovereignty would resolve the chronic problems that slavery's growth posed for national politics, Douglas sponsored the Kansas-Nebraska Act of 1854, which organized Kansas and Nebraska Territories and authorized territorial residents to determine slavery's status. But Douglas's optimistic projections were wildly off the mark. Because the Missouri Compromise of 1820 had prohibited slavery in these territories, the act shocked and enraged many northerners, who, as Lincoln later put it, "reeled and fell in utter con-fusion," but who each rose "fighting, grasping whatever he could first reach—a scythe—a pitchfork—a chopping axe, or a butcher's cleaver," and "struck in the direction of the sound."[68] Instead of solidifying party loyalties, the act fur-ther dissolved them, forcing many Illinoisans to chart a new political course.

Numerous voters joined a vibrant anti-Nebraska movement. In Madison, Peoria, Rock Island, and Stephenson counties, 81 percent of anti-Nebraska leaders were new to politics in 1854, spurred into action by the Kansas-Nebraska Act.[69] These new leaders found a sympathetic electorate. Illinois's voters elected anti-Nebraska candidates in five of the state's nine congressional districts that November, and enough anti-Nebraska state legislators to un-seat Democratic senator James Shields when the General Assembly convened several months later.[70] Meanwhile, the rapid emergence of anti-Nebraska nativists exacerbated the political chaos. Detesting both slavery and immi-grants, they established the Know-Nothing Party to strike at both. Although the party grew with astonishing speed throughout the North in the wake of the Kansas-Nebraska Act, mushrooming from 50,000 to 1 million members in only five months, it was not particularly vigorous in Illinois. Nevertheless, two of the five anti-Nebraska congressmen were Know-Nothings, and the others likely received Know-Nothing support. The state's politics had shifted profoundly. Illinois's voters, like those in the North generally, had decisively repudiated Douglas, the Kansas-Nebraska Act, and the Democratic Party.[71]

Illinois's Whig Party also hemorrhaged voters to the burgeoning anti-Nebraska movement. Although Whig state legislators had voted fourteen to four against endorsing the bill in February 1854, and subsequently the state's four Whig congressmen unanimously opposed its passage, the party was not a suitable vehicle for the widespread anti-Nebraska sentiment.[72] Whig congressman Richard Yates had predicted in March that the bill would rend party ranks, leaving only a "northern party and a southern party," and he was quickly proven prescient. Anti-Nebraska meetings were often nonpartisan and produced incongruous spectacles, such as Whig leader O. H. Browning writing anti-Nebraska resolutions that angry Democrats endorsed in Quincy. Such phenomena led a Jacksonville newspaper editor to marvel at the "perfect independence among men of all parties in the expression of their sentiments on this question."[73] Despite the Whigs' desire to corral anti-Nebraska voters, they could not do so easily, partly because proslavery southern Whigs had played an instrumental role in securing passage of the Kansas-Nebraska Act, partly because antislavery Democrats and Germans distrusted Whigs, and partly because the Know-Nothings and a fledgling antislavery Republican Party competed with them to recruit antislavery voters while poaching from their ranks. Ironically, the "northern party" Yates had predicted emerged at the expense of the Whigs.

By 1860, most Illinoisans and other northern voters had forged new loyalties to the Republican Party. Republicans promised to enact antislavery policies that would return the country to its founding principles of liberty. This appeal attracted slavery's most vehement northern opponents—the abolitionists—in addition to many voters who wanted the western territories to be free or sought to destroy slaveholders' power in national politics. Yet by voting Republican, northerners put the perpetuity of the Union in peril. No major party had previously proposed policies to produce slavery's ultimate extinction, and in this regard the Republican Party was truly radical.[74] For this reason, Stephen Douglas had repeatedly warned Illinoisans and other northerners that the Republican Party's success would drive southerners to secede. Nevertheless, enthusiastic northern voters flocked to the Republicans by 1860, when the party's presidential candidate, Abraham Lincoln, captured almost every northern state. Douglas's fear of southern secession soon proved prophetic. Only with the massive bloodletting of a civil war did antislavery politics finally triumph. The Emancipation Proclamation in 1863 and congressional passage of the 13th Amendment in 1865 reflected a transformation in northern politics. Emancipation of southern slaves had been almost unimaginable twenty years earlier, but the profound maturation and consolidation in northern antislavery sentiment since the late 1840s had made it possible.[75]

In contrast to the Republicans, the Whig and Democratic parties had not focused primarily on slavery. They typically fought over issues such as federalism, Indian affairs, economic policy, democratic theory, representation, suffrage, and partisan organizing. Those were important issues and deserved to be addressed. But slavery was so divisive that Whig and Democratic Party politicians preferred to ignore it. They were unable to do so completely for three reasons: slavery's enormous social, economic, and political significance in the South and the nation, which demanded and received powerful political representation whenever its interests were touched by government policy; the country's ceaseless expansion, which compelled politicians to formulate national policies for slavery's extension; and the intersection of slavery with the major Jacksonian issues of democracy and economic development. It was difficult for Americans who cared about democracy or economic opportunity to ignore slavery, and eventually both northern and southern voters endorsed politicians who reflected their respective views. For this reason alone, the Whig and Democratic parties were not stable, even though they were large, organized, and influential.

If the parties were not stable, however, historians ought either to discard the term "party system," which from its inception has implied regularity and durability, or at least modify their understanding of it. In regard to stability, Jacksonian-era parties have more in common with Jeffersonian-era parties, whose flowering was brief, than with the post–Civil War parties that have yet to be superseded. This should not surprise us. As Douglas Bradburn and Reeve Huston have shown in this volume, the emergence of a durable set of parties from an anti-partisan Constitution and political culture was a slow and protracted process. The country's parties did not emerge from the womb fully grown, and they developed unevenly and uncertainly. This is not to dismiss the remarkable things the parties accomplished: they provided a framework for political decision-making for much of the country's first seventy years, thus shaping the country's future in numerous ways, and furthermore developed ideas and practices that had far-reaching implications for American party politics. But they did not have the resources to survive the challenges they confronted. Neither the Whig nor the Democratic Party, for instance, had the institutional prestige, intersectional cohesion, unified leadership, or voter loyalty to negotiate the problems slavery posed to the nation. On that issue, voter support for the parties was conditional in both sections of the Union, and in both parties, throughout the antebellum era. The central political issues also varied dramatically during the heyday of the parties. The 1830s partisan debate was over banking and internal improvements; a decade later, party combat centered on national expansion and slavery. These changing headwinds did not reflect the caprice of politicians. They were the byproduct of extended dialogue between voters and politicians.

There is thus a better case for the dynamism than for the stability of the Jacksonian-era parties. Although the Whig and Democratic parties profoundly influenced antebellum politics, they remained subject to the preferences of the country's intensely mobile and participatory electorate, and consequently produced only about a decade of relatively stable political competition, and that only if discounting the Free Soil Party's rebellion in 1848. When this record is weighed against the massive upheaval produced by the Kansas-Nebraska Act, the parties arguably did more to destabilize than stabilize national politics. It is a slender branch on which to perch a party system. Realignment and party systems theory has helped historians to develop fruitful ideas about antebellum politics for fifty years. But now it is time to ask whether the emperor has been wearing clothes.

Notes

My thanks to Robert E. May, James Oakes, Jared Orsi, Daniel Peart, Adam I. P. Smith, and a University of Virginia Press peer reviewer for their contributions to this chapter.

1. For example, see Joel H. Silbey, *The Shrine of Party: Congressional Voting Behavior, 1841–1852* (Pittsburgh: University of Pittsburgh Press, 1967); Silbey, *Party over Section: The Rough and Ready Presidential Election of 1848* (Lawrence: University Press of Kansas, 2009); Michael F. Holt, *The Political Crisis of the 1850s* (New York: Wiley, 1978); Holt, *The Rise and Fall of the American Whig Party: Jacksonian Politics and the Onset of the Civil War* (New York: Oxford University Press, 1999); and

William E. Gienapp, *The Origins of the Republican Party, 1852–1856* (New York: Oxford University Press, 1987). On the presumed commitment of voters to parties, see Thomas B. Alexander, "The Dimensions of Voter Partisan Constancy in Presidential Elections from 1840 to 1860," in *Essays on American Antebellum Politics, 1840–1860*, eds. Stephen E. Maizlish and John J. Kushma (College Station: Texas A&M University Press, 1982), 70–121, and Jean H. Baker, *Affairs of Party: The Political Culture of Northern Democrats in the Mid–Nineteenth Century* (Ithaca, N.Y.: Cornell University Press, 1983).

2. V. O. Key Jr., "A Theory of Critical Elections," *Journal of Politics* 17 (February 1955): 3–18. Key's thesis was exploratory, and included insightful reservations and observations about his theory on pages 11, 16–18.

3. Walter Dean Burnham, "Party Systems and the Political Process," in *The American Party Systems: Stages of Political Development*, eds. William Nisbet Chambers and Walter Dean Burnham (New York: Oxford University Press, 1967), 288–98.

4. David R. Mayhew, *Electoral Realignments: A Critique of an American Genre* (New Haven, Conn.: Yale University Press, 2002), 7–33; Morris P. Fiorina, *Retrospective Voting in American National Elections* (New Haven, Conn.: Yale University Press, 1981), ix–x, 3–6.

5. Burnham, "Party Systems and the Political Process," 294.

6. Richard L. McCormick, "The Realignment Synthesis in American History," in *The Party Period and Public Policy: American Politics from the Age of Jackson to the Progressive Era* (New York: Oxford University Press, 1986), 64–88.

7. Richard P. McCormick, *The Second American Party System: Party Formation in the Jacksonian Era* (Chapel Hill: University of North Carolina Press, 1966), 5–6, 14, 353.

8. Holt, *Rise and Fall*, xiii.

9. Michael F. Holt, "An Elusive Synthesis: Northern Politics during the Civil War," in *Writing the Civil War: The Quest to Understand*, eds. James M. McPherson and William J. Cooper Jr. (Columbia: University of South Carolina Press, 1998), 116.

10. Glenn C. Altschuler and Stuart M. Blumin, *Rude Republic: Americans and Their Politics in the Nineteenth Century* (Princeton, N.J.: Princeton University Press, 2000), 47.

11. Holt, "An Elusive Synthesis," 126 (quotation); Holt, *Rise and Fall*, x–xi.

12. Ibid., xi–xii.

13. See, for instance, his detailed chapter on the election of 1844, and more generally his analysis of the Whig Party's internal tensions. Ibid., 162–207, xiii–xiv.

14. Fiorina, *Retrospective Voting*, ix–x, 3–19, 194–211. Fiorina believed that contemporary voters' power to discipline politicians and parties through retrospective voting was declining due to the onset of direct primaries, open caucuses, public financing, political action committees, television, congressional legislators' growing role as brokers between the government and constituents, and an increasing number of independent voters in the electorate, all of which weakened party power and loyalties. His arguments on this point are prescient and fascinating, but, whatever their

merits, he did believe that retrospective voting deeply shaped mid-twentieth-century American political history, and his theory seems applicable to the nineteenth century.

15. I do not mean to suggest that post–World War II political historians who interpret voter behavior using measurable data have necessarily rejected that approach, but their assumption of voter loyalty tends to push them in different interpretive directions.

16. Mayhew, *Electoral Realignments*, 43–64, 165 (quotations). He advances a welter of other arguments as well, but these are the most significant.

17. Ibid., 147–52, 147, 150 (quotations). Robert P. Saldin builds on Mayhew's analysis in "World War I and the 'System of 1896,'" *Journal of Politics* 72 (July 2010): 825–36.

18. Mayhew, *Electoral Realignments*, 153–62, 153 (quotation). He acknowledges the need "to detect patterns across American political history" (153), but his conceptualization of how to do it is classically historical.

19. In *Running on the Record: Civil War–Era Politics in New Hampshire* (Charlottesville: University Press of Virginia, 1997), Lex Renda uses retrospective voting theory to interpret nineteenth-century politics from the standpoint of New Hampshire's voters, but he cannot incorporate Fiorina's model fully.

20. Holt, *Rise and Fall*, xi, defends this focus on politicians and political activists. See also McCormick, "The Realignment Synthesis in American History," 79–80.

21. Congressional Research Service, *Congressional Careers: Service Tenure and Patterns of Member Service, 1789–2011*, 7 January 2011, http://assets.opencrs.com/rpts/R41545_20110107.pdf, 1–8. The percentage of congressmen who did not seek reelection ranged from 30–60 percent in those years. In contrast to the mid–nineteenth century, the average service time of contemporary congressmen is about ten years, and 90 percent run for reelection. Congressmen running for reelection in both eras, however, generally triumphed, with about 90 percent of mid-nineteenth-century and about 95 percent of contemporary congressmen succeeding.

22. Rosemarie Zagarri, "The Family Factor: Congressmen, Turnover, and the Burden of Public Service in the Early American Republic," *Journal of the Early Republic* 33 (Summer 2013): 283–316.

23. Solon J. Buck, *Illinois in 1818* (Springfield: Illinois Centennial Commission, 1917; reprint Urbana: University of Illinois Press, 1967), 195–97, 203–6.

24. John Craig Hammond, *Slavery, Freedom and Expansion in the Early American West* (Charlottesville: University of Virginia Press, 2007), 55–75, 150–68; George William Van Cleve, *A Slaveholders' Union: Slavery, Politics, and the Constitution in the Early American Republic* (Chicago: University of Chicago Press, 2010), 225–66.

25. Horatio Newhall to Isaac and Joel Newhall, 14 April 1824, Horatio Newhall Papers, folder 1, Abraham Lincoln Presidential Library and Museum (hereafter ALPLM); Thomas Ford, *A History of Illinois: From Its Commencement as a State in 1818 to 1847* (Chicago, 1854; reprint Urbana: University of Illinois Press, 1995), 32; John Reynolds, *My Own Times: Embracing Also the History of My Life* (Belleville, 1855; reprint Chicago, 1879), 155; James Simeone, *Democracy and Slavery in Frontier*

Illinois: The Bottomland Republic (DeKalb: Northern Illinois University Press, 2000), 245–46n3. The intensity of Illinoisans' antislavery attitudes in a state dominated by southern migrants helps to explain why the politics of slavery subsequently undermined Jacksonian party loyalties.

26. David Robson to William Shepherd and Robert Leslie, 6 August 1823, James and John Dunlop Papers, SC 432, ALPLM; John Reynolds to John Reynolds, 3 May 1823, John Reynolds Papers (quotation), SC 1264, ALPLM; Reynolds, *My Own Times,* 153.

27. "Aristides," *Illinois Intelligencer* (Vandalia), 24 May 1823; Alfred Cowles to Stephen B. Munn, 29 March 1823, box 5, folder 11, Lyman Trumbull Family Papers, ALPLM.

28. "An Old Resident of Illinois," *Edwardsville Spectator* (Illinois), 12 April 1823; A Friend to Freedom, "Another Convention Toast," *Edwardsville Spectator,* 19 April 1823; John Warnock, "To the Citizens of Fayette, Bond, and Montgomery Counties," *Illinois Intelligencer* (Vandalia), 30 July 1824.

29. Simeone, *Democracy and Slavery in Frontier Illinois,* 245–46n3.

30. Clarence Walworth Alvord, ed., *Governor Edward Coles* (Springfield: Illinois State Historical Library, 1920), 336–37.

31. George William Dowrie, *The Development of Banking in Illinois, 1817–1863* (Urbana: University of Illinois, 1913), 24–35.

32. Robert V. Remini, *Andrew Jackson and the Bank War* (New York: Norton, 1967), 82–83.

33. Robert W. Johannsen, *Stephen A. Douglas* (New York: Oxford University Press, 1973; reprint Urbana: University of Illinois Press, 1997), 38–44.

34. Robert W. Johannsen, ed., *The Letters of Stephen A. Douglas* (Urbana: University of Illinois Press, 1961), 29–30.

35. *Illinois Advocate and State Register* (Vandalia), 26 July 1834.

36. Johannsen, ed., *Letters of Douglas,* 24.

37. John Denis Haeger, "Eastern Money and the Urban Frontier: Chicago, 1833–1842," *Journal of the Illinois State Historical Society* 64 (Autumn 1971): 267–84; Paul W. Gates, *Landlords and Tenants on the Prairie Frontier: Studies in American Land Policy* (Ithaca, N.Y.: Cornell University Press, 1973), 48–71, 144–48.

38. Charles R. Clarke, ed., "Sketch of Charles James Fox Clarke with Letters to His Mother," *Journal of the Illinois State Historical Society* 22 (January 1930): 563.

39. Roy P. Basler, ed., *The Collected Works of Abraham Lincoln,* 8 vols. (New Brunswick, N.J.: Rutgers University Press, 1953), 1:7–8.

40. Rodney Owen Davis, "Illinois Legislators and Jacksonian Democracy, 1834–1841" (Ph.D. diss., University of Iowa, 1966), 110–22, 329–31. Items 3 and 5 in table 1 and items 2 and 3 in table 2 of the appendix show that the aggregate vote of Senate Democrats was 14–11 in favor of the two bank bills, while the aggregate vote of House Democrats was 37–31 in favor.

41. Howard Bodenhorn, *State Banking in Early America: A New Economic History* (New York: Oxford University Press, 2003), 48–52.

42. Johannsen, *Douglas*, 49–53; Dowrie, *Development of Banking*, 77–79, 104–9.

43. David Davis to unknown, 19 January 1840, box 1, folder A–2, David Davis Family Papers, ALPLM.

44. La Salle County Democratic Meeting, *Illinois State Register* (Springfield), 30 November 1839; "Resolutions of the Democratic State Convention," *Illinois State Register*, 21 December 1839 ("true channels"); Thomas Carlin, "Governor's Message," *Illinois State Register*, 27 November 1840 ("political slavery").

45. Dowrie, *Development of Banking*, 112–16, 123–26.

46. Norman E. Tutorow, *Texas Annexation and the Mexican War: A Political Study of the Old Northwest* (Palo Alto, Cal.: Chadwick House, 1978), 116–19.

47. James L. Huston, *Calculating the Value of the Union: Slavery, Property Rights, and the Economic Origins of the Civil War* (Chapel Hill: University of North Carolina Press, 2003), 27–32.

48. James Shields to Sidney Breese, 12 April 1844, box 1, folder 6, Sidney Breese Papers, ALPLM.

49. *Congressional Globe*, 27th Cong., 3rd sess., appendix, 86–91 (30 December 1842, 9 January 1843); *Illinois State Register* (Springfield), 14 June 1844.

50. Johannsen, *Douglas*, 139–51; Howard W. Allen and Vincent A. Lacey, eds., *Illinois Elections, 1818–1990: Candidates and County Returns for President, Governor, Senate, and House of Representatives* (Carbondale: Southern Illinois University Press, 1992), 113–15.

51. William R. Brock, *Parties and Political Conscience: American Dilemmas, 1840–1850* (Millwood: KTO Press, 1979), 114–150; Richard J. Carwardine, *Evangelicals and Politics in Antebellum America* (New Haven: Yale University Press, 1993), 133–152; William F. Moore and Jane Ann Moore, eds., *His Brother's Blood: Speeches and Writings, 1838–64, Owen Lovejoy* (Urbana: University of Illinois Press, 2004), 83; Basler, ed., *Collected Works of Lincoln*, 4:169.

52. *Congressional Globe*, 28th Cong., 2nd sess., appendix, 276 (15 January 1845).

53. *Telegraph* (Alton, Illinois), 22 June, 30 November 1844.

54. John Wentworth, *Free Tea, Free Coffee, Free Harbors, and Free Territory: Remarks of Mr. John Wentworth, of Illinois, Delivered in the House of Representatives, February 2, 1847* (Washington, D.C., 1847), 9–12.

55. Allen and Lacey, eds., *Illinois Elections*, 121–23; Thomas B. Alexander, "Harbinger of the Collapse of the Second Two-Party System: The Free Soil Party of 1848," in *A Crisis of Republicanism: American Politics in the Civil War Era*, ed. Lloyd E. Ambrosius (Lincoln: University of Nebraska Press, 1990), 25–28.

56. *Journal of the Senate of the Sixteenth General Assembly of the State of Illinois*, 1st sess., 16–44 (2–8 January 1849); *Journal of the House of Representatives of the Sixteenth General Assembly of the State of Illinois*, 1st sess., 18–55 (2–9 January 1849); *Journal of the House of Representatives of the Seventeenth General Assembly of the State of Illinois*, 1st sess., 69, 71–72, 126–34, 445–46 (15, 22 January; 14 February 1850); *Journal of the Senate of the Seventeenth General Assembly of the State of Illinois*, 1st sess., 4–6, 52–57, 101–2 (6, 14, 23 January 1851). Both the House and Senate

introduced a variety of resolutions on the slavery issue in 1851, but only the Senate resolutions passed both houses. The House members approved the Senate resolutions in one vote, while voting separately on each House resolution. Therefore the statistics above represent a cobbling together of votes on distinct resolutions that carried the same meaning despite differences in wording.

57. Johannsen, ed., *Letters of Douglas*, 272–82.

58. Arthur Charles Cole, *The Era of the Civil War, 1848–1870* (Springfield: Illinois Centennial Commission, 1919; reprint Urbana: University of Illinois Press, 1987), 92–98.

59. Kirk H. Porter and Donald Bruce Johnson, eds., *National Party Platforms, 1840–1956* (Urbana: University of Illinois Press, 1956), 17, 21.

60. The state's population was 157,445 in 1830, 476,183 in 1840, 851,470 in 1850, and 1,711,951 in 1860. John L. Andriot, ed., *Population Abstract of the United States*, vol. 1, *Tables* (McLean, Va.: Andriot Associates, 1983), 182.

61. Don Harrison Doyle, *The Social Order of a Frontier Community: Jacksonville, Illinois, 1825–70* (Urbana: University of Illinois Press, 1978; reprint Urbana: Illini Books, 1983), 92–108, 128, 261–63; David E. Schob, *Hired Hands and Plowboys: Farm Labor in the Midwest, 1815–60* (Urbana: University of Illinois Press, 1975), 150–72, 269.

62. Don Fehrenbacher, "Illinois Political Attitudes, 1854–1861" (Ph.D. diss., University of Chicago, 1951), 6–8.

63. Gienapp, *Origins of the Republican Party*, 37–67.

64. Stephen Hansen, *The Making of the Third Party System: Voters and Parties in Illinois, 1850–1876* (Ann Arbor: UMI Research Press, 1978), 11–20, 205–6. William Gienapp's statistical estimates using ecological regression suggest that Illinois's Whigs, Democrats, and Free Soilers did not switch parties between 1848 and 1852, but the documentary evidence indicates otherwise. See his *Origins of the Republican Party*, 482.

65. Barbara Lawrence and Nedra Branz, eds., *The Flagg Correspondence: Selected Letters, 1816–1854* (Carbondale: Southern Illinois University Press, 1986), 131.

66. Johannsen, ed., *Letters of Douglas*, 267–71, 267 (quotation).

67. Valuable entryways to the vast literature on the Kansas-Nebraska Act include Roy F. Nichols, "The Kansas-Nebraska Act: A Century of Historiography," *Mississippi Valley Historical Review* 43 (September 1956): 187–212; Johannsen, *Douglas*, 401–34; David Potter, *The Impending Crisis, 1848–1861* (New York: Harper and Row, 1976), 145–76; William W. Freehling, *The Road to Disunion*, vol. 1, *Secessionists at Bay, 1776–1854* (New York: Oxford University Press, 1990), 536–60; and Robert E. May, *Slavery, Race, and Conquest in the Tropics: Lincoln, Douglas, and the Future of Latin America* (New York: Cambridge University Press, 2013), 1–116. Douglas's motives will always remain to some degree shrouded in mystery. Some historians have contended that the bill's passage was deeply shaped by Douglas's presidential ambitions or financial interests as a land speculator. While these factors cannot be

entirely discounted, the bill was entirely consistent with his long-held expansionist sentiments, and its central purpose was eminently partisan and national: settling western territories as rapidly as possible.

68. Basler, ed., *Collected Works of Lincoln*, 2:282.

69. Hansen, *Making of the Third Party System*, 52–53.

70. Allen and Lacey, eds., *Illinois Elections*, 134.

71. Tyler Anbinder, *Nativism and Slavery: The Northern Know Nothings and the Politics of the 1850s* (New York: Oxford University Press, 1992), 43; Gienapp, *Origins of the Republican Party*, 122–26.

72. *Journal of the Senate of the Eighteenth General Assembly of the State of Illinois*, 2nd sess., 81 (23 February 1854); *Journal of the House of Representatives of the Eighteenth General Assembly of the State of Illinois*, 2nd Sess., 168 (25 February 1854).

73. *Congressional Globe*, 33rd Cong., 1st sess., appendix, 448 (28 March 1854); Theodore Calvin Pease and James G. Randall, eds., *The Diary of Orville Hickman Browning, 1850–1881* (Springfield: Illinois State Historical Library, 1925), 129–33; Paul Selby to Richard Yates, 8 April 1854, box 1, folder 5, Yates Family Collection, ALPLM.

74. Graham Alexander Peck, "Abraham Lincoln and the Triumph of an Antislavery Nationalism," *Journal of the Abraham Lincoln Association* 28 (Summer 2007): 1–27.

75. James Oakes, *Freedom National: The Destruction of Slavery in the United States, 1861–1865* (New York: Norton, 2013).

PART THREE

THE PLACE OF
PARTIES
— IN —
AMERICAN
POLITICS

★ KENNETH OWEN ★

Legitimacy, Localism, and the First Party System

For a party that supposedly laid the essential foundations of the American republic, the Federalists were tremendously insecure about their record. George Washington's Farewell Address—delivered at the end of what presidential experts routinely rank as one of the most successful presidencies in history—contained bleak warnings of the destruction awaiting the American republic were it not given "a fair and full experiment."[1]

Federalists greeted any sign of political dissent during the 1790s not only as politically misguided but also as fundamentally unpatriotic and antirepublican. While Federalist denunciation of the Democratic-Republican societies was most famously expressed in Washington's derisive dismissal of "self-created societies," essayists and pamphleteers likewise attacked the societies' principles and argued that they represented an attempt to introduce *imperium in imperio*. During debates over the ratification of the Jay Treaty, a meeting of Federalists in York County, Pennsylvania, bemoaned any action that "would betray a want of confidence in the Senate, and in the President." In other words, the populace had a right to deliberate on political affairs only up to the point that it approved of the government's actions.[2] If the legitimacy of the federal government was clearly established in the 1790s, then why did Federalist leaders display such anxiety about their exercise of power?[3]

Federalists believed in a hierarchical, deferential society in which those elected to national office would represent a "natural aristocracy" chosen for its self-evident talents and superior wisdom. In a governmental system predicated on (hard-won) popular sovereignty, however, their ability to exercise power rested fundamentally on the consent of the governed. The legitimacy of government, in other words, depended on a populace that, in the 1790s, was quick to elect new representatives when they felt politicians were acting against popular interests. Constituting new governmental structures was one thing; getting the people to support them was quite another. In order to establish the legitimacy of the new Constitution, federal politicians of the 1790s relied on a network of extra-governmental political institutions, often local in nature, through which ordinary citizens were able to constrain the actions of officials in higher levels of government.

Recent histories of the foundation of the American state have tended to stress the power of the institutions created by the federal Constitution. Max M. Edling's work on Hamiltonian visions of the "fiscal-military state," Brian Balogh on the power of the federal government from its earliest years, and Robin L. Einhorn on the development of taxation policy have all demonstrated that the federal government possessed considerable power in the 1790s — and was prepared to wield it.[4] While these studies help to correct the "myth of the weak American state," they focus heavily on high-level political and governmental systems, at the expense of examining why Americans were willing to grant such power. The federal government was not "a government out of sight." Excise systems, national banks, or ten thousand–strong militia forces were scarcely "invisible." Instead, the character of public debate focused on whether the federal government had the popular consent to institute these measures.

The expansion of the meaning of "political history" to encompass a wider range of actors, including women, African Americans, and lower orders of society, has been a productive trend in the history of the early republic over the last twenty years. These studies are mostly concerned with the structure and content of public debate. The processes through which citizens intended to use their direct agency to control the actions of government are less well understood.

Participation in public festivals and other institutions of an early American "public sphere" have drawn useful attention to modes of political discourse and demonstrated wide participation within political debates, but rely heavily on the idea of rational discourse allowing the best ideas to prevail, a point John L. Brooke emphasizes in his essay in this volume. Political legitimacy in the 1790s, however, did not emerge from an idealized form of intellectual debate.

Political legitimacy depended instead on being able to demonstrate popular support from representative institutions.[5] Claims to exercise governmental authority had to be carefully calibrated, balancing notions of "order" against conceptions of the exercise of popular power. If governments, whether state or local, could not demonstrate a close connection with organizations laying claim to expressing the will of the people, they found it difficult to continue to maintain authority.

The revolution created a political toolkit for converting popular anger over imperial policy into mechanisms of governmental and extra-governmental power. (By "mechanisms," I refer not to formal governmental institutions but rather means of channeling popular activism into political action.) They were used to prosecute a successful war effort and helped to institute new systems of government predicated on principles of popular sovereignty. Political identity in the new republic was the result of the creation of a vibrant political culture expressed through extra-governmental institutions that possessed a claim to representative legitimacy and that could serve as an expression of the will of the people.

These mechanisms encompassed a wide variety of political action, such as town meetings, county committees, petitioning, popular parades, election campaigns, and forms of civil disobedience extending to outright violence. Ordinary citizens carefully scrutinized their operation to ensure that resolutions passed by "the people" had representative legitimacy. These claims, though, were frequently contested. Violence was denigrated as anti-republican; town meetings were decried for being too small; parades were denounced for using public space for partisan purposes.

Such controversies underscore the importance of these mechanisms. There was no one ideal of a "representative body" that could supplant other competing claims in and of itself. Governmental representation was suspect because of representatives' seeking to aggrandize power; extra-governmental mobilization was suspect because it was impossible to prove the deliberative or representative character of these mechanisms. What lay at the core of the use of these means, though, was the idea that action in the name of an individual or a self-interested group was illegitimate, whereas action in the name of a community was the expected goal of a republican society.

Citizens accused one another of subverting these extra-governmental representative forms because if such abuses were left unchallenged, then the forms could be used to claim representative support for unrepresentative policies. This was partly a linguistic battle to define (and often restrict) membership of the political community. These mechanisms, however, garnered greatest potency by putting feet on the ground. Participation in such large numbers could not easily be ignored in a republican government, regardless of the perceived legitimacy of their participants. Politicians needed to engage carefully with this popular activism if they hoped to exercise authority in the early republic.

This chapter explores the importance of representative mechanisms in the politics of the 1790s through two case studies of political mobilization. The first study is of statewide electoral campaigns, specifically, the first two contested elections for governor of Pennsylvania. Although the focus of this case study is confined to the borders of a particular state, Pennsylvania's size and diversity helps to reflect the sorts of tactics used to define national politics. The second case study analyzes how political actors used extra-governmental mechanisms to mobilize support for and opposition to the ratification of the Jay Treaty. This debate highlighted the contested nature of many of the political mechanisms used by citizens in the early republic.[6] Yet despite their fractiousness and contention, the Jay Treaty debates show how control of extra-governmental mechanisms was fundamental to exercising public authority.

Although Federalists sought to restrict the role of popular activism in deciding public policy, they also engaged with extra-governmental bodies as they sought to establish the treaty as legitimate. The concerns of governmental officials with the popular meetings against the treaty show how the activism of ordinary citizens fundamentally framed national debate, participated in public policy formation, and thus constrained the actions of government. Men such as Alexander Hamilton or Frederick Muhlenberg were so concerned about influencing town meetings of no constitutional standing—at such potential risk to their public reputations—because they recognized the importance of actions being seen to have representative legitimacy outside of formal channels of government.

The relationship between governmental institutions and the people they represented was often testy. The existence of extra-governmental representative forms, however, allowed citizens and officials to communicate effectively with one another and bridge the gap between governmental stability and popular activism. Although town meetings and county committees were necessarily local in character, they could combine to form networks that allowed them to transcend parochial concerns. In contrast to the viewpoints of Stanley Elkins and Eric McKitrick, who defined typical communities of the 1790s as small and parochial, those who defended the interests of their towns and localities in political action were not just acting out of narrow-minded concern but consciously shaping a broader national debate.[7]

The familiarity of these extra-governmental modes of political action granted them legitimacy—another indication of the path-dependent nature of early U.S. politics outlined by Douglas Bradburn in his essay in this volume. In many cases, these types of activism had a longer heritage than the new constitutional structures introduced in the aftermath of the revolution.[8] This longevity gave the old forms stronger claims to political legitimacy than those used by party organizers like John Beckley, or newspaper editors like John Fenno or William Duane.[9] Town meetings and similar traditional forms of political action were often used for partisan purposes. But even when they were, the partisan dimension was blunted by the claim to speak for an entire community—a county or township—that had a "natural" legitimacy.

Ordinary citizens consequently retained their foundational importance within a more hierarchical political system. Despite the supposed conservatism of the federal Constitution, popular activism had a significant impact on national politics. National leaders relied on widespread mobilization to transmit their agendas and win electoral majorities. This reliance in turn allowed citizens to constrain the actions of their political leaders; suspicion of elite leadership was part and parcel of these mechanisms. In this way, a Constitution that aimed to introduce greater stability in government was still understood to be firmly grounded on the principles of popular sovereignty.

The Pennsylvania Gubernatorial Campaigns of 1790 and 1799

The gubernatorial election of 1790 was the first statewide election for a single position held in postrevolutionary Pennsylvania. The newly revised state constitution replaced the 1776 document's plural executive council (formed of one member from each county) with a single elected governor possessing powers far outstripping that of any individual under the first state constitution.[10] The revision of Pennsylvania's state constitution has traditionally been seen as a counterrevolution, in which the radically democratic 1776 frame of government was replaced with something more malleable by the forces of conservatism.[11]

The campaigns of Thomas Mifflin and Arthur St. Clair in September 1790, however, demonstrate that the famous names of the revolution—the men who supposedly changed Pennsylvanian politics forever with the revision of the 1776 constitution—actually lost power. The defeat of St. Clair, and the election of Mifflin, demonstrated the persistence of a political culture that demanded political leaders engage with popular political mechanisms.

Both candidates were well-known, and had a long political history in both state and federal politics. Mifflin was a former president of the Supreme Executive Council and had served at both federal and state constitutional conventions; St. Clair served as president of the Continental Congress before being appointed governor of the Northwest Territory. At first glance, the supporters of Mifflin and St. Clair seemed to subscribe to a politics of reputation and deference. Essayists, in considering the talents necessary for the new governor, highlighted skills such as "integrity, independence, . . . stability of character," and "a decent moral deportment."[12] The election campaign, however, demonstrated that reliance on reputation alone was insufficient to win popular support.

St. Clair's candidacy rested on his status as the favored candidate of Philadelphia's political elite. Illustrious names such as James Wilson, Robert Morris, Thomas Fitzsimons, and Benjamin Rush all announced their wholehearted support. And after a nominating meeting held in Philadelphia, it was not the volume of citizens that was cited as the key factor in his favor. Indeed, it was the support of one particular citizen that particularly stood out. A newspaper article announcing St. Clair's candidacy proudly declared, he possessed "the confidence of the PRESIDENT of the United States."[13]

Mifflin's campaign, by contrast, highlighted the popular support of the candidate. Instead of listing prominent individuals as his cheerleaders, Mifflin claimed the unanimous approbation of "a very numerous and respectable meeting of the Citizens of Philadelphia." His qualifications were framed not in terms of national government or character but in terms of service to the people of Pennsylvania. Although Mifflin was unquestionably a member of Philadelphia's elite, his supporters crafted a biography highlighting his wartime decision to break with the Society of Friends and fight for the patriot cause. "No elevation of rank has been sufficient to warp his mind from its original democratical biases: — No temptation of wealth has taught him to convert his official opportunities to personal emolument."[14] The inference was clear — Mifflin was receiving the support of a community that had freely deliberated on his merits, and one that he had served for many years in their interest.

Supporters of Mifflin and St. Clair quickly clashed with one another — not over the men's policies or their characters but over the legitimacy of their arguments for public support. St. Clair claimed to have held a meeting of numerous citizens of Philadelphia. His opponents said he did nothing of the sort. St. Clair's supporters were attacked for misrepresenting not only the size of his support but also its representative character. Only "between twenty and thirty" attended the meeting, "all of whom were . . . warmly attached to the federal government, and active in bringing about the present change in our constitution." They were so far from being biased by "'a considerable body of the citizens of Philadelphia' in their choice, that no one of our citizens, except members of the above named public bodies, attended the meeting."[15]

St. Clair's friends lambasted Mifflin in kind. "The meeting in Philadelphia which agreed to vote for General Mifflin was much more dictatorial. It consisted only of the select friends of General Mifflin, who were convened by printed cards; and yet the act of this selected meeting was offered to the counties, as the act of the citizens of Philadelphia."[16] Such a statement revealed the necessity of demonstrable popular support for electoral success in revolutionary Pennsylvania. Even in the immediate aftermath of the destruction of the 1776 state constitution, the very moment of their supposed political triumph, members of the social and economic elite needed to demonstrate their close engagement with extra-governmental activism to establish candidates as legitimately representative of the community at large.

Mifflin did just that, engaging seriously with town meetings and county committees. While St. Clair appealed to country gentlemen through public letters,[17] Mifflin's campaign organized meetings in Philadelphia, the Northern Liberties, and Delaware, Bucks, Chester, Philadelphia, and Lancaster counties. (These meetings would often also consider tickets for the concurrent legislative elections.)[18] This was no small feat for a campaign that had such limited time to organize! Such activity pointedly highlights the difference between the two campaigns. Mifflin's supporters subsequently portrayed St. Clair as the candidate of elitist gentlemen who hoped to use their political power for their own partial gain. Perhaps unsurprisingly, St. Clair was defeated resoundingly, with Mifflin winning by a margin of almost ten to one.[19]

Thus the supposed orchestrators of a counterrevolution in Pennsylvania found themselves defeated in the immediate aftermath of their triumph. The revision of the state constitution in 1790 did not herald the immediate introduction of hierarchical or deferential politics in Pennsylvania. Rather, a study of the 1790 election demonstrates the suspicion Pennsylvanians had for the politics of reputation. It also underlines the importance of building a network to unite citizens across an extensive and heterogeneous state. Ironically, Wilson, Rush, and others succeeded in amending the state constitution because of their appeals to popular sovereignty. If Federalists were to hope to succeed, even in a political landscape they had tried to tilt in their favor, then they would have to adopt more demonstrably representative and popular forms of political mobilization.

Campaigning strategies for the 1799 election were considerably more polished. These strategies nevertheless owed much to those utilized by Mifflin in 1790—popular engagement with extra-governmental political mechanisms and the mobilization of large numbers of citizens. The campaign appointed local bodies to coordinate campaigning efforts, thus underscoring the importance of representative legitimacy in establishing a candidate's qualifications for office. Most significantly of all, these strategies were not confined to Republican campaigning. The Federalist candidate, James Ross, consciously replicated the use of these representative forms. By 1799, it was clear that mobilizing popular support through participatory political mechanisms was the only reliable strategy for electoral success.[20]

Both campaigns took great care to choose their candidates in a manner demonstrably representative of the whole of Pennsylvania's political community. Republicans held meetings comprising elected officials and other interested citizens, designed to be as representative of the state as possible. A further committee, composed of three members each from the western, middle, and eastern counties of the state, and one member from Philadelphia, then scrutinized all nominations before a general meeting ratified the nomination of Thomas McKean.[21] Federalists similarly appointed a committee from twenty-one counties, which agreed to nominate James Ross of Pittsburgh, then serving as U.S. senator for Pennsylvania.[22] Both candidates appointed extensive committees of correspondence—overarching committees based in Philadelphia, followed by committees in every county.

These county committees explicitly delineated their members' duties. Sub-committees were appointed to organize each township's electoral support down to the last householder. A Chester County committee was exhorted to "use their best endeavors to induce every person in their township who feels himself interested in favor of Mr Ross, to attend at the election." The committee was "particularly requested to correspond with Col Gibbons (the corresponding member of the committee of Chester county) for the purpose of giving and receiving any information that may be necessary relative to the ensuing election."[23] Montgomery County went further still, calling on its committee members to visit "every man in the several townships."[24] McKean committees were similarly instructed. "If possible, all republican electors [should] be at their proper places at the time of election, with tickets prepared, to advance the election of the said candidate for governor, and other republicans to other offices."[25]

Committees stressed the importance of Pennsylvanian government not only in state or local matters but also in relation to the federal government. McKean's supporters lamented the loss of Pennsylvania's influence in the federal government following the appointments of John Adams. "We have not ever asked for our state president or vice president, yet we are left without one great influential office in the cabinet, the four executive departments."[26] Ross's partisans, for their part, warned that Pennsylvania's "wealthy, populous, commercial and extensive" position in the United States would necessitate acting as arbiter between "the eastern and southern parts of our country."[27] Although this was a state election, it was inseparable from national concerns.

These campaigning networks envisaged enormous political mobilization. Borough and township meetings encouraged correspondence with other committees and meetings throughout their county; county meetings in turn sat at the top of a statewide network. Those operating this system of committees and meetings made great efforts to be comprehensive. Republicans in Bucks County, for example, held two meetings: one in Buckingham township and one in the upper part of the county, in order to allow those who could not travel a great distance to "unite their efforts to promote the public interests in this interesting election."[28]

Citizens participated in these meetings enthusiastically and in large numbers. Organizers sought high attendance, publicizing meetings several weeks in advance, and scheduling them for the meeting of county courts or Fourth of July celebrations.[29] And though impossible to verify, reported attendance at individual meetings suggests an impressive degree of activism. In Bucks County, the Federalists appointed township committees numbering 182 people — nearly 10 percent of those who voted for Ross in the election. Engagement on the Republican side was larger still.[30] The two aforementioned meetings claimed attendances of 538 and "about 350" respectively.[31] Even allowing for exaggeration and dual attendance, a total attendance of 650 would represent more than a quarter of McKean's vote in October.[32]

The legitimacy of these meetings rested on their claims to being representative. Even taking a more skeptical view of attendance at the McKean Bucks County meetings, we would still find as much as one in ten of the eventual

electorate attending some form of semiofficial meeting—sufficient to lay claim
to speak in the name of their county. And only by speaking in the name of a
county or township could these meetings elevate themselves above the status
of interested groups. In other cases, efforts were made to demonstrate that the
resolutions offered by one township were shared further afield. A Hummel-
stown meeting was also attended by delegates from a meeting in a neighboring
township, who expressed their desire "to be considered as participating in the
measures of this meeting."[33] Although these gathering did not take place as
delegated meetings, it was important that they could be presented as representative of a wider community in some capacity.

To be sure, not all meetings were paragons of deliberative democratic virtue. Few meetings recorded deliberating or discussing the merits of both candidates. Many meetings asked supporters of the minority candidate to leave
before resolutions were officially approved. One set of resolutions explicitly rejected this practice: "such conduct, however fashionable, cannot be adopted by
republicans."[34] This highlights one limitation of extra-governmental activity,
which could be used not just to channel popular power but also to marginalize
those outside the mainstream.[35] Nevertheless, the continued importance of
these forms, and the contests over their use, demonstrate the desire of partisans of both sides to present themselves as representing the whole community
and not only a part thereof.

Attempts to hijack the accepted form of popular meetings caused controversy. A McKean supporter in Northampton County was attacked for seeking
to delay a popular meeting until more of his allies could attend. When an
attempt to filibuster Ross's supporters failed, Republicans were accused of
trying to unfairly disrupt the meeting by "seceding," "re-joining," and "making disorderly motions." They made a further attempt to hold a second meeting that night, "which was not to open until *all the aristocrats were gone*."[36]
Such fiercely contested resolutions demonstrate how important representative
forms were as vehicles of expressing the political sense of the community.
Corrupting those forms raised troubling questions about political legitimacy.

Nor were county committees and town meetings the only source of conflict
over representative legitimacy. The Ross campaign attracted significant op-
probrium when it attempted to use grand juries to bolster support. Whereas
town or county meetings were open for all to attend, grand juries were appointed by county sheriffs and so could less plausibly speak in the name of
the people. One essayist in the *Carlisle Gazette* wrote that "the reason of the

unanimity [of the grand jury] is very obvious — it is well known that sheriffs have the power of summoning juries, and not confined to any class of people, and if he is of the same complexion, why not exercise his power!"[37]

The Ross campaign's response was far from satisfying, calling the grand jurors "men the most respectable . . . for virtue and understanding."[38] As with the St. Clair letters to "leading gentlemen," Ross's partisans had missed the point of the controversy. It was not the character of the jurors but their unrepresentative nature that made them illegitimate political commentators. The attempt to use grand juries as campaigning organizations left Ross open to charges of being under "the influence of wealth, office, and other various means" — a slippery slope toward corruption, faction, and governmental dependency.[39]

Yet McKean supporters struggled with the constant need to reference governmental power back to the people. The strength of popular mobilization led Albert Gallatin to declare that "not a single person had enough influence to carry one county" in the state, and William Duane to argue "the great body of the people will not submit to be led."[40] This was memorably expressed in an address of Greene County citizens to Albert Gallatin during the debate over the Alien and Sedition Acts. Instead of congratulating Gallatin on his leadership, the committees instead thanked the people themselves for the good sense they had in electing such a man to office![41]

The 1799 gubernatorial campaign nevertheless demonstrates the importance of extra-governmental mechanisms in American politics in the years after the ratification of the federal Constitution. Although McKean won the election, he did so only by a narrow margin.[42] More significant than the result was the process of the electoral campaign. Success or failure rested in no small part on the ability to present a candidature as representative of the wider community. This process of organizing county meetings allowed citizens to transcend parochial interests and engage seriously in the construction of national politics.

By 1799, both parties engaged in this extensive popular mobilization. This belief in the importance of referencing power to local institutions was shared by both candidates in the election — forming a common language of politics that allowed ordinary citizens to maintain their control of governmental policy even as constitutional revision and population growth made offices less immediately representative than they had been in the revolutionary era. Although vestiges of the earlier appeal to reputation were still evident in the Ross campaign, by the end of the 1790s, Federalists had recognized the necessity of widespread and energetic engagement with popular mechanisms. Their changed tactics saw them come close to pulling off a famous victory in a state that was reliably Jeffersonian throughout the 1790s and 1800s.

Extra-Governmental Mechanisms and the Jay Treaty

Questions of institutional legitimacy also lay at the heart of popular activism outside of regular election periods. The Jay Treaty debates provide a striking example of the connections between local activism and federal policymaking in the 1790s. Negotiations with Britain, controversial from the moment of John Jay's appointment as diplomatic envoy, precipitated a political crisis almost as soon as news of Jay's negotiations reached America in early 1795.[43] Although the treaty was controversial on several grounds—attitudes to foreign policy, questions of economic development, and the relative powers of different branches of the government—this essay considers the importance of political mechanisms in the fight over the treaty. Despite the considerable policy issues at stake, an important part of the political debate revolved around the question of who could legitimately participate in policy formation.

Todd Estes has focused particular attention on the contribution and engagement of Federalists in the summer of 1795 and spring of 1796, arguing that Federalist mastery of the public sphere allowed them to prevail in securing ratification—even as they used this popular engagement to defend a restricted vision of political activism in the early republic. This analysis makes the important contribution of highlighting that Federalist political culture was not as restrictive as historians once believed.[44]

Yet it was the continued importance of political mechanisms that could speak with the voice of the community which forced Federalists to engage in popular activism, with the consequence that attempts to introduce a government based on reputation and deference were forced instead to filter their legitimacy through reference to local institutions.

No sooner did news of the Jay Treaty reach America than Republicans lambasted any hint of an alliance with Britain. In response, Federalists started to discredit attempts to scrutinize the negotiations in public. One writer, mocking the form of resolutions used by the Democratic-Republican societies the previous summer, sarcastically reprehended Jay "for not sending the treaty by a balloon." The societies were said to be keen to "discuss the treaty, Paragraph by Paragraph, whether the same arrive or not"; finally, "there being but one Member of this newly organized branch of the Democratic Society, he shall after signing the same as President, be a Committee to publish these resolutions."[45] Opponents of Federalist foreign policy were thus portrayed as a small group of agitators trying to find subversive means of exaggerating their support.

Federalists sought to deny the legitimacy of public scrutiny of governmental action, arguing instead that it belonged, alone, to the public officials entrusted with such powers by the federal Constitution. The Senate's adhering to a strict policy of secrecy regarding the treaty's ratification, however, somewhat undermined this argument. For many, the legitimate use of power in a republican polity did not need to be hidden from public view.

Despite Federalist efforts to discredit attempted public scrutiny, controversy erupted in the summer of 1795 when Virginia Senator Stevens Thomson Mason passed a draft copy of the treaty to the Philadelphia *Aurora*. Publication sparked a flurry of popular activity, with crowds burning effigies of John Jay and, in New York, throwing stones and bottles when Alexander Hamilton attempted to intervene in debate. Every major urban center and many minor ones held some sort of meeting to debate the principles of the treaty and to defend the right of the people to scrutinize the actions of government.

The summer of 1795 thus saw the further use of a variety of popular political mechanisms as opponents of the Federalists attempted to mobilize to prevent the Jay Treaty from being signed into law. These meetings not only inspired ordinary citizens to engage in the politics of the street; leading political figures also took a prominent part.[46] The use of meetings and committees to petition the president and Congress to alter their actions occasioned a large public debate over the proper place of popular activism in the governmental process. Although agitation against the Jay Treaty would ultimately fail to prevent its coming into force, the use of committee structures to organize political debate cemented the necessity of engaging with extra-governmental mechanisms in a republican governmental process.

To be sure, town meetings were not deliberative meetings dispassionately debating political matters. Yet although not the finest exemplars of rational discourse, they were organized in a manner designed to emphasize the power of ordinary citizens to deliberate on matters of public policy. To combat attempts to portray opposition as the first step on the road to mobocracy, organizers of the meetings took great pains to emphasize their respectable character. The first town meeting against the Jay Treaty, in Boston, for example, appointed a committee to draw up resolutions on the subject of the treaty, and demanded that the treaty be read publicly and in full before any resolutions were passed. These were important measures. An elected committee carried representative force. A public reading of the treaty prevented criticisms that the leaders of the meeting were simply attempting to rouse the passions of a mob. These institutions could not easily be dismissed as "self-created."[47]

The New York town meeting highlighted both the possibilities and problems of using representative forms to engage in political debate. An important factor underpinning the legitimacy of the form was that it could claim to speak the mind, and with the voice, of an entire community. This, however, left meetings vulnerable to divisions and dissensions that could be used to undermine that authority. This was certainly the case in New York City; partisans of both sides of the debate were present, and attempts to find out which side possessed the majority (including an attempt to physically divide the meeting into two sides) were inconclusive at best.

The centrality of the formal political process was reflected in the New York meeting's recognition of the necessity of swift action. An attempt to adjourn the meeting for further discussion similarly failed, for "it was probable a decision by the President of the United States would not be delayed." Those who had turned out in opposition to the treaty clearly saw attempts to introduce a period of further discussion as a delaying tactic intended to buy the silence of the meeting and thus tacitly support the president. "A body of 4000 industrious citizens could not be expected to attend a discussion which must necessarily have been so lengthy. . . . It was fairly presumable that the citizens assembled had read the treaty . . . and had made up their minds of the subject, and that they assembled not to discuss, but to give an opinion."[48]

These meetings were sizeable. Two Philadelphia town meetings numbered around five or six thousand citizens—the largest meetings that had been held in the State House Yard since 1779.[49] But it was not just attendance that made these meetings remarkable as a political phenomenon. Several of Pennsylvania's most prominent politicians were present, including Chief Justice Thomas McKean, Secretary of State Alexander Dallas, and other federal and state representatives.[50] As with the Boston meeting, the Philadelphia meeting elected a committee to draw up resolutions and a remonstrance to the president.

A second meeting discussed the committee's report, considered by paragraphs, so each substantive point carried the weight of public opinion. The adoption of the report was thus presented as the considered opinion of the people of Philadelphia. Proper observance of process was important in establishing the legitimacy of the town meeting. A properly constituted meeting prevented the Federalists from taunting their opponents as the unwitting dupes of a few designing men.

The town meetings firmly defended the right of the people to interpose in public debate. Hamilton's intervention in the New York meeting was heavily criticized for the lack of trust it placed in the people. "Instead of giving an opinion on the important question under consideration, [he wished] to pass a Resolve expressing an implicit reliance on the President and Senate. Were the principles contained in this resolution to be adopted in the United States, the Federal Constitution would be exchanged for an Oligarchy."[51] Similarly, the resolutions of the Philadelphia meeting began by declaring it the "constitutional right and patriotic duty" of citizens that they should "express the public sense of public measures."[52]

Essayists, too, strongly contended for the presence of extra-governmental activism. "It surely will not be contended by a *Republican*, that one man [an essayist] shall have more consideration and more rights than a number. . . . Any meetings in which the sense of the people can be collected, are republican and proper. . . . No-one will dispute their propriety, whose interest is not distinct from that of the whole people."[53] Such formulations are critical in understanding the locus of power in the early republic; they represent an understanding of politics that may have delegated the business of negotiations to officeholders but saw the root of all policy as emanating directly, not indirectly, from the people themselves.

The importance of the representative form of the town meeting is further underlined by alternative attempts to introduce supportive voices into the treaty debate. While Federalist essayists were often dismissive of town meetings and their claims to popular authority, President Washington responded swiftly and in detail to petitions sent to him by "Merchants' Committees" from the major seaport towns.[54] The notion of merchants or other trade groups forming their own committees had previously been used in times of political crisis.[55] The importance of representative claims, though, was underlined by the very fact that merchants chose to style themselves as "committees" rather than relying on their own personal reputations.

There was something curious, however, about supposedly representative bodies "disavowing" the resolutions of more numerous public meetings.[56] The

self-presentation of "Merchants' Committees" helped to strengthen opposi-
tional claims that supporters of the Jay Treaty were the wealthy protecting
their own special interests. "Does the President measure men's information
by their wealth?" asked one essayist. "Does he determine on their rights by the
quantum of bank stock, or six per cents they possess, that he thus introduces
casts among citizens?"[57] Washington's conduct treated the thousands who had
attended city meetings "in a lump" while "the flatterers of public measures
have received the most courteous attention." While opponents of the treaty
used town meetings because their size and diversity could carry weight as an
expression of public opinion, the actions of the government raised fears that
the government itself was beginning to form a separate interest from the community at large through its favorable response to less ostensibly representative
petitions.[58]

Opposition to the treaty very much depended on this cultivation of a system
of town meetings and committees, in keeping with established past practice.
These mechanisms were crucial, for it was hard for Federalists to portray a
series of public meetings and popularly selected committees as illegitimate
political voices. This popular outcry against the Jay Treaty forced the national
government to engage with this extra-governmental politics, for it ultimately
exposed a constitutional defect that could only be remedied through prece-
dent and agreed popular opinion.

Although much Federalist comment attempted to delegitimize popular
activism, it quickly became apparent that success in the treaty debate could
only succeed through a careful engagement in public debate. Federalists were
therefore forced to demonstrate that they possessed popular support, and thus
organized their own meetings. A York County meeting resolved that though
they considered "it the constitutional right of the citizens of the United States
to address the President by way of petition, memorial, or remonstrance, on any
subject, concerning which the Constitution has vested him with a negative or
affirmative . . . there may be certain situations in which it would be exceed-
ingly improper, and inconsistent with their duty so to do."[59] Popular agitation
against the treaty, moreover, "would betray a want of confidence in the Senate,
and in the President; that it would tend to weaken our government and give
foreign nations a bad opinion of its wisdom and stability."[60]

Such tactics placed opponents of the treaty on far shakier ground. The resolutions refused to deny the right of people to assemble against the treaty, but
used these forms of assembly to demonstrate support for constituted author-

ities. York Federalists thus moderated the enthusiasm and zeal of Republican advocates of this model of political community, pushing for general consideration of public measures without threatening the authority of constituted bodies too directly. Elections represented a fair chance for the community to have its input on public policy; popular power, if taken too far, would mean all decisions, no matter how important, could be second-guessed by local concerns.

Elections in 1795 tied the formal political process ever more closely to popular agitation. Opponents of the treaty—who already criticized the ability of one man to rule "with no other guide than his own will"—presented the election as a choice between "that which is for a King, and that which is for a republic."[61] In Philadelphia at least, such agitation appears to have been successful. Whereas the 1794 delegation to the state House of Representatives had been almost entirely Federalist, in 1795, only Republicans were returned.[62] At least some consideration had been given to the fact that senators were elected indirectly through the state legislature.[63]

This was not a debate about abstract notions of popular sovereignty—it was, instead, intimately linked to the political process. The entire population of a city could express its feelings at a town meeting, but if it could not direct that political energy into an institutional form, it would have no legal weight. It was of no practical use to suggest that citizens wait for the next presidential election to procure a change. The mobilization of the summer of 1795, and the subsequent Federalist mobilization of the spring of 1796 to ensure that the House of Representatives voted to fund treaty obligations, demonstrated the importance of extra-governmental mechanisms. As governmental bodies became more sophisticated in their operation, it became increasingly necessary to have demonstrable claims to popular activism. This was particularly significant in the Federalist era. By 1796, Federalists had already been forced to use the toolkit of popular mobilization to legitimize their own wielding of power.[64] Although there was always a tendency to rely on the politics of reputation, the 1790s showed increasingly that harnessing the strength of local movements was the only sure building block of any political program.

FEDERALISTS AND REPUBLICANS were united in the 1790s by their claims to uphold government by the people. To prove these claims, they needed to establish legitimate representative mechanisms through which they could demonstrate popular support for their policies. These forms of activism allowed leaders to take governmental action, safe in the knowledge that they were not acting as petty tyrants but rather as wise republican rulers. Yet concentrating on the role of leaders in analyzing the politics of the 1790s is misguided. Their reliance on the mechanisms of popular political activism rendered leaders dependent on ordinary citizens in ways which allowed the citizenry to turn popular sovereignty into a political practice, rather than merely a touchstone of revolutionary rhetoric.

The mechanisms used to demonstrate partisan support, however, were not strictly party operations in the way we would understand the term today. They did rely on the development of printing and postal networks to coordinate action over large areas, but the basic forms of political mobilization depended on personal connections and direct local activity. The success of town meetings, county committees, and other similar organizations rested on their claim to being representative of "the people" or "the community" as a whole.[65] Their potency relied on their claim to transcend narrow sectional or class interests. This drew on revolutionary and prerevolutionary traditions; Pennsylvania's revolution was one in which "the security and protection of the community" was placed front and center.[66] To speak in the name of the community, resolutions, committees, and town meetings had to conform to the notion that they were not ostensibly partisan but rather a meeting of citizens carrying out their duty of active consideration of political matters.

Consequently, the claim of any of the mechanisms analyzed in this chapter to truly represent "the community" cannot be fully substantiated. These meetings were likely, though not necessarily exclusively, male-dominated. Similarly, there was a certain degree of control inherent in such collective proceedings. These representative forms were nevertheless significant in that they established popular activism as the bedrock of the political process in the new republic. Even if a town meeting discussed resolutions drawn up by a political elite, these resolutions gained their sanction from the presence of thousands of citizens — who would have been free to reject any resolutions not in keeping with the temper of the times.

This was, therefore, not merely a linguistic debate over who constituted "the people." Instead, the practices of politics in the 1790s reinforced the notion that for government to speak in the name of the people, there was a necessary process. Legitimate governmental action was that which not only proclaimed to act in the interests of the people but also was seen to have been taken with the people's consent.

Furthermore, such a structure allowed the activism of local politics to be fundamentally connected to state or federal politics. This linked citizens to a political system increasingly distant from their everyday experiences. It was for this reason that the prerevolutionary and pre-Constitution traditions of participatory political action were so vital. As citizens adjusted to new forms of government, they used existing practices to make these forms understandable and to bring them under popular control. As several essays in this volume demonstrate, popular sovereignty did not simply mean participation in elections. Extra-governmental institutions were designed precisely with the intention of influencing the actions of government, and subjecting elected and appointed officials to popular scrutiny at all times.

The necessity of coordinating action across differing localities also caused problems for activists. What was the best means of effecting change? Town meetings were one expression of political feeling, but to be truly successful, they needed demonstrable results, either in voting out erring representatives or in affecting governmental policy. As would be seen later with the campaign against the Alien and Sedition Acts, failure to agree on a uniform national means of mobilization could fatally weaken a campaign.[67] Local campaigns, such as the gubernatorial elections of 1790 and 1799, were easier to keep in a cohesive form. Yet even fragmented national campaigns could force a change in rhetoric — as seen in Federalist campaigns that initially relied on language of supporting the president but quickly changed to present the Jay Treaty as the will of the people through their elected representatives. As a result, elected officials were forced to engage closely with the demands of their constituents. This, in turn, provided a means through which the energy of popular support in a particular locality could be transmitted to shape the contours of national debate.

These mechanisms were not, therefore, either blindly class-based or rigidly anti-governmental. Instead, they allowed the new forms of government to establish their legitimacy by creating a framework through which dissent and debate could shape the political process. Although these circumstances may make early republic politics appear more turbulent than a consideration of the high political principles of opposing elite leaders, they were fundamental in ensuring that new forms of government could demonstrate their connection with the people. The use of any one individual mechanism may have been challenged or considered illegitimate under certain circumstances. Taken as a whole, however, varying forms of popular activism ensured that political control remained in the hands of the people, as expressed through a complex formulation of governmental office and extra-governmental political activism. Whether looking at how the Washington administration refined its conduct to be more explicitly based on popular sanction, or at how election campaigns for state office in 1790 and 1799 evolved, one thing is certain. American politics and society had developed so that there was a popular political solution to the administrative challenges of republican government.

Notes

1. George Washington's Farewell Address (1796), Avalon Project, http://avalon.law .yale.edu/18th_century/washing.asp.

2. *Philadelphia Gazette,* 22 August 1795.

3. Stanley Elkins and Eric McKitrick, *The Age of Federalism: The Early American Republic, 1788–1800* (New York: Oxford University Press, 1995), 54; Richard Kohn, *Eagle and Sword: The Federalists and the Creation of the Military Establishment in America, 1783–1802* (New York: Free Press, 1975).

4. William J. Novak, "The Myth of the Weak American State," *American Historical Review* 113 (June 2008): 752–72; Max M. Edling, *A Revolution in Favor of Government: Origins of the US Constitution and the Making of the American State* (Oxford: Oxford University Press, 2003); Brian Balogh, *A Government out of Sight: The Mystery of National Authority in Nineteenth-Century America* (Cambridge: Cambridge University Press, 2009). Other relevant books to this discussion include Richard R. John, *Spreading the News: The American Postal System from Franklin to Morse* (Cambridge, Mass.: Harvard University Press, 1995), and Robin L. Einhorn, *American Taxation; American Slavery* (Chicago: University of Chicago Press, 2006).

5. Simon Newman, *Parades and the Politics of the Street: Festive Culture in the Early American Republic* (Philadelphia: University of Pennsylvania Press, 1997); David Waldstreicher, *In the Midst of Perpetual Fetes: The Making of American Nationalism, 1776–1820* (Chapel Hill: University of North Carolina Press, 1997); Len Travers, *Celebrating the Fourth: Independence Day and Rites of Nationalism in the Early Republic* (Amherst: University of Massachusetts Press, 1997). For related literature on printers and newspapers, see note 9, below.

6. This is particularly well demonstrated in Todd Estes, "Shaping the Politics of Public Opinion," *Journal of the Early Republic* 20 (Fall 2000): 393–422. His depiction of Federalist activism in 1795 and 1796, however, relies heavily on public debate in newspapers and less in an engagement with representative institutions.

7. Elkins and McKitrick, *Age of Federalism,* 54.

8. Saul Cornell, *The Other Founders: Anti-Federalism and the Dissenting Tradition* (Chapel Hill: University of North Carolina Press, 1999), talks about the importance of developing a "loyal opposition." The continuities in forms of political mobilization from before the revolution are an important part of this. See also David J. Siemers,

Ratifying the Republic: Antifederalists and Federalists in Constitutional Time (Stanford, Cal.: Stanford University Press, 2004).

9. Jeffrey L. Pasley, *"The Tyranny of Printers": Newspaper Politics in the Early American Republic* (Charlottesville: University Press of Virginia, 2001); Jeffrey L. Pasley, "'A Journeyman, Either in Law or Politics': John Beckley and the Social Origins of Political Campaigning," *Journal of the Early Republic* 16 (Winter 1996): 531–69; Andrew W. Robertson, *The Language of Democracy: Political Rhetoric in the United States and Britain, 1790–1900* (Ithaca, N.Y.: Cornell University Press, 1995); Marcus L. Daniel, *Scandal and Civility: Journalism and the Birth of American Democracy* (Oxford: Oxford University Press, 2009).

10. Constitution of Pennsylvania (28 September 1776), Avalon Project, http://avalon.law.yale.edu/18th_century/pa08.asp.

11. Robert Levere Brunhouse, *Counter-Revolution in Pennsylvania, 1776–1790* (Philadelphia: University of Pennsylvania Press, 1942); Owen S. Ireland, *Religion, Ethnicity and Politics: Ratifying the Constitution in Pennsylvania* (University Park: Pennsylvania State University Press, 1995); Terry Bouton, *Taming Democracy: "The People," the Founders, and the Troubled Ending of the American Revolution* (Oxford: Oxford University Press, 2006), Harry Tinkcom, *Republicans and Federalists in Pennsylvania, 1790–1801: A Study in National Stimulus and Local Response* (Harrisburg: Pennsylvania Museum and Historical Commission, 1950); Andrew Shankman, *The Crucible of American Democracy: The Struggle to Fuse Egalitarianism and Capitalism in Jeffersonian Pennsylvania* (Lawrence: University Press of Kansas, 2004); Sean Wilentz, *The Rise of American Democracy* (New York: Norton, 2006).

12. *Pennsylvania Gazette* (Philadelphia), 22 September 1790.

13. *Pennsylvania Gazette* (Philadelphia), 8, 15 September 1790.

14. "A Citizen," *Independent Gazetteer* (Philadelphia), 18 September 1790; *Pennsylvania Gazette* (Philadelphia), 22 September 1790.

15. *Pennsylvania Gazette* (Philadelphia), 22 September 1790.

16. *Pennsylvania Gazette* (Philadelphia), 29 September 1790.

17. Ibid.

18. *Pennsylvania Mercury* (Philadelphia), 11 September 1790; *Independent Gazetteer* (Philadelphia), 18 September 1790; *Federal Gazette and Pennsylvania Evening Post* (Philadelphia), 22 September 1790; *Aurora General Advertiser* (Philadelphia), 6, 7, 9 October 1790.

19. Pennsylvania 1790 Governor, State," A New Nation Votes: American Election Returns 1787–1825, http://elections.lib.tufts.edu/catalog/tufts:pa.governor.1790.

20. Kenneth Owen, "Political Community in Revolutionary Pennsylvania, 1774–1800" (Ph.D. diss., University of Oxford, 2011).

21. *Herald of Liberty* (Washington, Penn.), 13 May 1799. It appears that some members at the final general meeting attended in a representative capacity, having been nominated from an earlier meeting in Philadelphia.

22. *Philadelphia Gazette,* 11 April 1799.

23. *Gazette of the United States* (Philadelphia), 22 June 1799.

24. *Philadelphia Gazette,* 31 July 1799.

25. *Carlisle Gazette* (Pennsylvania), 28 August 1799.

26. *Herald of Liberty* (Washington, Penn.), 13 May 1799.

27. *Gazette of the United States* (Philadelphia), 5 March 1799.

28. *Claypoole's American Daily Advertiser* (Philadelphia), 11, 19 September 1799.

29. See, for example, *Oracle of Dauphin* (Harrisburg, Penn.), 10 July 1799; *Gazette of the United States* (Philadelphia), 18 July 1799; *Philadelphia Gazette,* 26 July 1799.

30. *Oracle of Dauphin* (Harrisburg, Penn.), 18 September 1799.

31. *Universal Gazette* (Philadelphia), 5 September 1799; *Claypoole's American Daily Advertiser* (Philadelphia), 19 September 1799.

32. It is difficult to ascertain the true attendance at any political meeting in this period. I have made an estimate here of around two-thirds of the claims made in newspaper reports of the popular meetings. This is based on experience of dealing with other large political meetings in Pennsylvania throughout the revolutionary era. Additionally, I have not found any accounts that contest the figures given—as the rest of this essay demonstrates, such contests were a regular feature of political debate in this period. Owen, "Political Community."

Bucks County election returns show 4,233 total votes in the election, with 2,058 for McKean and 2,175 for Ross. Pennsylvania Election Statistics Project, http://staffweb .wilkes.edu/harold.cox/gov/PaGov1799.html.

33. *Oracle of Dauphin* (Harrisburg, Penn.), 28 August 1799.

34. *Carlisle Gazette* (Pennsylvania), 28 August 1799.

35. The complicated relationship between top-down organizations and bottom-up activism is explored in detail by Douglas Bradburn in "A Clamor in the Public Mind: Opposition to the Alien and Sedition Acts," *William and Mary Quarterly,* 3rd series, 65 (July 2008): 565–600, and *The Citizenship Revolution: Politics and the Creation of the American Union, 1774–1804* (Charlottesville: University of Virginia Press, 2009).

36. *Gazette of the United States* (Philadelphia), 12 July 1799.

37. *Carlisle Gazette* (Pennsylvania), 14 August 1799.

38. *Gazette of the United States* (Philadelphia), 28 September 1799.

39. *Claypoole's American Daily Advertiser* (Philadelphia), 11 September 1799.

40. Sanford Higginbotham, *The Keystone in the Democratic Arch: Pennsylvania Politics, 1800–1816* (Harrisburg: Pennsylvania Historical and Museum Commission, 1952), 16.

41. Greene County Address to Albert Gallatin, September 1798, Albert Gallatin Papers, New-York Historical Society.

42. "Pennsylvania 1799 Governor, State," A New Nation Votes, http://elections.lib .tufts.edu/catalog/tufts:pa.governor.1799.

43. Jerald A. Combs, *The Jay Treaty: Political Battleground of the Founding Fathers* (Berkeley: University of California Press, 1970); Jonathan R. Dull, *A Diplomatic History of the American Revolution* (New Haven, Conn.: Yale University Press, 1985).

44. Todd Estes, *The Jay Treaty Debate, Public Opinion, and the Evolution of Early American Political Culture* (Amherst: University of Massachusetts Press, 2006);

Doron Ben-Atar and Barbara B. Oberg, eds., *Federalists Reconsidered* (Charlottesville: University Press of Virginia, 1998).

45. *Carlisle Gazette* (Pennsylvania), 11 March 1795.

46. *Massachusetts Spy* (Worcester), 22 July 1795; *Gazette of the United States* (Philadelphia), 23 July 1795; *Philadelphia Gazette*, 24 July 1795.

47. *Gazette of the United States* (Philadelphia), 17 July 1795; *Aurora General Advertiser* (Philadelphia), 17 July 1795; "Camillus," *Philadelphia Gazette*, 14 August 1795.

48. *Philadelphia Gazette*, 21 July 1795. A subsequent meeting is recorded in *Independent Gazetteer* (Philadelphia), 1 August 1795.

49. For more on the use of public space in Philadelphia, see Benjamin L Carp, *Rebels Rising: Cities and the American Revolution* (New York: Oxford University Press, 2007), 172–213.

50. *Aurora General Advertiser* (Philadelphia), 24 July 1795.

51. *Independent Gazetteer* (Philadelphia), 29 July 1795.

52. *Aurora General Advertiser* (Philadelphia), 24 July 1795.

53. Ibid.

54. *Jersey Chronicle* (Mount Pleasant), 8 August 1795; *Claypoole's American Daily Advertiser* (Philadelphia), 25 August 1795.

55. See Eric Foner, *Tom Paine and Revolutionary America* (New York: Oxford University Press, 2005), 145–83; Owen, "Political Community," ch. 2.

56. *Aurora General Advertiser* (Philadelphia), 18 December 1795.

57. *Aurora General Advertiser* (Philadelphia), 27 August 1795.

58. "Hancock," *Aurora General Advertiser* (Philadelphia), 27 August 1795. The term "flatterers" is used again by "Hancock" in *Aurora General Advertiser* (Philadelphia), 3 September 1795.

59. *Philadelphia Gazette*, 22 August 1795. York County petitioners sent a further remonstrance on the issue early the next year. *Gazette of the United States* (Philadelphia), 23 April 1796.

60. *Philadelphia Gazette*, 22 August 1795.

61. *Aurora General Advertiser* (Philadelphia), 1 October 1795.

62. Legislative Directories, Wilkes University Election Statistics Project, http://staffweb.wilkes.edu/harold.cox/legis/indexlegis.html.

63. *Aurora General Advertiser* (Philadelphia), 5 October 1795.

64. Estes, "Shaping the Politics," 416–22.

65. For more on printing and postal networks in this period, see John, *Spreading the News*, and Joseph M. Adelman, "The Business of Politics: Printers and the Emergence of Political Communications Networks, 1765–1776" (Ph.D. diss., Johns Hopkins University, 2010).

66. Nathan R. Kozuskanich, "For the Security and Protection of the Community: The Frontier and the Makings of Pennsylvanian Constitutionalism" (Ph.D. diss., Ohio State University, 2005).

67. Bradburn, "Clamor in the Public Mind." Similar problems are seen in the Whiskey Rebellion; see Owen, "Political Community," ch. 4.

★ TYLER ANBINDER ★

"Peaceably If We Can, Forcibly If We Must"

Immigrants and Popular Politics in Pre–Civil War New York

T he politics of the 1850s have probably been studied in more detail than that of any other decade in American history. It is surprising, then, that even though immigrants made up a larger portion of the electorate in this period than in any other in U.S. history, immigrants' political activity in these crucial years is not well understood. The impact of the Know-Nothing Party on the destruction of the so-called second party system, the place of nativism in the new Republican Party, and the Democrats' success at courting immigrant voters have all been thoroughly examined. But while immigration as a political issue in this period has been carefully studied, the nature of the immigrants' own participation in the political arena has received relatively little scholarly attention. We know that Irish Catholic immigrants voted overwhelmingly Democratic, but the nature of the relationship between Irish immigrants and native-born Democratic leaders remains something of a mystery. Irish immigrants are said to have been more politically active in this period than their German counterparts, but little evidence is typically presented to buttress such claims. Scholars generally suggest that while German and Irish Catholics tended to vote Democratic, Protestants from these places supported the Whig and Republican parties, but, again, we have little substantiation for such assertions. A comparison of popular politics in the German and Irish immigrant enclaves of pre–Civil War New York City enables us to better understand the nature of their political activity, how each group's political participation differed from that of native-born Americans and each other's, and what these facts tell us about the nature of antebellum politics and American democracy.[1]

New York City provides an excellent case study of popular politics in the Irish and German immigrant communities. In this period, New York had a larger Irish-born population than any other city in the world except Dublin, and its German-born population was larger than any but Berlin's. Two-thirds of adult New Yorkers in 1855 were foreign-born, meaning that German and Irish immigrants ought to have wielded tremendous political clout. Many Americans certainly believed that they did. One of Thomas Nast's most famous cartoons for *Harper's Weekly,* "This Is a White Man's Government" (1868), depicts what he contends are the three pillars of the Democratic Party. In the middle is Nathan Bedford Forrest representing the unrepentant South. To Forrest's left is German immigrant August Belmont, a New York banker, representing Wall Street "capital." And to Forrest's right is an Irish immigrant from New York's notoriously violent and impoverished Five Points neighborhood wielding a club labeled "a vote." Many Americans clearly associated New York's immigrants with politics and political power.[2]

New York's two major immigrant groups were physically situated very differently within the city. German immigrants concentrated in four of the city's twenty-two wards, in what would eventually become the Lower East Side but was known in the 1850s as "Klein Deutschland" (Little Germany). But in only three of these four wards (the 10th, 11th, and 17th) did the German-born truly dominate the immigrant population, and in none did they comprise a majority of the total adult population. In contrast, by 1855, there was no part of New York that did not have a large Irish immigrant population. Irish dominance within New York's immigrant population was declining, however. In 1850, Irish immigrants in New York outnumbered Germans by almost three to one, yet by the eve of the Civil War, the ratio of Irish to German immigrants had fallen to less than five to three. Nonetheless, because of Irish immigrants' wider dispersion, the city *felt* much more Irish than those numbers indicate, even in 1860. By that date, when 69 percent of the city's adult population was foreign-born, Irish immigrants constituted a plurality of the adult population in thirteen of the city's twenty-two wards, and immigrants comprised a majority of the adult population in twenty-one of twenty-two wards (see map 1).[3]

Because the Irish came to New York earlier and in greater numbers than the Germans, they were the first to become a political force in the city. It was most often the children of immigrants, however, rather than the immigrants themselves, who pursued political office and actively participated in the

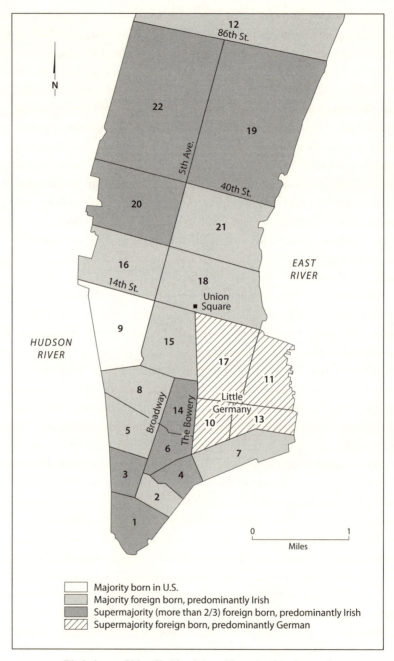

Birthplaces of New York's adult residents in 1860, by ward

political process. Like all New Yorkers in the early nineteenth century, Irish immigrants deferred to the city's prominent businessmen in political matters. Well-known merchants and manufacturers held the most important elective offices, even ward-level posts. With the adoption of universal white male suffrage, however, this deference began to wane. The election of the uneducated and uncultured Andrew Jackson as president in 1828 and his raucous inauguration the following year helped to inspire this political revolution. New York's election riots of 1834 marked the shift's climax on the local level, as Irish immigrants began to seize power over their local affairs. First in Five Points and then in other districts where the Irish were numerous, such as the East River waterfront, Irish Americans demanded a greater voice in determining how and by whom they were governed.[4]

Irish Catholic New Yorkers voted overwhelmingly for Democrats like Jackson. By the eve of the Civil War, non-Democratic candidates had trouble garnering even 15 percent of the vote in heavily Irish districts. Irish immigrants' support for the Democrats resulted from a number of circumstances. Democratic opposition to both the antislavery movement and to laws that would restrict the sale of alcohol drew many Irish immigrants to the Democratic fold. So too did the party's reputation as a friend of Catholic immigrants and an opponent of nativism. But substantive issues were rarely discussed during political contests in New York's Irish neighborhoods, which tended to follow the "low road" model of politics described in Andrew W. Robertson's essay in this volume. Platforms and policy statements are conspicuously absent from local political campaigns. Instead, the outcome of electoral battles in New York's Irish enclaves usually turned on the personal popularity of Democratic factional leaders, the ability of those leaders to deliver patronage to their followers, and the leaders' skills at using violence and intimidation at primary meetings and on election days to secure power and maintain it thereafter.

Just because New York's Irish Catholics were Democrats did not mean that Democrats welcomed Irish Catholics into their ranks, a fact exemplified by events in the spring of 1842. Until that year, public schools in New York City were run by a Protestant organization, the Public School Society. Its curriculum featured readings from the Protestant King James Bible, the singing of Protestant hymns, and textbooks that—according to Catholics—presented "the grossest caricatures of the Catholic religion, blaspheming its mysteries, and ridiculing its authority." As immigration increased their numbers, New

York Catholics complained bitterly about the overtly Protestant orientation of the schools, and asked that either religion be removed altogether or that the state fund Catholic schools to complement the ones run by the Public School Society.[5]

In April 1842, the New York legislature, attempting to mollify dissatisfied Catholics while simultaneously maintaining the support of Protestants content with the status quo, passed the Maclay Act, which created a new city-run public school system while leaving the Public School Society and its schools intact. The new system's policies on Bible reading and other contentious issues would be set by school boards popularly elected in each city ward. Neither side was satisfied with this act. Roman Catholic leaders such as Bishop John Hughes of New York believed that the immigrants would not receive fair treatment from the new boards, while Protestants perceived any changes to the prevailing system as capitulation to Catholic demands. One of these disappointed Protestants was Walt Whitman, then the young editor of a Democratic newspaper called the *New York Aurora*. Whitman condemned the Maclay Act as a "statute for the fostering and teaching of Catholic superstition."[6] Given the Democratic Party's reputation as the organization most sympathetic to the city's Irish Catholic immigrants, Whitman's comments may come as a surprise. But city Democrats actually split over the school question, with Protestant Democrats generally supporting the Public School Society. Whitman argued in the *Aurora* that New York Democrats should not submit to the ultimatums of Catholic leaders. "Shall these dregs of foreign filth—refuse of convents—scullions from Austrian monasteries—be permitted to dictate what Tammany *must* do?" If Democrats yield to "the foreign riffraff . . . in this case, . . . there will be no end to their demands and their insolence." The best way to teach the newcomers to respect American institutions, Whitman argued, was to resist Catholic educational demands.[7]

These Democratic divisions manifested themselves in the New York City municipal elections of 1842, which began just two days after passage of the Maclay Act. The 6th Ward, with its especially high concentration of Irish Catholic immigrant voters, was especially on edge. In the race for alderman, William Shaler captured the "regular" Democratic nomination, though a second Democratic ticket headed by former alderman Jim Ferris entered the fray as well. It was not unusual to find two Democratic candidates vying in a 6th Ward aldermanic race. But as the *New York Herald* pointed out,

All this quarrel arose out of the School question also. For Con Donohue [Donoho], the former Collector of the ward, was turned out by the Common Council for the part he took in the School Question. . . . When the nominations were made, Donohue was sacrificed and thrown overboard; on this his Irish friends rallied, made a new ticket, with Ferris at the head, to run it against Shaler, who had become very unpopular by his crusade against the little boys for crying Sunday newspapers.

The late entry into the contest of a third Democratic candidate, Shivers Parker, whom the *Herald* described as "the Bishop Hughes' candidate" (meaning that he probably favored using a portion of the city's school funds to finance Catholic schools), further complicated matters, raising the real possibility that the Whig nominee, earthenware manufacturer Clarkson Crolius Jr., might win the post.[8]

On election day, each faction attempted to prevent the supporters of the others from casting their ballots. "The fight," observed a reporter from the *Herald*, "was bloody and horrible in the extreme." Men were "so beaten about the head that they could not be recognized as human beings." A detachment of policemen, led by the mayor himself, arrived to quell the violence, but as soon as they left, thugs once again invaded the 6th Ward. Their goal, noted Whitman approvingly, was to rebuke "the outrageous insolence of [the ward's] foreign rowdies." Choosing their targets carefully, the rioters attacked the Orange Street grocery of Con Donoho "and injured it considerably." Then they moved uptown to Hughes's home, where rioters broke windows, doors, and furniture before authorities dispersed them. "Had it been the reverend hypocrite's head" that had been smashed, snarled Whitman, "instead of his windows, we could hardly find it in our soul to be sorrowful." The divisions among 6th Ward Democrats allowed Crolius to carry the race for alderman, giving the Whigs a one-vote majority on that board. Although a Democrat, Whitman rejoiced at his party's defeat in the contest for alderman, asserting that it would teach Tammany to resist Catholic demands.[9]

The "School Question" continued to simmer for the next couple of years. The ire that native-born Americans felt as immigrants criticized their school system led to the formation of the anti-immigrant American-Republican Party, which, in alliance with the Whigs, elected James Harper to the mayoralty in 1844. But with tens of thousands of immigrants arriving in the city annually, neither major party was willing to endorse the nativist agenda on a permanent basis. While the Whig dalliance with nativists further cemented Irish immigrants' ties to the Democrats, the Irish remained convinced that they would have to continue to battle within their own party to insure that their views were taken seriously and that their leaders won a fair share of the nominations.[10]

Who were these candidates for whom Irish New Yorkers fought so fiercely? Until about 1840, wealthy merchants and manufacturers such as Crolius had held most elective offices, even in wards with many immigrants. In some parts of the city, this remained the case into the 1850s. But by 1840, Irish immigrants had begun to develop a different kind of political elite, composed of saloonkeepers, grocers, policemen, and firefighters. The political power of these four groups resulted from their particular ability to influence voters. Saloonkeepers were the most respected men in immigrant neighborhoods. "The liquor-dealer is their guide, philosopher, and creditor," commented the *Nation* in 1875. "He sees them more frequently and familiarly than anybody else, and is more trusted by them than anybody else, and is the person through whom the news and meaning of what passes in the upper regions of city politics reaches them." Saloonkeepers could thus earn the gratitude and confidence of large numbers of tenement dwellers, gratitude that could be repaid as votes on election day. Liquor dealers also had the name recognition and financial resources to bid successfully for political office. Because many grocers derived a large proportion of their profits from the sale of alcohol, they too were well positioned for political advancement.[11]

Another route to political prominence ran through the volunteer fire department, one of old New York's most colorful institutions. A well-drilled fire company was just as likely to turn out in force to support a particular electoral slate as to extinguish a fire. The renowned fighters of the Irish fire companies were often the toughs who determined the outcome of primary meetings or general elections. Most companies admitted at least a few members to their exclusive ranks specifically for their fighting skills. Many of New York's Irish politicians first came to prominence as foremen of the city's fire companies, as did Tammany "Boss" William M. Tweed.[12]

Another path to political power wound its way through the police department. "There is no patronage . . . that a district leader desires so much and seeks so eagerly as places on the police force," noted postbellum attorney and reformer William M. Ivins. Politicos usually reserved positions in the police department for young men who had demonstrated party loyalty through pre-vious campaign efforts. In return for such a high-paying and secure job (about $12 per week in the mid-1850s, double what a day laborer could earn if he was lucky enough to get six days of work in a week), the officer was expected not only to continue laboring for the party at election time, but to contribute a portion of his salary to party coffers and use his influence to assist party mem-bers who might run afoul of the law. In this "unobtrusive and quiet way," Ivins recognized, a policeman could render "valuable service" to both the political benefactor who secured him his job and the party as a whole. Such "service" enabled many an Irish policeman to rise out of the ranks to both party leader-ship and elective office.[13]

A few Irish New Yorkers managed to claw their way to political power with-out first working in the police and fire departments or owning a saloon. An immigrant might, for example, approach a neighborhood political leader and promise to deliver the votes of a pair of large tenements or of those immigrants from a certain Irish county. Or he might offer the services of his gang to intim-idate the leader's opponents at a primary meeting or on election day. Whether he offered voters or fighters, this political aspirant would expect something in return. Some gang leaders asked for money, but the more politically ambitious sought patronage—jobs with the local, state, or federal government—either for themselves or for their allies. Patronage was one of the keys to increasing one's political clout, especially for those who could not count on the support of a fire company or saloon customers. The aspiring politician who could deliver jobs to supporters was in the best position to increase his own strength. This was especially the case in Irish neighborhoods, where steady jobs were so hard to come by.

By the end of the Civil War, these paths to political power had been sys-tematized into a relatively well-defined hierarchy, with the city's party "boss" at its apex. His lieutenants each controlled one of the city's assembly districts, and they in turn relied on the ward leaders. Every ward was divided into election districts, each headed by a single leader or a committee of ward cap-tains or "heelers." But before the Civil War, the situation was far more fluid. No boss anointed a ward or district captain in those years. Instead, factional leaders and their supporters fought (often literally) for control of each ward.[14]

However an Irish New Yorker had risen to prominence in his home district, to win elective office he had to parlay that prominence into a nomination. The leaders of each Democratic faction drew up a slate of candidates in advance of

the primary meeting (in heavily Irish neighborhoods, Democrats so outnumbered their opponents that the party always consisted of at least two factions
and sometimes more). By the 1850s, it was said that most candidates for significant offices such as alderman had to bribe these leaders to be assured a re-
alistic chance at a nomination. The faction leaders also chose nominees for the
minor ward offices (such as assistant alderman, constable, and school board
member) and candidates to represent the ward at nominating conventions for
city, state, and federal posts. With the ticket set, faction leaders had barely
enough time to mollify disappointed office-seekers before the ward primary
meeting, which typically took place three to four weeks before election day.

In a city that became renowned for its rough and bloody primary meetings, those in its Irish wards were the most violent of all. "Regularity in the
old Sixth was ofttimes only won by black eyes, torn coats, and dilapidated
hats," recalled J. Frank Kernan, a longtime New York political operative, in
his memoirs. "The knowing politicians of the ward never went well dressed
to a caucus meeting." The convention's very first vote was the most crucial,
because the faction that managed to elect the meeting's chairman controlled
the proceedings and could, with official sanction, use its fighters to "maintain order," the typical excuse given for expelling the weaker faction's members from the building. If its strongmen failed to appear promptly, disaster
loomed for even the most popular and seemingly invincible clique. "Once,"
Kernan remembered, "when John Emmons was the candidate [for alderman],
nothing gave him the victory but the fact that Bill Scally [a noted pugilist],
with Con Donoho and his men, arrived just in the nick of time to save the
chairman from going out of the window, and the secretary following him; but
their timely arrival changed the complexion of things, and sent the opposition
chairman and officers out through the same window." Candidates for even the
most prestigious offices could not sit idly by while hired bullies did the rough
work for them. Kernan observed that those nominees who did not "take a
hand with their friends in battling for their cause" at the primary meetings
would be derided as cowards and "lack votes on election days."[15]

On the day of the general election, scenes like those found at the primary
meetings would repeat themselves in Irish neighborhoods at each polling station. One might imagine that the general elections would be peaceful inas-
much as the Democrats far outnumbered their rivals in Irish wards, but there
were two reasons that violence might resurface. First, the losing faction in the
Democratic primary often stayed in the race as a "reform" ticket. Sometimes

these renegades would bring their toughs to the polls hoping to prevent the rival faction's supporters from voting and thereby carry the election. Even if Irish Democrats in a given district were not at war on election day, fighters were often stationed at the polls anyway to suppress the Whig or Republican vote. They did so less to insure a victory in the local races, in which the Democrats rarely had to fear defeat, but instead to decrease the citywide or statewide vote of those parties, especially when one of those contests was thought to be close.[16]

In contrast to Irish immigrants, who jumped enthusiastically into New York's political fray as soon as they were able, German immigrants seemed politically apathetic. The German newcomer "cares . . . little who governs and what is done over him," commented the *New York Times* in a typical assessment. Perhaps as a result, as late as the early 1850s, one finds very few German Americans other than August Belmont playing a prominent role in New York City politics. In Klein Deutschland, Irish surnames on ballots always far outnumbered Germanic ones, even in the ward-level party nominations. Until the mid-1850s, there never appeared more than one Germanic surname on any party's Klein Deutschland ballot, and such nominations were always for the lowest positions, such as constable or election inspector.[17]

New York's Germans did, however, maintain their own political organizations within each party, something the Irish never did. In the month or so before any given election, newspapers brimmed with announcements of meetings of German Democrats, Whigs, or Republicans. As election day drew near, these gatherings inevitably concluded with torchlight parades designed both to rally support for the party's ticket and increase the visibility of German immigrants on the New York political scene.[18]

Like the Irish, German New Yorkers voted overwhelmingly Democratic and did so for many of the same reasons. Germans were drawn to the Democratic Party in part because of its reputation as the friend of the immigrant. Even immigrants who had not yet arrived in New York when Harper was elected mayor in 1844 would have been reminded by other Democrats that the nativist publisher's victory had been made possible by the Whigs' decision to tacitly endorse Harper by withdrawing their own candidate. The Whigs in New York State were also perceived to be those most inclined to restrict or even ban the sale of alcohol, and Germans Americans abhorred the temperance movement just as vehemently as the nativist crusade.

German political apathy ended rather abruptly in 1854 when nativism, prohibitionism, and a third issue, slavery, simultaneously erupted in controversy. In the first months of the year, the New York legislature began to consider a bill, sponsored by Whig Myron H. Clark, that would have banned the sale of alcohol in the state (such statutes, modeled after one enacted in Maine in 1851, were known as "Maine Laws"). The bill passed both houses of the legislature in the first days of spring, but after what seemed like an eternity of indecision to New York's German population, Democratic Governor Horatio Seymour vetoed the measure. Temperance advocates vowed to continue fighting to enact a Maine Law, and a few months later, New York Whigs indicated their stance on the issue by nominating Clark for governor. New York's Germans vowed to make his defeat their highest priority.[19]

In the very months that the liquor prohibition bill was wending its way through the legislature in Albany, an equally controversial bill, one that would repeal a different kind of prohibition, was under consideration in Congress. That legislation, proposed by Illinois Senator Stephen A. Douglas and eventually known as the Kansas-Nebraska Act, would end the ban (in place since 1820) on slavery in most western territory acquired in the Louisiana Purchase. Instead, the settlers in each territory would vote on whether or not to allow slavery. Passage of the Kansas-Nebraska Act in May 1854 inspired unprecedented political fighting within the New York German immigrant community and brought a new group of leaders to the forefront of New York's immigrant politics.[20]

Just when the Maine Law and the Kansas-Nebraska Act were roiling New York politics, a new nativist political organization, the Order of the Star Spangled Banner, burst on the political scene, creating a third reason for German New Yorkers to become more politically active. The new group's supporters (dubbed "Know-Nothings" because when asked about the organization they feigned ignorance) demanded that immigrants be banned from elective or appointed political offices, that Protestants resist Catholic demands to make changes to the American school system, and that immigrants be required to wait twenty-one years, rather than five, until they could become citizens and vote. Although Know-Nothing leaders directed more of their venom at Irish immigrants, Germans also found the nativist movement insulting and repugnant, and vowed to fight the Know-Nothings and their agenda as well.[21]

Of the three issues that rocked the political landscape in 1854, temperance seems to be the one that motivated German voters the most. The Maine Law was omnipresent in both the German press and the mainstream media's reporting on German political activity. "GERMANS!—The pride of your fatherland, lager bier, is imperiled," cried the *New York Herald* as it implored them to vote the Democratic ticket on election day in November 1854. "Next they'll want your pipes." Addressing a crowd from atop a barrel on that same date, a German grocer warned that the Whigs wanted "to meddles mit te croceries and mit te lager bier places. I shall say you mush not vote to dem. I shall say eef you shall vote for dem my pizeness shall pe all proke, smash to pieces." Nevertheless, Clark won the governorship, prompting German New Yorkers to fear that the enactment of a prohibitory law was imminent. Germans denounced "the dark aims hidden under these pretended moral movements" and vowed to resist such legislation, "peaceably if we can, forcibly if we must."[22]

Such sentiments reflected more than the desire of Germans to drink and their merchants to retain an important part of their sales. That immigrants organized much of their political activity in their saloons and beer halls meant that prohibition would strike not only at immigrants' drinking habits but at their political power as well. Most immigrant political leaders could afford to run for office because of the income generated from the sale of alcohol. Germans also linked the temperance movement directly to anti-immigrant prejudice. These were the "dark aims" to which New York's Germans referred. Natives sometimes admitted as much, as when the *Herald* asserted that "the Know Nothing Order is the sign of the first movement against these . . . grog shop politicians." Perhaps with that same thought in mind, that German grocer speaking from atop a barrel predicted that "eef dem mans [the prohibitionists] pe made pig den all der Toichmans shall pe made so smaller as notings mitout lager bier." The Germans' social lives, economic well-being, and political clout would all suffer if "dey shall pe all dry up like ter Yankees."[23]

Those New Yorkers who hoped to pry German Americans away from the grip of the Democratic Party thought that the Kansas-Nebraska Act might make such a realignment possible. For while Seymour's veto had killed New York's Maine Law in April 1854, Congress had enacted the Kansas-Nebraska bill and President Franklin Pierce had signed it into law in May. Initial signs pointed to a great divide in New York's German community over the territorial legislation. When German Democrats called a meeting in February to demonstrate that the Teutonic newcomers supported the Nebraska bill, the gathering did not go according to plan. Much to the chagrin of the meeting's organizers, half of the two thousand Germans in attendance refused to endorse a German American who supported the legislation as meeting chairman. Yet the anti-Nebraska nominee for chairman could not secure a majority of the vote either. According to the *Herald,* the "yells" of those in attendance, "louder than the revelry among the imps of Pandemonium, prevented a decision in favor of any one." Pleas for "compromise and conciliation" fell on deaf ears. A German priest attempted to calm the crowd, but "he was received with cries of 'Down with Catholicism.' 'Down with the Pope.' 'Down with him.'"[24]

Such comments point up the religious divide within the German immigrant population that was relatively absent in the Irish community. While the overwhelming majority of Irish immigrants in New York were Catholics, the German newcomers were more split evenly between Protestants (primarily from northern states such as Prussia and Hanover) and Catholics from southern German states (such as Bavaria, Baden, and Württemberg), though New York's German community had more southern Germans than most major American cities with large German populations. New York's Germans, however, were better known for their *lack* of religious conviction than for devotion to any Christian denomination. "They are inclined to skepticism and irreligion," asserted the *New York Times* about the city's Germans in 1855, while another observer concurred that "a large portion belong to the school of Rationalism, and can scarcely be said to have any religion." Whatever the case, natives believed that Germans who were either Protestants or atheists might be weaned from the Democratic Party and converted to the antislavery cause.[25]

When the leader of the meeting's anti-Nebraska forces, brewer Erhard Richter, tried to address the audience from the speakers' platform, "a rush was made for it and it was upset and smashed into pieces and Richter laid sprawling upon the heads of the crowd." At this point, according to the *New York Herald*'s reporter, there "began a general fight. Men were tossed over heads, trampled under foot, and pulled and pummelled in every quarter." Some of the combatants attempted to raise a makeshift standard declaring, in German, "'No Slaves.' The fight then became terrific; some seized pieces of [a] broken table, knocked men over the head and brought blood from several." After two hours of this mayhem, the conclave dissolved without ever having come to order. While such scenes were common at primary meetings in Irish wards, this kind of bloodshed was unprecedented at a German political gathering in New York, reflecting the impassioned views of German New Yorkers on the slavery issue.[26]

The anti-Nebraska movement was important not only because it revealed fissures within the New York German community but also because it brought the city's "Forty Eighters," leaders of the failed German revolutions of 1848 who had fled to the United States to avoid arrest, into New York politics for the first time. On the 3rd of March, the German opponents of the Nebraska bill held their own meeting, and again the hall was packed with several thousand participants. "Lager bier," reported the *Herald*, "flowed in abundance, and the majority of the sons of the 'Faderland' appeared to show their contempt for all prohibitory liquor laws" by consuming "copious draughts of that refreshing beverage." After the assemblage elected Richter chair of the meeting, German "Turners," members of a liberal gymnastic society that had supported the 1848 revolutions, marched into the hall accompanied by their band "playing the 'Marseillaise,' and bearing the red republican flag. They were received with a tremendous outburst of enthusiasm." Next,

> another detachment . . . succeeded in making an entrance, bearing the tri-colored revolutionary flag of Germany, which also obtained its share of applause. Then came several banners, one inscribed "No Slavery," another, "No Maine Liquor Law," and a third was a caricature intended as a lampoon on the editor of the *Staats Zeitung*, who made himself obnoxious to a portion of the Germans by his support of Mr. Douglas's bill, and also upon the lady of the proprietor of that journal. The two figures were coarsely daubed with black paint.

At these and subsequent German antislavery meetings, the featured speakers were almost always "the most eminent of the martyrs of the German Revolution of 1848." At this initial gathering, according to the *Herald*, these ex-revolutionaries denounced the Nebraska bill "in the most unmeasured language, and every opprobrious epithet in the vocabulary was heaped upon it most unsparingly."[27]

Tammany Hall made sure to stage a German pro–Kansas-Nebraska Act rally a few weeks later that drew an even larger crowd than the anti-Nebraska meeting. But fearing nevertheless that German defections might cost them the some contests in the 1854 elections, Democrats for the first time in years put German Americans on their citywide tickets (in 1845, they had nominated William F. Havemeyer, the son of German immigrants, to run against the nativist Harper). In 1854, the larger Democratic faction, the "Softs," selected paint magnate Daniel F. Tiemann (the child of German immigrants) for the post of almshouse governor. The other Democratic faction, the "Hards," also nominated a second-generation German American, C. Godfrey Gunther (a wealthy fur merchant), for the same post. Tiemann won. "The German Democrats," as the *Times* later put it, were no longer willing "to quietly give their votes and get none of the spoils." The Whigs, meanwhile, nominated a German American for commissioner of streets and lamps. These were relatively insignificant posts, but that Germans received any citywide nominations at all indicated that their votes were now considered both important and potentially up for grabs.[28]

Given the Whigs' past support for nativism and temperance, their leaders understood why few German immigrants would vote for their candidates. Yet with the demise of the Whigs and the rise of the Republican Party, which put antislavery above all other issues, Republicans thought that they would win a large portion of the New York German vote. German Republicans organized large rallies in the city for the 1856 Republican presidential nominee, John C. Frémont. At these gatherings, those heroes of '48 would address New York's German immigrants in their native tongue, exhorting them to be faithful to the republican cause in Germany by joining the Republican Party in the United States. Frederick Hecker, who in 1848 had led the failed attempt to overthrow the government of Baden, told a New York audience that the "honor of the German name and of the German nation, and the hatred of aristocratic arrogance and tyranny, make it the sacred and imperative duty of every German to enter the lists against Slavery and Slaveocracy." Another exile argued that "we have not come to this country in order to go hand-in-hand with those who stand in the same category with our aristocrats at home." A few weeks before the election, the *New York Times* (a Republican paper) confidently predicted that "the majority of Germans in New-York were now with the Republicans."[29]

But election day proved that the *Times* predictions had been wildly over-optimistic. In no part of Klein Deutschland did Frémont come close to defeating Democrat James Buchanan. The *Times* tried to sugarcoat the results, defying mathematical logic by insisting that "in several of the strong German Wards of this City probably full *one-third* of the Germans voted with the Republicans." But the estimate by a German paper that only six thousand New York Germans had cast Republican ballots was probably closer to the mark.[30]

Why did the antislavery movement fail to motivate German New Yorkers to switch parties? Germans seemed to believe that the Republican Party was as tainted with nativism and prohibitionism as the Whig Party had been. The many instances in which Republicans cooperated with northern Know-Nothings made it impossible to cast a vote for free soil without also tacitly endorsing Know-Nothingism. "If you Americans will but present to the Germans a truly free party—free in every respect—you will be sure to command their votes, and you might count upon their best aid in forming such a party," commented one German American in explaining the reluctance of the immigrants to cast Republican ballots. Other Germans cited the liquor issue as the decisive one, since many upstate Republican candidates for the legislature in 1856 were vowing to enact imbibing restrictions. Republicans' occasional anti-Semitic attacks on the most prominent German immigrant Democrat in New York, August Belmont, could not have helped endear Germans to the Republican organization.[31] German Republicans asked their countrymen to at least support the antislavery party for posts that did not involve enforcement of the liquor laws, but such pleas went largely unheeded.[32]

Germans' association of the Republican Party with liquor restrictions seemed to be confirmed after the Republicans won statewide races in the 1856 elections. With support for radical temperance measures such as outright prohibition fading, the Republican-controlled legislature instead enacted legislation closing New York's saloons on Sundays and imposing steep licensing fees on all establishments that sold alcohol. Fearing that New York City's police would not enforce the statutes, the legislature in early 1857 also disbanded the force and replaced it with a state-run police unit from which immigrants were largely excluded and whose ranks were filled with former Know-Nothings (whose party had disintegrated by the end of 1856).[33]

German New Yorkers now made good on their vow to resist temperance legislation with violence if necessary. When the new police officers came to Klein Deutschland to enforce the Sunday closing law just days after the new statute went into effect in July 1857, the Germans there rioted in an attempt to drive the lawmen out of the neighborhood. The Germans became enraged when one of the inexperienced policemen attempting to restore order in the 17th Ward shot a bystander dead. These events, as well as New York Republicans' attempts in the same legislative session to extend the waiting period before immigrants could vote, reinforced the notion in Germans' minds that Republicans were prohibitionists and nativists, and helped the Democrats to maintain their grip on the vast majority of the German vote in the city.[34]

While we know that there was a significant antislavery element in New

York's German immigrant population, it is far more difficult to gauge Irish immigrants' views of "the peculiar institution." Except for the rare reference to the issue by an Irish American candidate for political office, we have no means of judging how the Irish immigrants perceived slavery, though we can try to infer their views on the subject by consulting the city's Irish, Catholic, and Democratic press. These newspapers consistently argued that both abolitionism and the more moderate movement to prevent the creation of additional slave territory threatened the survival of the nation. "We are totally opposed to Abolitionism in every shape;—not because we desire to perpetuate slavery, but to preserve the Union," announced the *Irish-American* in 1853. "That slavery is inconsistent with the Declaration of Independence and our Republican Constitution we will not affect to deny," its editors admitted four years later. But they argued that Americans had been "forced to accept the 'Institution' of slavery" as part of the compromises that created the nation, and that those pledges could not subsequently be broken.[35]

Some New York Democrats argued that slavery was beneficial to blacks and whites alike. The *Day Book,* a Democratic paper aligned with Mayor Fernando Wood, who was especially popular among the city's immigrant population, asserted that "'slavery,' or negro subordination to the will and guidance of the superior white man, is a law of nature, a fixed truth, an eternal necessity, an ordinance of the Almighty, in conflict with which the efforts of human power sink into absolute and unspeakable insignificance." Free blacks such as those in New York had been better off as slaves, argued the newspaper's editors, because now they were still subordinate to whites but were not guaranteed the subsistence of food, clothing, and shelter that slave owners provided.[36]

Irish Americans also frequently justified their opposition to abolitionism on the grounds that it would hurt the movement to liberate Ireland. Daniel O'Connell, who fought to repeal the Act of Union that had bound Ireland politically to the United Kingdom, spoke out against American slavery in the early 1840s. "The black spot of slavery rests upon your star spangled banner," O'Connell wrote, "and no matter what glory you may acquire beneath it, the hideous, damning stain of Slavery remains upon you; and a just Providence will sooner or later, avenge itself for your crime." After O'Connell's repeal movement fizzled, many Irishmen cited his diversion into abolitionism as the cause of his difficulties. The *Irish-American* claimed that his statements on slavery "WERE THE FIRST — THE VERY FIRST — CAUSES OF THE DIVISIONS" that fractured the repeal forces. "American sympathy was a 'mighty fact' be-fore then," stated the journal, but subsequently, "division, disunion, distrust, contention, [and] personal bitterness" doomed the repeal movement to failure. Abolitionists ought to focus their attention on the 6 million "white slaves" in Ireland, insisted the *Irish-American*, before interceding on behalf of the 3 million black slaves in the United States.[37]

Irish Catholics often alluded to abolitionists' prejudice against them to jus-tify their refusal to endorse the antislavery movement. "Irishmen have no [more] bitter enemies, Catholics no fiercer foes, than are nine-tenths of the American Abolitionists," insisted the *Freeman's Journal* in 1843. "Dark, sullen, ferocious bigots as they are, they abhor the name of Ireland and Catholicity." In the mid-1850s, when the Know-Nothing Party scored major electoral vic-tories in the Northeast where abolitionism was strongest, the *Irish-American* asked why "the citizens of New England, who spend their money, their time, their talents, in endeavoring to make the negro free, are so opposed to the 'foreigner?'"[38]

While the extent to which the average Irish immigrant discussed the slavery issue is impossible to determine, by the mid-1850s it had clearly became a com-mon topic of political conversation even for Irish immigrants. Even the editors of the New York *Irish-American*, a nonpartisan journal that focused its political coverage on Ireland and rarely discussed American elections, felt compelled to admit in early 1858 that Kansas, Stephen A. Douglas, and the Lecomp-ton constitution dominated "thought, talk, and writing, North and South. . . . Few sounds are uttered without these all-absorbing names being heard." This was the case in New York's immigrant enclaves too, because whether one supported Buchanan or Douglas on the issue of slavery in the Kansas consti-tution, this issue had begun to determine nominations for elective office and many patronage appointments.[39]

By the late 1850s, however, immigrant New Yorkers, especially the Irish, began to demand prestigious elective offices as well as patronage positions. In 1858, when the Irish insisted on two of the dozen or so positions on the city-wide ticket, native-born and German immigrants complained that "the ticket would be entirely too Irish." But the Irish prevailed, electing John Kelly as sheriff and John Clancy as city clerk (both were the children of Irish immi-grants). A German immigrant running on the Republican ticket won election as an almshouse governor in that same year, not because he drew more Ger-mans than usual to the Republican ticket, but because the nomination of a

popular Irish immigrant, James Lynch, on the insurgent Mozart Hall Democratic ticket caused the Democratic vote to be more evenly divided than usual,
allowing the Republican to win this race (by this point the Democratic division between Softs and Hards had been replaced by a Tammany Hall–Mozart
Hall divide). Henceforth, Irish and German Americans would receive larger
shares of the citywide nominations than had previously been the case, as the
various parties and factions strove to win the hearts and minds of immigrant
voters.[40]

Just weeks after the contests of 1858 had been decided, New Yorkers began
discussing the upcoming presidential election of 1860, knowing that a Republican victory might bring about southern secession. This possibility even
became a cause for alarm in immigrant enclaves that had once paid relatively
little attention to national issues and contests. In early 1859, for example,
Clancy could be found at his favorite Five Points saloon regaling the tavern's
patrons with his enthusiasm for the candidacy of Douglas, the "little giant"
from Illinois. Douglas had just won reelection to the U.S. Senate over Republican Abraham Lincoln, a name few New York immigrants would have recognized before that contest. Yet Lincoln, like most Americans, knew about Five
Points. When he visited New York a year later to give a campaign speech, he
found time to take a tour of the famous neighborhood. He said that the cheer-
ful optimism he encountered at one of the district's Sunday schools "inspired
me — [has] given me courage. . . . I shall never forget this as long as I live."[41]

Lincoln, however, did not inspire New York's immigrants. The city's leading Catholic newspaper, the *Freeman's Journal,* though nominally nonpartisan, took the unusual step of endorsing the "fusion" ticket opposing Lincoln
in the 1860 presidential race. "It is not the business of the political power to
settle moral questions," the *Journal* argued when explaining its decision. Only
when a majority of Americans North and South could be brought by "moral
suasion" to oppose slavery would it be appropriate for politicians to interfere
with the institution. Democrats directed other arguments at immigrant voters, including a circular in German aimed at immigrant tailors stating that "if
Lincoln is elected to-day, the bread will be taken out of the mouths of your
children. The trade with the South will be entirely destroyed, and that is the
mainstay of your occupation. . . . Vote to maintain yourselves and your children, and let the negro take care of himself." A newspaper ad directed at "Irish
and German laborers" predicted that "if Lincoln is elected to-day you will
have to compete with the labor of four million emancipated negroes. . . . The

North will be flooded with free negroes, and the labor of the white man will be depreciated and degraded. . . . Go to the polls, every man of you, and cast your votes against Lincoln and abolitionism. Vote early." New York's immigrants apparently found such arguments convincing. Lincoln managed to poll a respectable 40 percent of the vote in the most heavily German ward in the city, but that was a smaller proportion of votes than the district had polled for the hopeless candidacy of Whig Winfield Scott in 1852. In the 4th and 6th Wards, those with the highest concentrations of Irish immigrants, Lincoln could muster only 13 percent of the vote. Lincoln won the election, but he did so without much support from New York City's immigrant community.[42]

Looking at the political crisis of the 1850s from the vantage point of New York's immigrants suggests a number of lessons for those who seek to understand the history of American popular politics. First, even though more than half of the electorate in New York City was foreign born, immigrants wielded relatively little political power within the parties themselves. Immigrants almost never held elective office and rarely secured nominations, even for minor positions. In almost every instance, it was the children of immigrants who were the Irish and German Americans contesting elections. German Americans were especially underrepresented in elective office. Even in races for ward-level positions in Klein Deutschland, German Americans rarely secured nominations until the late 1850s. Irish surnames, in contrast, were commonly found on antebellum New York electoral tickets, but Irish Americans nonetheless complained that they received the least important nominations and were barred from positions of real authority in both government and the Democratic Party. Such complaints persisted until well after the Civil War. But things could have been worse. In Philadelphia, another city with a large Irish immigrant population, native-born political leaders in 1853 "reformed" the city government in a manner that sharply reduced Irish Democrats' rising political power, as Andrew Heath details in his chapter in this book.

Second, German Americans' relative political impotence in New York did not result, as has often been posited, from a lack of interest in American politics. New York's Germans were avid political organizers, holding meetings and rallies as often as did their Irish American counterparts. One reason German immigrants may not have wielded as much clout as the Irish was that the Germans were not willing to use violence to wrest power from entrenched ward heelers. It often took violence (or at least intimidation) to win nominations at primary meetings and gain positions in the hierarchy of Tammany

Hall, and while the contemporary record reveals numerous melees through which Irish immigrants seized local nominations from native-born Democratic leaders, no such incidents occurred involving German New Yorkers. Germans did grow violent when debating temperance and slavery, but they would not fight with fellow Democrats for nominations in the manner that the Irish did.

Finally, the national political issues that captivated most Americans during the 1850s seem to have had relatively little appeal to immigrant New Yorkers. The question of whether and to what extent slavery should be allowed to expand into the territories is almost wholly absent from New York's ethnic press. Although Irish immigrants were renowned for their opposition to the antislavery movement, their New York newspapers were strangely silent on the leading national political issue of the day. More Germans than Irish opposed the extension of slavery, but that stance did not convince Germans to change partisan allegiances as long as Republicans were also perceived to be the party of nativism and prohibition. Only at the very end of the 1850s did the slavery issue take center stage in New York City's immigrant communities. This occurred in part because fighting within the Democratic Party over Kansas became so intense that even local patronage appointments now required a promise to tow the Buchanan administration line on this issue. The increasingly real threat of disunion and its economic implications may have also made the slavery issue more relevant to immigrants than it had ever been before.

It may also be the case that in attempting to prove their devotion to their new homeland, immigrants preferred to steer clear of issues that so bitterly divided native-born Americans. Furthermore, having not lived in the United States long enough to have developed sectional identifications, immigrants may have felt far removed from the slavery debate. Even today, immigrants tend to be motivated to become politically active primarily by issues that directly affect them. One of the twentieth century's best-known Irish American politicians, Thomas P. "Tip" O'Neill, once famously said that "all politics is local." That seems to have been the case for Irish and German immigrants in antebellum New York City as well.

Notes

1. My estimate that immigrants made up a larger percentage of the electorate by 1860 than they would in subsequent years was reached as follows: While immigrants made up 1 percent more of the total U.S. population in 1870, 1890, and 1910 (14 versus 13%), the fact that the freedmen could vote in 1870 would have reduced the immigrants' share of the electorate. In 1890 and 1910, far fewer immigrants sought naturalization than in the antebellum years, reducing the number of immigrants who could vote. On the destruction of the second party system, see Michael Holt, *The Political Crisis of the 1850s* (New York: Norton, 1978); William Gienapp, "Nativism and the Creation of a Republican Majority," *Journal of American History* 72 (December 1985): 529–59; Gienapp, *The Origins of the Republican Party, 1852–1856* (New York: Oxford University Press, 1987); Tyler Anbinder, *Nativism and Slavery: The Northern Know Nothings and the Politics of the 1850s* (New York: Oxford University Press, 1992); and Ronald P. Formisano, "The Invention of the Ethnocultural Interpretation," *American Historical Review* 99 (April 1994): 453–77. On the Democrats' success at courting Irish voters, see Amy Bridges, *A City in the Republic: Antebellum New York and the Origins of Machine Politics* (Ithaca, N.Y.: Cornell University Press, 1984); Steven Erie, *Rainbow's End: Irish-Americans and the Dilemmas of Urban Machine Politics, 1840–1985* (Berkeley: University of California Press, 1990); Thomas O'Connor, *The Boston Irish: A Political History* (Boston: Northeastern University Press, 1995); Tyler Anbinder, *Five Points: The Nineteenth-Century Neighborhood That Invented Tap Dance, Stole Elections, and Became the World's Most Notorious Slum* (New York: Free Press, 2001); and James Connolly, *An Elusive Unity: Urban Democracy and Machine Politics in Industrializing America* (Ithaca, N.Y.: Cornell University Press, 2010).

2. "This Is a White Man's Government," *Harper's Weekly,* 5 September 1868, 568.

3. Robert Ernst, *Immigrant Life in New York City, 1825–1863* (1949; reprint Syracuse, N.Y.: Syracuse University Press, 1994), 193; 1850 1% Census Sample from Steven Ruggles et al., *Integrated Public Use Microdata Series: Version 5.0* (Minneapolis: University of Minnesota, 2010), http://usa.ipums.org/usa/index.shtml. Nativity of population by ward in 1860 is based on the 1860 manuscript population schedules compiled by the author from ancestry.com.

4. Anbinder, *Five Points,* 7–13, 26–32; Paul Weinbaum, *Mobs and Demagogues: The New York Response to Collective Violence in the Early Nineteenth Century* (Ann Arbor: UMI Research Press, 1979), chs. 1–2; Paul Gilje, *The Road to Mobocracy: Popular Disorder in New York City, 1763–1834* (Chapel Hill: University of North Carolina Press, 1987), 121–72.

5. "The Proposed State School Law," *Freeman's Journal* (New York), 27 October 1849, 2.

6. *New York Aurora,* 11 April 1842, in Joseph J. Rubin and Charles H. Brown, eds., *Walt Whitman of the "New York Aurora"* (State College, Penn.: Bald Eagle Press, 1950), 68; "Public Schools," *New York Herald,* 11 April 1842, 2; "Alderman Jones

on the School Question," *New-York Tribune*, 12 April 1842, 2; Edwin G. Burrows and Mike Wallace, *Gotham: A History of New York City to 1898* (New York: Oxford University Press, 1999), 630–31. See also Joann Krieg, *Whitman and the Irish* (Iowa City: University of Iowa Press, 2000), ch. 3.

7. Rubin and Brown, eds., *Walt Whitman of the New York Aurora*, 58–59, 67–68.

8. "The Terrible Election Riot in the Sixth Ward," *New York Herald*, 14 April 1842, 2.

9. Rubin and Brown, eds., *Walt Whitman of the New York Aurora*, 77, 78, 80; "Election Riots," *New-York Tribune*, 13 April 1842, 2; "The Terrible Election Riot in the Sixth Ward," *New York Herald*, 14 April 1842, 2.

10. Lewis Dow Scisco, *Political Nativism in New York State* (New York: Columbia University Press, 1901), 45–47; Eugene Exman, *The Brothers Harper* (New York: Harper and Row, 1965), 183.

11. "Boss Government," *The Nation*, 4 November 1875, 288; Richard B. Stott, *Workers in the Metropolis: Class, Ethnicity, and Youth in Antebellum New York* (Ithaca, N.Y.: Cornell University Press, 1990), 239; Matthew P. Breen, *Thirty Years of New York Politics Up-to-Date* (New York, 1899), 233.

12. New York Board of Aldermen, *Documents* 25 (1858): doc. 6, pp. 53–54, 161, 171; J. Frank Kernan, *Reminiscences of the Old Fire Laddies* (New York, 1885), 23–24, 501; "Owen W. Brennan," *New York Times*, 30 October 1884, 5; *Manual of the Corporation of the City of New York for 1855* (New York, 1855), 168.

13. William M. Ivins, *Machine Politics and Money in Elections in New York City* (1887; reprint New York: Arno Press, 1970), 13–14, 25; *Manual of the Corporation of the City of New York for 1856* (New York, 1856), 225; "The Process of Electing Mr. Wood," *New-York Tribune*, 20 October 1856, 4.

14 Ivins, *Machine Politics*, 9–11; Breen, *Thirty Years*, 39–43.

15. Kernan, *Reminiscences*, 49–50. On the influence of money and fighters in securing nominations citywide, see "Democratic Ratification Meeting," *New York Herald*, 29 October 1850, 8; "The Primary Meetings—Horrible Developments of Bribery, Corruption, and Fraud," *New York Herald*, 30 October 1850, 2; "The Death of Bill Poole," *New York Herald*, 10 March 1855, 4; and Breen, *Thirty Years*, 40–43. For comparisons to other cities, see Richard Bensel, *The American Ballot Box in the Mid–Nineteenth Century* (New York: Cambridge University Press, 2004), 138–86.

16. Anbinder, *Five Points*, 151–54.

17. "Political Notices," *New York Times*, 28 October 1852, 5; "Germans and Education," *New York Times*, 29 June 1855, 4; "At a Meeting of the German Democratic Republican Citizens of the First Ward," *New York Herald*, 4 November 1850, 1; "The Irish Vote," *New York Herald*, 29 November 1852, 4; "The German Vote," *New York Herald*, 31 October 1852, 2.

18. "The Irish Vote," *New York Herald*, 29 October 1852, 4; "A German Republican Procession Atrociously Assaulted," *New York Herald*, 9 October 1856, 4; "Torchlight Procession," *Evening Post*, 26 October 1852, 2.

19. Anbinder, *Nativism and Slavery*, 76–78; Gienapp, *Origins of the Republican Party*, 148; John Krout, "The Maine Law in New York Politics," *New York History* 17 (1936): 260–72.

20. David Potter, *The Impending Crisis, 1848–1861* (New York: Harper and Row, 1976), 145–76; Michael Holt, *The Rise and Fall of the American Whig Party* (New York: Oxford University Press, 1999), 804–30.

21. "Germans and Know-Nothings," *New York Times*, 16 June 1855, 4; "The Germans and Education," *New York Times*, 29 June 1855, 4; Anbinder, *Nativism and Slavery*, ch. 2.

22. "Germans!" *New York Herald*, 7 November 1854, 4; "Scenes of Election Night," *New York Times*, 8 November 1854, 5; "The Germans on K.N.'s and the Maine Law," *New York Times*, 25 May 1855, 3.

23. "The Know Nothings and the Southern Democratic Members of Congress — A Great Mistake," *New York Herald*, 8 January 1855; "Scenes of Election Night," *New York Times*, 8 November 1854, 5.

24. "Meeting of the German Democrats," *New York Herald*, 24 February 1854, 8. On the relationship between the Forty Eighters and the abolition movement, see Mischa Honeck, *We Are the Revolutionists: German-Speaking Immigrants and the American Abolitionists after 1848* (Athens: University of Georgia Press, 2011), and Daniel Nagel, *Von Republikanischen Deutschen zu Deutsch-Amerikanischen Republikanern: Ein Beitrag zum Identitätswandel der Deutschen Achtundvierziger in den Vereinigten Staaten 1850–1861* (St. Ingbert, Ger.: Röhrig Universitätsverlag, 2012).

25. "Germans and Know-Nothings," *New York Times*, 16 June 1855, 4; Thomas Low Nichols, *Forty Years of American Life*, 2 vols. (London, 1864), 2:69; W. J. Rorabaugh, "Rising Democratic Spirits: Immigrants, Temperance, and Tammany Hall, 1854–1860," *Civil War History* 22 (June 1976): 142; Jay P. Dolan, *The Immigrant Church: New York's Irish and German Catholics, 1815–1865* (Baltimore: Johns Hopkins University Press, 1975), 68–86. Origins of German immigrants in various American cities is based on Joseph C. G. Kennedy, *Population of the United States in 1860: Compiled from the Original Returns of the Eighth Census* (1864; reprint New York: Norman Ross, 1990), 608–15, with the exception of Milwaukee data, which is from the author's own database of German immigrant origins and destinations based on a sample of New York immigrant ship registries from 1846 to 1854, National Archives, Washington, accessed via ancestry.com. The religious divide in the German community also explains why the school question did not become as big an issue in the German community as it was in the Irish — many Germans were happy with the Protestant-oriented schools set up by the Public School Society or the schools set up under the Maclay Act, which in New York City had very little religious content.

26. "German Meeting on the Nebraska Bill," *New-York Tribune*, 24 February 1854, 5; "Meeting of the German Democrats," *New York Herald*, 24 February 1854, 8; *Trow's New York City Directory for 1855–56* (New York, 1855), 696.

27. "Great German Fremont Meeting," *New York Herald*, 4 March 1854, 8; "The

German Anti-Slavery Meeting Last Night," *New-York Tribune,* 4 March 1854, 4; "Grand German Demonstrations," *New York Times,* 4 March 1854, 8; "Great German Fremont Meeting," *New York Times,* 22 August 1856, 1.

28. "New York: The Latest Returns," *New York Times,* 11 November 1854, 1; "Still Another Party! The German Democrats in the Field," *New York Times,* 24 September 1855, 1; "William F. Havemeyer," *New York Times,* 21 October 1872, 8; "Obituary: Ex-Mayor C. Godfrey Gunther," *New York Times,* 24 January 1885, 5; "Biographical Sketches: Hon. Daniel F. Tiemann, Mayor of the City of New York," *United States Democratic Review* 42 (November 1858): 420–36.

29. "From a German to the Germans," *New York Times,* 23 July, 1856, 1; "Great German Fremont Meeting," *New York Times,* 22 August 1856, 1; "Germans in America," *New York Times,* 9 October 1856, 4; "German Republican Meeting," *New-York Tribune,* 8 October 1856, 5; "Tremendous Gathering of the Germans in Favor of John Chas. Fremont for President," *New York Herald,* 22 August 1856, 1.

30. "The German Vote," *New York Times,* 7 November 1856, 1; "The German Vote and the Presidential Election," *New York Times,* 25 November 1856, 3. Comparison of the 1856 voting results in Klein Deutschland to those of the previous four years suggests that few Germans had changed their allegiances since 1852.

31. "Slidell, Belmont, and Buchanan," *New York Times,* 12 June 1856; "The Germans," *New York Times,* 22 October 1856, 4; "The German Vote and the Presidential Election," *New York Times,* 25 November 1856.

32. "German Republicans," *New York Times,* 5 November 1855, 4.

33. Paul Weinbaum, "Temperance, Politics, and the New York City Riots of 1857," *New-York Historical Society Quarterly* 59 (July 1975): 246–50.

34. Ibid., 258–63; "Another Terrible Riot in Second Avenue," *New York Herald,* 13 July 1857, 1; "The Seventeenth Ward Riot," *New York Herald,* 14 July 1857, 1; "The City Riots," *New York Herald,* 15 July 1857, 1; "Riot in the Seventeenth Ward," *New-York Tribune,* 13 July 1857, 5; "The Second Avenue Riot," *New-York Tribune,* 14 July 1857, 6; "The Seventeenth Ward Riots," *New York Tribune,* 15 July 1857, 4; "Mass Meeting of the Germans to Organize an Independent Political Party," *New York Times,* 14 October 1858, 5; "The German Republicans on the Twelfth Section," *New York Times,* 1 September 1859, 8; *Staats Zeitung,* 1 November 1858; Anbinder, *Nativism and Slavery,* 254–57.

35. "Irish Abolitionists," *Irish-American,* 29 October 1853, 2; "Northern Abolitionists," *Irish-American,* 31 January 1857, 2.

36. *Day Book,* 11 November 1857.

37. "O'Connell and the Slavery Question," *New York Evening Post,* 23 June 1843, 2; "Father Mathew Kidnapped in Boston," *Irish-American,* 12 August 1849, 2; "The Abolitionists at Syracuse," *Irish-American,* 17 May 1851, 2; "Mrs. Stowe in Cork," *Irish-American,* 11 June 1853, 2.

38. "Mr. O'Connell's Speech," *Freeman's Journal,* 22 July 1843, 4; "Northern Abolitionists," *Irish-American,* 31 January 1857, 2.

39. "Kansas and Senator Douglas," *Irish-American,* 9 January 1858, 2.

40. Anbinder, *Five Points*, 292–95; "For Governor of the Almshouse," *New York Times*, 29 November 1858, 1; "The Results of Yesterday's Election," *New-York Tribune*, 8 December 1858, 4.

41. *Leader*, 9 October, 6 November 1858, 12 March 1859; Anbinder, *Five Points*, 235–36.

42. "The Importance of the Issue," *Freeman's Journal*, 6 October 1860, 4; "That Dastardly System of Intimidating Poor Mechanics," *New-York Tribune*, 1 November 1860, 4; "Workmen Not Slaves," *New-York Tribune*, 3 November 1860; "Irish and German Laborers," *New York Herald*, 6 November 1860, 5.

★ ANDREW HEATH ★

Small Men, Best Men, and the Big City

Reconstructing Political Culture in Antebellum Philadelphia

I n September 1851, municipal reformers gathered in Philadelphia to re-view the progress of their campaign to consolidate the 2-square-mile city proper and its burgeoning suburbs under one government. The charter revision, first proposed after two huge riots in 1844, had gradually won the backing of merchants, manufacturers, and professionals; these self-styled "best men" made up the officers at the meeting, and having secured pledges from both the Whig and Democratic parties to back the scheme in the state legislature the previous fall, they had expected success. As the *Evening Bulletin* declared after the elections, "the question of the union of the city and districts" had been settled.[1]

In Harrisburg, though, the new charter had been quietly killed during the spring session, and the Executive Consolidation Committee blamed the Philadelphia delegation. Their support, its report to the meeting complained, was "so limited" they "could not pass a bill purely local in its character, and upon the passage of which their own character, as well as that of the political party to which they belonged, and their own reputation as legislators, was in a great degree involved." The only legislator in attendance, Edward A. Penniman, reacted angrily to these accusations. As a journeyman coach-trimmer in the mid-1830s, he had cut his teeth as a leader of the militant General Trades' Union, a movement that had briefly united Philadelphia's artisans and laborers, and won a series of spectacular victories over the city's employers. When the Panic of 1837 fractured the brief moment of working-class unity, he followed the well-trodden path for radicals into the Democratic Party, and by the late 1840s was editing the Jacksonian daily *The Spirit of the Times*. His journal's acerbic attacks on Philadelphia's high society—its correspondents included George Lippard, author of the scurrilous city mystery novel *The Quaker City* and the founder of a radical brotherhood that denounced the reign of "Capital and avarice"—helped to win it a strong following among workingmen, but it did little to endear its owner to the hostile audience at the meeting. In a retort that one of his critics decried as full of "extreme violence and excitement," he accused the Consolidation Committee and its allies of a "base libel." His denunciations of the "liars," "slanderers," and "villifiers" present did not go down well. As he tried to speak, he was subject to "considerable interruption" from the floor, and attendees voted down a resolution that would have absolved him of blame for the bill's demise. The meeting concluded with a speech by Judge Anson V. Parsons, who urged attendees to select "a ticket apart from politics" and "sweep the Democratic, the Whig and the Native parties to the winds."[2]

Just under three years later, reformers took up Parsons's baton. With the backing of the Whig editor Morton McMichael, whose *North American and United States Gazette* was widely read in the drawing rooms of the city's economic elite, supporters of consolidation broke free from party trammels and nominated an independent ticket at the polls. Led by the wealthy attorney Eli Kirk Price; the locomotive builder Matthias Baldwin; and the first president of the Pennsylvania Railroad, William C. Patterson, the ticket triumphed in the state elections, winning all eight of the city's legislative seats and sending a state senator to Harrisburg. Over the following weeks, consolidators met regularly at the Board of Trade to draw up a new charter. Shepherded through the state senate by Price, the bill they drafted was signed into law in February 1854. That June, when the consolidated government came into being, the city annexed not just its adjacent districts but the entire county, expanding in the process by over sixty-fold while collapsing dozens of independent jurisdictions into one. Mill towns, romantic suburban retreats, and thousands of acres of farmland were drawn into the domain of the new municipality, making Philadelphia in territorial terms the largest city in the Union.

Although the consolidation movement triumphed against the backdrop of what Michael F. Holt has called a "widespread revolt" over politics as usual in the early 1850s, it is usually read as a purely local measure: a belated response on the part of the city's businessmen to the series of riots that had visited the city during preceding decades. After restoring order, Samuel Bass Warner argued, the economic elite retired to the counting house, leaving the field of politics to the specialist. Warner's account is more or less affirmed in several other works on the midcentury city, which stress the private orientation of wealthy citizens and their disengagement from municipal politics. While historians sometimes disagree on whether they are describing a willing withdrawal or a reluctant retreat, most concur that across the big metropolitan centers of the Northeast, genteel citizens played an ever-decreasing role in local politics between the Jacksonian era and the Civil War. In modernizing city government—leaving it, that is, in the hands of experts and party leaders—the consolidation movement merely hastened this process.[3]

We must be careful, though, not to confuse effect with intent. Reading backward from after the Civil War, when Philadelphia's Republican leaders had acquired a stranglehold on the reformed city government, it is tempting to see the Consolidation Act as a pact between aspiring machine politicians and supine businessmen: a minor footnote in the "routinization" of party politics to which John L. Brooke refers in his essay in this volume. Looking forward from the 1851 meeting, though, the rise of boss rule does not seem preordained. Riding the rising tide of antiparty sentiment, reformers set about redrawing not only the metropolitan boundaries but also the rules of the political game. They were not aiming to elevate the political specialist but instead transform the social character of the city's representation. For some, at least, consolidation was a way to restore the rule of the "best men."[4]

The movement for a new city charter rested first and foremost on a critique of the way politics was practiced in a metropolis undergoing rapid social and economic change. Consolidators believed that men like Penniman had mastered a political style peculiarly well-suited to the patchwork quilt of districts and boroughs woven onto the map of Philadelphia county. In neighborhoods over which the economic elite no longer exercised moral or political authority, so-called wire workers built fiefdoms through control over local governments, taverns, and riotous fire companies and street gangs. Such "petty sovereignties"—always an obstacle for state-builders to overcome—stood between citizens and the metropolitan interest, degrading the character of the former and inhibiting the pursuit of the latter. The consequence, reformers argued, was a divided and decrepit system of local governance, which left Philadelphia ill-equipped to compete with its rivals in the race for population and wealth.[5]

The style of immigrant and working-class politics was so well-adapted to a divided and distended metropolis that to challenge it might seem futile. Yet as Kimberley K. Smith has argued in a study that draws heavily on Philadelphian sources, the antebellum decades witnessed a protracted struggle over the legitimacy of different forms of political expression: a battle, in short, to define the rules of the game. Rioting, for instance, which up to the 1830s was sometimes seen as an acceptable form of protest, was less tolerable to respectable citizens a couple of decades later. Instead, educated citizens insisted democracy should "mean informed, reasonable people cordially debating important issues in the public arena." But while Smith's work underscores the very real fears Americans harbored that voters might join mobs or succumb to the wiles of silver-tongued demagogues, her interest is more on the discourse than the practice of politics. By focusing on texts rather than movements, meanwhile, she has less to say on the social character of reform, and disputes the salience of class.[6]

While my analysis, therefore, differs from Smith's in several crucial respects, I want to build on her work here by showing how the consolidation movement's redrawing of political boundaries—both in terms of the territorial and administrative reach of municipal power—can be read as an attempt to remake the practice of politics. By the 1840s, as Smith points out, the problems that beset the city were frequently blamed on disorderly and degraded homes in a reform literature that saw family and civil government as intimately interlinked.[7] The assumption that well-ordered households would produce good citizens has a history that stretches back at least as far as the American Revolution, but in the age of the "Great City," reformers argued that in the absence of clean, comfortable houses, urban residents would be pushed out into the open. There, in neighborhoods beyond the reach of the economic elite, they would be exposed to a host of debilitating environmental and institutional influences. Somehow, citizens needed domesticating, ensuring they learned their politics in the cathartic realm of the home rather than the turbulent world of the street.[8]

The solution for many of the Philadelphians who supported consolidation lay in an aggressive extension of public power, giving reformers the weapons to destroy the petty sovereignties that were both an obstacle to and a reason for reform, embark on a program of urban improvement designed to uplift the city's residents, and encourage working-class citizens to acquire salubrious homes of their own, not least through putting in place the infrastructure to sustain rapid suburban expansion. Each of these designs aimed to draw citizens away from the orbit of the "small men" of neighborhood politics, of the type described by Tyler Anbinder elsewhere in this book. By no means all reformers shared these hopes. Plenty backed a new city charter in the hope it would deliver cheaper government, strengthen the police, and boost the value of unimproved real estate. But several of the more influential figures in the movement—including Eli Kirk Price and Morton McMichael—saw the household, the urban environment, and political practice as entwined, and concluded that a local state with the power to remake either of the first two could improve the other. "Urban planning discourses," Margaret E. Farrar reminds us in her recent book on the building of Washington, D.C., "not only create subjects but also create citizens."[9] Read in this vein, charter revision was not just an attempt to rewrite the rules of city politics; it was also an opportunity to transform the terrain on which it was played and the character of its participants.

What more ambitious consolidators sought, indeed, was a structural reformation of the urban polity; they saw themselves as architects of a political system and urban environment capable of producing a public culture worthy of Philadelphia's metropolitan scale. In this regard, their designs went well beyond what we know of their peers elsewhere in the 1850s, as frustration with "politics as usual" hurt Whigs and Democrats across the North. Retrenchment, not expansion, is the word used most often in making sense of the objectives of these reformers. Philadelphians like Price and McMichael imagined something quite different: political regeneration through urban reconstruction. They did not do so, as bourgeois New Yorkers would later attempt, by contesting suffrage rights, nor did they anticipate the path charted by Progressive reformers, who used the model of the business corporation to reorient municipal politics from the ward to the metropolis. Rather, they designed a republic in miniature in which the social and institutional configuration of the city itself would elevate dignified leaders. In short, they tried to find a way to make democracy work for them.[10]

The Politics of the Street

A few days before Edward Penniman confronted his critics, a correspondent in the *North American* called on Philadelphia to keep pace "with the progress and refinement of the age" by creating a municipal park. Although such plans for metropolitan improvement circulated widely among the economic elite over the course of the early 1850s, they were more often discussed than enacted. Seduced by rapid growth, burgeoning real estate values, and booster designs to make the city the central place in America's continental empire, property owners readily embraced the social and aesthetic order of what David Schuyler has called "the new urban landscape," a cityscape of airy boulevards and genteel public squares. "We should have our Parks, Fountains and Columns," one citizen argued in 1852, but Philadelphia would not become the "Paris of America" without consolidation and a "different class of men at the head of affairs." It was a familiar lament: reformers believed that across the metropolis, "small" politicians lorded over petty fiefdoms with little thought for the public good of the city.[11]

By 1853, consolidators had concluded that the divide between their metropolitan aspirations and the seemingly petty preoccupations of the city's political class could not be bridged, and looked on enviously at rival cities less hamstrung by democratic propriety. That November, McMichael's paper wrote admiringly of the vast improvements that over the following two decades would transform Paris into what David Harvey has called "the capital of modernity."[12] While the journal grudgingly acknowledged that such projects required a form of "absolute rule" not "in all respects desirable," it nevertheless wished "some of the energetic spirit of enterprise and progress displayed in the works of Louis Napoleon" could be "infused into our citizens and our municipal councils." The problem lay in how to do so in the era of the common man. In 1837, a constitutional convention made the vote the exclusive privilege of white men and opened new offices like the mayoralty to public ballot. By the 1840s, Whig, Democratic, and Native party members had established party organizations in the metropolis, and if they lacked the hierarchical structure that would come to characterize postbellum political machines, they were strong enough to thrust men wealthy citizens derided as uncouth and unlettered into positions of power. "This," the *North American* concluded, "is the grand defect of our system, social and political; and it is one that, being inherent, cannot be cured."[13]

Or could it be? That same week, McMichael attended as usual a meeting of the Consolidation Committee. Its delegates' ostensible aim — the union of the "city proper" with its outlying districts — masked their grander ambition of building a new political culture. Over the preceding decades, the cluster of self-governing boroughs and districts to the north and south of corporate Philadelphia had grown at a far greater rate than the metropolitan core, threatening to reduce William Penn's original settlement, as the committee's victorious candidate for the state senate, Eli Kirk Price, revealingly put it, to "an appendage of her colonies." The contrasting ratios of growth, however, were merely the symptoms of a profound social transformation. At midcentury, most wealthy Philadelphians still lived in the city proper; the bulk of workingmen and laborers, on the other hand, lived beyond its borders, where work was near and rent cheap. These divisions may have been less pronounced than the segregation that would mark the twentieth-century metropolis but were real enough for citizens to see the county map as a social tapestry: the truculent Irish weavers of Kensington; the Germans with "Louis Napoleon" moustaches who lived alongside native-born artisans in Northern Liberties; the "proletaires" of Southwark eking out a living on the waterfront; and the combustible amalgam of fugitives from famine and slavery in "miserable, misguided and misgoverned" Moyamensing. As the final description suggests, the suburbs had a distinct political character: more democratic both in temperament and party affinity than the city proper. That the latter was sometimes referred to as the "Whig Gibraltar" prior to 1854 is telling. As Price's imperial metaphor suggests, its genteel residents cast themselves as defenders of order, resisting the papist, leveling tendencies that lurked just beyond the city line. For some of them, consolidation was an act of self-defense: subduing a wild frontier marred by rioting and disease.[14]

The contrast Philadelphians drew between the city and its "colonies" at midcentury was the consequence of a commercial and democratic transformation that, in consigning journeymen and laborers to hidden alleys and remote suburbs at the very moment they were winning new rights as citizens, weakened bonds of deference. Midcentury writers waxed nostalgically about the old days of the productive household when apprentices looked to their masters for political guidance as well as induction into the mysteries of the craft, contrasting this hazily remembered golden age to a present in which spatial divisions magnified social ones. Journalists and reformers frequently reminded their middle-class readers how few had any firsthand experience of the "infected districts" and "plague spots" that lined the corporate boundaries of the city. Their sensationalist prose filled in the gaps, depicting a netherworld physically proximate but morally remote from Philadelphia proper—a Dickensian realm in which rickety tenements and filthy streets mirrored the benighted condition of the people. The disease, disorder, and degradation they portrayed served as compelling evidence that the citizens of the likes of Moyamensing were incapable in their present condition of self-government. In this regard, the patchwork quilt of districts and boroughs conjured into being by legislative fiat were not arbitrary lines on a map. They were the political expression of real social divisions, with each municipality a law unto itself.[15]

Reformers eager to understand the ways politics worked in working-class suburbs tended to look beyond the local governments to the institutions and spaces that sustained them. What could account, they asked, for the sway figures like Penniman held over working-class voters? Evangelicals and racial pseudoscientists had their own answers—the susceptibility of "Celtic" immigrants to the corrupting influence of rum, for instance, or the casual intermixture of blacks and whites in impoverished neighborhoods—but the consolidators who wrote on the subject often drew a direct link between the physical degradation of suburban districts and the moral fiber of their inhabitants. "Why has 'the street schoolmaster—the Devil'—so many pupils?" one doctor asked in 1855. Boys, he answered, were driven onto the streets by the "sickening effluvia" emanating from their homes in teeming courts and alleys, while those who did dare to stay in their households were morally contaminated by the absence of privacy as a consequence of overcrowding. The political implications troubled him, for it was those children that would grow up to make "our nominations and control our elections." "The street is their home," the editor of the *Philanthropist* argued of the metropolitan poor, "for there lies all the chief attractions and incentives of action." Conceived as a classroom— a place to learn the rules of citizenship—the streets left much to be desired. From cobblestoned corners young men gravitated to a set of institutions woven into the fabric of primarily working-class neighborhoods: the houses of fire companies, the haunts of street gangs, and the taverns of ward heelers, each one a source of civil disorder, a forum for political intrigue, and an incubator of the muscular fraternal spirit that seemed to swing elections.[16]

Consolidators saw petty sovereignties—whether in the form of independent districts and boroughs that lined the city proper or increasingly working-class institutions like fire companies—as fragmenting what ought to have been an indivisible metropolitan interest. Like nativists wary of Catholics' loyalty to a foreign power, they feared such bodies would either capture the government or conspire to undermine it. One reformist tract called volunteer firemen "a power in the State, an '*imperium in imperio*,'" while gangs too were suspected of harboring political ambitions. In a novella from 1847, young men predict that, like the "Jacobins," the "Killers' Club, from a mere party organization, *will sway parties and dictate to the whole country*." Paradoxically, though, given these national ambitions, the territorial reach of what were seen as bastard scions of America's associational culture was worryingly limited for reformers with metropolitan aspirations. "Our strength lies in the district of Moyamensing," the Killers' leader proclaims, "and Moyamensing must be our stronghold." Pluck Hill, a neighborhood in northern Philadelphia populated by what one newspaper called "Black Dutch and wild Irish," was even reputed to have its own "queen," an unlicensed tavern keeper named Kit McCluskey who got "to rule on" every disturbance.[17]

Figures like McCluskey, in inverting the class and gender hierarchies cherished by the midcentury middle class, illustrate both the difficulties "best men" faced in establishing authority over working-class space, and their concerns that territory they could not control undermined their visions for the wider metropolis. The obvious place they could play a part in the political process was at ward-level delegate elections, which by the late 1830s had become the first stage in the process of choosing candidates for municipal, state, and federal office. But these meetings were held on the terrain of firemen, gang members, and tavern keepers, and a Whig paper complained in 1853 that they had "been abandoned to a very small portion of the whole taxable inhabitants of each ward — to men too often the least competent and honestly disposed to represent the wish and general welfare of the many." Like other journals, the newspaper implored respectable readers to show up, but few did. Their absence, though, did not necessarily mean they were turning away from politics; rather, it implied their rejection of a particular political culture.[18]

The remote and mysterious nature of the district ward meeting made it virtually impossible for the genteel reformer to participate without compromising his integrity. First, he had to live in a suburb to attend, at a point when most wealthier citizens still resided in the old city proper. Even if he was eligible to participate, he would have to go somewhere he would not "habitually visit" to mix with men who "may not be of the number he would daily concert with." As the conservative essayist J. Francis Fisher later pointed out, this often meant the "frequenting of low taverns," places reformers by midcentury were blaming for a whole host of evils.[19] For a class cultivating their own ideas of manners and politics, the social character of the delegate meeting was anathema to them. Those who did attend, indeed, became complicit in a system consolidators longed to dismantle. The *Sunday Dispatch* suggested in this vein that to win a nomination a candidate "must fawn and cringe to ignorant delegates, and implore their sweet voices; he must flatter some and bully others; he must lie, equivocate, and promise fearlessly and rashly; he must banish all self-respect, impose upon himself every degradation, and crawl amidst the meanest things." The best men, in short, could not play by the same rules as the small men: to do so meant sacrificing their claims to character on the altar of power. Those who slavishly adhered to the partisan line, the *Public Ledger* warned, "cannot be independent, cannot have moral courage enough to contend merely for *right*."[20]

But in abandoning delegate meetings, consolidators feared, they were leaving city politics to men who lacked the synoptic vision to transform Philadelphia into the London or Paris of America. "They are the great men of their respective localities," one paper sarcastically complained, but their myopia left them incapable of realizing the potential of the metropolis. To reformers, it seemed, the constituents these partisans answered to were firemen and gangsters rather than men of property and standing; their gaze pointed them not in the direction of genteel avenues but the "hovels" of Moyamensing's Bedford Street, the so-called Five Points of Philadelphia.[21]

"Oh that we had among our prominent citizens, and especially among our Councilmen, *one* that had the prescience to see our future, and the philanthropy and nerve requisite to do battle for its right direction," the merchant J. B. Okie argued in March 1852, in a familiar plea for urban improvement. "Such a man would, like all martyrs to a good cause, have to contend against serried ranks of ignorance, prejudice and passion; but it would reap for him in the end undoubted success and honor, and a name enduring as his city's greatness." The search for what David M. Scobey has called a "heroic" city builder was quixotic for reasons the economic elite understood all too well: the very forces that led Okie to conclude such a figure was needed ensured he could never be elected. Reformers instead embraced ever more desperate measures. Well before the *North American* was calling for a dose of the treatment Louis Napoleon and his city planner Georges-Eugène Haussmann had prescribed for Paris, other papers were urging vigilance committees to seize power in Moyamensing, cast out the district's board of commissioners, and restore the rule of law.[22]

It is in such debates that power and class intersected in the antebellum metropolis. Parties themselves may have been heterogeneous social coalitions, but the style of politics they practiced left a bitter taste in the mouths of the economic elite. Wealthy opponents from across the partisan divide — and prosperous Whigs and Democrats both joined the movement for civic union —

could happily forget their differences over the tariff or slavery extension in the bipartisan but bourgeois world of the Board of Trade, gentlemen's clubs, and the Consolidation Committee. They were less willing to mix with their party allies in the taverns and firehouses of Philadelphia's outlying districts. Yet it was in the latter, reformers feared, that the city's destiny was being determined. The critique of metropolitan politics was therefore enmeshed with a critique of the social space of the working-class neighborhood, which produced citizens unworthy of the democratic privileges they enjoyed, and partisan operatives more than willing to use their influence over these citizens. Rowdy suburbs sustained a style of politics impenetrable to respectable reformers, and generated government that jarred with designs to transform Philadelphia into a genteel city.

The Politics of the Home

Encoded within consolidators' critiques of street politics lay a path to reform. If degraded citizens and working-class institutions sustained ward heelers, severing the link between the two offered a way to restore the best men to their rightful place at the apex of the political ladder. Reformers aimed here to "carry away" what one journal called the "miasmatic heaps which poison the political atmosphere" by domesticating the practice of politics.[23]

By midcentury, the domestic ideal was virtually ubiquitous in middle-class culture. Evangelical Protestantism and the breakdown of the artisanal household had changed the meanings wealthier Americans attached to home. Counterposed to the masculine realm of the marketplace, the household became a cathartic retreat, a "quiet refuge from the rush and roar of life" in the words of one essayist. Within it, the tender influences of the mother reigned supreme. "Women are to make home the happiest place in the world," Price argued a decade after consolidation, "and husbands and sons are there to find their happiness, and to cultivate kindness and the courtesies of life." Like its near-ancestor, the late eighteenth-century cult of "republican motherhood," antebellum domestic ideology gave woman formally excluded from the public sphere of politics the important role of rearing virtuous citizens.[24] But the home's importance to the cultivation of good citizenship, reformers believed, did not just lie in the moral influence of the middle-class lady, for home-ownership also imposed a duty on the man to look after his family. "The moral man is sensible of the duties he owes to his wife, his children, society, and himself," argued the political economist Henry C. Carey. "His place is home."[25] The imperative of providing both material comfort and justice to one's dependents could easily become a rehearsal for participation in the broader realm of public life.

In a sense, this made the home another petty sovereignty, albeit one quite distinct from "Queen" Kit's Pluck Hill or "Jacobin" Moyamensing, for sound "family government," as Price and other reformers called it, was a miniature rather than an inversion of their natural political order. When consolidators sketched out the proper lines of authority in the household, they tended to follow the familiar precepts of midcentury domesticity, reserving an important role for the housewife in a "dual reign" with her husband. From this harmonious division of labor came benefits that extended well beyond the home. One reformer, for example, suggested that as the oldest "government on earth," it was the source from which all other forms of authority had sprung. The link between power in the private realm of the family and the public realm of politics endured into the Civil War era. "The moral power of a people is just in proportion to the combined virtuous influences which exist in the homes of that people" argued the Germantown *Telegraph* in 1854. The first post-consolidation mayor, Robert T. Conrad, was even more forthright. *"Home virtues,"* he insisted, "are not only the loftiest, but the only virtues, for those dispensed elsewhere are born at home."[26]

If this was the case, however, then the converse was equally true. Just as good homes produced healthy cities, bad homes produced sickly ones. Certainly reformers pointed to a lack of domestic mores to explain urban disorder. "The want of proper family government," one essayist put it, "is one of the most serious evils of our land," while others worried that thanks to poor parenting, vice was being handed down from generation to generation. In places like Moyamensing's Bedford Street, reformers saw the apparent absence of proper home life as both a symptom and cause of the district's malaise. It was "the homeless and traitors to home," Price proclaimed, who menaced the metropolis.[27]

Consolidators like Price believed that removing citizens from the didactic space of the streets and immersing them in the cathartic influences of home life offered a way to rewrite the rules of Philadelphia's political culture. To the *North American*, for instance, a metropolis built around the small house could expect to reap rewards in the form of less "dependence," "more sound public spirit," and greater "prudence and wholesome conservatism." From the late 1840s, then, reformers came forward with a slew of proposals to firm up the city's domestic terrain. The *Public Ledger*, one of the first journals to back consolidation and, according to one historian, the "voice of the city's respectable classes," made the case for strengthening government's role. As "the progress of humanity" rested on the provision of "home attraction," it argued, the state had the power to provide housing, and proposed that councils use the vacant lots bequeathed to the city by the late merchant Stephen Girard to build model dwellings for workingmen. In 1847, the paper also urged an unnamed district, almost certainly Moyamensing, to purchase "half of the lots now covered with shanties, hovels and pig-pens," level them, then cover the vacant land "with well built houses" for lease at "moderate rents." Eight years later, though now admitting the end would be ideally achieved through private enterprise, the same paper envisaged a reconstructed Bedford Street district as a "'Paradise Regained' in our midst." Demolition, it insisted, was one of the best ways to "protect the health, and consequently the morals of the community."[28]

Such designs existed only on paper, not least because the local state lacked the unity to bring them into fruition. But many reformers in the early 1850s did help to sponsor dozens of homestead associations, which purchased real estate for small family dwellings on the metropolitan frontier, and led calls for the creation of surrogate domestic spaces like almshouses and parks.[29] When wealthy citizens tried to bequeath land for a park to the city in 1856, they spoke of the need for a place in which Philadelphians of all classes "can feel at home." That same year, a pamphleteer argued that a new pleasure ground was vital to the "political stability of our institutions." Price, who after the Civil War became a leading figure on the Fairmount Park Commission, had expressed similar ideas before consolidation when he urged the city government to buy up a large suburban estate and cordon off its grounds for a series of evenly spaced public squares. Careful planning, he proposed, would augment the "health, culture and happiness" of the people; impress them "with the belief that their welfare is best cared for by those whom they elect to govern"; and make them "better citizens."[30]

Reformers were in no position to enact such plans in the early 1850s— indeed, the estate that interested Price lay beyond the city proper's territorial jurisdiction—but they did lobby city and state authorities to tear up the institutional fabric that sustained street politics. The pressure they applied here was closely tied to the cause of consolidation. The failure of Edward

Penniman's cohort to push annexation through the legislature in 1851 spurred a handful of reformers to nominate a city ticket for the fall election of that year. The independent movement failed, but at the end of 1852, a small band of reformers, several of them veterans of the struggle to unite the city and districts, launched a campaign to abolish the turbulent volunteer fire companies. At their first public meeting in February 1853, many of the city's leading merchants, manufacturers, and attorneys were listed among the officers. As owners of property and buyers of labor, they were well aware of the costs of fire in the form of insurance premiums and absenteeism.

But if calculations about real estate and productivity underpinned the calls for a "paid fire department," the men "of family" who spearheaded the movement also saw professionalization as a moral and political reform. Ridding the suburbs of the companies, they believed, would force citizens swayed by the "clannish" politics of the engine house to return to their homes. This would in turn deprive local politicians of the very institutions that had been the springboards for their ascent. By the summer of 1853, the reformers' campaign hinged on political arguments that chimed well with the national anti-partisan mood. A body of volunteers, one pamphleteer argued, that had "obtained an undisputed ascendancy over our party organizations" needed to be broken up, "whether it be agreeable to party managers or not." "In a republic," another claimed, "no class of men should be allowed, if prevention is possible, to grow up into a political power." With the question to be decided at the polls, a line of attack that drew on the familiar tropes of republican hostility to parties had proven appeal to independent voters. But anti-partisanship was more than merely a language of legitimation, for reformers believed that ridding the suburbs of the volunteers would starve the "small men" of the nourishment they needed to survive. In early August, they nominated Price as their candidate for the state senate.[31]

As the campaign against the volunteer firemen gathered strength, consolidators stepped up their own efforts. By July 1853, correspondents to the city's leading newspapers were calling for an independent ticket to take on the "formidable phalanx" of politicians who had blocked a union of the city and its districts in the past. The "sad and evil degeneracy" of the city's representation, a Whig journal argued, was no longer tolerable, and a few days after Price's nomination by advocates of a paid fire department, a public meeting concluded with reformers vowing to break free from party lines. Price himself was picked to lead the consolidation ticket, effectively uniting two reform movements that already overlapped in both membership and ambition, and over the following weeks, erstwhile Whigs and Democrats proudly proclaimed their readiness to vote for the independent slate. "Our citizens may be supine in political matters," one remarked, "but if awakened, they will show that they are not in slavery to the present corrupt party organization." On the eve of the election, the *North American,* a bellwether for the city's wealthy Whigs, joined the stampede in favor of consolidation. Lauding the "men of the best talent and information, and of elevated social position" on Price's ticket, the paper called the reform "a general and thorough remedy of all existing evils and imperfections in our municipal affairs."[32]

The break with party lines in 1853 was not absolute, but as Morton McMichael's journal suggested, it was markedly different in social character to its rivals. Eli Kirk Price and Matthias Baldwin were among a number of independents chosen, but several others, including the county senate candidate, were drawn from the ranks of the regular nominees. Still, whereas the regular Whig ticket, the *Evening Bulletin* argued, had been "condemned by all right-thinking men as utterly unworthy, in point of morality and capacity, of the support of an enlightened community," the reform candidates were "all first rate names," boasting an "average of talent, dignity and efficiency" so "much above that of most of our recent representatives at Harrisburg."[33] Such claims were hardly uncommon in a political culture in which statements of character mattered, but consolidation candidates were, as a whole, considerably wealthier than their rivals. In this regard, their movement had united merchants, manufacturers, and professionals against a way of practicing politics alien to them.

The Nation of Philadelphia

In the October contest, the reformers emerged triumphant. Price and his allies were certainly helped by circumstances peculiar to 1853: an off-year election, a nationwide surge in antiparty sentiment, and the rising tide of political nativism. But whatever the reasons for their success, the movement's leaders look quite unlike the familiar profile of antebellum reformers. While they spoke in the same republican idiom as the second party system's other malcontents, their prescriptions were often very different. In place of retrenchment in municipal affairs, they called for a dramatic expansion of both the territorial and administrative reach of the state. Reform for them rested on enlarging the scope of government power so the city could be ordered more effectively. In doing so, they hoped, the miasmas of ward politics would be blown away.

Consolidation, above all then, offered Price and his allies the tantalizing prospect of remaking the city's political space. The new government they hoped to create would have the strength to weaken the institutional foundations of the ward politicians' strength; to build—or at least to encourage the building of—new homes for workingmen; and to extend improvements to the vacant meadows of the metropolitan frontier, where, in a localization of the safety-valve thesis, erstwhile "denizens of the tenement houses" could learn the virtues of family government in spacious and salubrious new surroundings. By destroying petty sovereignties like districts, fire companies, and gangs, and by hastening the process of urban decentralization, consolidators imagined that citizens would regain the independence they required to act in pursuit of the metropolitan interest.[34]

Or rather, perhaps, the enlargement of Philadelphia would restore older bonds of deference and give the "best men" a competitive advantage in municipal politics. "Wire pullers," consolidators argued, were weedlike growths on the district system, for their power could only take root in petty fiefdoms. Their determination to protect these enclaves explained much of the opposition to consolidation. "Men of limited capacity," one journal argued, "are in dread of becoming obscure in a large city." Bigness, in contrast, already thrust the "best men" to the fore; at-large offices like the mayoralty still went to citizens of standing. It was not only the lure of high office that accounted for this phenomenon, reformers believed, but the weakness of parochial loyalties when voting overrode ward boundaries.[35] Consolidators, having rewritten the rules of local politics and elevated the position of the municipal legislator, would surely exploit such favorable conditions and fulfill their traditional civic obligations. Price's report on consolidation to the state senate in early 1854, for example, predicted that, in a united city, "men of large experience and stake in the community" would serve in councils.[36]

Consolidators, therefore, envisaged their reform leading to a changing of the guard in the city's political leadership. Ward politicians, one optimistic resident of the city proper anticipated, "will lose power and influence and have to crawl back to their original place of obscurity and insignificance." Having deprived such figures of the stranglehold they exerted over voters, men possessing "liberality and enlightenment . . . in accordance with the spirit of the age" would soon rise to the top. This did not mean an end to partisan

competition. "We aim not at the extinction of parties," a paid fire department pamphlet had argued honestly enough, "but at their reform."[37] But that
"reform" would ensure the preeminence of the "best men" of each faction:
legislators with the independence and foresight to act not in the interest of
the ward or party but to legislate for the city as a whole. With consolidation,
Philadelphians would not need an emperor to appoint a Baron Haussmann;
the new political terrain would simply thrust capable men to the fore. The city
could be imperial in scale and form yet republican in government.

Within a few days of Price's victory in 1853, the Executive Consolidation
Committee gathered for the first of their weekly meetings to draft a bill. The
process seemed an object lesson in how politics should work. If the reform
ticket had posited freedom from the "trammels of party" as a political virtue,
supporters of the movement were determined to continue that theme as they
hammered out the legislation. Historian Michael P. McCarthy has claimed
that the fall meetings show the healthy degree of "community involvement,"
but a careful scrutiny of the participants reveals that besides a few elected
officials, most of the attendees were drawn almost exclusively from the upper
tier of Philadelphia society. Among them was the millionaire druggist George
Carpenter, the industrialist Samuel Vaughan Merrick, and the president of
the Board of Trade, Frederick Fraley. Representation transcended partisan
lines, but as the Germantown *Telegraph* put it, the "ablest and best men" were
firmly in the ascendant. Their weekly deliberations stood in stark contrast to
what reformers saw as the corrupt and brutish practice of ward politics. "It
may assuredly be affirmed that no measure of legislation ever enjoyed the
benefit of a more thorough and enlightened process of preparation for the final
action of any deliberative body," the *North American* noted.[38]

The bill they drew up secured several of their objectives: strengthening
the power of the mayor, making the provision of parks and public squares a
responsibility of the city, and abolishing vital positions in ward politics. By
extending the territorial reach of the government from 2 square miles to well
over 100, it created a city government with the financial and political muscle
to set about remaking urban space and citizenship.

In this regard, the 1854 annexation underscored an emerging bourgeoisie's
hostility to the partisan style. The economic elite saw consolidation as a way
to rewrite the rules of politics through redrawing political space. These ambitions helped to bring their class together, yet it would be misleading to characterize the new charter as purely the work of wealthy merchants, manufactures,

and professionals, for in drawing up the bill, compromises had to be made. While the city was given the power to take control of the fire department, it was not required to do so. Instead, the reform would depend on backing from councilors who themselves relied on firemen's support. Localism too could not be entirely eradicated. Instead of resting on representation at large from across the city, the new councils were to be elected from twenty-four wards. The wards, though considerably larger than their predecessors, nevertheless provided a path back to power for the "small men" who saw potential too in the opening of new offices to popular vote. Meanwhile, the powers the enlarged city enjoyed over urban space were latent. Their effective use, reformers quickly realized, would depend on representation and finance.

With hindsight, the results are not surprising. While consolidation did enable the kind of large-scale public works projects the *North American* championed ("Haussmann must have emigrated to Philadelphia," wrote one despairing citizen a few years after the Civil War), it did so without restoring the "best men" to municipal power. Instead, as Peter McCaffery has shown, ward politicians retained their influence at the local level while becoming cogs in increasingly centralized machines, with new city bosses distributing the resources of the enlarged local government to maintain their positions. This forced reformers to make a difficult choice: support a corrupt Republican Party, which after winning power in 1858 had navigated Philadelphia through the treacherous waters of sectional strife relatively unharmed and embellished, or rebuild the movement that had won office in 1853. McMichael, who served as mayor after the Civil War, chose the former while never completely cutting his links to his old allies; many others opted for the latter, and former consolidators flocked to the reform movements that flickered briefly in the 1870s. Their lack of success was entirely predictable given a message of retrenchment that hardly resonated with middle-class voters dependent on suburban improvements and an enduring reluctance to muddy their hands in ward politics. "I'd rather have one good worker round the polls on election day," one Republican candidate told a journalist in 1871, "than all the [Union] League put together."[39]

Price, by now anointed the "Father of Consolidation," remained aloof from both the Republican Party and the reform movement, though he frequently suggested his sympathies lay with the latter. In 1873, the Historical Society of Pennsylvania commissioned him to write a history of the 1854 charter, and at the end of a rather disorganized amalgam of reminiscence and correspondence, he cast the independent ticket of 1853 as an exemplary warning to postbellum politicians. "What was then done can and will be done, again and again, rather than that chronic corruption shall exist in public places," he prophesized. It is telling that he chose to frame his study with an argument about the nature of politics. Most historians, in contrast, have read the act in terms of law and order or modernization. Price's history suggests that even after the Civil War, the idea of urban society as an essentially political construct lingered. But there was also a sense of discontinuity when he reflected that "though the limits of the City expanded at a bound, the minds of the citizens could not be so suddenly enlarged." Consolidators in the early 1850s had hoped that extending the realm of government would broaden the horizons of voters and thrust the "best men" to the fore. Optimistic about the democratic potential of the American republic, yet anxious about their own place within it, Philadelphia's reformers help us to bridge the gap between the Federalist elite and the Gilded Age and Progressive era's bourgeoisie. When the reformers' designs for a miniature republic failed to materialize, they either had to make their peace with the party system or retreat into the unimaginative conservatism of retrenchment.[40]

Notes

1. *Evening Bulletin* (Philadelphia), 9 October 1850. All subsequent newspaper citations refer to journals published in Philadelphia unless otherwise stated.

2. *Public Ledger,* 18 September 1851; *Sunday Dispatch,* 21 September 1851.

3. Michael F. Holt, *Political Development from the Age of Jackson to the Age of Lincoln* (Baton Rouge: Louisiana State University Press, 1992), 270; Sam Bass Warner Jr., *The Private City: Philadelphia in Three Periods of Its Growth* (Philadelphia: University of Pennsylvania Press, 1987), 79–98, 100–102, 152–56. On consolidation, see also Howard Gillette Jr., "The Emergence of the Modern Metropolis: Philadelphia in the Age of Its Consolidation," in *The Divided Metropolis: Social and Spatial Dimensions of Philadelphia, 1800–1975,* ed. William W. Cutler III and Howard Gillette Jr. (Westport, Conn.: Greenwood Press, 1980), 3–25. On privatism elsewhere in the nineteenth-century American metropolis, see Robin L. Einhorn, *Property Rules: Political Economy in Chicago, 1833–1872* (Chicago: University of Chicago Press, 1991).

4. The only historian to deal with consolidation principally as a political reform argues it was crafted in the spirit of Jacksonian democracy. See Michael P. McCarthy, "The Philadelphia Consolidation of 1854: A Reappraisal," *Pennsylvania Magazine of History and Biography* 110 (October 1986): 531–48.

5. The idea of "petty sovereignties" is used to make sense of state formation and

the plantation in the Civil War–era in Stephanie McCurry, *Confederate Reckoning: Power and Politics in the Civil War South* (Cambridge, Mass.: Harvard University Press, 2010), 219–20.

6. Kimberley K. Smith, *The Dominion of Voice: Riot, Reason, and Romance in Antebellum Politics* (Lawrence: University Press of Kansas, 1999), vii–viii, 51–52, chs. 2–4.

7. Ibid., 58, 60. On government as a keyword in this era, see Daniel T. Rodgers, *Contested Truths: Keywords in American Politics since Independence* (New York: Basic Books, 1987), ch. 4.

8. On the relationship between household and civil government, see Linda K. Kerber, *Women of the Republic: Intellect and Ideology in Revolutionary America* (Chapel Hill: University of North Carolina Press, 1980); Paula Baker, "The Domestication of Politics: Women and American Political Society, 1780–1920," *American Historical Review* 89 (June 1984): 620–47; and Rebecca Edwards, *Angels in the Machinery: Gender in American Party Politics from the Civil War to the Progressive Era* (Oxford: Oxford University Press, 1997). On the environmental sources of moral disorder, see, for example, Stanley K. Schultz, *Constructing Urban Culture: American Cities and City Planning, 1800–1920* (Philadelphia: Temple University Press, 1989), 112–13; David Schuyler, *The New Urban Landscape: The Redefinition of City Form in Nineteenth-Century America* (Baltimore: Johns Hopkins University Press, 1986), 6; and Paul S. Boyer, *Urban Masses and Moral Order in America, 1820–1920* (Cambridge, Mass.: Harvard University Press, 1978). The point about domestication is also made in Peter C. Baldwin, *Domesticating the Street: The Reform of Public Space in Hartford, 1850–1930* (Columbus: Ohio State University Press, 1999).

9. Margaret E. Farrar, *Building the Body Politic: Power and Urban Space in Washington, D.C.* (Urbana: University of Illinois Press, 2008), 13.

10. On retrenchment in the 1850s, see Amy A. Bridges, *A City in the Republic: Antebellum New York and the Origins of Machine Politics* (Chicago: University of Chicago Press, 1980), 38, and Edward K. Spann, *The New Metropolis: New York City, 1840–1857* (New York: Columbia University Press, 1981), 50. On later reform traditions, see Sven Beckert, "Democracy and Its Discontents: Contesting Suffrage Rights in Gilded Age New York," *Past and Present* (February 2002): 116–57, and Samuel P. Hays, "The Politics of Reform in Municipal Government in the Progressive Era," *Pacific Northwest Quarterly* 55 (October 1964): 157–69.

11. "W," *North American*, 9 September 1851; "R," *Public Ledger*, 12 February 1852. On midcentury urbanism, see Schuyler, *New Urban Landscape;* David M. Scobey, *Empire City: The Making and Meaning of the New York City Landscape* (Philadelphia: Temple University Press, 2002).

12. David Harvey, *Paris: Capital of Modernity* (London: Routledge, 2003).

13. *North American*, 8 November 1853; Peter McCaffery, *When Bosses Ruled Philadelphia: The Emergence of the Republican Machine, 1867–1933* (State College: Pennsylvania State University Press, 1993), 2–16.

14. Pennsylvania, General Assembly, Senate, Select Committee on the Consolidation of Philadelphia, *Consolidation of the City of Philadelphia: Report of the Se-*

lect Committee (Philadelphia, 1854), 5; Warner, *Private City*, 50; *North American*, 31 October 1857; George Taylor Rodgers, ed., "'Philadelphia in Slices' by George G. Foster," *Pennsylvania Magazine of History and Biography* 93 (January 1969): 38; *Sunday Dispatch*, 24 June 1849; Frank Gerrity, "The Disruption of the Philadelphia Whigocracy: Joseph R. Chandler, Anti-Catholicism, and the Congressional Election of 1854," *Pennsylvania Magazine of History and Biography* 111 (April 1987): 168.

15. *A Full and Complete Account of the Late Awful Riots in Philadelphia* (Philadelphia, 1844), 16; *North American*, 19 January 1854. For an example of a sensationalist urban sketch, see *Mysteries and Miseries of Philadelphia* (Philadelphia, 1853).

16. *Prize Essays on Juvenile Delinquency, Published under the Direction of the Board of Managers of the House of Refuge, Philadelphia* (Philadelphia, 1855), 110, 155; *Evening Bulletin*, 25 January 1855. On the fire companies, see Bruce Laurie, "Fire Companies and Gangs in Southwark: The 1840s," in *The Peoples of Philadelphia: A History of Ethnic Groups and Lower-Class Life, 1740–1940*, ed. Allen F. Davis and Mark H. Haller (Philadelphia: Temple University Press, 1973). Amy S. Greenberg, *Cause for Alarm: The Volunteer Fire Department in the Nineteenth-Century City* (Princeton, N.J.: Princeton University Press, 1998), downplays class but does not look closely at Philadelphia. For treatments of immigrant and working-class politics from the bottom up, see Harry C. Silcox, *Philadelphia Politics from the Bottom Up: The Life of Irishman William Mcmullen, 1824–1901* (Philadelphia: Balch Institute Press, 1989).

17. *Evening Bulletin*, 27 May 1853; *The Almighty Dollar; or, The Brilliant Exploits of a Killer: A Thrilling Romance of Quakerdelphia* (Philadelphia, 1847), 15–16; Poulson Scrapbooks, vol. 9, Library Company of Philadelphia, Philadelphia.

18. *North American*, 16 August 1853.

19. *North American*, 10 September 1859; J. Francis Fisher, *Reform in Our Municipal Elections: A Plan Suggested to the Tax Payers of Philadelphia and New York* (Philadelphia, 1866), 25.

20. *Sunday Dispatch*, 2 September 1849; *Public Ledger*, 21 July 1847.

21. *Public Ledger*, 3 March 1846; *North American*, 9 August 1859.

22. *Sunday Dispatch*, 9 June 1850; "J.B.O.," *North American*, 12 March 1852; Scobey, *Empire City*, 189; *Public Ledger*, 16 June 1849.

23. *Sunday Dispatch*, 28 July 1850.

24. *Prize Essays on Juvenile Delinquency*, 53; Eli Kirk Price, "The Family as an Element of Government," *Proceedings of the American Philosophical Society* 9 (1863): 318. On domesticity, see, for example, Mary P. Ryan, *Cradle of the Middle Class: The Family in Oneida County, New York, 1790–1865* (Cambridge: Cambridge University Press, 1981), and Lora Romero, *Home Fronts: Domesticity and Its Critics in the Antebellum United States* (Durham, N.C.: Duke University Press, 1997), 1–2.

25. Henry C. Carey, *The Harmony of Interests: Agricultural, Manufacturing, and Commercial* (Philadelphia, 1865), 202.

26. Price, "Family as an Element of Government," 315–16; *Prize Essays on Juvenile Delinquency*, 54; *Telegraph* (Germantown), 13 December 1854; Robert Conrad, *An*

Address Delivered before the Literary Societies of Pennsylvania College, Gettysburg, September 15, 1852 (Philadelphia, 1852), 28.

27. *Prize Essays on Juvenile Delinquency,* 59; Price, "Family as an Element of Government," 318. See also Scobey, *Empire City,* 186.

28. *North American,* 4 July 1856; *Public Ledger,* 14 May 1847, 30 August 1854. On the *Ledger,* see Noel Ignatiev, *How the Irish Became White* (New York: Routledge, 2005), 152. This was a vision Philadelphian reformers shared with Frederick Law Olmsted, who advocated the housing of New York's poor as a means of civilizational uplift. See Scobey, *Empire City,* 180.

29. Andrew Heath, "'Every Man His Own Landlord': Working-Class Suburban Speculation and the Antebellum Republican City," *Journal of Urban History* 38 (November 2012): 1003–20.

30. Price, "Family as an Element of Government," 319; Baldwin, *Domesticating the Street; Fairmount Park Contribution* (Philadelphia, 1856), 3; Charles S. Keyser, *Lemon Hill in Its Connection with the Efforts of Our Citizens and Councils to Obtain a Public Park* (Philadelphia, 1856), 22; "E.K.P." [Eli Kirk Price], *North American,* 28 October 1851.

31. *North American,* 25 February 1853; *Evening Bulletin,* 27 May 1853; "Paid Fire Department" (1853), Eli Kirk Price Family Collection, Archives and Special Collections, Waidner-Spahr Library, Dickinson College, Carlisle, Penn.; *Evening Bulletin,* 27 May 1853; Eli Kirk Price, *The History of the Consolidation of the City of Philadelphia* (Philadelphia, 1873), 21; J. T. Rothrock, "Biographical Memoir of the Late Eli K. Price, L.L.D.," *Proceedings of the American Philosophical Society* 23 (1886): 584.

32. "F.T." [Francis Tiernan?], *Public Ledger,* 14 July 1853; *North American,* 29 July, 7 October 1853; "A Whig Subscriber," *Evening Bulletin,* 6 October 1853.

33. *Evening Bulletin,* 20 September, 8 October 1853.

34. *North American,* 10 October 1861.

35. *North American,* 10 September 1859, 10 October 1861; *Sunday Dispatch,* 23 September 1849; *Sunday Dispatch,* 9 June 1850, 17 August 1851.

36. *North American,* 21 February 1854; "Franklin," *Public Ledger,* 19 November 1850; Pennsylvania, *Consolidation of the City of Philadelphia,* 12.

37. "J.S.P." [Jacob S. Price?], *North American,* 26 November 1853; "T. O'N.," *Sunday Dispatch,* 1 January 1854; "Paid Fire Department," Price Family Collection.

38. *Evening Bulletin,* 1 October 1853; McCarthy, "Philadelphia Consolidation," 546; *Telegraph* (Germantown), 2 November 1853; *North American,* 15 December 1853.

39. "Penn," *Telegraph* (Germantown), 29 March 1871; McCaffery, *When Bosses Ruled Philadelphia,* esp. ch. 3; *Sunday Morning Times,* 24 September 1871. See also Howard Gillette, "Corrupt and Contented: Philadelphia's Political Machine, 1865–1887" (Ph.D. diss., Yale University, 1971).

40. Price, *History of the Consolidation,* 120, 136.

PART FOUR

A FRESH
PERSPECTIVE

★ JOHANN N. NEEM ★

Two Approaches to Democratization

Engagement versus Capability

T he nineteenth century is often thought of as a golden age for American politics. There is no doubt that voter turnout in the antebellum era was astounding. Historians have documented a time when ordinary citizens actively followed politics and cared so deeply that their identities were shaped by parties.[1] Women, too, were part of this partisan world.[2] In *Self-Rule*, Robert H. Wiebe expressed his amazement: "Not only did *everybody* participate, but everybody *participated*."[3] In *The Partisan Imperative*, Joel H. Silbey argued that parties were the central organizing principle of American political life.[4] William Gienapp concurred: "Perhaps at no time . . . did politics occupy a more central role in American life than during the period 1840–1860."[5] Lurking within this historiography, however, is a profound problem that political historians have not adequately addressed: whether or not voting rates—and *engagement*—measure the quality of democratic public life.[6]

This essay argues that engagement is insufficient to understand democratization. Rather, historians must understand to what extent ordinary people could affect the outcomes of political deliberation and policymaking. Building on work by Amartya Sen, I argue that political historians need to do a better job examining the actual *capabilities* of ordinary citizens to affect political outcomes.[7] To Sen, freedom must lead "to the expansion of the 'capabilities' of persons to lead the kinds of lives they value—and have reason to value." An accurate measure of freedom would gauge "the ability of people to help themselves and also to influence the world."[8] For political historians, this means that the existence of the right institutions—fair elections, the rule of law, a broad suffrage, and political parties—is insufficient to demonstrate actual democratization. Instead, as Sen writes, "We have to seek institutions that *promote* justice, rather than treating the institutions themselves as manifestations of justice."[9] Conceptually this means that historians must evaluate to what extent elections, voting, and political parties actually furthered citizens' abilities to shape politics. In doing so, political historians can learn from historians whose subjects have lacked the vote, including women, laborers, African Americans, and reformers organized outside of the formal party system.

The more able citizens are to influence outcomes, the more democratic the society. As Sidney Verba and his coauthors write, citizens must have both "the *motivation* and the *capacity* to take part in political life."[10] Wiebe agreed that "voting is not enough" to define democracy; citizens "need government officials who respond to popular decisions."[11] Engagement, or motivation, therefore, is only the beginning of an accurate measurement of democracy. Following engagement must come actual civic capabilities—the ability of citizens to deliberate and then influence public policy.

The Engagement Paradigm and Its Critics

The engagement paradigm still reigns among political historians. Yet since the 1997 publication of two articles by Glenn C. Altschuler and Stuart M. Blumin, there has been an undercurrent of concern as to whether high engagement truly proves that society was becoming more democratic.[12] More recent explorations of the future of political history suggest a consensus that it has failed to demonstrate a relationship between elections or voting and political outcomes. Whether in response to Altschuler and Blumin, or to a broader concern about political history's status in American history, historians have sought to innovate beyond the older tradition of focusing exclusively on parties and elections.[13]

In a 2004 *Journal of Policy History* roundtable, three prominent scholars —Richard R. John, Julian E. Zelizer, and Joanne B. Freeman—offer some guidance. Rather than help political historians study parties and elections more effectively, however, each takes the opportunity to suggest abandoning the project altogether. John urges historians to turn from elections to political economy, concluding that institutions, including such formal institutions as the state but also cultural norms, had a greater impact on politics than elections.[14]

Zelizer argues that the emergence of the theory of American political development (APD) oriented scholars to formal structures and how those structures shaped preferences and political and economic outcomes. Rather than voters expressing their preferences through elections, APD scholars talk about how policies "restructured the long-term interests of politicians and interest groups." Zelizer urges looking "beyond the act of voting to understand how and why citizens try to influence politics," and "what types of participation seem to catch the eye of public officials, as well as the institutional roles and regulations that foster or stifle different types of citizen participation." Rather than assume a causal relation between engagement and outcomes, historians can learn from APD's institutional focus and ask not just *whether* citizens were engaged but also what kinds of engagement affected politics.[15]

Like John and Zelizer, Freeman argues that the party paradigm ignores the broader structural categories that determine political outcomes. To Freeman, the analytical lens is political culture, "the study of patterns of shared values, assumptions, and behaviors associated with public life." Invoking three 1997 books—Len Travers's *Celebrating the Fourth*, Simon Newman's *Parades and the Politics of the Street*, and David Waldstreicher's *In the Midst of Perpetual Fetes*—Freeman concludes that political outcomes were not determined by voter preferences via political parties but rather by broader ideological and cultural frames.[16]

The year 2004 also saw the publication of the essay collection *Beyond the Founders: New Approaches to the Political History of the Early American Republic*, an ambitious effort to reimagine the era's political history. The impetus for the collection was the editors' distaste for "founders chic," the revival of interest in elite Founding Fathers in a way that ignored decades of historical scholarship on ordinary people.[17] *Beyond the Founders* sought to demonstrate that political outcomes were shaped by ordinary as well as elite Americans from diverse backgrounds. To understand how ordinary people influenced politics, the editors and contributors brought together social, cultural, and political history.

The editors' introduction reinforces themes expressed by John, Zelizer, and Freeman. They argue that to connect ordinary people to politics more effectively, one must look at political culture, norms, and institutions. The editors take seriously what they call "cultural politics," meaning the ways in which ordinary people gave expression to their political commitments through cultural forms. While the importance of culture cannot be denied, many of the essays fail to connect cultural expressions of identity to the ability to exercise political power, however. For example, Jeffrey L. Pasley, David Waldstreicher, and Albrecht Koschnik focus on the roles of parties and associations in shaping political identities and engaging voters. All three prove that politics is expressed culturally, but they do not connect that process to political outcomes.[18]

Other essays in the collection move in the right direction. Andrew W. Robertson argues that as parties developed complex procedures to reach out to voters, they slowly eroded cultural practices premised on deference, encouraging voters to think of themselves as equal stakeholders in politics. Although Robertson uses voting rates (engagement) as a proxy for democratization, he recognizes that we must connect the formation of political identities to actual practices, a point echoed by Rosemarie Zagarri in her chapter about women in politics.[19]

John L. Brooke's essay in the volume offers guidance toward a better measure of democratization. Drawing on the ideas of Jürgen Habermas, Brooke argues that we must be concerned with who shapes political decisions and the role of power in affecting outcomes. By bringing civil society and its public sphere into the picture, Brooke proposes a synthesis that includes formal political institutions as well as the activities of ordinary people out of doors. In civil society and the public sphere, myriad groups interact and seek to influence each other. At some point, these interactions must be boiled down to the actual doings of politicians. It is here where the new meets the old. While anybody can seek to persuade voters and leaders, actual policy decisions are made by politicians and judges in formal institutions.[20]

Only two essays in the collection take the step Brooke advocates, and each provides a model to rethink political history. Richard Newman argues that African Americans, denied access to the formal institutions of political power, had to find alternate ways to shape outcomes. Following broader trends in American society, they developed mass organizations and a press, and hosted rallies and parades to mobilize their constituents. Unlike other political historians, Newman does not assume that mobilization was enough since his subjects were often denied access to the ballot box. Thus, as discussed in more detail below, Newman takes the next step and shows how African Americans relied "on print to exert political influence."[21] In short, because they lacked the vote, African Americans had to develop political capabilities that could impact elections and laws.

Reeve Huston's essay on the relationship between anti-renters in New York and the party system offers a nuanced analysis of the relationship between ordinary citizens and political parties. Huston makes clear that anti-renters could exercise political autonomy from parties and that their political capabilities were initially learned by participating in partisan organizations, rallies, and activities, positing a link between parties and the development of political capabilities:

> The emergence of two-party democracy had a momentous and ironic outcome at the grass roots. To win support in the leasehold districts, the Whigs and Democrats offered tenants powerful social and political ideas and trained large numbers of estate residents as political organizers. The anti-renters turned these skills and teachings to uses that most Whigs and Democrats found threatening. In the process, both groups helped change the character of farmers' movements in the United States.[22]

Parties taught citizens how to exert political influence, a lesson that anti-renters used against those very parties. Finally, Huston argues that anti-renters learned their lessons so effectively that when party leaders proved unresponsive, anti-renters rejected parties and embraced traditional rural protest. In response, parties had to alter platforms and, in some cases, embrace anti-rent ideas to gain votes. The result was a dynamic process combining grassroots organizing and party activity that illuminates how anti-renters, as voters, learned to pressure party leaders and shape policy.[23]

Both Newman and Huston connect ordinary people's actions to actual influence over the political system. This is where political history needs to go, and Brooke makes clear what is at stake: consent. In the American tradition, consent is the basis of freedom; its absence means that one is subject to a foreign will and that one's life, liberty, and property are insecure.[24] In response to both skeptics like Altschuler and Blumin, and "new institutional" scholars like John and Zelizer, political historians must demonstrate that the nineteenth century was indeed an age in which ordinary citizens could exercise meaningful influence on the state.

Civil Society

Unlike political historians, who have been able to use voting as a proxy for capability, students of civil society's actors—social reformers, women, and laborers—have had to demonstrate that their subjects could influence the political system. In the decades after 1810, reformers, women, and laborers together developed a "grassroots public sphere" in which ordinary people forged mass social movements through voluntary associations and print media. These efforts required new civic skills. Students of American democracy need to understand how these skills were learned and how citizens used them to affect political outcomes.[25] This section examines how different groups developed their civic skills and assesses whether these new capabilities affected public policies. Historians of civil society broadly defined have done a better job connecting the political activity of ordinary people to political outcomes than have historians of parties and elections.

For a long time, historiography on reform movements focused on "social control," the desire of elite ministers and their evangelical followers to impose their middle-class religious values on less privileged populations. Less appreciated is how the emergence of the Benevolent Empire made it possible for citizens to develop the civic capabilities that, in time, they would use to participate in politics on their own terms. As Theda Skocpol argues, the Benevolent Empire's most important institutions were federal in nature, comprising a central, or parent, association usually composed of an elite set of officers and dozens to thousands of local auxiliaries around the nation.[26] This federal structure had democratic implications. Far from controlling their auxiliaries, parent associations were dependent on their auxiliaries' voluntary participation. A broad cross section of middle-class women and men formed and joined these associations and, in turn, learned how to be participants in civic life.

Three specific movements can be used to understand citizens on the make: Sabbatarianism, temperance, and antislavery. Other associations, including missionary and Bible societies, were also important, but for brevity's sake, I am focusing on those that were primarily political in orientation.

Since Alexis de Tocqueville, we have considered associations to be schools of democracy, but we are less aware of how citizens learned to associate in the first place. In the early days of reform, activists had to teach recruits about associations, how they were formed, what offices needed filling, how to raise funds, and how associating could impact politics.[27] The reform movement saw a series of technological innovations as ministers and citizens learned what Elisabeth S. Clemens calls new "organizational repertoires" which proved effective in a political system that responded to public opinion. Effective reformers used techniques designed to influence particular political structures and interests.[28] By assuming that influencing public opinion would influence elections, ministers taught citizens strategies suitable for a mass electoral democracy.[29] As Mark Voss-Hubbard writes, "Organizations teach members how to think and act politically in certain ways but not others."[30]

The shift from an elite-driven political system to a grassroots one that relied on developing citizens' civic capabilities can be seen by comparing the two phases of the Sabbatarian movement. The first began in 1810 when Congress mandated that post offices be open whenever mail arrived, including Sundays. Northern ministers initiated an effort to petition Congress for redress. By the end of 1815, about one hundred petitions had reached Congress. Although the petitions were signed by local citizens, most were undertaken by ministerial initiative and emerged from the top down.[31] By the late 1820s, however, the religious community had developed new strategies to pressure political leaders. In 1828, ministers established the General Union for the Promotion of the Christian Sabbath. While this group's origins were also top down, it mobilized and organized significantly larger numbers of men and women in more localities around the country, leading John to call it "unabashedly democratic—and, indeed, almost populistic." The new movement sought to form as many associations and send as many petitions as possible to Congress. To do so, ministers directed their efforts not at political elites but at citizens, exhorting them to become involved. Rather than "coercion," Reverend Lyman Beecher argued that the movement's success depended on "public sentiment." Each citizen would have to make her or his own decision about whether to become involved.[32] The result of this effort was impressive. By 1829, 467 petitions had reached Washington; by 1831, the number had topped 900. The Sabbatarian movement spoke in the name of, and relied on the actions of, ordinary people. It taught many Americans that they could shape the social order.[33] While Sabbatarianism did not prove successful, it established new modes of mobilization that would be picked up by later reformers.

The most successful reform in numbers and political influence was temperance. Its storyline is not that different from Sabbatarianism. The Massachusetts Society for the Suppression of Intemperance (MSSI) was at its 1813 founding largely elite, but the directors knew that they had to reach out to the broader public, and they relied on print to do so. While their first annual report was circulated only among themselves, by their third annual meeting, they were printing two thousand copies in order to encourage people in all the state's towns to organize associations. The number of reports grew consistently; by 1826, they were printing six thousand reports and asking clergymen to read them before their congregations. These reports were civic primers. In the eighteenth century, associations were often limited to elite men who held public office; now ministers urged ordinary congregants to take initiative and taught them how to do so.[34] Print was important in another way: like parties, reformers used print to frame issues for voters.[35]

The MSSI was largely genteel. Some ministers, therefore, turned to an even more democratic association, the American Temperance Society (ATS). The ATS, Ian Tyrrell wrote, "encouraged the formation of state temperance societies, but most important were the county and local organizations," which kept temperance in the public sphere. The ATS printed tracts, circulated annual reports, and sponsored a newspaper. Drawing from revivalism, the ATS argued that "all believers were equal in spirit" and thus equally responsible for taking action in civil society.[36]

Although the ATS's membership was middle class, the number of women and men that became involved was astounding and, from a civic perspective, transformative.[37] As people organized, they made a difference. Within five years, the ATS had 2,200 societies with 170,000 members; by 1833, there were 6,000 societies with a million members. Only Alabama, Louisiana, Illinois, and Missouri lacked state chapters.[38] Massachusetts reformers pressured electoral candidates and leaders to support prohibition, producing new legislation. In 1831, legislators limited the ability of common victuallers to sell alcohol, producing such a backlash that it was repealed the next year. But grassroots reformers continued to exert pressure, and in 1835, Whigs authorized counties to elect commissioners to make local decisions. By 1838, seven counties had gone dry. That same year, Whigs passed an unpopular "15-gallon law," prohibiting alcohol sales in small amounts.

The 15-gallon law helped cost Whigs reelection, and Whig analysts blamed the temperance movement, demonstrating citizens' ability to influence Whig leaders. Whigs accused their leaders of being "SUBSERVIENT to a moral and religious fanaticism that will, under our present form of government, destroy *any* political party that suffers itself to become contaminated with anticonstitutional views and feelings."[39] Whigs had been seduced by a question that did not belong in "the political arena."[40]

Yet because of the local election of commissioners, by 1850 all counties had embraced prohibition. In short, local organizing had reformed local public opinion, which then filtered upward, reversing the assumptions of earlier movements that worked from the top down.[41]

Temperance advocates pressured the political system effectively in other states, too. Starting at the local level and working up, activists secured prohibition in twelve northern states and territories by 1855.[42] Their success depended on developing citizens' capabilities to influence public policies. In addition to associations, temperance advocates relied on petitions. In Massachusetts, a petition with 156,000 signatories was presented to the legislature. An 1853 New York petition had over 300,000 signatures; a Michigan petition had 70,000 signers, including many women.[43] Evaluating why temperance and prohibition proved successful, Tyrrell concluded, "The degree of success which prohibitionists achieved before 1850 was a tribute to the importance of the process of agitation and an example of the power which well-organized groups could exert in a liberal-democratic political system."[44]

The Sabbatarian and temperance movements demonstrate how ministers developed their congregants' civic skills, but the antislavery movement shows how these capabilities enabled citizens to exercise political agency. In two recent books, Richard S. Newman's *The Transformation of American Abolitionism* (2002) and Susan Zaeske's *Signatures of Citizenship* (2003), we learn how antislavery developed civic capabilities.[45]

Newman argues that between the revolution and the 1830s, "what began as an elite abolitionist movement in Pennsylvania during the Post-Revolutionary period yielded to an egalitarian movement based in Massachusetts during the early 1830s." This transformation had profound implications for ordinary citizens, black and white, female and male. Elite Pennsylvanians following American independence had formed the Pennsylvania Abolition Society, which sought to parlay its elite members' status into support for slavery's abolition. Its members did not reach out to the public but rather directly petitioned Congress. By the 1830s, however, William Lloyd Garrison and many lesser-known activists of poor and middling origins had learned to organize people like themselves to exert pressure on policymakers from below. Newman's story explores the democratic implications of this change.

The antislavery activists' 1830s "mass action strategy," Newman writes, "necessitated tactical innovations," both to develop citizens' capabilities and to ensure that their efforts would influence political leaders. In Massachusetts, activists formed associations in town after town, traveled around giving lectures, and distributed pamphlets and other print material to influence the public sphere. Newman attributes the shift in strategies to religious revivalism's

"democratizing both religion and society."[46] These claims are not themselves
novel; what is important about Newman's work is that he next examines how,
exactly, abolitionists developed their movement and why and how it impacted
public life.

Newman begins his story among black Americans in Massachusetts. Because of racial segregation, distinct religious patterns, and marginalization
from mainstream political life, black activists had already developed distinct
strategies before Garrison became involved. In particular, whereas white activists had tended to be respectful of their fellow white slaveholders, black
activists "injected moralism and emotionalism into the fight against racial
oppression." They appealed to the heart because they could not appeal to
courts or political leaders. In the decades before 1831, black activists used their
speeches and publications to "fight slavery in the public realm."[47]

Blacks moved beyond exhortation to organization. First, much of the social
capital required to organize effectively was present in postrevolutionary black
churches, benevolent societies, debating clubs, and self-help organizations.[48]
In 1826, Massachusetts citizens formed the General Colored Association to
secure black freedom and justice. Its members included such prominent citizens as David Walker, author of the *Appeal in Four Articles: Together with
a Preamble to the Colored Citizens of the World* (1829). The association and
other lesser-known black organizations mobilized the black population, and
sought to influence white citizens as well. The group ensured that white citizens would hear radical antislavery positions as well as criticism of the elite-
led American Colonization Society. Black men and women had an impact
on humanitarian-minded white reformers, most notably Garrison, who acknowledged that both his conversion to immediate abolition and his ability
to form the New England Antislavery Society depended on black words and
organizational support.[49]

Once some whites had been converted, they borrowed both from black
strategies and rhetoric and from their own experience in the Sabbatarian,
temperance, and other movements. Just as black Americans had learned to
organize, elite white ministers taught their congregants how to organize.
Garrison benefited from both sources of civic education.[50] Activists sought to
change public opinion; they focused on citizens first, political leaders second.
By forming associations, sponsoring traveling lecturers, and helping to pool
capital to support antislavery newspapers and distribute pamphlets, organizers

reached out to every citizen in the state. The New England Antislavery Association hired agents to help organize new associations both to influence each town's public sphere and to develop further the capacity of the parent association to exert pressure at higher levels. The central goal was to change public opinion.[51] Newman's work focuses not just on antislavery beliefs but also on how activists developed new organizational repertoires that proved influential.

By focusing on the relationship between antislavery petitions and political identity, Zaeske explores how the "mass action strategies" Newman identifies transformed women's understanding of their civic role. As in Sabbatarianism, one goal of a petition in an era before scientific polling was to give elected leaders a sense of where public opinion was headed. A petition with significant numbers of signatures indicated a widely shared opinion, petitioners implied. Denied the vote, petitioning was, Zaeske writes, "One of the few civil rights [women] were understood to possess."[52] And because her subjects could not use voting as a proxy for democratic capability, Zaeske must prove that petitioning mattered.

Zaeske argues that petitioning connected the transformation of public opinion to elected political leaders via a signed piece of paper. Although at first women couched their petitions in traditional rhetoric — that of a supplicant — in fact antislavery women became increasingly adamant that their moral voices be heard. And we know that the effect of growing numbers of petitions had a profound impact in Congress, leading in 1836 to the gag rule. Members of Congress, in short, were forced to respond to the grassroots pressure of the public sphere. But as important, the very act of joining an association and signing a petition mattered for female citizens. It not only taught them how to shape public affairs but, by signing their names, enabled women to see themselves as citizens with capabilities and helped them become informed participants in the print and oral public spheres. "By entering public dialogue on the issue of slavery, women transformed themselves from private individuals into public actors who operated independent of male guardians," Zaeske concludes.[53] She demonstrates that petitioning developed female civic identities and capabilities, and, by connecting the grassroots public sphere to the halls of power, forced state and national leaders to respond.[54]

Antislavery transformed northern public opinion. By 1860, northern voters supported a sectional party and elected Abraham Lincoln president. That same year, Democrats divided sectionally over slavery, aiding Lincoln's election and demonstrating that the slavery issue, which both parties had long sought to avoid, had been forced into the public sphere by activists.[55]

In addition to examining the mobilization of women as part of social reform and antislavery, many historians have sought to understand how women became influential political actors. While Zagarri makes a strong case that the revolution opened a space for formal female participation in politics, most historians have emphasized instead the gradual development of female civic capabilities over the decades following American independence.[56] As Paula Baker wrote, "From the time of the Revolution, women used, and sometimes pioneered, methods for influencing government from outside electoral channels," including crowd activities, petitioning, forming associations, and lobbying legislatures. Baker rightly asked her readers to explore "the interaction between women's political activities and the political system itself."[57] While elite women could shape politics via their relationships with elite men, other women had to learn to be citizens.[58]

The first step in political democratization was to develop women's intellectual abilities. Historians have long recognized that women after the revolution were seen as playing a vital civic role. The republic required educated, virtuous citizens. Given that most early education happened at home, women would have to consider their homes civic institutions. Although this role did not challenge separate spheres ideology, it did offer women a place in the era's political thought. Educating children required educated mothers. In female academies across the new nation, young women, many for the first time, received formal education which, as Mary Kelley writes, transformed female consciousness. As more women learned about history and politics, they became not just better mothers but also more capable of thinking as citizens.[59] Outside of school, women gained civic literacy through reading magazines and discussing them.[60]

While for some women being a mother was its own reward, for others education resulted in a desire to be more active in the polity. Some women were participants in partisan parades and events, and to this extent, parties fostered female civic engagement.[61] But denied the vote, and often denied for cultural reasons meaningful access to partisan settings, the majority of active women focused on social reform, where they developed their capabilities. Ministers, as they looked out on increasingly female congregations, played an important role in politicizing women by urging them to form associations and exhort their husbands, neighbors, and in time political leaders on vital moral issues. Women joined the temperance, antislavery, and other reform movements in record numbers. When some northerners sought to prevent Cherokee removal, ministers asked women to sign petitions and send them to Congress. By gaining access to education and learning how to form associations, women became agents in the grassroots public sphere, and made their wills known to political leaders.[62]

There is, of course, some question as to whether women's political activity had any impact on male political leaders, given that women could not vote, but historians have suggested that women's voluntary work was not ignored. It was precisely because women gained real civic capabilities in civil society—the use of associations and petitions—that they had an impact on public opinion. Historians have had to demonstrate how women found ways of being politically effective. Thus, Zaeske focuses on the political response petitions engendered. Mary Ryan has found that the effort to regulate sexuality and curtail prostitution in antebellum cities derived in no small part from evangelical women's activities.[63] Various studies of moral reform confirm this conclusion. By forming an association, influencing each other, and then reaching out to other citizens through personal contacts and print, women shaped public opinion and cultural norms in ways that informed public policies.[64]

Historians of labor have also had to make a case for the political impact of their subjects. Sean Wilentz's now classic *Chants Democratic* argues that laborers' participation in associational life helped them to organize collectively for political purposes, going beyond strikes to partisan politics. Emerging from both their existing craft association traditions and through participation in social reform and parties, both New York City's master craftsmen and wage laborers gained the skills necessary for collective action during the first three decades of the nineteenth century. These skills were put to good use in pressuring political leaders during the New York workingmen's movement in 1829–30, in which workers formed a party that challenged both Democrats and National Republicans. The party's very existence demonstrates that workers were developing their civic capabilities.[65]

Although New York's workingmen's movement failed as a party, it, and similar movements in Philadelphia and Boston, forced other political parties to reach out to workers as a voting bloc. Despite the movement's quick demise, New York's Democrats responded to some of the workers' demands, including abolishing imprisonment for debt, reforming the militia system, and, in New York City, passing a mechanics' lien law. Wilentz concludes that "the lesson, for practical politicians, was clear: no party could succeed nationally—unless it could appeal to the voters aroused by the Working Men and address their concerns."[66] Ronald Schultz came to the same conclusion for Philadelphia's Workingmen's Party. Despite good showings at the polls in 1829, it soon eroded or was assimilated into the Democratic Party. But, Schultz writes, "the mainstream Democratic party moved quickly to incorporate Workingmen's reforms into their platform, and in the course of the 1830s established free public schools, abolished imprisonment for debt, and staunchly supported the working-class ten-hour movement." Democrats had learned that organized workers could pose an electoral threat and vowed to "never again ignore the interests and desires of city craftsmen."[67] Of course, workers also used associations to engage in other forms of collective action, including strikes. These efforts helped workers to develop civic capabilities by allowing them to practice the art of organizing. And these efforts resulted in political responses that demonstrated organized labor's potential power.[68]

Working people developed hybrid associational forms that combined the techniques of artisanal craft governance, social reform, and party. Thus, in Massachusetts, laborers' agitation for a ten-hour workday in the 1850s borrowed heavily from temperance and other social reform movements' organizational repertoire, including hosting conventions; setting up ten-hour auxiliary locals in industrial towns tied together through a parent association (the State Central Committee); and facilitating mass print petition drives to politicize members, on the one hand, and to pressure lawmakers, on the other. Workers also drew on their own traditions to organize strikes to pressure employers and policymakers to act. The ten-hour movement, Mark Voss-Hubbard concludes, resulted in "innovative organizational vehicles, a vibrant print culture, and ultimately new political solidarities around the single issue of labor reform."[69]

The history of third parties reinforces the claim that citizens developed their civic capabilities in civil society. The Anti-Masonic Party originated in areas where evangelical reformers were particularly active. They initially formed "people's committees" that looked and acted much like other associations before making the move into politics. Thus they had a grassroots base quite distinct from the top-down origins of the major parties.[70] Similarly,

Bruce Laurie has demonstrated that the Liberty and Free Soil parties in Massachusetts owed much to the organizational knowledge of antislavery activists who had developed their civic skills and organizational capabilities prior to entering formal political life.[71] The Workingmen's Party drew from artisans' own associational traditions, originating at the grassroots, and relied on the voluntary activity—thus developing the civic skills—of workingmen and -women.[72] In Know-Nothingism, "politics followed organization form," as Know-Nothings copied the model of nonpartisan fraternal associations before mobilizing members for political purposes; nativist lodges created new civic networks and political identities that could be mobilized for electoral purposes.[73] Equally important, third-party builders could rely on their stock of social capital—the network of associations, and thus engaged citizens, that had been created by social reformers.[74] This is not to discount the importance of parties. First, parties offered activists a model of how to move from reform into politics. Second, third parties benefited from the know-how of political leaders, including editors, who joined them. Parties thus offered a template for action, and partisan defectors brought their own political knowledge with them, helping third parties to be more formidable than otherwise might have been possible.[75]

The history of third parties offers another important lens to understand democratization. Third parties help to trace whether citizens' grassroots mobilization can alter public policies. In the case of Know-Nothings, party leaders passed laws in the four core areas of concern—nativism, antislavery, temperance, and political reform. At the same time, their ability to dislodge existing partisan and economic interests was more limited.[76] In many cases, citizens who participated in third-party movements either abandoned their parties when political efforts proved ineffective or when major parties responded to and coopted third parties' positions. In such cases, we see how the civic skills citizens learned in civil society enabled them to threaten the major parties' dominance, forcing party leaders to respond by accommodating third parties' demands or, in the case of the relationship between anti-Masons and northern Whigs, or Know-Nothings and the Republican Party, to fuse existing movements like Know-Nothing nativism into a winning political coalition.[77] In effect, by combining organizational forms learned in civil society and from observing existing parties, citizens could reshape party platforms and coalitions, and in doing so, affect elections and public policies.

Jacksonian Backlash

The best evidence we have that the reformers were effective is that the political system *did* respond. When temperance advocates sought to limit liquor sales, liquor sellers and their supporters organized rival associations in civil society; sellers had to compete for public opinion and influence with their opponents.[78] When Sabbatarians sought to prevent Sunday mail delivery, Jacksonians balked at privately organized associations seeking to restore the union between church and state. When antislavery activists sought to prevent slavery's spread, Jacksonians sought a gag rule, refused to deliver abolitionist mail in the South, and even, at times, resorted to violence. The political system's sometimes hostile response proves both that the new civil society's legitimacy was contested and that organizers affected parties' abilities to dominate public deliberation.

The Jacksonian backlash points to another interpretive possibility. In the face of both their Whig opponents and the proliferation of new associations in civil society, many Jacksonians defended a more populist understanding of democracy, in which "the people" were a coherent entity with shared values and interests. From this perspective, far from furthering democratization, the pluralism of civil society threatened it. The Democratic Party would have to serve, in Wilentz's words, as "the constitutional party of the sovereign people," the people's agent in a corrupt world.[79] If true, this means that scholars should also take seriously the continued—and perhaps increasing—salience of what Michael Kazin has called "the populist persuasion," and trace whether organizations like the Democratic Party proved effective not just in mobilizing supporters but in developing those voters' capabilities to resist organized interests.[80]

More importantly, such a perspective would ensure a necessary caution to those inclined to idealize civil society. The older "social control" school, after all, saw in associations a threat to democracy. The middle-class membership of many reform associations meant that middle-class values influenced American politics. And here, class does matter. Middle-class volunteers sought to reform not just themselves but the working people below them, who they believed drank too much and lacked the values and discipline to be good Americans. At times, these reforms were animated by a deep anti-Catholicism; at other times, by a general class bias. Associations may have developed their members' civic capabilities, but we must also think about who were the objects of an association's outreach, and what specific goals or policies specific associations advocated. As John Brooke reminds us, associations could challenge hegemonic power, but through their cultural influence, they could also reinforce it.[81]

Associations, moreover, no better reflected public opinion than did parties. Associations mobilized specific groups of citizens for specific purposes. Given their organizational power, they were as likely to skew as to represent the majority's values. As Mancur Olson Jr. taught us, civic action is a collective action problem. The narrower an interest, the easier it is to mobilize stakeholders; the broader the interest — and the public interest is the broadest interest — the harder it is to organize. Moreover, with the growth of the state's administrative apparatus and regulatory duties — itself a response to the changing economic and social conditions of industrialization — civil society was as (if not more) likely to be composed of professional lobbyists representing "interests" as it was to be composed of citizens organizing for grassroots change.[82] In such a context, it is also worth asking whether parties serve as democratic countervailing powers against the corrupting potential of associations, since parties, unlike associations, have to forge a majority.

Politics and Political Capability — Some Ideas

Political historians can learn from historians of civil society. We need to know better how deliberation in civil society and its public sphere affected voters' actions and, in turn, the decisions of party leaders and elected officials. We need to assess to what extent engaged voters were manipulated by political elites, and to what extent those same elites depended on voters capable of having a real impact on public policies.

To be democratic, parties must be more than patronage machines. Some have suggested that parties' primary role was to give money to those within their networks, including offering government positions to loyal partisans.[83] If this was the case, parties may have served a useful function, but they were not serving democracy. Yet even if parties were primarily about winning office (a big if), parties had to convince voters to vote. Parties thus were active agents within civil society and its public sphere. According to Joel Silbey, parties "framed the agenda" in order to win votes. They, moreover, were essential to a mass democracy because they helped to organize the diverse interests and values of civil society into coherent voting blocs capable of governing.

Without parties, the will of the people would be too diffuse to gain clear expression, and voters would be rendered powerless. Thus parties, even if their primary goal was to get elected, served a vital democratic function.[84] From a capability perspective, however, we still need to know whether when political parties framed the issues, they furthered deliberation or reinforced the existing assumptions and biases of the electorate, thus reducing voters' abilities to deliberate in a meaningful fashion.[85]

A capability approach must also test how effective voters were in shaping policies. We cannot take this link for granted. In fact, Richard P. McCormick found little connection between elections and policies, concluding that government shaped politics rather than the other way around.[86] But can citizens be an independent variable? This is the question the capability approach poses, and, as Michael F. Holt argues, "what linked grass-roots voters to actions of the state" ought to be "at or near the top of any agenda."[87]

Parties helped voters to care. Like other associations, they relied on print and exhortation to excite voters about public affairs. Engagement is a vital first step to civic activity. Voters who were not interested would never go through the trouble of developing their capabilities.[88]

The "new political history" approach of measuring voter behavior can offer some guidance. This work explores how different groups responded to parties' efforts to frame the political agenda. Relying on significant empirical analysis, it has helped us to understand the correlation among religion, ethnicity, economic interest, and partisan coalitions. The new political history, however, was designed to identify the specific social characteristics that correlated with votes, but not to gauge how and why voters' preferences were shaped.[89] As Daniel Feller writes, "Conceptualizing politics as group behavior and then mediating that behavior through such categories as class, religion, ethnicity, or even party can produce an inadvertent but insidious reductionism. It leads us to think of political belief and political practice as wholly dependent variables."[90] We need a better framework to make sense of the data that the new political historians have uncovered, one that moves beyond behavior to agency: did individuals and groups make real choices that had an impact on the political system?[91]

The "new new political history" offers little guidance here because, as discussed above, it also focuses on engagement. Although the lens of analysis shifted from voting rates and correlations to cultural questions about partisan identity, new work does not answer whether citizens were truly capable of having a political influence. While parties spurred engagement, we still do not know if they took the next step and developed voters' capabilities. Here, political historians must fill in some of the gaps. We have too long considered engagement a proxy for actual democratization. Historians in civil society, on the other hand, have had to make a case for their subjects' political influence. We ought to do the same for parties.

One place where such a case can be readily made is for party activists. Even if most voters were not involved in party operations, parties as organizations still developed the capabilities of those that did join. Parties, like other civic associations, were federal in character, which meant that they required national leaders but also local volunteers. At the local level, party activists learned how to take part in and shape politics. To this extent, parties were like other associations, developing members' civic skills.[92] There is still some debate as to how democratic parties in the second party system were. If the first party system was organized from the top down, were things different during the age of mass parties? Holt's work demonstrates that local and state party associations had significant leeway to shape their platforms to appeal to their particular constituents.[93] A capability approach would build on Holt to understand how local party activists both gained new civic skills by participating in parties and whether these local activities affected platforms and policies.

Parties, like associations in civil society, had two tiers. There was an inner group of local, state, and national activists who gained civic capabilities through participating in party work, and a broader set of voters. Parties served the same democratizing function for this inner group as did other associations for their members. But like other associations, parties reached out to a broader public. Through their local activities and print, parties sought to convince voters to support them. They challenged and were challenged by other associations. They built coalitions and found their coalitions challenged by others. In this sense, parties *as associations* promoted democratization for their members; we need not hold parties to a higher standard than we hold other associations.

The challenge, of course, is that parties must govern. Parties run candidates who are chosen by voters. They were, and remain, more than mere "civic associations." Thus the stakes are high. Even if parties developed the civic capabilities of their activists, it is vital that we figure out to what extent they also developed citizens' capabilities.

Finally, we might look more closely at how local government functioned. Thomas Jefferson famously celebrated the ward republic, while Tocqueville saw the seeds of American democracy in New England's town halls. Local politics, whether partisan or not, might have been a foundation for developing civic capabilities. Just as becoming involved in the local auxiliary of an association or party developed one's capabilities, election to local offices could do the same. Existing local histories and new ones oriented around the question of capability might help us to understand what role local governing institutions played in fostering citizens' abilities to govern themselves.

Exemplary Books

Four recent books can help us to start imagining a political history with capability at its center. The first, Ronald P. Formisano's *The Transformation of Political Culture* (1983), shows how delicate party coalitions were in the early republic. Massachusetts leaders were constantly reconstructing themselves in response to organized interests in civil society. Formisano concludes, "Parties had acquired lives of their own, but the citizenry still possessed the capacity to undo what had been done in its name."[94] To Formisano, democratization happened in civil society (although he does not use the term), where citizens' capabilities were developed. Parties served as mediating devices that responded to, or limited, popular pressures. Parties per se did not develop democratic capabilities; in fact, parties had to be consistently challenged by the grassroots in order for them to serve their democratic purposes.

In *Evangelicals and Politics in Antebellum America* (1993), Richard Carwardine argues that evangelicals were America's most influential "subculture," and that they played a vital role in shaping politics. Churches and voluntary associations were critical for "political socialization" because they "offered an example of how the world might be changed through systematic agitation" and encouraged "voting, and responsible and dutiful citizenship." Because evangelicals judged politicians and policies by their values, and because they were organized, their ethical concerns found their way into politics. Party leaders could not ignore antislavery, anti-Catholicism, temperance, and education, and thus they could not avoid the very issues that frustrated parties' efforts to sustain national coalitions.[95] Carwardine's study makes clear that evangelicals, thanks to effective organization and mobilization, had the capability to influence elections, party platforms, and policy outcomes.

If Formisano and Carwardine look to parties' responses to external pressures, in *Rise and Fall of the American Whig Party* (1999), Michael Holt returns to more traditional terrain. He studies local and state electio. why the fortune of elected leaders depended quite heavily on both the how partisans used to mobilize voters and the actual policies leaders promote and enacted. In short, federalism mattered; voters cared about state-level distributive and regulatory policymaking and held leaders accountable. Holt thus suggests that voters did exercise civic capability during elections. Even if party conventions and organizations were controlled by party elites—as Glenn Altschuler and Stuart Blumin argue—those elites' hold on power was not as secure as their analysis would make one think.[96] Instead, like Formisano, Holt emphasizes parties' relative weakness because party dominance was challenged consistently by third-party movements. Leaders in the party period had to be responsive to voters.[97]

Voters did impact policies. Holt's Whig leaders at the national and state levels were constantly involved not only in mobilizing voters but also in trying to read them and figure out how to sell their platform to a skeptical public. Holt's book thus offers historians the strongest case yet that voting mattered. Yet Holt is unclear as to how voters participated in deliberation. How did voters themselves determine what values and policies they thought worth supporting? Holt's argument emphasizes that voter *engagement* increases when parties present distinct, divergent platforms. But these partisan distinctions can reflect as well as distort voters' actual preferences.

In *Columbia Rising* (2010), John L. Brooke, unlike Holt, focuses on the deliberative realm. Brooke frames his argument around the assumption that democratization should mean that more people get to participate in the act of consent: in deliberating, framing, and shaping the policies by which they are governed. Brooke recognizes that there was a formal public sphere made up of legally equal, enfranchised citizens, a sphere that expanded over the first decades of the nineteenth century to include most white men. Political parties sought votes from the formal public sphere. But women, African Americans, tenant farmers, laborers, and reformers participated in a broader public sphere through which they made their values and interests known, and through which they could pressure voters and leaders. In turn, political leaders and the state relied on their power to impose their values and interests in the informal public sphere, what might be termed an imperfect hegemony.

Brooke moves our discussion forward by exploring how civil society worked as a "*flywheel*" between people and their government." With the exception of enslaved people, whose consent was coerced, in civil society consent was ᴜgh cultural norms, but also challenged by organizations that general mobilized citizens around competing values and interests. It was this give-and-take, in which the disenfranchised were both victims and agents, that deliberation took place in the informal public sphere. Brooke concludes that it was in civil society, and not through parties, that citizens most effectively developed the social capital, or "skills in associated action that lead to wider positive social outcomes." Reformers, by organizing to shape culture and opinion, may have been more effective at developing citizens' capabilities than party leaders.[98] Brooke thus offers a way to integrate civil society's history into political history.

THE CURRENT STATE of the field suggests that parties' contributions to democratization were through engagement and issue clarification, but that it was in civil society that citizens gained the capabilities necessary to shape deliberation and policy outcomes. It was the active work of civic organizers that fundamentally reshaped Americans' relationship to politics. In social movements, citizens learned the skills they needed to organize to shape public opinion and pressure political leaders. Civil society's leaders gave citizens the capabilities needed to impact public life at a time when parties were responsive to changes in public opinion. Voting in elections may be the most important political act in a democracy, and studying the exercise of political power is equaled only by studying economic power, but voting may also be merely the tip of a democratization process that took place in civil society rather than in traditional politics.

This does not mean that parties were unimportant. Had partisan competition not existed, voters might not have been motivated to go to the polls and express their will, and voters might have chosen leaders according to deference and personality rather than platform. Parties also mediated between citizens and the state. They shaped political identities in ways that gave citizens a stake in politics. We know that party competition encouraged engagement. What we now need to know is the extent to which parties encouraged or discouraged Americans' political capabilities.

Notes

1. There are many approaches to the identity question. To such historians as Jean Baker and Albrecht Koschnik, parties as political institutions were themselves shapers of identity; to the "new political historians," preexisting ethnocultural identities determined partisan affiliation. Whichever way the causal arrow pointed—and probably it went both ways—it meant that partisan affiliation was deeply held.

2. See, for example, Elizabeth R. Varon, "Tippecanoe and the Ladies, Too," *Journal of American History* 82 (September 1995): 494–521; Rosemarie Zagarri, *Revolutionary Backlash: Women and Politics in the Early American Republic* (Philadelphia: University of Pennsylvania Press, 2007); and Ronald J. Zboray and Mary Saracino Zboray, *Voices without Votes: Women and Politics in Antebellum New England* (Durham: University of New Hampshire Press, 2010).

3. Robert H. Wiebe, *Self-Rule: A Cultural History of American Democracy* (Chicago: University of Chicago Press, 1995), 61.

4. Joel H. Silbey, *The Partisan Imperative: The Dynamics of American Politics before the Civil War* (New York: Oxford University Press, 1985), ch. 4, esp. 64–67. See also Wiebe, *Self-Rule,* and Lynn Hudson Parsons, *The Birth of Modern Politics: Andrew Jackson, John Quincy Adams, and the Election of 1828* (New York: Oxford University Press, 2009), on the transition from the politics of deference to the mass political system of the post-1828 era. For a discussion of the historiography, see the introduction to this volume. Older analyses include William G. Shade, "Politics and Parties in Jacksonian America," *Pennsylvania Magazine of History and Biography* 110(October 1986): 483–507, and Daniel Feller, "Politics and Society: Toward a Jacksonian Synthesis," *Journal of the Early Republic* 10 (Summer 1990): 135–61.

5. William Gienapp, "'Politics Seem to Enter into Everything': Political Culture in the North, 1840–1860," in *Essays on American Antebellum Politics, 1840–1860,* ed. Stephen E. Maizlish and John J. Kushma (College Station: Texas A&M University Press, 1982), 14–69. See also Michael Schudson, *The Good Citizen: A History of American Civic Life* (New York: Free Press, 1998), 110–32.

6. Here I build on concerns raised some time ago by Richard L. McCormick in "The Party Period and Public Policy: An Exploratory Hypothesis" (1979), in *The Party Period and Public Policy: American Politics from the Age of Jackson to the Progressive Era* (New York: Oxford University Press, 1988), 197–227.

7. Amartya Sen, *Development as Freedom* (New York: Oxford University Press, 1999); Sen, "Equality of What?" (Tanner Lecture on Human Values, Stanford University, 22 May 1979), http://tannerlectures.utah.edu/_documents/a-to-z/s/sen80 .pdf. See also Martha C. Nussbaum, *Women and Human Development: The Capabilities Approach* (New York: Cambridge University Press, 2000); Nussbaum, "Aristotelian Social Democracy," in *Liberalism and the Good,* ed. R. Bruce Douglass et al. (New York: Routledge, 1990), 203–52; Nussbaum, "Capabilities as Fundamental Entitlements: Sen and Social Justice," *Feminist Economics* 9 (2003): 33–59; Nussbaum,

"Constitutions and Capabilities: 'Perception' against Lofty Formalism," *Harvard Law Review* 121 (November 2007): 4–97; and Carole Pateman, *Participation and Democratic Theory* (Cambridge: Cambridge University Press, 1970). Charles Tilly, *Democracy* (New York: Cambridge University Press, 2007), offers a similar claim, namely that democratic institutional structures matter in conjunction with clear modes through which ordinary people are consulted and can influence policy.

8. Sen, *Development as Freedom*, 18.

9. Amartya Sen, *The Idea of Justice* (Cambridge, Mass.: Harvard University Press, 2009), 82.

10. Sidney Verba, Kay Lehman Schlozman, and Henry E. Brady, *Voice and Equality: Civic Voluntarism in American Politics* (Cambridge, Mass.: Harvard University Press, 1995), 3.

11. Wiebe, *Self-Rule*, 8–9, 256–57.

12. Glenn C. Altschuler and Stuart Blumin, "Limits of Political Engagement in Antebellum America: A New Look at the Golden Age of Participatory Democracy," *Journal of American History* 84 (December 1997): 855–85; Altschuler and Blumin, "'Where Is the Real America?': Politics and Popular Consciousness in the Antebellum Era," *American Quarterly* 49 (June 1997): 225–67. Their findings were subsequently published as *Rude Republic: Americans and Their Politics in the Nineteenth Century* (Princeton, N.J.: Princeton University Press, 2000).

13. Joel H. Silbey, "The State and the Practice of American Political History at the Millennium: The Nineteenth Century as a Test Case," *Journal of Policy History* 11 (1999): 1–30.

14. Richard R. John, "Farewell to the 'Party Period': Political Economy in Nineteenth-Century America," *Journal of Policy History* 16 (2004): 117–25. John echoes McCormick, "Party Period and Public Policy."

15. Julian E. Zelizer, "History and Political Science: Together Again?" *Journal of Policy History* 16 (2004): 126–36. On these points, see also Theda Skocpol et al., "How Americans Became Civic," *American Political Science Review* 94 (September 2000): 527–46, and Elisabeth S. Clemens, *The People's Lobby: Organizational Innovation and the Rise of Interest Group Politics in the United States, 1890–1925* (Chicago: University of Chicago Press, 1997).

16. Joanne B. Freeman, "The Culture of Politics: The Politics of Culture," *Journal of Policy History* 16 (2004): 137–43. For a broader discussion of the idea of political culture, see Ronald P. Formisano, "The Concept of Political Culture," *Journal of Interdisciplinary History* 31 (Winter 2001): 393–426. See also Len Travers, *Celebrating the Fourth: Independence Day and the Rites of Nationalism in the Early Republic* (Amherst: University of Massachusetts Press, 1997); Simon Newman, *Parades and the Politics of the Street: Festive Culture in the Early American Republic* (Philadelphia: University of Pennsylvania Press, 1997); and David Waldstreicher, *In the Midst of Perpetual Fetes: The Making of American Nationalism, 1780–1820* (Chapel Hill: University of North Carolina Press, 1997).

17. David Waldstreicher, "Founders Chic as Culture War," *Radical History Review* 84 (Fall 2002): 185–94.

18. Jeffrey L. Pasley, "The Cheese and the Words: Popular Political Culture and Participatory Democracy in the Early American Republic"; David Waldstreicher, "Why Thomas Jefferson and African Americans Wore Their Politics on Their Sleeves: Dress and Mobilization between American Revolutions"; and Albrecht Koschnik, "Young Federalists, Masculinity, and Partisanship," all in *Beyond the Founders: New Approaches to the Political History of the Early American Republic*, ed. Jeffrey L. Pasley, Andrew W. Robertson, and David Waldstreicher (Chapel Hill: University of North Carolina Press, 2004), 31–56, 79–103, 159–79. For a similar critique, see William G. Shade, "Déjà Vu All over Again: Is There a New New Political History?" in Pasley et al., eds., *Beyond the Founders*, 387–412. We should not dismiss the importance of understanding identity formation and political culture. See also John L. Brooke, "Reason and Passion in the Public Sphere: Habermas and the Cultural Historians," *Journal of Interdisciplinary History* 29 (Summer 1998): 43–67.

19. Andrew W. Robertson, "Voting Rites and Voting Acts: Electioneering Ritual, 1790–1820," in Pasley et al., *Beyond the Founders*, 57–78; Rosemarie Zagarri, "Women and Party Conflict in the Early Republic," in Pasley et al., eds., *Beyond the Founders*, 107–28.

20. John L. Brooke, "Consent, Civil Society, and the Public Sphere in the Age of Revolution and the Early American Republic," in Pasley et al., eds., *Beyond the Founders*, 207–50.

21. Richard Newman, "Protest in Black and White: The Formation and Transformation of an African American Political Community during the Early Republic," in Pasley et al., eds., *Beyond the Founders*, 180–294, 201 (quotation).

22. Reeve Huston, "Popular Movements and Party Rule: The New York Anti-Rent Wars and the Jacksonian Political Order," in Pasley et al., eds., *Beyond the Founders*, 355–86, 362 (quotation).

23. As Reeve Huston, *Land and Freedom: Rural Society, Popular Protest, and Party Politics in Antebellum New York* (New York: Oxford University Press, 2000), 7, puts it in response to Altschuler and Blumin: "Rather than being simply represented, coopted, or cynically amused by partisan activists, the anti-renters' relationship to those [partisan] activists was a dialectical one, in which each appropriated and reshaped the ideas, demands, and platforms of the other." *Land and Freedom*, esp. 131–94, provides a more detailed, substantive examination of the themes raised in Huston's *Beyond the Founders* essay. On the anti-rent movement, see also Charles W. McCurdy, *The Anti-Rent Era in New York Politics and Law, 1839–1865* (Chapel Hill: University of North Carolina Press, 2001), which examines why the political and legal systems found it so difficult to respond to anti-renters' demands.

24. Brooke, "Consent, Civil Society"; Gordon S. Wood, *The Creation of the American Republic, 1776–1787* (Chapel Hill: University of North Carolina Press, 1969).

25. The term and discussion of the "grassroots public sphere" is from Johann N.

Neem, *Creating a Nation of Joiners: Democracy and Civil Society in Early National Massachusetts* (Cambridge, Mass.: Harvard University Press, 2008), ch. 4. Mark Voss-Hubbard, *Beyond Party: Cultures of Antipartisanship in Northern Politics before the Civil War* (Baltimore: Johns Hopkins University Press, 2002), 60–68, also recognizes the importance of the development of new organizational forms in civil society. See also Schudson, *Good Citizen*, 98–109.

26. Theda Skocpol, *Diminished Democracy: From Membership to Management in American Civic Life* (Norman: University of Oklahoma Press, 2003), 20–73; Michael P. Young, *Bearing Witness against Sin: The Evangelical Birth of the American Social Movement* (Chicago: University of Chicago Press, 2006), 54–85; Neem, *Creating a Nation of Joiners*, 90–99; Donald G. Mathews, "The Second Great Awakening as an Organizing Process, 1780–1830: An Hypothesis," *American Quarterly* 21 (Spring 1969): 23–42.

27. Neem, *Creating a Nation of Joiners*, ch. 4; Conrad Edick Wright, *The Transformation of Charity in Postrevolutionary New England* (Boston: Northeastern University Press, 1992).

28. Clemens, *People's Lobby;* Neem, *Creating a Nation of Joiners*, 81–82. See also Charles Tilly, "Repertoires of Contention in America and Britain, 1750–1830," in *The Dynamics of Social Movements: Resource Mobilization, Social Control, and Tactics*, ed. Mayer N. Zald and John D. McCarthy (Cambridge, Mass.: Winthrop, 1979), 126–55, and Young, *Bearing Witness*, 10–38.

29. On public opinion, see Brooke, "Consent, Civil Society," and Gordon S. Wood, "The Democratization of Mind in the American Revolution," in *Leadership in the American Revolution* (Washington, D.C.: Library of Congress, 1974), 63–88. For elite ministers and public opinion, see Neil Brody Miller, "Proper Subjects for Public Inquiry: The First Unitarian Controversy and the Transformation of Federalist Print Culture," *Early American Literature* 43 (March 2008): 101–35; Jonathan Sassi, *A Republic of Righteousness: The Public Christianity of the Post-Revolutionary New England Clergy* (New York: Oxford University Press, 2001), 121–44, 163–95.

30. Voss-Hubbard, *Beyond Party*, 12.

31. Richard R. John, "Taking Sabbatarianism Seriously: The Postal System, the Sabbath, and the Transformation of American Political Culture," *Journal of the Early Republic* 10 (Winter 1990): 538–39, 542–43. For Sabbatarianism, see also Bertram Wyatt-Brown, "Prelude to Abolitionism: Sabbatarian Politics and the Rise of the Second Party System," *Journal of American History* 58 (September 1971): 316–41, and James Rohrer, "Sunday Mails and the Church-State Theme in Jacksonian America," *Journal of the Early Republic* 7 (Spring 1987): 53–74.

32. [Lyman Beecher], *The Address of the General Union for Promoting the Observance of the Christian Sabbath, to the People of the United States, Accompanied by Minutes of the Proceedings and in Its Formation* (New York, 1828); John, "Taking Sabbatarianism Seriously," 538. For the religious/theological foundations for civic activism, see Young, *Bearing Witness*, 86–117. A similar story can be told for the anti-Masonic movement of the late 1820s and early 1830s. As Steven C. Bullock, *Revolutionary*

Brotherhood: Freemasonry and the Transformation of the American Social Order 1730–1840 (Chapel Hill: University of North Carolina Press, 1996), 294–95, argues, anti-Masonic leaders—many of whom were Sabbatarians as well—transformed the public sphere by placing "public opinion and conscience at the heart of their thinking."

33. John, "Taking Sabbatarianism Seriously," 538. See also Johann N. Neem, "Creating Social Capital in the Early American Republic: The View from Connecticut," *Journal of Interdisciplinary History* 39 (Spring 2009): 471–95.

34. On the Massachusetts Society for the Suppression of Intemperance, see Neem, *Creating a Nation of Joiners*, 87.

35. The very formation of an association helped to create the problem it sought to resolve by defining it and establishing an institution determined to address it. On this point, see Wright, *Transformation of Charity*. On the role of print, see also David P. Nord, *Faith in Reading: Religious Publishing and the Birth of the Mass Media in America* (New York: Oxford University Press, 2004).

36. Ian Tyrrell, *Sobering Up: From Temperance to Prohibition in Antebellum America, 1800–1860* (Westport, Conn.: Greenwood Press, 1979), 66–67, 74–77. On women in the temperance movement, see also Barbara Leslie Epstein, *The Politics of Domesticity: Women, Evangelicalism, and Temperance in Nineteenth-Century America* (Middletown, Conn.: Wesleyan University Press, 1981), 89–114.

37. Robert L. Hampel, *Temperance and Prohibition in Massachusetts, 1813–1852* (Ann Arbor, Mich.: UMI Research Press, 1982), 25–44.

38. Tyrrell, *Sobering Up*, 87.

39. *Columbian Centinel* (Boston), 16 November 1839, quoted in Hampel, *Temperance and Prohibition*, 87.

40. *Atlas* (Boston), 16 March 1839. See also 5 August, 16 November 1839.

41. Neem, *Creating a Nation of Joiners*, 157–58; Hampel, *Temperance and Prohibition*, 45–78; Tyrrell, *Sobering Up*, 91–115, 227–43; Bruce Laurie, *Beyond Garrison: Antislavery and Social Reform* (New York: Cambridge University Press, 2005), 227–29.

42. Tyrrell, *Sobering Up*, 252.

43. Ibid., 279.

44. Ibid., 225–89, 372 (quotation). See also Voss-Hubbard, *Beyond Party*, 88–104. The temperance movement also inspired the working-class Washingtonian movement. Building on their own artisanal traditions and learning from middle-class reformers, the Washingtonians demonstrated how the knowledge of association, once learned, could enable citizens to become influential shapers of opinion. The movement began when six Baltimore artisans formed the Baltimore Temperance Society in 1840; by the end of 1841, the movement claimed 12,000 Baltimore followers, 10,000 in New York City, 5,000 in Boston, and 200,000 throughout the North. Even if the movement was not explicitly political, and even if it soon split into competing factions as middle-class members sought to purge less respectable workers, its importance lies in its educative role. Artisans had learned how to generate networks for

cooperating across space—what in today's parlance is known as social capital—in order to achieve broad goals. See Tyrrell, *Sobering Up*, 159–224; Hampel, *Temperance and Prohibition*, 103–28.

45. Richard S. Newman, *The Transformation of American Abolitionism: Fighting Slavery in the Early Republic* (Chapel Hill: University of North Carolina Press, 2002); Susan Zaeske, *Signatures of Citizenship: Petitioning, Antislavery, & Women's Political Identity* (Chapel Hill: University of North Carolina Press, 2003). See also Laurie, *Beyond Garrison*, esp. 17–48, and Daniel Carpenter and Nicole Topich, "Contested Boundaries of Representation: Patterns of Transformation in Black Petitioning in Massachusetts, 1770–1850," in *Democracy, Participation and Contestation: Civil Society, Governance and the Future of Liberal Democracy*, ed. Emmanuelle Avril and Johann N. Neem (Abingdon, Eng.: Routledge, 2014), ch. 14.

46. Newman, *Transformation of American Abolitionism*, 6–8.

47. Ibid., 86–87. See also Timothy Patrick McCarthy, "'To Plead Our Own Cause': Black Print Culture and the Origins of American Abolitionism," in *Prophets of Protest: Reconsidering the History of American Abolitionism*, ed. Timothy Patrick McCarthy and John Stauffer (New York: New Press, 2006), 114–44.

48. Newman, *Transformation of American Abolitionism*, 87. For the importance of these institutions in developing the social capital necessary for a mass movement, see Theda Skocpol et al., *What a Mighty Power We Can Be: African American Fraternal Groups and the Struggle for Racial Equality* (Princeton, N.J.: Princeton University Press, 2006).

49. Newman, *Transformation of American Abolitionism*, 100–106.

50. Ibid., 120–28; Neem, *Creating a Nation of Joiners*, 164–71.

51. As Newman, *Transformation of American Abolitionism*, 131–75, writes, "Mobilize people in a republic and the republic would have to change its laws on slavery" (154).

52. Zaeske, *Signatures of Citizenship*, 1. See also Julie Roy Jeffrey, *Silent Army of Abolitionism: Ordinary Women in the Antislavery Movement* (Chapel Hill: University of North Carolina Press, 1998), and Anne M. Boylan, *The Origins of Women's Activism: New York and Boston, 1797–1840* (Chapel Hill: University of North Carolina Press, 2002).

53. Zaeske, *Signatures of Citizenship*, 8.

54. For how petitioning continued to be a powerful political tool, both in shaping women's political identities and their capability to shape public affairs during and after the Civil War, see Wendy Hamand Venet, *Neither Ballots nor Bullets: Women Abolitionists and the Civil War* (Charlottesville: University Press of Press, 1991).

55. Johann N. Neem, "Taking Modernity's Wager: Tocqueville, Social Capital, and the American Civil War," *Journal of Interdisciplinary History* 41 (Spring 2011): 591–618; John L. Brooke, "Cultures of Nationalism, Movements of Reform, and the Composite-Federal Polity," *Journal of the Early Republic* 29 (Spring 2009): 1–33.

56. Zagarri, *Revolutionary Backlash*. In Zagarri's framework, as the revolutionary moment passed, women shifted to nonpartisan social reform, a step backward. Other

scholars have emphasized the ways in which this backward step enabled women to shape the outcomes of politics.

57. Paula Baker, "The Domestication of Politics: Women and American Political Society," *American Historical Review* 89 (June 1984): 620–47, 621 (quotation).

58. Catherine Allgor, *Parlor Politics: In Which the Ladies of Washington Help Build a City and a Government* (Charlottesville: University Press of Virginia, 2000).

59. Linda Kerber, *Women of the Republic: Intellect and Ideology in Revolutionary America* (Chapel Hill: University of North Carolina Press, 1980); Nancy Cott, *The Bonds of Womanhood: "Woman's Sphere" in New England, 1780–1835* (New Haven, Conn.: Yale University Press, 1977); Mary Kelley, *Learning to Stand and Speak: Women, Education, and Public Life in America's Republic* (Chapel Hill: University of North Carolina Press, 2006); and J. M. Opal, "Exciting Emulation: Academies and the Transformation of the Rural North, 1780s–1820s," *Journal of American History* 91 (September 2004): 445–70.

60. Susan Branson, *These Fiery Frenchified Dames: Women and Political Culture in Early National Philadelphia* (Philadelphia: University of Pennsylvania Press, 2001), 21–53; Carolyn Eastman, *A Nation of Speechifiers: Making an American Public after the Revolution* (Chicago: University of Chicago Press, 2010), esp. 53–82. See also Zboray and Zboray, *Voices without Votes*.

61. Branson, *Fiery Frenchified Dames*, 56–99; Zagarri, *Revolutionary Backlash*. For some of the limits of women's involvement in partisan public life, see Mary P. Ryan, *Women in Public: Between Banners and Ballots, 1825–1880* (Baltimore: John Hopkins University Press, 1998), 19–57, and Daniel Walker Howe, *What Hath God Wrought: The Transformation of America, 1815–1848* (New York: Oxford University Press, 2007), 606–8.

62. Daniel Carpenter and Colin D. Moore, "When Canvassers Became Activists: Antislavery Petitioning and the Political Mobilization of American Women," *American Political Science Review* 108 (August 2014): 479–98; Neem, *Creating a Nation of Joiners*, 96–99, 103–7; Kathleen D. McCarthy, *American Creed: Philanthropy and the Rise of Civil Society, 1700–1865* (Chicago: University of Chicago Press, 2003), 30–48. For some of the tensions between different women activists, see Boylan, *Origins of Women's Activism;* Nancy Hewitt, *Women's Activism and Social Change: Rochester, New York, 1822–1872* (Ithaca, N.Y.: Cornell University Press, 1984).

63. Ryan, *Women in Public*, 95–129.

64. Allgor, *Parlor Politics;* Boylan, *Origins of Women's Activism;* Hewitt, *Women's Activism;* Mary P. Ryan, *Cradle of the Middle Class: The Family in Oneida County, New York, 1790–1865* (Cambridge: Cambridge University Press, 1981), 105–44; Deborah Van Broekhoven, *The Devotion of These Women: Rhode Island in the Antislavery Network* (Amherst: University of Massachusetts Press, 2002).

65. Sean Wilentz, *Chants Democratic: New York City and the Rise of the American Working Class, 1788–1850* (New York: Oxford University Press, 1984), esp. 172–216.

66. Sean Wilentz, *The Rise of American Democracy: Jefferson to Lincoln* (New York: Norton, 2005), 347–58.

67. Ronald Schultz, *The Republic of Labor: Philadelphia Artisans and the Politics of Class, 1720–1830* (New York: Oxford University Press, 1993), 231–32.

68. For Massachusetts's Workingmen Party, see Ronald P. Formisano, *The Transformation of Political Culture: Massachusetts Parties, 1790s–1840s* (New York: Oxford University Press, 1983), 222–44, and Arthur B. Darling, "The Workingmen's Party in Massachusetts, 1833–1834," *American Historical Review* 29 (October 1923): 81–86.

69. Voss-Hubbard, *Beyond Party*, 81–85, 83 (quotation).

70. Ronald P. Formisano and Kathleen Smith Kutolowski, "Antimasonry and Masonry: The Genesis of Protest, 1826–1827," *American Quarterly* 29 (Summer 1977): 139–65; Bullock, *Revolutionary Brotherhood*, 277–279; Paul Goodman, *Towards a Christian Republic: Antimasonry and the Great Transition in New England, 1826–1836* (New York: Oxford University Press 1988), 3–19; Wilentz, *Rise of American Democracy*, 272–279; Ronald P. Formisano, *For the People: American Populist Movements from the Revolution to the 1850s* (Chapel Hill: University of North Carolina Press, 2008), 65–115, 141–58; Neem, *Creating a Nation of Joiners*, 108–13.

71. Laurie, *Beyond Garrison*. On Massachusetts anti-Masonry, see also John L. Brooke, *The Heart of the Commonwealth: Society and Political Culture in Worcester County, Massachusetts, 1713–1861* (New York: Cambridge University Press, 1989), 319–52.

72. Laurie, *Beyond Garrison*, 125–52; Formisano, *For the People*, 82–89.

73. Voss-Hubbard, *Beyond Party*, 12–13, 105–37; Formisano, *For the People*, 198–214; Richard Carwardine, *Evangelicals and Politics in Antebellum America* (New Haven, Conn.: Yale University Press, 1993), 199–204, 218–34.

74. On this point, Laurie's discussion in *Beyond Garrison* of the Liberty Party's emergence out of the existing antislavery movement is particularly strong. Social capital acts as a fund from which individuals can draw to accomplish their goals. In the case here, civil society's networks furthered democratization by enabling people to have a real impact on public affairs. Social capital therefore may also be one of the fundamental preconditions for citizens' civic capabilities. For a discussion of social capital, see Robert Putnam, *Bowling Alone: The Collapse and Revival of American Community* (New York: Simon and Schuster, 2000).

75. In a sense, parties served as "fields." Frederick J. Blue, *No Taint of Compromise: Crusaders in Antislavery Politics* (Baton Rouge: Louisiana State University Press, 2005), and Voss-Hubbard, *Beyond Party*, esp. 71–104, 117–37, both do an excellent job of showing how third parties combined the organizational repertoires of both civil society activists and professional politicians.

76. Voss-Hubbard, *Beyond Party*, 141–77; Tyler Anbinder, *Nativism and Slavery: The Northern Know Nothings and the Politics of the 1850s* (New York: Oxford University Press, 1992), 127–61.

77. Formisano, *Transformation of Political Culture*, has made this case quite convincingly. See also Formisano, *For the People*, 150–58; Voss-Hubbard, *Beyond Party*, 178–216; and William E. Gienapp, *The Origins of the Republican Party, 1852–1856* (New York: Oxford University Press, 1987).

78. Kyle Volk, "The Perils of 'Pure Democracy': Minority Rights, Liquor Politics, and Popular Sovereignty in Antebellum America," *Journal of the Early Republic* 29 (Winter 2009): 641–79; Eric R. Schlereth, "Fits of Political Religion: Stalking Infidelity and the Politics of Moral Reform in Antebellum America," *Early American Studies* 5 (Fall 2007): 288–322.

79. Wilentz, *Rise of American Democracy,* 516–17. See also Gerald Leonard, *The Invention of Party Politics: Federalism, Popular Sovereignty, and Constitutional Development in Jacksonian Illinois* (Chapel Hill: University of North Carolina Press, 2002), and Marvin Meyers, *The Jacksonian Persuasion: Politics and Beliefs* (Stanford, Cal.: Stanford University Press, 1957). On the Jacksonian backlash against civil society, see Neem, *Creating a Nation of Joiners,* 140–71; McCarthy, *American Creed,* 123–64; and John L. Brooke, *Columbia Rising: Civil Life on the Upper Hudson from the Revolution to the Age of Jackson* (Chapel Hill: University of North Carolina Press, 2010), 339–41, 449–50.

80. Michael Kazin, *The Populist Persuasion: An American History* (New York: Basic Books, 1995).

81. Brooke, "Consent, Civil Society." See also Oscar and Mary Handlin, "Restrictive Associations," in *The Dimensions of Liberty* (Cambridge, Mass.: Harvard University Press, 1961), 113–32, and Christine Stansell, *City of Women: Sex and Class in New York, 1789–1860* (New York: Knopf, 1986).

82. Mancur Olson Jr., *The Logic of Collective Action: Public Goods and the Theory of Groups* (Cambridge, Mass.: Harvard University Press, 1965); Joel H. Silbey, *American Political Nation* (Stanford, Cal.: Stanford University Press, 1991), 232–51; Skocpol, *Diminished Democracy;* Verba et al., *Voice and Equality,* esp. 186–227; Kay Lehman Schlozman, "Citizen Participation in America: What Do We Know? Why Do We Care?" in *Political Science: The State of the Discipline,* ed. Ira Katznelson and Helen V. Miller (New York: Norton, 2002), 433–61, esp. 443–46; Kay Lehman Schlozman and John T. Tierney, *Organized Interests and American Democracy* (New York: HarperCollins 1986), 58–87; Alice O'Connor, "Bringing the Market Back In: Philanthropic Activism and Conservative Reform," in *Politics and Partnerships: The Role of Voluntary Associations in America's Political Past and Present,* ed. Elisabeth S. Clemens and Dough Guthrie (Chicago: University of Chicago Press, 2011), 121–50. A good overview of the development of interest group theory in American political science can be found in Andrew McFarland, "Interest Group Theory," in *The Oxford Handbook of American Political Parties and Interest Groups,* ed. L. Sandy Maisel and Jeffrey M. Berry (New York: Oxford University Press, 2010), 37–56; Frank R. Baumgartner and Beth L. Leech, *Basic Interests: The Importance of Groups in Politics and Political Science* (Princeton, N.J.: Princeton University Press, 1998); and Schlozman and Tierney, *Organized Interests.*

83. See, most recently, Richard R. John, "Private Enterprise, Public Good?: Communications Deregulation as a National Political Issue, 1839–1851," in Pasley et al., eds., *Beyond the Founders,* 328–54.

84. Silbey, *American Political Nation,* 64, 72–73.

85. Another way of framing this question is to ask whether parties served the deliberative function Habermas would support, and therefore the development of democratic capabilities, by helping citizens think through issues thoughtfully, or whether, as George Lakoff, *The Political Mind: Why You Can't Understand 21st-Century Politics with an 18th-Century Brain* (New York: Viking, 2008), argues, political parties simply reinforced our existing preconceptions instead of helping us to rethink our understanding of issues.

86. Richard P. McCormick, *The Second American Party System: Party Formation in the Jacksonian Era* (Chapel Hill: University of North Carolina Press, 1966), 17, 216–20. See also Robert H. Wiebe, *The Opening of American Society: From the Adoption of the Constitution to the Eve of Disunion* (New York: Knopf, 1984), 349–52.

87. Michael F. Holt, *Political Parties and American Political Development: From the Age of Jackson to the Age of Lincoln* (Baton Rouge: Louisiana State University Press, 1992), 23.

88. Silbey, *American Political Nation*, ch. 5; Robertson, "Voting Rites"; Jeffrey L. Pasley, *"The Tyranny of Printers": Newspaper Politics in the Early American Republic* (Charlottesville: University Press of Virginia, 2001); Waldstreicher, *In the Midst of Perpetual Fetes;* Albrecht Koschnik, *"Let a Common Interest Bind Us Together": Associations, Partisanship, and Culture in Philadelphia, 1775–1840* (Charlottesville: University of Virginia Press, 2007); Michael F. Holt, *Political Crisis of the 1850s* (New York: Norton, 1978).

89. Ronald P. Formisano, "The Invention of the Ethnocultural Interpretation," *American Historical Review* 99 (April 1994): 453–77, esp. 464.

90. Feller, "Politics and Society," 159. See also Paul Bourke and Donald DeBats, *Washington County: Politics and Community in Antebellum America* (Baltimore: Johns Hopkins University Press, 1995).

91. Sen, *Idea of Justice*, 241–47. On the importance of agency in shaping capability outcomes, see David A. Crocker and Ingrid Robeyns, "Capability and Agency," in *Amartya Sen*, ed. Christopher W. Morris (Cambridge: Cambridge University Press, 2010), 60–90.

92. On this point, see Pasley, *Tyranny of Printers*, 10–11; Wilson Carey McWilliams, "Parties as Civic Associations," in *Party Renewal in America: Theory and Practice*, ed. Gerald M. Pomper (New York: Praeger, 1980), 51–68; J. Mills Thornton III, *Politics and Power in a Slave Society: Alabama 1800–1860* (Baton Rouge: Louisiana State University Press, 1978), ch. 3; Harry Watson, *Jacksonian Politics and Community Conflict: The Emergence of the Second Party System in Cumberland County, North Carolina* (Baton Rouge: Louisiana State University Press, 1981), 213–45; and Wiebe, *Self-Rule*, 78–82.

93. Holt, *Political Crisis;* Michael F. Holt, *The Rise and Fall of the American Whig Party: Jacksonian Politics and the Onset of the Civil War* (New York: Oxford University Press, 1999).

94. Formisano, *Transformation of Political Culture*, 22–23.

95. Carwardine, *Evangelicals and Politics*, xvii, chs. 6–8.

96. Holt, *Rise and Fall*. On this point, see also Gienapp, "Politics Seem to Enter into Everything," 47–51. Holt's point is reinforced when we remember that party leaders devoted significant amounts of time to challenging the legitimacy of civil society membership organizations for being special interests, demonstrating party leaders' fears that associations in civil society challenged parties' abilities to dominate deliberation. See Neem *Creating a Nation of Joiners*, 114–71.

97. See also Holt, *Political Parties*, 27–29.

98. Brooke, *Columbia Rising*, 6, 452.

Afterword

P olitical history, once ascendant then deeply unfashionable, has undergone a resurgence in recent years. It has reinvented itself in part by reflecting the concerns of today's historical profession with language and identity, and in part by restating the obvious truth that we cannot understand a society that was self-consciously founded on the principle of popular sovereignty without understanding formal as well as informal power relations. The challenge now for political historians, exemplified by this volume, is to understand the interactions between, on the one hand, people, policies, and institutions, and, on the other, less tangible elements of politics like culture, class, and ideology. All historical analysis is, on some level, about understanding the relationship between "event" and "structure," to borrow terms deployed by John L. Brooke in his essay in this book. For those of us who attempt to conceptualize the politics of the United States before the Civil War, this means, among other things, working out how the practice of American democracy shaped—and, within limits, was shaped by—the agency of political actors.

One conclusion that can certainly be drawn from this collection of essays is that previous efforts to conceptualize this relationship are lacking in some respects. Over the past half century, such efforts, beginning with Walter Dean Burnham's model of electoral equilibrium punctuated by periodic moments of critical realignment, have invariably focused on political parties as the primary agents of American democracy.[1] The concept of "party systems" appeared to resolve an apparent paradox that confronted Burnham's generation: if the defining feature of American history was a consensus over basic liberal values, as Louis Hartz had famously argued, how might that be reconciled with the evident reality of the sometimes rapid and wrenching changes generated by a liberal capitalist system?[2] Burnham's answer was that the political balance periodically adjusted to reflect new socioeconomic or ethno-cultural realities; tensions that originated outside the reigning party system gradually built up until they burst through the institutional dam in a "critical election," destroying one partisan regime, creating another, and reconnecting politicians and voters. In fact, as this book shows, parties were both more and less than Burnham imagined. "Less" because they were not the hegemonic forces he—and subsequent historians—thought: other modes of mobilizing, and giving voice to, political constituencies mattered too, in varying degrees. And "less" also because, while party leaders always sought regularity, consistency, and a measure of control over the political system, this was an aspiration that often fell short of reality. Parties were not just contesting for power among themselves; the approach to politics they represented was itself part of the contest. Yet parties were also, in a sense, "more" than Burnham imagined because they were not mere mirrors of the given social relations of an era (until a critical election forced a realignment). Parties were certainly reflective—to varying degrees—of socioeconomic and ethno-cultural tensions among the population at large, but they were also more than that: like all institutional arrangements, they developed their own distinctive agendas, and played an important part in defining the realms of the politically possible.

The clarity and coherence offered by grand narratives such as realignment theory is illusory, but the danger in rejecting such narratives is that we are all too easily left with a historical brand of nominalism in which politics becomes no more than a series of contingent events with the unchecked agency of political actors generating constant flux. Scholars of a systematizing bent find the study of politics by historians frustrating for precisely this reason; certainly, close contextualization and specificity is necessary, but it is also incumbent on us to try to make sense of change through time. This book offers some illustrations of how that might be done. The story that emerges here is one of Americans experimenting with different ways of maximizing their political capability. The American Revolution, building on a tradition of self-government in the colonial period and channeling powerful ideas about liberty, opened up the potential for the participation in government-making of almost all white men and, with important limits, some other members of society, too. In the early nineteenth-century world, this presented a breathtakingly original template for nationhood. We have not attempted to track the ups and downs, the "ins" and "outs," of politics in this period, focusing primarily on the practice of politics rather than its outcomes. But the practice was itself, in an important sense, also the outcome, since so much of it involved defending, extending, or defining the nature of the democratic polity. Practicing democracy, in the variety of forms set out in these pages, was, to a great extent, what politics was about.

Taken together, the essays here suggest several directions for future research. The first is the need for more study into the extent to which the political choices that shaped the development of American democracy were structured by preexisting institutional arrangements. The notion that such arrangements create patterns and expectations of behavior that influence, whether consciously or not, how people participate in politics has been embraced with some enthusiasm by political scientists under the umbrella of "path dependency." This concept is applied here explicitly by Douglas Bradburn in his reassessment of the origins of the United States' first national parties, which shows how both the particular forms that they took and the more durable dualist tradition in which they operated were decisively shaped by Americans' preexisting political experiences, both personal and culturally received. But Bradburn's is not the only essay to highlight the influence of institutional arrangements on political choices. Kenneth Owen demonstrates that in deciding among different modes of political action during the 1790s, Americans were often guided less by their newly written constitutions than by the older heritage of collective mobilization stretching back to the revolution and beyond: what Charles Tilly has elsewhere called their "repertoires of contention."[3] And while acknowledging an "organizational revolution" as a key point of differentiation between the Jeffersonian and Jacksonian political landscapes, Reeve Huston nonetheless cautions against any characterization of the latter as "a single, more or less unitary democracy, centered on partisan mobilization," when in reality it remained subject to variations in circumstance, alliances, and arrangements that long predated its formation. Meanwhile, John L. Brooke offers an alternative perspective on this approach, by investigating under what conditions existing institutions, in his case the Whig and Democratic parties, might lose their power to structure political choices in a moment of "liminal rupture."

Huston's chapter also points to the importance of local context in shaping both the nature and meaning of political activity that was national in scope. This is a theme that recurs throughout the volume, and is surely deserving of further study. Indeed, it is impossible for a single collection of essays such as this to detail comprehensively the numerous regional variations that made up the patchwork of American democracy during this period.[4] Yet still, there are indications here of how such research might proceed. Andrew W. Robertson complicates the conventional narrative of a nationwide trajectory toward universal manhood suffrage during the first decades of the nineteenth century by detailing the ways changes to suffrage requirements were decided on a state-by-state basis, with local considerations the primary determinant. Daniel Peart performs a similar task for political parties, showing how the relationship between party organization and popular participation was profoundly conditioned by the circumstances in which it took place. And both Andrew Heath and Tyler Anbinder demonstrate, in different ways, the impact of class and ethnic divisions on the practice of democracy amid antebellum communities.

Finally, there is a need to better understand how the pursuit of specific and tangible outcomes, a category that includes but also transcends the distributive policymaking identified by Richard L. McCormick, shaped the practice of democracy.[5] In virtually every essay in this volume, we find examples of Americans pursuing such outcomes, whether in relation to issues at the top of the national agenda, as in the cases of the Hamiltonian financial program (Bradburn), the Jay Treaty (Owen), the Second Bank of the United States (Peck), and the Fugitive Slave Act (Brooke); state-specific concerns, such as the right to vote in New Jersey (Robertson) and the legal status of slavery in Illinois (Peart); or local matters, like the distribution of patronage in New York City (Anbinder) and the ratification of a new municipal charter in Philadelphia (Heath). The essays by Robertson and Peck, in particular, remind us that while we have emphasized the role that party systems play in defining and directing political activity, we must also acknowledge how far political activity in pursuit of specific and tangible outcomes determines the waxing and waning of party competition. "Party," to update Ronald P. Formisano's formulation, is neither a wholly dependent nor a wholly independent variable.[6] In this respect, Johann N. Neem's essay provides an especially fitting end to the volume, with its plea for a redirection of future research away from the quantity and quality of political engagement in the electoral sphere, on which so much has been written over the past half-century, and toward what he calls "capability," that is, the extent to which "ordinary people could affect the outcomes of political deliberation and policymaking." Such a project would combine the sum of our existing knowledge of parties and elections, the staples of traditional political history, with the findings of an emerging scholarship on civil society broadly defined, in the service of meeting Walt Whitman's challenge cited in our introduction: to better understand the practice, and the meaning, of democracy in the United States from the Constitution to the Civil War.

Notes

1. Walter Dean Burnham, "Party Systems and the Political Process," in *The American Party Systems: Stages of Political Development,* ed. William Nisbet Chambers and Walter Dean Burnham (New York: Oxford University Press, 1967), 277–307.

2. Louis Hartz, *The Liberal Tradition in America* (New York: Harcourt, 1955).

3. Charles Tilly, "Repertoires of Contention in America and Britain, 1750–1830," in *The Dynamics of Social Movements: Resource Mobilization, Social Control, and Tactics,* ed. Mayer N. Zald and John D. McCarthy (Cambridge, Mass.: Winthrop, 1979).

4. For a recent volume that discusses one such set of regional variations, see William A. Link et al., eds., *Creating Citizenship in the Nineteenth Century South* (Gainesville: University Press of Florida, 2013).

5. Richard L. McCormick, "The Party Period and Public Policy: An Exploratory Hypothesis," *Journal of American History* 66 (September 1979): 279–98.

6. Ronald P. Formisano, "Deferential-Participant Politics: The Early Republic's Political Culture, 1789–1840," *American Political Science Review* 68 (June 1974): 483.

CONTRIBUTORS

TYLER ANBINDER is Professor of History at George Washington University. His first book, *Nativism and Slavery: The Northern Know Nothings and the Politics of the 1850s*, won the Avery Craven Prize of the Organization of American Historians. He is also the author of *Five Points: The New York City Neighborhood That Invented Tap Dance, Stole Elections, and Became the World's Most Notorious Slum.*

DOUGLAS BRADBURN, founding Director of the Fred W. Smith National Library for the Study of George Washington at Mount Vernon, is an award-winning teacher and author. In addition to many articles and book chapters, he is the author of *The Citizenship Revolution: Politics and the Making of the American Union, 1774–1804*, and coeditor of *Early Modern Virginia: Reconsidering the Old Dominion.*

JOHN L. BROOKE is Humanities Distinguished Professor of History at the Ohio State University. He is the author of *Columbia Rising: Civil Life on the Upper Hudson from the Revolution to the Age of Jackson*, which was awarded the 2011 SHEAR Book Prize.

ANDREW HEATH is Lecturer in American History at the University of Sheffield. His work on the urban history and political culture of Civil War–era America has appeared in *Civil War History*, the *Journal of American History*, and *American Nineteenth Century History*. He is currently completing a book on the reconstruction of Philadelphia between 1837 and 1877.

REEVE HUSTON teaches history at Duke University. He is the author of *Land and Freedom: Rural Society, Popular Protest, and Party Politics in Antebellum New York* and *The Early American Republic: A History in Documents*. He is currently working on a book on the transformation of American political practices between 1812 and 1840.

JOHANN N. NEEM is Professor of History at Western Washington University. He is the author of *Creating a Nation of Joiners: Democracy and Civil Society in Early National Massachusetts.*

KENNETH OWEN is Assistant Professor of History at the University of Illinois, Springfield. His research focuses on political mobilization and the ways in which Americans attempted to link ideas of popular sovereignty to institutions of governmental power during and following the American Revolution. He received a doctorate from the University of Oxford in 2011 for his dissertation "Political Community in Revolutionary Pennsylvania, 1774–1800."

DANIEL PEART is Lecturer in American History at Queen Mary University of London. He is the author of *Era of Experimentation: American Political Practices in the Early Republic* and "Looking beyond Parties and Elections: The Making of United States Tariff Policy during the Early 1820s" in the *Journal of the Early Republic*. He is working on a book about lobbying and the making of U.S. tariff policy between the War of 1812 and the Civil War.

GRAHAM A. PECK is Associate Professor of History at Saint Xavier University. He has published three articles on Abraham Lincoln and Stephen A. Douglas in the *Journal of the Abraham Lincoln Association* and currently has a book under contract on antebellum Illinois politics.

ANDREW W. ROBERTSON is Deputy Executive Officer of the History Program at the Graduate Center of the City University of New York (CUNY) and also teaches at Lehman College, CUNY. He is the author of *The Language of Democracy: Political Rhetoric in the United States and Britain, 1790–1900*, and coeditor of *Beyond the Founders: New Approaches to the Political History of the Early American Republic* and the forthcoming *Oxford Handbook of Revolutionary Elections in the Americas, 1800–1910*. He is presently at work on a book about Jeffersonian Democracy.

ADAM I. P. SMITH teaches history at University College London. He is the author of *No Party Now: Politics in the Civil War North*, and his current work is on conservatism in nineteenth-century America.

INDEX

abolitionism, 5–6, 14, 63, 65, 82–87, 151, 157–58, 161–62, 212–15, 255–56, 262. *See also* antislavery

Ackerman, Bruce, 74

Adams, John, 38, 40–41, 107, 181

Adams, John Quincy, 3, 124, 133–34

African Americans, 81–82, 84–85, 86, 174, 248, 250; political engagement of, 5–6, 57, 63–64, 122n24, 256–57, 267; suffrage of, 54–55, 56, 113–19

Albany Evening Journal, 59

Aldrich, John H., 123

Alien and Sedition Acts, 105, 108, 183, 191

Alton Telegraph, 158

Altschuler, Glenn, 9–10, 18n42, 18n44, 143n54, 147–48, 248, 251, 267, 271n23

American Colonization Society, 63, 256

American-Republican Party, 201–2

American Tract Society, 63

American Temperance Society, 254. *See also* prohibitionism; temperance

Ames, Fisher, 31

anti-Catholicism, 73, 78, 151, 200, 201, 206, 208, 213, 229, 262, 266. *See also* evangelicalism; nativism

Anti-Masonic Party, 64, 65, 260–61, 272n32

anti-partisanship, 6, 7, 14, 50, 54–55, 60–61, 76, 132–33, 137–38, 153, 162, 223–24, 235, 236–37, 261. *See also* political parties

antislavery, 14–15, 73, 76–79, 82–89, 130–34, 145, 151–53, 157–59, 161–62,

165n25, 199, 208–13, 216, 255–58, 261, 262, 266, 276n74. *See also* abolitionism; "convention question" (Illinois); Foster, Stephen; Stowe, Harriet Beecher

"Appeal of the Independent Democrats" (1854), 73, 79–80, 90n3

"Appeal to the Women of the Free States" (Stowe), 88

associations, 6, 10, 51, 54–55, 57, 63–64, 66n4, 71n33, 115, 130–31, 229–30, 234, 250–66, 273n35, 273n44, 279n96

Bailyn, Bernard, 75

Baker, Paula, 258

Baldwin, Matthias, 223, 236

Baltimore Patriot, 112

Bancroft, George, 3, 120n2

banking, 30, 33–34, 76–77, 104, 106, 150, 151, 153–55, 159, 163, 166n40, 174; Second Bank of the United States, 76–77, 284

Banks, Nathaniel P., 88–89

Beecher, Henry Ward, 87

Beecher, Lyman, 253

Belmont, Angus, 197, 205, 211

Bensel, Richard, 12, 18n42

Benson, Lee, 4

Blackstone, William, 113

Blumin, Stuart M., 9–10, 18n42, 19n44, 143n54, 147–48, 248, 251, 267, 271n23

Bolingbroke, Henry St. John, Viscount, 36

Breese, Sidney, 156

Britain, impact on American politics, 1, 2, 30, 35–36, 39, 84, 100, 110–11, 184
Brown, Richard D., 136
Browning, O. H., 161
Buckingham, Joseph T., 129, 135–36, 137–38, 143n54
Burnham, Walter Dean, 4, 125, 126, 131, 136, 139n11, 140n17, 146–48, 281–82
Burr, Aaron, 107

Cabot, George, 31
Calhoun, John C., 138
Carey, Henry C., 232–33
Carlisle Gazette, 182–83
Carpenter, George, 238
Carwardine, Richard, 266
Casey, Zadoc, 154
Chicago Journal, 158
civil society, 11, 13, 250, 251–61, 263–66, 267–68, 276n74, 279n96, 285; civic rituals, 5, 48, 50–53, 57–60
Civil War, 72–74, 162
citizenship, 2, 6, 57, 118, 229, 232, 238, 266
Clancy, John, 213, 214
Clark, Myron H., 206
Clarke, Charles, 154
Clay, Henry, 80, 134
Clemens, Elizabeth S., 252
Collini, Stefan, 11
Columbia County (New York), 51, 55
Columbian Centinel, 112
Compromise of 1850, 73–74, 80–83, 86–87, 159–60. *See also* Fugitive Slave Law
Conrad, Robert T., 233
Consolidation Act (Philadelphia), 224, 238–39. *See also* Executive Consolidation Committee (Philadelphia)
Constitution (Kansas), 213
Constitution (Pennsylvania), 177, 179–80, 183–84
Constitution (United States), 1–2, 3,

25–26, 53–54, 80–81, 87, 157–58, 174, 177, 185, 187, 188, 254; drafting of, 26–29; and partisanship, 31–32, 33–34, 37–38, 76, 162–63; ratification of, 31, 35; and slavery, 72–73, 76, 80, 88, 89, 212; twelfth amendment (1804), 23–24; thirteenth amendment (1865), 162
constitutional conventions (state), 56–57, 61, 77, 102–3, 113, 117, 121n9, 227
"convention question" (Illinois), 130–31, 133–34, 142n36, 151–53
Cook, Edward M., Jr., 38
Cowles, Alfred, 152
Crolius, Clarkson, Jr., 201

Davis, David, 155
Day Book, 212
deference, 3, 50–52, 54, 106, 126, 134, 136, 173–74, 178, 179–80, 184, 199, 228, 237, 250, 268; scholars' views on, 5, 16n16, 121n11, 140n14, 143nn50–51, 143n54, 269n4. *See also* gentry politics; neighborhood politics
Democratic Party, 3, 5, 48, 59, 62, 73, 78, 79–80, 85, 88, 145–46, 150–51, 153–63, 222, 259–60, 262, 282; divisions within, 200–201, 204–5, 209–10, 213–14, 257–58; immigrant voters and, 197, 199, 203–4, 207–8, 211, 214–15; Republican Party, competition with, 205; Whig Party, competition with, 4, 46, 48, 61–62, 72–73, 76–77, 82, 146, 155, 159, 160, 205, 231–32
Donoho, Carl, 201, 204
Douglas, Stephen, 79, 80, 87, 88, 119, 153, 159, 160–61, 161–62, 206, 213, 214
Douglass, Frederick, 83, 85
Duane, William, 177, 183
Durkheim, Emily, 75, 76

Edling, Max M., 174
education, 199–200, 256–57, 258–59, 266

Einhorn, Robin L., 12, 174
election: 1790 gubernatorial (Pennsyl-
    vania), 177–80, 191; 1799 guberna-
    torial (Pennsylvania), 180–84, 191,
    194n32; 1800 presidential, 23, 113;
    1802 state (New Jersey), 115–16; 1803
    state (New Jersey), 117; 1807 state
    (New Jersey), 117–19; 1820 presiden-
    tial, 124, 133; 1822 state (Illinois),
    133; 1824 convention referendum
    (Illinois), 130–31, 133–34, 153; 1824
    presidential, 124–25, 133–34, 137,
    152; 1828 presidential, 3, 99, 100, 103,
    125, 199; 1840 presidential, 125; 1840
    municipal (New York), 200–201; 1844
    presidential, 157; 1848 presidential,
    78, 158; 1850 congressional, 159–60;
    1851 state (Pennsylvania), 222, 235;
    1853 state (Pennsylvania), 235–36;
    1854 state (Pennsylvania), 222–23;
    1854 congressional, 78–79, 88–89,
    209–11; 1856 presidential, 78; 1858
    congressional, 213–14; 1860 presiden-
    tial, 78, 214–15, 257–58
elections, 41n1, 88–89, 140n17, 150,
    165n21; congressional, 105–6, 126–
    27, 131–32, 134–35, 143n47; guber-
    natorial, 60, 110–11, 115, 126–27,
    131–32, 134–35, 143n47, 191; issues
    and, 12–14, 38, 61–62, 100, 104–5,
    106–9, 111–12; party organization of,
    48–51, 60, 63–64, 77–79, 130–31, 199,
    202, 203–5, 207, 209, 239; popular
    participation in, 37, 54–57, 78–79, 82,
    126–27, 131, 189, 202–4, 250; presi-
    dential, 60, 104, 125, 134–35, 137;
    scholars' views on, 2–3, 4, 5, 7–14,
    77, 99, 100–101, 120n2, 146–49, 248–
    49, 282. See also political parties;
    political practices; turnout
Emancipation Proclamation, 162
"Era of Good Feelings," 124–26, 130,
    138

Estes, Todd, 184
evangelicalism, 57, 64, 82, 137–38, 150,
    157, 229, 232, 252, 255–56, 259, 260,
    266. See also Sabbatarianism
Evening Bulletin, 222, 236
events: politicization of, 53, 149, 258;
    transformative impact of, 24–25, 72,
    73, 75–76, 77, 79, 80, 81, 89, 282
exceptionalism, 62, 99, 119–20
Executive Consolidation Committee
    (Philadelphia), 222–23, 227, 232, 238
expansionism, 12, 73, 80, 151, 155–57,
    160, 162, 163, 168n67, 216. See also
    antislavery

Farrar, Margaret E., 226
federalism, 33–34, 81, 162, 266–67
federal government, scholars' views on,
    104, 174, 252
Federalist 10 (Madison), 32
Federalist Party, 7, 27, 31, 44n46, 111–12,
    124, 126–27, 128, 136, 173–74, 176,
    184; and popular mobilization, 50–52,
    105, 108, 180, 181, 183–84, 185–86,
    188–89, 191, 192n6; Republican Party,
    competition with, 5, 23, 37, 38, 40,
    49–52, 55, 62–63, 105, 107–12, 114–15,
    119, 124–25, 128, 130, 136, 146, 182–
    84, 184–85, 188–89
Federal Republican, 112
Feller, Daniel, 264
Ferris, Jim, 200–201
fire-companies: New York, 202–3; Phil-
    adelphia, 225, 229, 230, 235, 238, 239
Fisher, J. Francis, 230
Fitzhugh, George, 55
Foner, Eric, 73
Ford, Thomas, 152, 157
Formisano, Ron, 8, 10–12, 46, 47, 52, 53,
    82, 266–67, 284
Foster, Stephen, 74, 82, 84–87, 89
Fraley, Frederick, 238
franchise. See suffrage

Freeman, Joanne B., 49, 248, 249
Freeman's Journal, 213, 214
Free Soil Party, 73, 78, 163, 261. *See also* expansionism; Liberty Party
Frémont, John C., 89, 210
French Revolution, 1, 40, 51, 62–63, 111–12
Fries's Rebellion, 62–63
Fugitive Slave Law, 74, 80–82, 83, 88, 89, 92n27, 284. *See also* Compromise of 1850

Gallatin, Albert, 183
Garfield, James, 83
Garrison, William Lloyd, 255, 256
Gazette of the United States, 107
General Trades' Union, 222
General Union for the Promotion of the Christian Sabbath, 253. *See also* Sabbatarianism
gentry politics, 49–52, 57, 67n10. *See also* deference
Giddings, Joshua, 83
Gienapp, William E., 8, 48, 168n64, 247
Girard, Stephen, 234
Glover, John, 88
Gunther, C. Godfrey, 210

Habermas, Jürgen, 5, 74, 250, 278n85. *See also* "public sphere"
Hamilton, Alexander, 7, 28–35, 40–41, 42n12, 104, 108, 175, 176, 185, 187, 284; scholars' views on, 26–28
Hankinson, Joseph, 115
Hardin, John J., 157–58
Harper, James, 201
Hartford Convention, 124. *See also* War of 1812
Hartz, Louis, 281
Harvey, David, 227
Havemeyer, William P., 209
Hecker, Frederick, 210

Hillhouse, James, 23–24, 40
Historical Society of Philadelphia, 239–40
Hoar, George Frisbie, 79
Hofstadter, Richard, 7, 50, 67n10
Holt, Michael F., 4, 8, 73, 147–48, 223, 264, 265, 266–67, 279n96
Holton, Woody, 62
Howe, Daniel Walker, 100, 123

Illinois Intelligencer, 137
immigrants, 6, 11, 150–51, 159, 197, 199–200, 208, 219n25, 228, 229; and abolitionism, 212–13, 216; hostility towards, 73, 78, 151, 159–60, 229; and office-holding, 202–4, 214; political engagement of, 150, 157, 196, 197–99, 202–3, 205–7, 208–9, 210–11, 213–14, 215–16, 217n1. *See also* fire-companies; migration; nativism; "school question" (New York)
Independent Chronicle, 112
Indians, suffrage of, 54, 64
Irish-American, 212–13
Ivins, William F., 202–3

Jackson, Andrew, 3, 57, 58, 59, 60, 62, 99, 100, 120n2, 125, 134, 153, 154, 199
Jay, John, 83, 184–85
Jay Treaty, 63, 104, 136, 173, 176, 184–88, 191, 284
Jefferson, Thomas, 7, 26–27, 29–32, 34, 40, 51, 53, 107, 109–10, 112, 265
John, Richard R., 248, 253

Kansas-Nebraska Act, 73–74, 78–79, 87–89, 160–61, 163, 206, 207, 208–9
Kazin, Michael, 262
Kelley, Mary, 258
Kelly, John, 213
Kernan, J. Frank, 204
Keyssar, Alexander, 100

King, Rufus, 31

Koschnik, Albrecht, 6, 50, 249–50

Know-Nothing Party, 6, 14, 78–79, 160–61, 196, 206–7, 211, 213, 261

Laurie, Bruce, 261, 276n74

Leggett, William, 2–3

Liberty Party, 56, 78, 82, 157, 261, 276n74. *See also* abolitionism; antislavery; Free Soil Party

Lincoln, Abraham, 1, 7, 119, 154, 157, 160, 162, 214–15, 257–58. *See also* Republican Party (Lincoln's)

Linn, James, 116

Lippard, George, 223

Lovejoy, Owen, 157

Lynch, James, 213–14

Maclay, William, 31

Maclay Act, 200, 219n25. *See also* "school question" (New York)

Madison, James, 2, 3, 29, 31, 32–35, 37, 38, 39–41, 124; scholars' views on, 26–28

Maine Law, 206–7

Mason, Stevens Thomson, 185

Massachusetts Society for the Suppression of Intemperance, 253–54

Mathisen, Erik, 61

McCaffery, Peter, 239

McCarthy, Michael P., 238

McCormick, Richard L., 4, 11–12, 100, 125, 128, 131–32, 147, 264, 285

McCurry, Stephanie, 6

McKean, Thomas, 180–83

McKluskey, Kit, 230

McMichael, Morton, 223, 226, 227, 236, 239

McPherson, James, 74

McRoberts, Samuel, 156–57

Merrick, Samuel Vaughan, 238

Mexican War, 78, 85, 157–58

Middling Interest, 129–30

Mifflin, Thomas, 177–80

migration, 155–56, 159–60. *See also* expansionism; immigrants

militia, 6, 50, 107, 128

Missouri Crisis, 76, 124, 152

Monroe, James, 124, 133

Morris, Lewis, 36

Muhlenberg, Frederick, 176

National Era, 82

Native Americans. *See* Indians

nativism, 78–79, 88–89, 150, 151, 159, 196, 199, 205–6, 210–11, 216, 236, 261; and hostility toward immigrants, 73, 78, 151, 159–60, 229. *See also* Know-Nothing Party

neighborhood politics, 197, 199, 202–4, 224–27, 237. *See also* deference; gentry politics; politics practices

New England Antislavery Society, 256

New-England Galaxy, 129, 135–36, 137

Newman, Richard S., 250, 255–57

Newman, Simon, 50, 249

newspapers, 13, 53, 78, 104, 158, 187, 254, 256; and political mobilization, 34, 37–38, 48, 51–52, 54, 55, 58–61, 106, 107, 112, 116, 119, 124, 128, 136, 177, 194n32, 205–7, 212, 216

New York Aurora, 200

New York Herald, 200–201, 207, 208, 209

New York Times, 8, 205, 208, 210

North American and United States Gazette, 223, 226, 227, 231, 233, 236, 238, 239

North, Douglass, 24

Northrup, Solomon, 83

Novak, William, 12

Okie, J. B., 231

Olson, Mancur, Jr., 263

Otis, Harrison Gray, 130, 138

Panic of 1837, 78, 155, 222

Party Period, 4–5, 77, 125–26, 128, 132–33, 267

Parker, Shivers, 201

Parker, Theodore, 88–89

Parsons, Anson V., 223

Pasley, Jeffrey, 5, 7–8, 10, 11–12, 13–14, 49–50, 52, 125, 126, 136, 249–50

"path dependency," 8, 283

Patterson, William C., 223

Penniman, Edward A., 222–23, 224, 226, 229, 234–35

Pennsylvania Abolition Society, 255

Pessen, Edward, 9

petitions, 37, 80–82, 87–89, 92n27, 122, 134, 175, 185, 187, 188, 195n59, 253, 255, 257–60

Philadelphia Aurora, 185

Philanthropist, 229

Pierson, Paul, 24

Pinckney, Charles Cotesworth, 107

Pole, J. R., 100, 117

political parties, 2–15, 23–24, 25–34, 38–39, 46–65, 72–74, 105–8, 126–33, 135–38, 145–51, 227–30, 236–40, 263–66, 268, 284–85; colonial tradition of, 35–37, 282; democratization and, 1, 3–4, 7–8, 13, 15, 47, 49–50, 54–55, 61, 99, 118, 123, 138, 143n51, 146, 247, 265–66, 268, 281; organisation of, 2–3, 4–5, 10–12, 13–14, 47–48, 54, 57–63, 64–65, 76–80, 104–6, 116–17, 128–31, 135–37, 153, 177, 190, 204–5, 227, 235–36, 262; party systems and, 4, 7–10, 46, 47, 64, 76, 100, 123, 126–27, 142n33, 145–49, 162–63, 196, 240, 250–51, 265, 281–82; popular engagement with, 7–10, 12–14, 48–49, 50–53, 65, 106–8, 151, 155, 159–60, 164n14, 165n25, 202–3, 228, 229–30, 232, 265–66, 268, 269n1; scholars views on, 2–5, 7–12, 18n42, 46–51, 52,

72–73, 123, 125–27, 249–51, 263–64, 266–68, 278n85, 279n96, 284; third parties, 54–55, 64, 259–61, 276n75. *See also* anti-partisanship; deference; elections; gentry politics; neighborhood politics; Party Period; suffrage; turnout; *and specific parties*

political practices, 1–3, 11, 13–14, 54–55, 71n33, 106–7, 128–29, 174, 176–77, 181–83, 185–87, 191–92, 224–25; colonial tradition of, 3, 35–37, 44n47, 113, 134, 143n51, 191, 282; scholars views on, 7–8, 19n44, 48–51. *See also* associations; militia; political parties; "public sphere"; riots; rituals, civic; town meetings

Polk, James K., 157, 159

popular sovereignty, 2–3, 15, 79, 138, 158, 160, 173–74, 175, 179–80, 189–91, 281

Price, Eli Kirk, 223, 226, 228, 232–40

prohibitionism, 13, 199, 202, 206–7, 211, 216, 253–55. *See also* temperance

Public Ledger, 231, 234

"public sphere," 5–6, 10, 62, 74–75, 77–78, 87, 174, 184, 232, 250–59, 263, 267–68, 271n32

Pulteney, William, 36

Quaker City, The, 223

Quasi War, 105

Ratcliffe, Donald, 47, 51–52, 59

reform movements, 11, 13, 44n19, 55–57, 63–64, 102, 130, 143n54, 159, 204–5, 222–40, 248, 251–54, 258–62, 267–68, 273n44, 274n56. *See also* abolitionism; antislavery; associations; Sabbatarianism; suffrage: reform of; temperance

religion. *See* evangelicalism

republicanism, 7, 34, 40–41, 124, 137–38,

154, 173, 175–76, 180–81, 185, 187, 189–
90, 192, 209, 232–33, 235, 236, 238
Republican Party (Jefferson's), 7, 23,
37–38, 50–52, 57, 62–63, 100, 111–19,
124–26, 128, 129, 130, 136; Federalist
Party, competition with, 5, 23, 37,
38, 40, 49–52, 55, 62–63, 105, 107–
12, 114–15, 119, 124–25, 128, 130, 136,
146, 182–84, 184–85, 188–89; popular
mobilization and, 105, 106–9, 116–17,
180–84, 189, 259; scholars views on,
5, 46–47, 49–50
Republican Party (Lincoln's), 14, 73,
78–79, 86, 87–89, 145, 151, 161–62,
196, 205, 261; and Consolidation Act
(Philadelphia), 224, 239; Democratic
Party, competition with, 205; 1860
presidential election, 78, 214–15, 257–
58; and immigrant voters, 210–16;
scholars views on, 47
revivalism. *See* evangelicalism
Reynolds, John, 152
Rice, Thomas D., 84–85, 87
Richmond Enquirer, 76
Richter, Erhard, 208–9
riots: New York, 199; Philadelphia, 222,
225
Ritchie, Thomas, 76
rituals, civic, 5, 48, 50–53, 57–60. *See
also* political practices
Robson, David, 152
Ross, James, 180–83
Russell, Benjamin, 124, 128
Ryan, Mary, 259

Sabbatarianism, 6, 252, 253, 255–57,
262, 272n32. *See also* antislavery;
evangelicalism; temperance
Schlesinger, Arthur, Jr., 3, 46, 120n2
"school question" (New York), 199–
200, 201–2
Schultz, Ronald, 260

Schuyler, David, 227
Scobey, David M., 231
Second Bank of the United States,
76–77, 284
Second Party System, 145–49, 162–63
Sen, Amartya, 247–48
Seymour, Horatio, 206–7
Sewell, William H., Jr., 75–76, 77, 80
Shaler, William, 200–201
Shields, James, 156, 160
Silbey, Joel, 4, 7, 48, 77, 125–26, 128,
130, 247, 263
Skocpol, Theda, 252
Smith, Kimberly K., 225
Smith, William Loughton, 30–31
social capital, 256, 261, 268, 274n44,
276n74
Sons of Liberty, 6
Spirit of the Times, 222–23
St. Clair, Arthur, 177–79
Stowe, Harriet Beecher, 74, 82–84,
86–87, 88, 89
suffrage, 46–47, 54–56, 61, 99–100, 104,
108, 109, 114, 117–19, 121n7, 121n9,
162, 199, 257, 284; reform of, 100,
102–3, 226; restrictions on, 113–15
Sumner, Charles, 79, 83, 89
Sunday Dispatch, 230–31

Taylor, John, 124–25, 134
Taylor, Zachary, 80–81
Telegraph (Germantown), 233, 238
temperance, 6, 14, 63, 151, 150, 205–7,
210–11, 216, 253–56, 259–61, 262, 266,
273n44. *See also* prohibitionism
Tiemann, Daniel F., 209–10
Tocqueville, Alexis de, 1, 99, 119–20,
252, 265–66
town meetings, 19n44, 63, 175–77, 179,
182, 185–91, 194n32
Travers, Len, 249
Treasury Department, 28–31, 33

True American, 116–17
turnout, 5, 7, 8–10, 13, 48, 53, 60–61, 65,
    99–111, 117–19, 125–26, 131–32, 135,
    137, 140n17; in congressional elec-
    tions, 105–6, 126, 127, 131–32, 134–35,
    143n47; in 1824 Illinois convention
    referendum, 133–34; in gubernatorial
    elections, 110–11, 126, 127, 131–32,
    135, 143n47; and party mobilization,
    104–5, 116–17; and political issues,
    145, 151–52, 164n14, 267; in presi-
    dential elections, 124–25, 137; in state
    elections, 115–19, 125. *See also* elec-
    tions; political parties
Tweed, William M., 202
Tyrrell, Ian, 254, 255

Uncle Tom's Cabin (Stowe), 74, 82–84,
    86–89
United States Telegraph, 59

Van Buren, Martin, 2–3, 7, 41, 58–60,
    76–77
Van Cleve, Benjamin, 115
Verba, Sidney, 248
Voss-Hubbard, Mark, 6, 253, 260

Waldstreicher, David, 7, 50, 249–50
Walker, David, 256
Walpole, Robert, 36
Warner, Samuel Bass, 223–24
War of 1812, 110, 124, 126–27
Washington, George, 29–34, 53, 57,
    124, 173, 187, 188, 192
Weber, Max, 50, 75
Webster, Daniel, 80, 82

Weed, Thurlow, 60
Wiebe, Robert H., 247, 248
Wilentz, Sean, 3, 47, 100, 120n2, 123,
    259–60, 262
Wilson, Henry, 89
Wilson, James J., 116
Wheaton, Ellen, 83
Whig Party, 48, 56–59, 61–62, 76–77,
    145–46, 147–48, 150–51, 154–55,
    156–63, 196, 222, 223, 226, 227–28,
    230, 231–32, 235–36, 251, 254, 261,
    262; collapse of, 78–79, 82, 161–62,
    168n64; Democratic Party, compe-
    tition with, 4, 46, 48, 61–62, 72–73,
    76–77, 82, 146, 155, 159, 160, 205,
    231–32; and immigrant voters, 201–3,
    205–7, 210, 214–15; scholars' views
    on, 4, 5, 8, 14, 266–67, 283
Whiskey Rebellion, 31, 62–63
Whitman, Walt, 1, 200, 201, 285
women, 82, 85, 88, 174, 232–33, 247–48;
    political engagement of, 5–6, 64,
    66n4, 116–17, 250–61, 267, 274n56;
    suffrage of, 54, 56, 57, 100, 113–18
workingmen's movement, 259–60
Workingmen's Party (Philadelphia), 54,
    64, 260–61

XYZ Affair, 105

Yates, Richard, 161

Zaeske, Susan, 255, 257, 259
Zagarri, Rosemarie, 5, 114, 125, 250,
    258, 274n56
Zelizer, Julian E., 248–49, 251